POPULAR MUSIC IN FRANCE
FROM *CHANSON* TO TECHNO

Popular Music in France from *Chanson* to Techno

Culture, Identity and Society

Edited by
HUGH DAUNCEY and STEVE CANNON

ASHGATE

Published by
Ashgate Publishing Limited
Gower House
Croft Road
Aldershot
Hants GU11 3HR
England

Ashgate Publishing Company
Suite 420
101 Cherry Street
Burlington, VT 05401-4405
USA

Ashgate website: http://www.ashgate.com

British Library Cataloguing in Publication Data
Popular music in France from chanson to techno : culture,
    identity and society. - (Ashgate popular and folk music
    series)
    1. Popular music - France - History and criticism
    I. Cannon, Steve II. Dauncey, Hugh, 1961–
    782.4'2164'0944

Library of Congress Cataloging-in-Publication Data
Popular music in France from chanson to techno : culture, identity, and society / edited
by Steve Cannon and Hugh Dauncey.
        p. cm. -- (Ashgate popular and folk music series)
    Includes bibliographical references and index.
    ISBN 0-7546-0849-2 (alk. paper)
    1. Popular music--France--History and criticism. 2. Popular culture--France--History.
    3. Music--Social aspects. I. Cannon, Steve, 1963– II. Dauncey, Hugh, 1961– III. Series.

    ML3489 .P67 2003
    781.64'0944--dc21

                                                    2002028149

ISBN 0 7546 0849 2

Printed and bound in Great Britain by MPG Books Ltd, Bodmin, Cornwall.

Contents

List of Contributors

Philippe Birgy is Maître de conférences at the University of Toulouse Le Mirail.

Steve Cannon is a Senior Lecturer in Film Studies at the University of Sunderland.

Hugh Dauncey is a Senior Lecturer in French at the University of Newcastle upon Tyne.

Geoff Hare is a Senior Lecturer in French at the University of Newcastle upon Tyne.

Philippe Le Guern is Maître de conférences at the Université d'Angers.

Christopher Lloyd is a Senior Lecturer in French at the University of Durham.

David Looseley is a Reader in French at the University of Leeds.

Richard Middleton is Professor of Music at the University of Newcastle upon Tyne.

Mat Pires is a Lecturer at the British Institute in Paris at the University of London.

Phil Powrie is Professor of French Cultural Studies at the University of Newcastle upon Tyne.

Keith Reader is Professor of Modern French Studies at the University of Glasgow.

Robynn J. Stilwell is Assistant Professor of Music at Georgetown University.

Philippe Teillet is Maître de conférences at the University of Rennes.

Chris Tinker is Lecturer in French Studies at Heriot-Watt University.

General Editor's Preface

The upheaval that occurred in musicology during the last two decades of the twentieth century has created a new urgency for the study of popular music alongside the development of new critical and theoretical models. A relativistic outlook has replaced the universal perspective of modernism (the international ambitions of the 12-note style); the grand narrative of the evolution and dissolution of tonality has been challenged; and emphasis has shifted to cultural context, reception and subject position. Together, these have conspired to eat away at the status of canonical composers and categories of high and low in music. A need has arisen, also, to recognize and address the emergence of crossovers, mixed and new genres, to engage in debates concerning the vexed problem of what constitutes authenticity in music and to offer a critique of musical practice as the product of free, individual expression.

Popular musicology is now a vital and exciting area of scholarship, and the Ashgate Popular and Folk Music series aims to present the best research in the field. Authors will be concerned with locating musical practices, values and meanings in cultural context, and may draw upon methodologies and theories developed in cultural studies, semiotics, poststructuralism, psychology and sociology. The series will focus on popular musics of the twentieth and twenty-first centuries. It is designed to embrace the world's popular musics from Acid Jazz to Zydeco, whether high tech or low tech, commercial or non-commercial, contemporary or traditional.

Professor Derek B. Scott
Chair of Music
University of Salford

Visit Project Pop:
http://www.music.salford.ac.uk/music2/web/projects/FDTLpop/welcome.htm

Abbreviations

ADAMI	Société pour l'administration des droits des artistes et musiciens interprètes
BAFTA	British Academy of Film and Television Arts
BDS	Bureau de diffusion sonore du ministère des Affaires Etrangères
BMG	Bertelsmann Group
CEO	Chief Executive Officer
CLT	Compagnie Luxembourgeoise de Télédiffusion
CSA	Conseil Supérieur de l'Audiovisuel
DEP	Département des études et de la prospective
e.p.	Extended Play
FCM	Fonds pour la création musicale
FFI	Forces françaises de l'intérieur
FMBL	French Music Export Office
FNAC	Fédération nationale d'achat (des cadres)
LVF	Legion of Volunteers against Bolshevism
MCM	Montants compensatoires monétaires
MFM	Modified Frequency Modulation
MIDEM	Marché international du disque, de l'édition musicale et de la vidéo-musique
MP3	Moving Picture Experts Group (audio layer) 3
MTV	Music Television
OAS	L'Organisation de L'Armée Secrète
ORTF	Office de Radiodiffusion-Télévision Française
PCF	Parti Communiste Français
R & F	*Rock & Folk*
RFM	Radio Station
RMC	Radio Monte-Carlo
RTF	Radiodiffusion-Télévision Française
RTL	Radio-Télévision Luxembourg
SACD	Société des auteurs et compositeurs dramatiques
SACEM	Société des auteurs, compositeurs et éditeurs de musique
SCCP	Société civile pour l'exercice des droits des producteurs phonographiques
SDRM	Société pour l'administration du droit de reproduction mécanique
SER	Services des études et recherches
SLC	*Salut les copains*

SNEP	Syndicat national de l'édition phonographique
SPEDIDAM	Société de perception et de répartition des droits des artistes-interprètes de la musique et de la danse
SPPF	Société civile des producteurs de phonogramme en France
SPRE	Société pour la perception de la rémunération équitable
TF1	Télévision Française Un
TPS	Télévision par satellite

Introduction

Music, modernization and popular identity

Richard Middleton

Polyphonic music always says 'we', according to one of T. W. Adorno's more memorable aphorisms. For that matter, monophonic music does so too, even when sung or played solo, for the act of performance itself presupposes dialogue, while the semiotics of musical utterance are unthinkable outside pre-existing regimes of cultural conventions. Music is irreducibly social. Why, then, have musicians and music analysts so often denied this – or at least proceeded as if it were not true, attempting to seal music in its own hermetic space? The answer to this question is itself socially specific. It lies in the development, from the late eighteenth century in Europe, of so-called 'autonomous music', a music that – so it was claimed – makes sense only in its own terms and transcends the effects of all social settings. This development was part and parcel of a broader constellation of changes: the rise to a dominant status of instrumental (as against vocal) music; the emergence of a concept of musical 'works' (rather than practices), self-sufficient and historically transfinite; the construction of a canon of 'masterpieces' associated with a selective list of (white, male) Great Masters; the political and economic success of a hegemonic bourgeois fraction, much of whose cultural capital was tied up in this music world, while at the same time their claims to natural authority were well served by the music's apparent universality of value.

There was not much space in this world-picture for popular music. Indeed, for the rulers of this world, it was precisely popular music's social messiness, its sticky historical specificity, that constituted it as a Low-Other, legitimating the claims of Art through its difference.[1] But the assumptions of this world also made it problematic to think out the terms of *any* sociology of music at all. One response from sociologists was blandly positivist: counting sales, instruments, concert attendances and so on, and reducing musical meaning to basic social facts. The opposite approach to this – most famously represented by Adorno – was to take autonomy seriously but to read social meaning as sedimented in the

---

[1] See Middleton, Richard (2000), 'Musical Belongings: Western Music and Its Low-Other', in *Western Music and Its Others: Difference, Representation and Appropriation in Music*, Berkeley, CA: University of California Press, 59–85.

1

historically formed musical materials themselves, albeit in mutating and always contradictory ways. Adorno's position is flawed by his refusal to accept that popular music's distance from his favoured high modernism might be anything other than ideologically mystificatory; but his account remains of huge significance, not least for his insistence that music's value lies in its truth-claims – its capacity to transcribe (if also to mis-scribe) the complexities of social subjectivity in the era of late capitalism.

When popular music studies began to emerge as a discipline, in the 1970s, it drew most obviously on approaches in the social sciences. Yet the almost universal distrust of Adorno hampered this engagement from the start. While the few interested musicologists grappled with the legacy of the autonomy position, scholars coming to popular music from social and cultural studies have only slowly come to terms with the particular requirements that music (as against sport, or TV, or family structures, etc.) imposes. Interestingly, two of the most helpful contributions to the debates over theory and method have come out of France. Jacques Attali's 'political economy of music', entitled *Noise*, is indebted to Adorno; music is intimately embedded in mechanisms of power and ideology, but not, Attali agrees, as a mere superstructural mirror:

> Music is a credible metaphor of the real. It is neither an autonomous activity nor an automatic indicator of the economic infrastructure ... Undoubtedly music is a play of mirrors in which every activity is reflected, defined, recorded, and distorted. If we look at one mirror, we see only an image of another. But at times a complex mirror game yields a vision that is rich, because unexpected and prophetic.[2]

However, Attali also draws on Foucault, constructing a historical schema made up of a series of 'orders', each of which, as music channels the violence of 'noise' into acceptable structures of sound, mirrors, motivates, stands for the mode of organization of power in a particular type of political economy. Moreover, such is music's speed of development that, far from being simply responsive, it is prophetic: 'It is a herald, for change is inscribed in noise faster than it transforms society.'[3] Thus the order of *repetition*, sweeping through the world in the shape of mass reproduction, especially in recorded pop music, prefigures the meaningless stockpiling of commodities which is generalized in the system of advanced capitalism. But, for Attali, this order is already in conflict with the embryonic order of *composition* – a utopian practice of individualized do-it-yourself music-making – and this conflict lays before us the broader battle to be fought out within the networks of global capitalist society.

Attali's argument works at a schematic (indeed, sometimes apocalyptic) level, and he offers rather little guidance to interpretation of day-to-day practice or

---

[2]   Attali, Jacques (1985), *Noise: The Political Economy of Music*, trans. Brian Massumi, Manchester: Manchester University Press, 5.

[3]   Ibid.

specific musical texts. Here the work of Antoine Hennion comes to our aid. Hennion's core point is that, actually, music does not exist as such; that is to say, it is impossible to speak of 'music itself' since our speaking cannot help but create it in one form rather than another: music is constituted by the discourses which construe it and the practices which situate it. Thus 'it must be strictly forbidden to create links when this is not done by an identifiable intermediary';[4] what generates understanding of music and forms the topic of our investigations is the network of *mediations* – endless yet quite particular – that embed and embody it. In the advanced societies today, this network is huge in scope, for people use, value and discuss music in an enormous variety of ways, while this object of their discourse and practice occupies a multitude of homes and follows a maze of routes.

In one sense, Hennion's desire to focus down on the minutiae of mediation places him at the opposite extreme from Attali. Yet they agree about the social power of music. Although Hennion has no excitable theory of music's prophetic capacity, he has called for the replacement of the sociology of music by a 'musicology of society'; his point is that, by attending closely to the complex and fluid ways in which music features in people's lives, we can read something about their social world: 'Music is active within social life, it has "effects", then, because it offers specific materials to which actors may turn when they engage in the work of organising social life. Music is a resource – it provides affordances – for world building.'[5] Even if we might think that this statement should be glossed with a more explicit psychological as well as sociological dimension – for 'world building' takes place inside as well as outside – and even though we may find the thrust overly voluntarist – as if actors can simply decide how to use music, outside the constraints and pressures of those frameworks that form both it and them – this seems a good starting point for the study of popular music and identity. It is strictly forbidden, we might suggest, to examine popular music with a view to deciphering there representations of identity that have already been laid down elsewhere; rather, we should be looking for mechanisms of practice and orders of discourse through which sites of musical work contribute to the construction, maintenance and dissemination of identities.

These sites are 'modern'. The autonomy issue; the problematizing of the relationship between 'music' (or, more broadly, 'culture') and 'society'; artistic claims to critical or truth-value; secular usages of music in the service of 'technologies of the self' (world-building, identity-formation): these are all, in the

---

4   Antoine Hennion, quoted in DeNora, Tia (2000), *Music in Everyday Life*, Cambridge: Cambridge University Press, 4. The most readily accessible introduction by Hennion himself to his own theory is 'Music and Mediation: Towards a New Sociology of Music', in *The Cultural Study of Music: A Critical Introduction*, ed. Richard Middleton, Trevor Herbert and Martin Clayton, London and New York: Routledge, 2003, 80–91.
5   De Nora, *Music and Everyday Life*, 44.

forms outlined above, features of a specific historical phase taking off in the late eighteenth century – the phase of 'late modernity'. And the reflexiveness apparent both in current theories and current vernacular practices of music betoken a typically late-modern separation of spheres (politics, culture, economics, psychology, etc.) together with the equally characteristic fluidity, fragmentation and distancing of consciousness that goes with this. Integral to the whole historical development is the appearance of 'popular music' itself as we moderns understand the term (or as we understand it in anglophone countries; French lacks a direct equivalent, and *musique populaire* is closer to what in Britain came to be known as folk music). Although there is no terminological uniformity across the modernizing European (and New World) societies, in all of them an important part of the historical rupture lay in the evolution of new ways of thinking about vernacular musical practices. These new ways pointed in several different directions – towards new concepts of democracy, figuring 'the people' as a central political actor; towards processes of industrialization, urbanization and an accompanying commercialization of culture, figuring music as commodity; towards a new impetus in the building, consolidation and self-expression of nation-states, figured in part through a revaluation of musical heritage (manifested in folk song collecting and the like). But while this reveals the internal contradictions that were built into the new territory mapped by 'popular music' from its very beginnings, it does not alter the fact that, considered as a whole, this territory was located in opposition to a cultural interlocutor, situated within elite social realms. 'Popular music', however it is defined, lives as an Other, defined through its difference from its cultural and artistic betters. It is shunned, feared, policed, appropriated, desired, exoticized, constantly manipulated as an instrument of social control, ideological mystification, collective fantasy, self-abasement or gratification, resistance, patriotism and financial enrichment. While the setting within which these processes have played out has mutated constantly over the past 200 years as a result of social, economic and technological changes, the basic structure of the action – a staging of alterity, within an intricate network of socio-political and psychological operations – has not. On this level, the identity-question posed by popular music remains as it has been since Rousseau and the Revolution: who are the people?[6]

In France as elsewhere, the locale where popular music's difference is shaped has of course been intensely variable, ranging from the imagined village of tradition, through seedy café and variety hall, the cabaret of nostalgia and regret, the political theatre of national and proletarian anthem, to transatlantic images of modernization and rebellion, in jazz and hip hop. These multifarious patterns have been over-determined by larger narratives, most notably the impact of

---

[6]   This theme is explored in more detail in Middleton, Richard (2003), 'Locating the People: Music and the Popular', in *The Cultural Study of Music*, ed. Middleton, Herbert and Clayton, 251–62.

centralized production and mass-media dissemination, sounding the death, apparently, of Barthes's 'musica practica' (but also, arguably, precipitating its rebirth at the hands of guitar-playing singer-songwriters, do-it-yourself punks and home-studio techno-boys); the rise to dominance of Tin Pan Alley and then Anglo-American pop, with dramatic and provocative impacts in non-anglophone countries such as France; and the increasing incorporation of national scenes of production, practice and taste into trans-national, even global systems of accumulation, exchange and imagination. Ever since the shocking incursion of American rock'n'roll, France has been at the forefront of attempts to defend local musical interests and values against the threat of a homogenized 'McMusic'. But there are multiple ironies here. France is not only a relative periphery within the global media system but also a centre: after all, it was the first state to establish an agency for musical copyright protection – the *Société des auteurs, compositeurs et éditeurs* set up in 1851. Today, most successful musicians from francophone colonies and ex-colonies come – have to come – eventually to Paris, to perform and to record. The *zouk* genre inhabits a transatlantic circuit conjoining its birthplace in Guadeloupe and Martinique, and its production centre as a world music style, Paris; the *rai* stars from Algeria make their names on the global stage via French recordings, performances and marketing. But there is a lengthy history behind such contemporary cases, for they are inseparable from the legacy of colonialism and the 'orientalism' that went with it. For Bizet, in *Carmen*, the 'orient' lay in Spain, while for Debussy, strolling round the *Exposition Universelle* in Paris in 1889, it was located in Japan, Indo-China and Java. These exotic references can be linked to others – to the simple melodies of the people valorized by Rousseau as memories of that primitive scene which saw the birth of language in song; or, by contrast, to the Parisian 'negrophilia' of the 1920s, for which jazz, tango and singer-dancer Josephine Baker represented precisely a new spirit of modernity. Indeed, if we read Paul Gilroy's concept of the 'black Atlantic' as a way of interpreting the colonial *inside* of the imperialistic West and linking it to the far-off outside, we can see how Low- and Black-Others interconnect, and why this master-trope of difference lies at the core of the self-understanding of modernity itself.[7]

In the era of 'world music', this history contextualizes a still important issue of exactly whose identity is celebrated in these global musical movements, and at whose expense. The 'cultural imperialism' thesis, in its cruder forms at least, has long been discredited; the network of response, hybridity and multiple centres of power is too intricate for it to deal with.[8] Within the French history, the

---

[7]   Gilroy, Paul (1993), *The Black Atlantic: Modernity and Double Consciousness*, London: Verso.

[8]   See e.g. Laing, Dave (1986), 'The Music Industry and the "Cultural Imperialism" Thesis', *Media, Culture and Society*, **8** (3), 331–41; for an excellent case study illustrating the complexity, see Stokes, Martin (2003), 'Globalization and the Politics of World Music', in *The Cultural Study of Music*, ed. Middleton, Herbert and Clayton, 297–308.

varied responses to Anglo-American sources represented by, say, the jazz of the *Quintette du Hot Club de France*, the folk-rock of Alain Stivell, or the idiosyncratic dance-electronica of Air make the point. The question, then, is not one to be staged in a simple binaristic form: (homogenizing) global system versus (authentic) local traditions; rather, we should think of variegated responses to complex and unevenly manifested pressures. This is a view which, in James Clifford's words, sees the world not as 'populated by endangered authenticities – pure products always going crazy. Rather it makes space for specific paths through modernity.'[9] However, this space should not be imagined either as home to a happy, utopian pluralism. Lazily, we often imagine 'world music' as simply a pop music marketing category or perhaps as just that cornucopia of 'other' music brought to us by globalization. But, as Philip Bohlman has argued,[10] 'world music' is an idea with a long history, founded on the trope of 'encounter'; and those encounters that make history, and thus 'world music' – French missionaries describing the songs of New World cannibals, subsequently discussed by Montaigne, just as much as *Deep Forest* and other recent recordings of 'pygmy pop'[11] – are always structured in dominance. A country like France stands, fascinatingly, in more than one role and at more than one level in this multivalent system. If popular music is good to think (and feel) with, and offers rich materials and thickly mediated settings with which to do identity work, we need to recognize that the identities in question are not only malleable and multi-faceted, but also multi-levelled – *layered* by structures of power.

9   Clifford, James (1988), *The Predicament of Culture: Twentieth-Century Ethnography, Literature and Art*, Cambridge MA: Harvard University Press, 5.
10   Bohlman, Philip (2002), *World Music: A Very Short Introduction*, Oxford: Oxford University Press.
11   See Feld, Steve (2000), 'The Politics and Poetics of Pygmy Pop', in *Western Music and Its Others: Difference, Representation and Appropriation in Music*, ed. Georgina Born and Dave Hesmondhalgh, Berkeley, CA: University of California Press, 254–79.

Chapter 1

The study of popular music between sociology and aesthetics: a survey of current research in France

Philippe Le Guern

Placed within the general framework of the sociology of art, the sociology of music, and in particular the sociology of the most 'contemporary' forms of musical production, appears in France to have been relatively neglected.[1] The neglect for this field of research can for example be measured by the number of articles devoted to it in academic journals: although *Actes de la Recherche en Sciences Sociales* was quick to show an interest in the production of symbolic forms, a survey of articles published in the journal between 1975 and 1997 (119 numbers) reveals that only six articles were devoted to music (five dealing with classical music and one with country music) and that, in comparison, the literary field and that of art were much better covered. In the *Revue Française de Sociologie* the treatment of different artistic disciplines is statistically less biased against music, but the subject was nevertheless covered only twice between 1981 and 2000 in a total of more than 500 articles (one article on jazz and one on contemporary music). The perusal of bibliographies of French work in sociology allows similar conclusions to be drawn; for example, in the dozen or so pages of a recent bibliography claiming an exhaustive coverage of studies on music, only three references are to be found to French articles and books specifically dealing with rock or with *musiques actuelles*, in stark contrast with the much greater number of studies produced by Anglo-Saxon researchers on the same subjects.[2]

---

[1]   There is a great variety of terms describing the music discussed in this chapter, such as 'popular music', 'musiques actuelles' ('contemporary' musics), 'musiques amplifiées' ('amplified' musics), 'le rock' (rock or pop of all kinds, in the UK/US senses), 'variétés' (varieties). The discussion given in this chapter takes a very broad view of what popular music is in France, but focuses on musics which are *not* taught in official Academies of music (*conservatoires*), which form part of the cultural industries, and which are the objects of mass rather than restricted consumption.

[2]   See the Bibliography provided by Hennion, Antoine, Maisonneuve, Sophie, and Gomart, Emilie (2000), *Figures de l'amateur. Formes, objets, pratiques de l'amour de la musique aujourd'hui*, Paris: La Documentation française. Attention should also be drawn

Such a situation has lead Patrick Mignon, for example, to emphasize that 'research interest in rock is new in France, but the pioneering nature of French work on the subject should not lead anyone to imagine that we are are doing anything more than discovering an America already comprehensively explored'.[3] Danièle Pistone uses another source to arrive at a similar conclusion, since in consulting the CD-Rom *Doc-Thèses* covering PhDs awarded in France between 1972 and 1999 he finds merely three theses dealing with music out of a total of 341 devoted to sociology overall.[4]

How can this apparent lack of interest in *musiques actuelles* be explained? Several reasons can doubtless be suggested: on the one hand, in contrast with classical music, the least legitimated forms of music do not predispose *musiques actuelles* to become acceptable objects of study – as Erik Neveu has pointed out (not without humour), 'why waste serious academic work on minor topics while Hobbes and the sociology of voting behaviour still have so much to tell us? What does an interest in rock reveal apart from a questionable desire to distinguish oneself?' On the other hand, the criticisms that have accompanied the growth of rock music and the dangers of anomie predicted by some intellectual commentators (such as Alain Finkielkraut and Alan Bloom)[5] has helped contribute to the undervaluing of rock music as a worthy object of study. Moreover, whereas important studies of the role of government policies in general and cultural policy in particular in the encouragement of musical scenes and the record industry do exist, for example, rare are the ethnographic works which analyse record companies themselves or musicians. This may suggest that practical difficulties (which are not, of course, the monopoly of the study of music) are to blame, and do not allow the establishment of a cumulative body of knowledge, enabling us to produce a subtle understanding of the musical artist and to reflect the full complexity of the world of musical art. Another difficulty is that the meaning of the categories most usually used to describe musical styles (*musiques vivantes, amplifiées, actuelles*) vary according to whether they are coined and used by institutions as disparate as musical criticism, specialist magazines, record companies, or public policy emanating from central or local government. To fully understand the nuances of these terms it would doubtless be necessary to study the visions these categories obey and the divisions which held them apart. A further difficulty relates to the problem whether and how sociologists should take into

---

to one of the few French periodicals devoted to rock and other popular music styles, entitled *Volume!* (Editions Mélanie Séteun), which commenced publication in 2002.

[3]   In Mignon, Patrick and Hennion, Antoine (eds) (1991), *Rock: de l'histoire au mythe*, Paris: Anthropos, coll. Vibration, 6.

[4]   Pistone, Danièle (2000), 'De l'histoire sociale de la musique à la sociologie musicale: bilans et perspectives', in Anne-Marie Green (ed.), *Musique et sociologie. Enjeux méthodologiques et approches empiriques*, Paris: L'Harmattan, coll. Logiques sociales, 83.

[5]   Finkielkraut, Alain (1987), *La défaite de la pensée*, Paris: Gallimard.

account the supposedly special nature of the musical act itself, and, for example, the value of collaboration between sociology and musicology.[6]

The analysis of *musiques actuelles* as a social and cultural phenomenon is criss-crossed by a series of questions which are properly sociological: the legitimacy of cultural goods; music as a vector of the construction of identity; methodological choices between paradigms of the sociology of domination (Bourdieu) and the sociology of 'worlds of art' (Becker); or, further, attempts to go beyond the determinist sociology which relates the structure of tastes and socioeconomic position through a sociology of 'love of music' or 'ceremonies of pleasure';[7] the pertinence of the distinction between 'savant' and 'populaire', in other words between music which is 'serious' and music which is 'not serious'. Additionally, we should not forget the peculiar position which those who come to study this kind of subject find themselves occupying, since the struggle to study rock is similar to that required to study female, proletarian, or black perspectives on history.[8]

Without aspiring to an exhaustive survey, and by concentrating on a number of major academic journals, this chapter proposes a summary of the current state of French research on the sociology of *musiques actuelles* (distinct from classical music or contemporary music) in France. This summary will cover work on the conditions of music production itself (the socio-political context and the workings of the systems of production), and the conditions of music's reception (systems of mediation such as radio, concerts, accompanying discourses such as the 'Rock press') studies of the music-consuming public and of the uses to which music is put. From such a summary, it will transpire that a study of 'rock' needs to address at least three significant series of questions: firstly, how can one measure the impact of *musiques actuelles*, particularly amongst young audiences and those driven by the tenets of counter-culture – how far is rock a music which is indissociably linked to a certain phase of life? Secondly, how can one analyse the origin and development of rock music in France other than as a spontaneous phenomenon – what is the role played by 'the Art world' (the recording industry and the media etc.) in the social production of this kind of music? And how can one take account of musical genres or musical practices left in the shadows such as amateur musicians or musicians in the Métro? Finally, what are the typologies which obtain within the musical field (*musiques actuelles, vivantes, amplifiées*) and according to what principles do they operate?

---

6   Green (ed.), *Musique et sociologie*, 224.
7   Hennion, Antoine (1996), 'L'Amour de la musique aujourd'hui: une recherche en cours sur les figures de l'amateur', in Alain Darré (ed.), *Musique et politique. Les répertoires de l'identité*, Rennes: Presses Universitaires de Rennes, coll. Res Publica, 47.
8   See Mignon and Hennion (eds), *Rock: de l'histoire au mythe*, 264.

Typologies and terminology: 'musiques actuelles', 'musiques vivantes', 'musiques amplifiées'

The issue of typologies and of how to label the different styles of music is one of the major preoccupations of the sociology of music. We can, for example, point out the variability of genres and styles of music covered by the common-denominator term of 'rock'. Today, the label 'rock' is widely attributed. Thus one can find within the same musical landscape of 'rock' both rap and 'new age' music diametrically opposed to each other. Catherine Dutheil remarks – in a survey of bands in Nantes – that the profusion of musical styles to which rock bands lay claim reflects a logic of belonging in which it is important to assert one's identity and originality as a band, a process which can go so far as to invent new styles or new descriptions of musical style, such as 'hard-blues'.[9] More generally, it is the category 'rock' which is problematic: does it represent a pure, original style of music and how can distinctions be made between different genres of music where there are so many similar styles?

The opposition drawn between 'serious music' and 'non-serious music' is similarly problematic: the important contribution to this debate made by Pierre-Michel Menger's study of musicians raises the question of the divide which seems to exist between 'legitimate' musics and those which are less legitimate or not legitimate at all. Menger's analysis, which combines economics and sociology, deals with work in music and artistic careers and deals precisely with composers of so-called 'serious' music since 1945. Menger's analysis notably leads him to define 'la musique populaire' *negatively* as a music of mass consumption, in contradistinction to music of restricted consumption. He reveals that in the musical field, the question of defining artistic domains and their boundaries is above all an issue of money, 'since a "serious" repertoire, by a more or less complex machinery of revalorisation is advantaged in the drawing up of rights in order to marginally rectify the socio-economic imbalance between the two opposing markets'.[10] In contrast to 'rock' but also to classical or 'serious' music, it is jazz that is considered by Béatrice Madiot as a musical genre which is intermediate between what can be legitimated and what is legitimate, an intermediate object in the social hierarchy of musical value between 'serious music' and *musique populaire*.[11] A survey carried out by Madiot of 95 jazz musicians provides a possibility of apprehending – negatively – the social representation of 'rock' since although 'rock' appears hard to define, its musical characteristic which is the most often cited is its sound, and sound is followed by rhythm and then by its choice of instruments, of which the

---

9   Dutheil, Catherine (1991), 'Les musiciens de rock nantais', in Mignon and Hennion (eds), *Rock: de l'histoire au mythe*, 150–51, 153.
10   Menger, Pierre-Michel (1983), *Le paradoxe du musicien*, Paris: Flammarion, 28.
11   Madiot, Béatrice (1991), 'Les musiciens de jazz et de rock', in Mignon and Hennion (eds), *Rock: de l'histoire au mythe*, 183–93.

guitar is the unchallenged symbol. But in addition to these considerations of style, Madiot finds that rock has particular features as a genre, such as energy and a technical simplicity.[12] Thus an initial criterion in the definition of 'rock' could seem to be the value attached to instantaneousness and the present, this value being found notably in the primacy given to the desire to technically master an instrument and the excessive importance attached to representations such as authenticity, energy, instinct and impulse.[13]

It is also possible to define 'rock' within the framework of a teleological approach: Seca, for example, concludes that the purpose of rock music is to engender a 'state of trance', in other words to uncover emotions by exaggerating them in a type of aesthetic rapport with music which is relatively novel.[14] Another purpose of rock music may also be to create markers of recognition and affinity – in other words new identities for social groups. Rock music can also serve various other purposes, for example at the level of local government policy: economic at Belfort with the *Eurockéennes* festival, or, as Mignon has stressed, linked to issues of identity at Givors, with politics and publicity at Rennes, Belfort and Agen – with the Florida festival – cultural at Rennes, Poitiers, Lille and Montpellier, or social, like the first political measures taken in favour of rock. Yet another purpose of rock music can be to enable the re-creation of 'local memory' as in the case of the *Musée de la musique populaire* at Montluçon.[15]

In the final analysis, it is probably the constructivist viewpoint which offers the richest resources for understanding the category of 'rock' music. In looking at the social invention of the notion of 'rock' music, Mignon demonstrates that 'rock' is not a closely defined isolated object but is rather the result of collective activities, thus: 'Rock can be defined as the network of all those individuals who are necessary to the production of what is called "rock" – the musician, the fan, the record-buyer, the music critic, the concert organiser, the instrument salesman and repairer, the record producer, the sound engineer, the academic who analyses trends in society and the chargé de mission for rock at the Ministry of Culture.'[16] In this perspective, rock and its history can be analysed as a succession of different systems of collective actions and compromises on what one agrees to define as rock, or again as the juxtaposition of specific interests (of musicians, the media, music industry employees, the market, critics and commentators) which propose a series of definitions and representations of which rock is the subject (for example – rock is more 'authentic' than varieties, more

---

[12]   Ibid., 188.
[13]   See Teillet, Philippe (1991), 'Une politique culturelle du rock', in Mignon and Hennion (eds), *Rock: de l'histoire au mythe*, 236.
[14]   Seca, Jean-Marie (1988), *Vocations rock*, Paris: Le Méridien.
[15]   Brandl, Emmanuel (2000), 'La sociologie compréhensive comme apport à l'étude des musiques amplifiées/actuelles régionales', in Green (ed.), *Musique et sociologie*, 282–83.
[16]   Mignon, Patrick (1991), 'Paris/Givors: le rock local', in Mignon and Hennion (eds), *Rock: de l'histoire au mythe*, 197.

'representative' of *mouvements sociaux)*. More specifically, this framework of analysis close to constructivist sociology enables Mignon to draw up an inventory of factors which allow the existence of a rock music *à la française* tied, for example, to 'the sedimentation of old musical practices, the invention of local worlds of rock music and to its ability to involve local politics and cultural, social and educational institutions'.[17] Similarly, Philippe Teillet also opposes an essentialist definition of rock music, explaining that as a generic expression covering often contradictory terms, 'rock' exists only through the discourses (historical, critical, media) of which it is the object and which create it.[18] It is thus possible to identify elements in the discourses about rock which construct the identity of rock music and which permit the exclusion of artistic suggestions which go too far.[19] This is an identity which is defined *negatively* (neither a component of mass culture, nor a component of elite culture) or *positively* (authentic music, heterogeneous music, music of multiple borrowings). Tracing the birth of the terminologies used to describe rock and its multiple forms also means taking into consideration the social construction of its referents expressed in cultural policies at various levels, from the Ministry of Culture down to the regional or local level, as Mignon,[20] Teillet[21] and E. Brandl[22] have indicated, but also those contained within activities of commentary, particularly in the rock press.[23] In this respect, Teillet demonstrates how and why the French regional decentralized authorities favour the term 'musiques amplifiées' whereas the Ministry of Culture prefers 'musiques actuelles', these choices reflecting the positions occupied by these musics and the power relationships at different levels of cultural policy. Concerning the apparatus of commentary (particularly the

---

[17]   Ibid., 199.

[18]   See Teillet, 'Une politique culturelle du rock', 218.

[19]   Ibid., 220.

[20]   Mignon, 'Paris/Givors: le rock local', 197–216; and Mignon, Patrick (1997), 'Evolution de la prise en compte des musiques amplifiées par les politiques publiques', *Politiques publiques et musiques amplifiées*, Adem, FL: Gema, 23–31.

[21]   Teillet, Philippe (1999), '"Musiques amplifiées", "musiques actuelles", "musiques populaires", "musiques d'aujourd'hui", etc. ou la querelle des principes de vision et de division', in *Actes des 2ème rencontres nationales Politiques publiques et musiques amplifiées/actuelles*, La Scène. *Le Magazine professionnel des spectacles*, Hors série, Ed. Millénaire, Avril, 115; and Teillet, Philippe (2002), 'Eléments pour une histoire des politiques publiques en faveur des musiques amplifiées', in Philippe Poirrier (ed.) (2002), *Les collectivités locales et la culture; les formes de l'institutionnalisation, 19ème–20ème*, Paris: La Documentation Française/Comité d'histoire du ministère de la Culture.

[22]   Brandl, Emmanuel (2000), 'La sociologie compréhensive comme apport à l'étude des musiques amplifiées/actuelles régionales', in Green (ed.), *Musique et sociologie*, 256–300.

[23]   See Teillet, Philippe (2002), 'Les cultes musicaux. La contribution de l'appareil de commentaires à la construction de cultes; l'exemple de la presse rock', in Philippe Le Guern (ed.), *La célébration. Œuvres cultes et culture fan*, Rennes: Presses Universitaires de Rennes, coll. Le sens social.

specialized press), Teillet also shows how references and norms such as 'immediacy' and 'ephemerality' have been instituted with the aim of characterizing rock music. He also shows how it is the interiorization of models coming from persons of reference and characterized by their spontaneity, impulsiveness or even juvenility, which nowadays allows the legitimation of (and the admission of the legitimacy of) what is ephemeral, and penalizes what claims too visibly the desire to endure. He suggests that it is this hierarchization which produces the difficulty for rock musicians to enjoy both credibility and a long career.[24] The constructivist approach to the definition of the category of 'rock' finds perhaps its most developed form in Mignon's article 'Rock et rockers: un peuple du rock?' in which he suggests the field of rock is 'an interesting case of contagion of representation'[25] which deals as much with the values vehicled by rock (youth, rebellion) as with the practices with which it is associated (the idea according to which it is young people who produce and consume rock). Mignon demonstrates that there is need for a dual process of deconstruction and construction of the object of rock music in order to question the truths upon which discourses on rock are based (coherence, the spontaneity of its production, its universalist or specific vocation) and everything which underpins the idea of a rock culture.[26] In this way, Mignon demonstrates that rock culture is the product of a collective action associating a large number of agents, and not merely a group of people – either 'youth' or music business executives – and that in this perspective, rock is a heterogeneous object which produces itself through a series of successive compromises between differing definitions.

However, without wanting to ignore the fact that rock is also the product of a discourse about performance, Olivier Donnat suggests that he cannot adhere totally to a viewpoint which aims to contest the unifying character of the category 'rock'.[27] In fact, despite internal differentiations which make rock a protean object, one can consider that this music – with its own history, its own specialist critics, its stars – brings together a universe of references and symbols which everyone recognizes as rock.

Being a musician: from learning to doing

Studying musicians as a group raises obvious difficulties for sociologists considering music, mostly for practical reasons. Firstly, because they are difficult

---

[24] Teillet, Philippe (1996), 'L'Etat culturel et les musiques d'aujourd'hui', in Alain Darré (ed.), *Musique et politique. Les répertoires de l'identité*, Presses Universitaires de Rennes, coll. Res Publica, 120.

[25] Mignon, Patrick (1996), 'Rock et rockers: un peuple du rock?', in Darré, *Musique et politique*, 73.

[26] Ibid., 75.

[27] Donnat, Olivier (1994), *Les Français face à la culture*, Paris: La Découverte.

to understand or observe (especially in the case of styles of music taught outside music academies or learned 'on-the-job'), the ways in which musicians learn to play are an elusive subject for sociological analysis, which therefore often concentrates on rehearsal or concerts. Moreover, there are few studies which succeed in describing the development of musicians' careers in a diachronic perspective, since most investigations are snapshots supported by statistical material and by interviews, but which only seldom manage to follow the changes and development of musical 'careers'.

The interactions governing the life of a rock group have for example been observed by Catherine Dutheil in a major provincial town (Nantes) in a study which allows the deconstruction of the main stereotypes which habitually (since the vogue for black leather jackets in the 1960s) define the cliché of the rock musician. Firstly, the musicians are not so young, secondly, they do not predominantly come from working-class families, and thirdly, most of them have educational qualifications. This data on 'rockers' as a group allow us to 'nuance what has sometimes been called "the rock life-style" or also "rock culture", which can now be seen less as a break with society (tied to a particular age-group or social class) and more as an art of living in parallel, to the side of normal society'.[28] Dutheil reveals that rock musicians in Nantes as a group are characterized by other sociological variables such as gender division – with a marked over-representation of males – to such an extent that gender is more important as a marker than social class. Another lesson drawn from the study is that the musicians are mostly musically self-taught and that playing music actually requires input of money rather than providing an income. Finally, Dutheil exposes the internal workings of the rock bands she studied, which were typified by a high turnover of groupings of musicians (average life of a band two years), by financial insecurity (often linked to an inability to develop a commercial outlook) and a symbolic division between members of the band based on the instruments played which determines musicians' roles within the band (for example, the bass guitar is the least prestigious, since it gives little scope for virtuoso playing and, in contrast with the guitar, does not allow composition).

The production of music in a location which is sited outside the usual confines of musical dissemination has been studied by Anne-Marie Green in an ethnographic analysis of musicians in the Paris Métro.[29] This study is underpinned by a number of significant theoretical choices, of which the first is the use of the term *musiques vivantes* to describe the musics played in the Métro – this is intended to take into account the diversity of forms of production and reception of music (including music played outside the usual locales such as

---

[28]   Dutheil, Catherine (1991), 'Les musiciens de rock nantais', in Mignon and Hennion (eds), *Rock: de l'histoire au mythe*, 150–51.
[29]   Green, Anne-Marie (1998), *Musiciens de métro. Approche des musiques vivantes urbaines*, Paris: L'Harmattan, coll. Logiques Sociales.

concert halls) as a challenge to those who 'wish to enclose music in hallowed locations and to assert that outside these places there is not music but simply "noise" for the common people'.[30] The second significant choice underpinning the study concerns that of the place and the function of such musics in urban public spaces such as the Métro. More generally, Green's theoretical framework aims to reconsider Bourdieu's notion of the *habitus* and of social determination by investigating an approach to life (and to a life in music) which diverges from the usual pattern of musical and aesthetic factors. In order to develop such a theoretical framework, she makes particular reference to Marc Augé's notion of 'non-lieux' (non-places) and Michel de Certeau's 'arts de faire' (arts of doing). According to Green, listening to live music in the Métro, as an untypical practice, is a source of new kinds of sociability, which although ephemeral, nevertheless break free from the functional dimensions of strictly public places by allowing the possibility of finding pleasure almost serendipitously.[31] Green draws up a typology of musicians playing in the Métro and takes into account their motivation and interest in playing in such an environment, but, at the same time, she seems to hesitate between a relatively beatific vision of Métro musicians as a group (they represent a unified social grouping, they assert their cultural identity) and a definition of them which reintroduces the theory of domination (there is a hierarchy of musics and of street musicians, their career is often viewed as a kind of obstacle course). At the end of her analysis, Green proposes a triple conclusion illustrating the status of *musiques vivantes* overall (of which music in the Métro is merely one instance): the relative autonomy of this kind of music (it escapes the control of the music business); the modification of the usual context of musical reception (outside radio, records, the concert hall) allows the development of new forms of sociability; the break with the preconceptions about the musician as artist and clichés about the 'meaning of music', 'musical talent' and the reintroduction of the idea of musicians' social function.

In the same way that those musics which are wrongly considered as 'marginal' (such as 'rock') have been neglected by academic study, so have musical practices deemed 'ordinary' (*ordinaire*), 'daily' (*quotidien*) or 'amateur'. In this area, however, a number of studies stand out.

The first study that must be mentioned is the book-record produced by Marc Touché, in which he studies the origins and development of *musiques amplifiées* in order to rediscover practices and forms of sociability generally ignored through a field-study of the history of electronic amplification in the late 1950s and early 1960s in Annecy.[32] The study is presented in four parts: firstly, Touché considers the involvement of public policy, notably at the local level, at a time

---

30   Ibid., 208.
31   Ibid.
32   Touché, Marc (1998), *Mémoire Vive*, Annecy: Association Musiques Amplifiées/Le Brise Glace.

when musical practices had been spreading and diversifying; secondly, he presents extracts of interviews which through a series of case histories of various individuals retrace the development of electronic amplification; thirdly, he reconsiders the conditions under which rock bands make music in an analysis of musical rehearsal not only as a stage in the musical process but also as a social issue; finally, the study addresses the question of specialized infrastructures for musical practices, the equality of access to them for all and the attitude of the municipal authorities towards this issue.

Methodologically, the study relies on a series of interviews and the analysis of a corpus of documents from the period concerned, but despite the difficulties inherent in such attempts at reconstituting history, Touché's erudite attention to the story of electronic amplification and the development of musical techniques (participant statements on the early days of amplification or on the spread of the first electric instruments are particularly informative) enable him to show to what extent they determine the form and end-products of musical practice. One of the musicians questioned relates: 'I started playing guitar all through summer 1960, it was a 99 franc guitar, and I played it all the time. The same year we found the group "les Merry-Set" ... We wired up the guitar to radios with big speakers to give ourselves amps ... We generally rehearsed in flats during the afternoons and all the time at weekends.'[33] How does the idea of creating a group arise? How do groups organize the division of tasks, and particularly, the allocation of instrumental roles? How do musicians start doing music through buying equipment or finding rehearsal rooms? How are repertoires, access to concerts, to recording and to a professional status organized? Touché's interviews give a flavour of the daily aspects of musical practices and ordinary sociability at the scale of a town such as Annecy contextualized in their social environment (friends, families, networks of musicians, associations), in their institutional environment (town council, churches, youth clubs, compulsory schooling until 16, military service, and for some the war in Algeria) and in their technical environment (progressive electrification of households, ownership of a record players, transistor radios, the presence of a jukebox).[34]

By emphasizing in particular the act of rehearsing, Touché's aim is to relocate the social and technical conditions of musical practice within the field of the representation of music. The strength of this approach is the way it allows the review of a number of stereotypes and ideological constructions which clutter the study *musiques amplifiées*. Firstly, for example, the practice of these kinds of music is not necessarily the monopoly of young people or of those from working-class backgrounds, since a sociological study of musicians using amplified sound demonstrates, on the contrary, that they involve male practitioners of various ages drawn from a variety of social milieux. In any case, engaging in the practice of

---

[33]   Ibid., 38–39.
[34]   Ibid., 6.

music appears as an element which plays a highly structuring role in the everyday lives and sociability of individuals 'whether it is for a few years during adolescence or during an entire lifetime (choice of partner, housing, work, networks of friends, social solidarities built around common musical interests, the auditory and musical education of children)'.[35] Another cliché that Touché's study addresses is that which states that the ambition to use as many decibels as possible is an inherent feature of *musiques amplifiées* – in reality, it seems that what may appear to be an aesthetic choice is actually the consequence of specific practical constraints: 'A number of groups play loud not for aesthetic motives, but in order to make themselves heard in a magma flow of noise resulting from the clash between their own sound and unfavourable acoustic surroundings.'[36] Finally, Touché's work shows how rehearsal is a markedly revealing indicator of the effects and issues raised by the linguistic labelling of different categories of music ('musiques amplifiées', 'actuelles', 'vivantes'): amongst the practitioners, the never-ending renewal of categories and typologies is an instrument of social distinction through criteria of identity, age and so on. Thus the category 'musiques amplifiées' cannot simply denote a sole musical genre, but rather those genres which share sound amplification. Similarly, the category 'musiques actuelles' is equally questionable since in addition to the fact that not all music played nowadays is necessarily amplified, 'using the term *musiques actuelles* amounts to a declaration of war on classical institutions, by suggesting that they have no longer any meaning whereas they are completely relevant'.[37] Moreover, using the expression 'musiques actuelles' can suggest that these musics have no history.

The study made by Antoine Hennion, Sophie Maisonneuve and Emilie Gomart lets light in from another perspective on those musics which have been left in the shadows. The theoretical basis of this work emphasizes the limitations of critical sociology, accused of reducing aesthetic pleasure to a mere social construct.[38] Thus, understanding the tastes and practices of these amateur musicians 'enables us to see that it is impossible to be satisfied with explanations of "beauty" in terms of conventional products of collective action, or of art in terms of belief or *illusio* to use Bourdieu's famous term'.[39] The amateur musician is here defined in a less restrictive way than the traditional sense of someone who practices music for leisure rather than professionally – amateur practices can reflect forms of attachment to the works or (artistic) skills which are highly developed. In addition, observing the ways in which music is accessed and consumed reveals the role played by these activities in the construction of identities: musical passions are ritualized, they can be associated with important

---

[35] Ibid., 87.
[36] Ibid., 85.
[37] Ibid., 95.
[38] See Hennion, Maisonneuve and Gomart (2000), *Figures de l'amateur.*
[39] Ibid., 30.

moments in anyone's life, strategies of listening are many and varied (from the Walkman for adolescents to the hi-fi stereo for music aficionados) and musical taste is indissociable from a heterogeneous ensemble of 'practices of passionate enthusiasm' such as dance, fashion, social and even sexual relations.

Jean-Marie Seca has studied musicians and *musiques alternatives* within the framework of a questionnaire survey supported by observation and interviews of 106 groups.[40] Reference to 'underground' – which covers a musical field which is rather extensive, ranging through rock, punk and rap, but sharing a common opposition to musics with a strictly commercial purpose – allows Seca to address the issue of music as a model of mediation for minority groups, or groups which feel they are 'deviant'. He investigates particularly the meaning of a representation which blends at one and the same time an attitude of revolt and one of sincerity on the part of those who lay claim to it – how does one build the vocation of being a rocker? How do the careers of certain rockers evolve? What are the modes of apprenticeship, of work, of rehearsal which construct the identity of underground musicians? Seca particularly reveals the motivations which lead musicians to choose the repertoire of *musiques alternatives*, showing that a common characteristic of these musicians is often a refusal of hierarchy and of the usual structures of socialization. In this way, the representation of underground artistic activity is highly idealized and contrasted with professional musical activities which are more 'conventional'. The minority stigma of underground musics thus operates as an element which serves to distinguish these musicians. The laying claim to authenticity is a constant feature of underground musicians but it should not be seen merely as a consequence of the experience of these artists as a minority group. Seca shows that such claiming of authenticity also has uses in developing careers: given that success requires an understanding and knowledge of the market and that 'making it' is as unpredictable as there are understandings of what success is, presenting underground music as a kind of workshop activity imbued with purity and authenticity allows musicians to make a virtue of necessity if success eludes them. Essentially, for Seca, 'All these genres simply repossess the model of the *artiste maudit* – of which Van Gogh is the prototype – and re-arrange it to suit their circumstances.'[41] The dialectical opposition between pure and impure leads to the denouncing of forms of music deemed too commercial, official or conventional, since according to these criteria impure musics are devoid of emotion and revolt, lacking in message and aesthetically routine. Opposed to these musics – for the agents of the underground – 'pure' styles define themselves by their degree of sincerity. However, the position occupied by underground musicians is often more ambivalent than this dialectical opposition

---

[40]   Seca, Jean-Marie (2001), *Les musiciens underground*, Paris: PUF, coll. 'Psychologie sociale'.
[41]   Ibid., 95.

might suggest, in that the quest for aesthetic approval ('purity') does not automatically exclude the search for commercial success and stardom. Thus the ways in which groups function are significant: the size of the group is a factor which determines how it can make music (from rehearsal with several players, through solitary composition using computers); technical requirements are not necessarily simply those of using instruments but can also include other forms, such as scratching or DJ mixing. It is also evident that groups' careers are built from fumblings to find the successful formula for working together – constant attempts to find more and more available (and increasingly expensive) rehearsal space, the invention of a more and more personal musical style, rehearsals playing for friends, then small concerts, then self-produced records. In any analysis, in contrast to the myth of musical giftedness and of spontaneous artistic creation, these tentative steps suggest that all musical activity is accompanied by a representation of music and by considerations of commercialization, competition and potential audience.

The transition from rehearsal to concert also offers an opportunity to understand the purist ethic to which many musicians lay claim. This is what is investigated by Frédéric Saumade in his description of a rock concert.[42] He identifies the features specific to this highly ritualized presentation and the way in which the audience's assessment of the concert revolves around three main issues: the sound, instrumental technique and energy. Saumade shows that the concert is interesting in the way that it requires its spectators to be at the *right* distance from the stage – far from the stage the fan is also distanced as much as possible from the musicians, but for those fans who are the most enthusiastic about the star, nearness to the stage (which can involve a physical ordeal, given the crush of the crowd and the levels of noise) is a sign of passionate intensity. For the musicians the expression of rock music, characterized by the simplicity of chords and the repetition of themes and rhythms, can be considered as a way of repeating time and extending the duration of the concert, or, moreover, seeking a trance-like state and its effects, in which the surpassing of oneself becomes something shared by both musicians and the audience.

The question of emotions and trances is also at the heart of the analyses made by Morgan Jouvenet on the work of DJs: 'The DJ adapts to his audience, but in another sense, his work is to discretely inform the demands of his listeners ... in short, it's a matter of "shared delirium".'[43] The example of the DJ is also interesting in that the work of DJs partially deconstructs the theories sanctifying the 'author' and the finished and unalterable 'work', since it plays with musical elements which are fragmentary and transformable. For all that, however, this

---

[42]   Saumade, Frédéric (1998), 'Le rock, ou comment se formalise une passion moderne', in Christian Bromberger (ed.), *Passions ordinaires*, Paris: Hachette Littératures, 309–29.
[43]   Jouvenet, Morgan (2001), 'Emportés par le mix. Les DJ et le travail de l'émotion', *Musique et émotion*, Terrain 37, septembre, 48.

deconstruction is only relative, since, as Jouvenet shows, within the profession of DJ-ing normative rules and values distinguish between mere 'technicians' and DJs able to develop an individual aesthetic style (who are deemed more 'noble' and closer to the traditional model of what is expected of an artist). Essentially, it is studying the ways in which DJs acquire their *savoir-faire* that the distinction between mere 'record-pushers' and the others can be understood. Being a good DJ means more than simply acquiring a technical mastery of the equipment, but also being able to adapt the music to the place, the audience and the time. To become a good DJ it is practice in context (rather than alone) which is necessary, allowing the DJ to augment his knowledge of links between musical forms and reactions of audiences and at the same time constructing a personality as an artist.[44] It is in this way, also, that DJs can be lead to compare themselves with shamans, since their musical performance has constantly to adapt itself to changing circumstances and aim to elicit emotions which culminate in a trance-like state. In other words, the sociology of music here starts to cross over with the aesthetic theory of emotions.

The musical field: from public policies to the record business

The study of the politics of rock – notably marked in France by reference to Jack Lang (minister of Culture) and the cultural policy overall implemented between 1981 and 1986 and then renewed in 1997 – has enabled an analysis of the diachronic development of France's cultural discourse. Philippe Teillet has drawn a number of conclusions from this: firstly, access to cultural heritage is no longer the sole priority of the state, since it is now also inclined to encourage the development of individual cultural practices; secondly, cultural policy no longer aims exclusively to encourage the preservation for posterity of works of art, since rock is also promoted by the state, even though it is characterized by the expression of desire and by immediacy. More broadly, this widening of the cultural field to all arts – including those of the 'everyday' – makes reference to Michel de Certeau's definition of 'la culture au pluriel' (plural culture). The question thus arises of how the state can intervene in a sector which is apparently problematic because of the way in which rock is 'a composite phenomenon, both musical and social' and also because it is 'unsuited to the usual forms of cultural policy' and therefore at any kind of 'institutionalization'. As Teillet has demonstrated, the state attempts to avoid the risk of institutionalizing rock through its actions: 'its interventions are short-term and target the music business as live spectacle in order to help its regeneration and diversity.'[45] More generally, it can be seen how rock music challenges the usual patterns of action of cultural

---

44   See ibid., 49.
45   Teillet, Philippe (1991), 'Une politique culturelle du rock', 227.

policy, since its ephemeral and protean nature – not necessarily conforming with the usual aesthetic norms – obliges the Ministry of Culture to structure its interventions less in terms of preserving works of art than of encouraging individual artistic expression. As Vincent Dubois has reminded us: 'on 10 May 1982, the terms of the Ministry of Culture's brief are changed to replace "masterpieces" with "art by all".'[46]

Concerning the recording industry, it is to be noted that with the exception of studies of an economic nature devoted to the record business, there has been little or nothing said about record companies themselves. The work undertaken by Hennion, even if it is now somewhat dated given the developments which have since affected the music business (in particular the arrival of MP3), still represents something of an exception in this area of study.[47] Hennion's study is structured chronologically to follow the different stages of the production and marketing of a record and presents itself as a series of ethnographic observations on the organizational structure and activities characteristic of record companies. Rather than being simply descriptive, however, the study aims to discover whether 'hits' are the result of rationalization, anticipation or the formatting of the tastes of the 'general public'. What is a 'hit' and how is it made? In order to answer this question, Hennion analyses the structure and workings of the field of the recording industry, establishing initially that the tendency towards the concentration of record companies is not automatically – and contrary to the generally accepted idea – the cause and the symptom of cultural globalization: 'Even if the oligopoly of huge world-wide companies is exclusively Anglo-Saxon, it would be wrong to conclude from this that the UK and US are culturally dominant.'[48] In fact, according to Hennion, within the French subsidiaries of these multinational companies can be seen a 'Frenchifying' of teams and methods of work, and, moreover, from the standpoint of production, it seems uncertain to talk of standardization or industrial uniformity. On the contrary, indeed, there appears to exist a diversification of musical genres and consuming publics and in addition, the difference between small and large record companies cannot simply be presented as a conflict in which the bigger companies win. The system seems more complex, allowing the independent labels room for manoeuvre, enabling them to be more than mere subcontractors of highly specialized sectors of the record business overall.

According to Hennion, the record company is fundamentally better at *producing*, *exploiting* and *maintaining* success than it is at *inventing* it. In fact, the three possible ways in which record companies act to manage musical

---

[46] Dubois, Vincent (1999), *La politique culturelle. Genèse d'une catégorie d'intervention publique*, Paris: Belin, coll. Socio-Histoires.
[47] Hennion, Antoine (1981), *Les professionnels du disque. Une sociologie des variétés*, Paris: Metaile.
[48] Ibid., 207.

success suggests a threefold typology of activities: (i) the exploiting of pre-existing tastes, of stable musical genres and accepted musical styles (this implies managing a back-catalogue on the basis of a relationship between artists and their fans which is already established and a supply and demand which are already known); (ii) a long-term policy of inventing artistic careers (creating musical 'rents' by gambling on the eventual durable success of artists whose initial sales are disappointing); (iii) the statistical management of 'hits' which are accepted to be inherently unpredictable (short-term policies requiring the ability to react quickly to unexpected successes and the acceptance of a balance between calculated risks and regular income).

But the analysis of the formal properties of a song is not enough to explain its success or failure. The expectations of the public – who invest the song with its meaning – must also be taken into account. But the public, by stating its preferences, also defines itself: 'By ranking the genres, the listeners also rank themselves.'[49] In other words, recording success cannot, in Hennion's view simply be envisaged as a new variant of the concept of a manipulated public: 'Politicians in a sort of imaginary democracy instituted by songs, the record producers do not manipulate the public, but rather poll its every move ... the producers' power is not to impose recognition of a record on the public, but to suggest it.'[50]

These remarks on the structure and internal workings of record companies must be amplified by some more general comments on the structure of the musical field in France. A volume by Mario d'Angelo presents music in France as a system – in other words as a series of relations between distinct spheres of activity (artistic, political, economic, media) – and provides quantitative examples of this system of interdependencies.[51] For example: in 1995 the SACEM (the French recording rights organization) covered 24,900 music artists of whom 95 per cent were French; in terms of the supply of concerts, from 1984, the Ministry of Culture has instituted a campaign to encourage the creation of *locales* for the staging of rock and variety concerts in towns, but for the mid-1990s, however, figures underline the still dominant position of Paris over the provinces in terms of the staging of rock, varieties and jazz concerts. The analysis of the channels of distribution of music reveals a phenomenon of concentration with the disappearance of local record shops and the monopoly of hypermarkets and specialized shops such as FNAC and Virgin, who in 1994 accounted for 80 per cent of record sales. D'Angelo also addresses the impact of the media on the

---

[49]   Ibid., 226.
[50]   Ibid., 324.
[51]   D'Angelo, Mario (1997), *Socio-économie de la musique en France. Diagnostic d'un système vulnérable*, Paris: La Documentation française. Useful on this topic is also Guibert, Gérôme and Migeot, Xavier, 'Les dépenses des musiciens de musiques actuelles: éléments d'enquêtes réalisées en Pays-de-Loire et Poitou-Charentes', in Teillet, P. (1999), *Politiques publiques et musiques amplifiées actuelles*, hors série *La Scène*; Guibert, Gérôme (2001), 'Industrie musicale et musiques amplifiées', in *Chimères*, **40**, 103–16.

structure of the musical field, in particular the effect of the 1981 law on the 'freeing of the airwaves' which contributed to developing the market for radio listening via more closely focused supplies of music and new radio concepts targeting more segmented audiences.[52] The target audiences for the major radio networks are easily identifiable, and it can be seen that they focus primarily on young listeners (below 35), and in this respect, the question can be raised to what extent radios such as Skyrock, Fun Radio or NRJ have been the indispensable instruments of the massive spread of English-language musics. This is the very issue that led, in 1994, to the implementation of quotas of French-language music on the radio, which stipulated 40 per cent of Francophone music (half of which to be new talent or production) in programmes classified as varieties and prime-time.

A sociology of reception: the mediation of music and its audiences

Are *musiques actuelles* inseparably tied to the 'youth' audience? This is the question raised by Erik Neveu in a study of the social determinants of the rock phenomenon, and more particularly, of the nature of an audience whose social identity is supposedly principally defined by age. Neveu underlines the significance of the ideological discourses – especially the idea that rock expresses counter-culture and adolescent aspirations – which have somehow 'legitimated this reading of rock based on the elevation of youth to a quasi-class'.[53] Neveu's argument targets particularly Paul Yonnet's assertion that young people's interest in rock correlates to a disaffection with traditional forms of politics and politicization and that rock is therefore expressive of a true 'youth' class conscience.[54] Whereas Yonnet relies on young people's later-and-later entry into the working population as an explanatory factor, Neveu concentrates on demonstrating the sociologically illusory nature of the claim that rock is exclusively the preserve of the young. The results of this first survey of French cultural practices reveal, in effect, that since the 1960s rock music does not involve solely working-class adolescents but preponderantly middle-class and upper-middle class students and adolescents from urban areas. Based on statistics provide by the Ministry of Culture in 1973 on the cultural practices of the French, Neveu shows that the spread of rock does not simply occur in an undifferentiated way within a homogenous 'youth' population. In this context, the rural–urban split, the degree of educational qualification and the socio-professional status of individuals reveal significant differences. For example, individuals from working-class backgrounds go less frequently to concerts than

---

[52]   Ibid., 68.
[53]   Neveu, Erik (1991), '"Won't get fooled again?" Pop musique et idéologie de la génération abusée', in Mignon et Hennion (eds), *Rock: de l'histoire au mythe*, 53.
[54]   Yonnet, Paul (1985), *Jeux, modes et masses*, Paris: Gallimard.

families whose person of reference is in senior management or a profession, with a differential of frequency ranging from 100 per cent to 200 per cent in extreme cases. The second argument – which contradicts the idea that rock is consumed by a homogenous audience of young people – involves the diversity of ways in which consumers appreciate this kind of music. This reflects the way in which rock (and its subdivisions, from pop to hard rock) can lend itself to a *cultured* reading typical of the process of legitimation by social groupings of considerable cultural capital of forms of art hitherto considered inferior, but also to a process of extreme devaluing when it is presented as a musical genre which is essentially *working class*. The final argument against the illusion of rock associated solely with adolescence deals with the imaginary homogeneity of the youth protest movement in the 1960s, supposedly co-terminous with the ideology of the pop movement during the same period. In reality, this movement was more disparate than it has appeared, also involving the fraction of youth disaffected by its discovery that educational achievement was not synonymous with upward social mobility. Here arises a major theme of pop music protest targeting the family, the institutions of socialization and particularly the school system. More widely, it also raises the issue of the homology between the agents of the pop scene and the general public.

The surveys of the cultural practices of the French undertaken by the *Département des études et de la prospective* in 1973, 1981, 1989 and 1997 contribute numerous details on the evolution of the uses of music and of rock in particular. The data analysed in 1994 by Olivier Donnat thus reveal how the conditions of reception of music are closely linked to the technological change (Walkmans, CDs and so on) which has so much facilitated the consumption of music. Moreover, this increasing access to music is marked very strongly by generational aspects, since today's younger generations listen to more music than their parents born in the post-war baby boom, who themselves listen to more music than their own parents. But to understand fully the implications of this veritable transformation, one must keep in mind not only the spread of the practice of listening to music amongst young people but also the role played by this practice in the creation of identities, which manifests itself as a mix of genres and musical categories particularly evident in the way in which the music business creates a musical market which is ever more segmented. In this context, one can again raise the question of the homology between classical music/educated audiences and rock-variétés/working-class audiences and consider how, in a period when jazz is undergoing a relative 'elitization' (predominantly male listeners, urban and educated), rock is apparently marked by a form of 'classicization' affecting several generations of its audience (since more than half of those who frequently listen to rock are over 25 and more than a quarter over 35). Equally, listening to rock music is not a characteristic which differentiates starkly between different groups since it seems to affect all social milieux, although Donnat qualifies this 'federative dimension' of rock by adding that the attending of rock concerts mirrors geographical and social disparities much more closely than the listening to records concerning, for example, principally urban and educated individuals. On the other hand, however, for Donnat the term 'rock' covers such a multiplicity of musical forms that an analysis of listening to rock that focuses on content, distinguishing for example between the singers and groups actually listened to, reveals differences in behaviour and taste between social milieux and between generations – thus fans of rock amongst workers and foremen are more likely only to like rock and to favour either rock-variétés or, on the contrary, the purest forms of rock such as hard rock, whereas managerial rockers favour pop music classics of the 1960s and 1970s.[55] Overall, it can be seen that this quantitative study of rock audiences shows that rock is not just a musical genre of young people – among other reasons because young people (the original public) have aged, but continue, in part, to like this music. It is because of this that it is also important to take account of the effects of institutionalization and consecration that rock has undergone.

Antoine Hennion has revealed the characteristics of the rock scene through a series of ethnographic studies. He has distinguished between rock and classical concerts by comparing a Pretenders concert and a performance of Richard Strauss at the Paris Opéra. The aim of this comparison is to understand the meaning of the performances as collective constructions shared with the audience within the context of a rethinking of the classical terms of Durkheim's problematization of belief. Hennion shows that the differences and similarities between rock and classical music are most clearly revealed by the bodily attitudes of the listeners (*attitudes corporéelles*) which associate the audience with the performance: 'The moving body or the body immobile. Rock is an empty stage, in the way that opera is an altar. In opera one holds oneself still and projects everything forwards; in rock one mobilises oneself with others, and through successive waves of the crowd, moves towards the front rows, almost onto the stage to replace the actors of the drama.'[56] However, the notion of collective violence is also a way of comparing these two types of performance, for example in opera, violence is contained by an audience careful to respect the codes of behaviour (polite applause etc.) and by their physically ascetic immobility, even discomfort, frozen in their seats. Hennion also looks at the ways in which one listens, ways which are revelatory of the characteristics of the rock stage: in contrast with a series of mediations (records, radio and TV appearances) which publicize the rock musician, the rock stage – the test of live performance – can be described as the cancelling out of intermediaries: 'an artist and an audience face to face "live" – whatever the status attributed to this as founding

---

[55] Donnat, Olivier, *Les Français face à la culture*, 228.
[56] Hennion, Antoine (1991), 'Scène rock, concert classique', in Mignon and Hennion (eds), *Rock: de l'histoire au mythe*, 106.

myth or durable illusion ... the truth of a live concert of unique intensity ... And this rapport with "something else" sought by the "fan" gets closer and closer to the sole escape available, the physical relationship with body of the singer, as its presentation on stage suggests as a possibility – possibility of course rejected, the stage is an altar which distances as much as it presents.'[57]

Conclusion

The research in the sociology of *musiques actuelles* in France appears mainly characterized by a series of questions firstly about cultural policies, and secondly about the formation of tastes and emotions. These questions sometimes bring the sociology of music into partnership with aesthetics. The lack of interest in the socioeconomics of the recording industry, which – unlike publishing – has not been the object of any focused study, is a surprising feature, especially since the concentration of major recording companies and the freedom of access to an ever-growing catalogue of titles facilitated by MP3 technology has had considerable impact on the economics of culture (when, for example they undermine the status of the 'author' or of the distribution system). In the same vein, the influence of the economy of media and publicity needs some analysis – is it possible to talk of a 'sub-field of music' when the processes of production and dissemination are ever more closely integrated and economic concentration seals the interdependence of the film, musical and televisual sectors? And what is to be said of the role of critical commentators (specialized newspapers, radio and TV channels) which nowadays have the power to fashion record industry success?

---

[57]   Ibid., 109–110.

Chapter 2

In from the margins: *chanson*, pop and cultural legitimacy

David Looseley

In the English-speaking world, French popular music is sometimes more sinned against than sinning. Despite its diversity and the international success of some of its most esteemed performers – from Maurice Chevalier in Hollywood and Jacques Brel at Carnegie Hall (1963 and 1965), to the recent UK chart showings of what Philippe Birgy calls 'French electronica', or techno – old prejudices die hard. For many Britons alive in the 1960s and 1970s, the word *chanson* (used in English but exotically ill-defined), tends to evoke Piaf, Aznavour, perhaps even the Singing Nun (Sœur Sourire); while allusions to 'French pop' are usually taken to mean Johnny Hallyday (now at retirement age), Mireille Mathieu (in her 50s), or the 'French punk' Plastic Bertrand (who was actually Belgian) and prompt snorts of derision, though occasional figures like Françoise Hardy or Serge Gainsbourg fare slightly better in UK affections. Such embedded perceptions are entertaining but irritating and will not be shifted overnight by academic writing. But I want at least to clarify the terminology a little by examining the relationship between French *chanson* and French pop socio-historically. My premise is that this relationship tells us a good deal about French cultural history and French cultural values, and more specifically about the process by which an imported popular-cultural form may become 'legitimate' in French public discourse: worthy of being taken seriously or treated indulgently, studied in schools or specialist arts establishments, even publicly subsidized; worthy in fact of marching under the political banner of the French cultural exception.

Pop was not, of course, the first Anglo-Saxon music to invade France, for jazz had disembarked with the American troops posted there during the First World War, just as it did again in 1944, in the form of be-bop and swing. By the Liberation, Paris had in fact already developed a rich jazz culture, made up of French musicians like Django Reinhardt, Boris Vian and Claude Luter, American jazzers who played there regularly (Sidney Bechet even settled in France in 1949), and venues like the Hot-Club de France with its associated critics Hugues Panassié and Charles Delaunay, passionately divided over bebop.[1] Nevertheless,

---

[1]   This debate between Delaunay and Panassié is examined in Gumplowicz, P. (1995), 'Au Hot Club de France, on ne faisait pas danser les filles', in P. Gumplowicz and J.-C.

French popular music has above all been associated with the indigenous song form, famous at home and abroad as *la chanson française* but difficult to pin down. At its most inclusive, it unexceptionally denotes words set to music; at its most exclusive, it connotes a set of cultural assumptions about what French song *ought* to be. In this second, prescriptive sense, the genre is chiefly defined in opposition to something: jazz to an extent, variety (*les variétés* in French, i.e. commercial easy listening), and most of all pop. Hence the tendency today – in everyday conversation, the specialist press, the classification practices of some record stores – to distinguish between *chanson* on the one hand and *variétés françaises*, *le rock français* and most recently *la techno* on the other. *Chanson* is in fact set apart (positively or negatively) by a process of 'distinction' in the broadly Bourdieusian sense. Christophe Conte, for example, music editor of the respected popular-culture magazine *Les Inrockuptibles*, remarked in an interview in 2001: 'The mainstream in England is rock. In France it's *chanson*'; and he went on to speak of an incipient shift away from 'the club tradition' represented by Daft Punk, and a 'return to the magic of *chanson*'.[2] Yet although such distinctions are made confidently and spontaneously, when one asks what exactly they are founded upon, the answers are seldom as clear-cut.

The beginnings of this binary distinction can be tracked back to the Second Empire, as public singing began to be transformed into a professional activity and public listening into a commodity. In the first half of the nineteenth century, *chanson* was largely an amateur activity pursued in singing clubs (*caveaux* for the middle classes, *goguettes* for the workers) which met in the back rooms of Paris cafés and restaurants, like the celebrated Rocher de Cancale still visible in the rue de Montorgueil not far from the Pompidou Centre. In such venues, members would meet once a month to dine and sing each other's new compositions. These were often topical satires sung to well-known melodies. The *caveaux* therefore became associated with dissident republicanism and the *goguettes* with working-class revolutionism or anarchism. But, mid-century, three institutional innovations transformed the situation.

The first came in 1851 with the creation of the *Société des auteurs, compositeurs et éditeurs musicaux* (society of music authors, composers and publishers), or SACEM, formed to protect performing rights by identifying the composers of melodies and lyrics and remunerating them for public performances of their work. This introduced popular music to the notion of intellectual property, whereas previously a songwriter would sell a song to a music publisher for a flat fee and receive nothing more for it. With the coming of the SACEM, popular songwriting thus became a way of making a living,

Klein (eds), *Paris 1944–1954. Artistes, intellectuels, publics: la culture comme enjeu*, Série Mémoires no. 38, Paris: Éditions Autrement, 167–82.
[2]   Conte, C. (2001), interview, *Time Out Paris Free Guide*, 'The Music Issue', Autumn, 15–17, 17.

especially if the songwriter also performed, and singing in public became a commercial transaction. The second innovation came in 1852, when the new emperor, Napoléon III, attempted to repress the revolutionary spirit of 1848 by subjecting all public gatherings to police authorization, effectively killing off both *goguettes* and *caveaux*. In their place came the famous *cafés-concerts*, of *caf'conc'*, once described as 'the Opera-house of the people and its *Comédie Francaise*'.[3] The most famous were in Paris: L'Eldorado, Le Ba-ta-clan, Le Moulin Rouge, Les Folies-Bobino, or Le Divan Japonais where Yvette Guilbert made her name; but the phenomenon also spread to the other big cities: Bordeaux, Lyon, Marseille. In the *caf'conc'*, singers were among the entertainment offered to customers who bought a drink, alongside ventriloquists, conjurors, and others. The singers were classified into recognizable types and their repertoire was often comic or bawdy. Audience participation was common as it had been in the *goguettes*, and as it remained on street corners too, where itinerant singers would sell simple sheet music known as *petits formats* (small-formats), so that passers-by could sing them themselves. However, the noise and bustle of a busy café meant that lyrics became less important and more basic – all the more so given the poorly educated nature of much of the audience. As Coulonges writes: 'Under these conditions, it is quite obvious that, from this rudimentary audience, rudimentary artists were content to elicit the most rudimentary reactions, to exploit the most rudimentary emotions by seeking out their simplest manifestations; the aim was to make people laugh or make them cry.'[4]

The third innovation, in March 1867, was the lifting of a ban on performing in costume and with props in drinking houses, imposed after lobbying from the theatre profession fearful of competition. The removal of the ban allowed *cafés-concerts* to hire comic performers who sang in character, like Dranem or one of his imitators, a very young Maurice Chevalier. The effect was to push *chanson* further away from collective participation towards spectatorship and it was completed when music hall (imported from Britain) and the glossy Paris revues of the Folies Bergère and the Moulin Rouge took over from the *caf'conc'* in the first two decades of the twentieth century. In the halls, customers were no longer served drinks and seated at tables but were physically demarcated as an audience. This segregation of the performer helped create the first real *chanson* stars,

---

[3]   E. Heros, quoted in Vernillat, F., and Charpentreau, J. (1977), *La Chanson française*, 2e édition revue et corrigée, Que Sais-Je?, no.1453, Paris: Presses Universitaires de France, 45.

[4]   Coulonges, G. (1969), *La Chanson en son temps de Béranger au juke-box*, Paris: Les Editeurs Français Réunis, 252. For fuller accounts of the café-concert, see also Dillaz, S. (1973), *La Chanson française de contestation: des barricades de la Commune à celles de mai 1968*, Paris: Seghers; and Dillaz, S. (1991), *La Chanson sous la Troisième République, 1870-1940*, Paris: Tallandier; and Caradec, F., and Weill, A. (1980), *Le Café-concert*, Paris: Hachette.

remote and untouchable but dedicated to giving the public the light entertainment it supposedly craved. Chevalier was one such star, Mistinguett another, Piaf a third. Stardom in the true sense was thus a twentieth-century phenomenon, though star identities still drew on the conventions of the *café-concert*, which had evolved a set of stock characters. The *chanteur fantaisiste* of the mid-twentieth century, singing in character with a prop, a costume or just a stylized manner (Les Frères Jacques, Marcel Amont, Yves Montand, Charles Trenet) still referred back intertextually to the costumed clown and *comique-troupier* (comic soldier) figures of Polin, Mayol and Dranem. Similarly, Piaf's waif-like stage presence, her little black dress and red neckerchief ('a fragile bundle of emotions caught in a simple white spotlight', as Hawkins describes her), looks back through Fréhel and Damia to the melodramatic *pierreuse* of Angèle Moreau in the nineteenth century, with whom originated the theatrical street style of the *chanson réaliste* (realist song).[5] However, in Piaf and the *chanson réaliste*, the element of costume or stylized play-acting taken from the *café-concert* has withered and the singer has become tightly identified with her role, just as the 1920s or 1930s movie star has with hers, 'The star', writes Edgar Morin, 'is not only an actress. Her characters are not only characters. Cinema characters contaminate stars. Conversely, the star herself contaminates her characters.'[6]

Alongside this 'starisation' as Morin calls it, a different *chanson* trope was germinating during the inter-war years which would eventually blossom in the 1950s. While the star turn sang what it was assumed the audience wanted to hear, a more 'authentic' singer-songwriter figure emerged, deemed to be singing what he (less often she) wanted to express. This change came about progressively, however, beginning with two transitional figures, Mireille and Charles Trenet, both of whom wrote and performed their own material but were still quite clearly cast as commercial entertainers. The gaiety and tunefulness of their early songs owed a good deal to the *fantaisistes* of the *café-concert*, especially in Trenet's case whose stage look – the merrily popping eyes and comically battered hat of his 'singing fool' persona (*le fou chantant*) – remained for 70 years. But what was different about these two performers was, on the one hand, the influence of jazz which gave their work the cosmopolitan freshness of modernity; and on the other, the playful literacy of their lyrics. Trenet's whimsical themes and delicate word-play made for a sparkling combination of surrealism with a kind of scat-singing, though with sound and sense always skilfully balanced as in the semi-onomatopoeic *Débit de lait, débit de l'eau* [Water-seller, milk-seller]. At the same time, Trenet was able to hint at a repressed melancholy which the weepy

[5]   Quotation from Hawkins, Peter (2000), *Chanson: the French Singer-Songwriter from Aristide Bruant to the Present Day*, Aldershot: Ashgate, 79; Coulonges, G. (1969), *La Chanson en son temps de Béranger au juke-box*, Paris: Les Editeurs Français Réunis, 32. The *chanson réaliste* also harks back to the social realism of Aristide Bruant (1851–1925).
[6]   Morin, E. (1972), *Les Stars*, Paris: Seuil (3rd edn), 36, my own translation.

chanson réaliste achieved only rarely. Towards the end of his life, he was hailed as a poet, a term which helps measure just how far *chanson* had come from the coarser days of the *café-concert*. Significantly, however, as we shall see, this consecration as an artist was a long time coming in Trenet's case and, even as late as 1983, did not help him win the seat on the *Académie Française*, the bastion of the literary establishment, for which he had eccentrically applied the year before. In his case at least, there were still limits to how far the cultural establishment was ready to accept *chanson* as literature, as Jean Mistler, 'perpetual secretary' of the *Académie* at the time, made painfully clear, putting Trenet firmly in his place: 'I consider that the *Académie*'s reaction is entirely as it should be, and I hope that next time a few serious writers apply.'[7] Yet this was not the end of the story, either for *chanson*'s aesthetic consecration or for Trenet himself.

After the Occupation and the rise of jazz, Existentialism and the smoke-filled Left-Bank cabaret, a triumvirate of singer-songwriters, Georges Brassens, Jacques Brel and Léo Ferré, emerged, whose work today, long after their deaths, remains the pinnacle of achievement in *chanson*. All three declared their debt to Trenet but took his initiatives further; and the work of all three was fairly rapidly classified as 'poetic song' or 'text-song' (*chanson poétique, chanson à texte*). Where Trenet's playfulness prevented his official consecration, Brel, Brassens and Ferré steadily acquired a different persona, that of artist rather than entertainer. The archetype here was Brassens, the taciturn, no-nonsense refuser of compromise, writing the songs – and wearing the moustache – of a mythical peasant craftsman and famously uncomfortable on stage with the star persona inflicted upon him.

By the early 1960s, the big three had become the first singer-songwriters to be anthologized in the Seghers *Poètes d'aujourd'hui* (poets of today) series. Their lyrics were studied in schools and appeared on *baccalauréat* syllabuses and they themselves received the plaudits and lamentations of Ministers or Presidents when they died: Brel in 1978, Brassens in 1981, and Ferré in 1993. Indeed, with the help of the untimely departures of the first two and the funereal consecration they received, Brel, Brassens and Ferré have become national myths, and so too has *chanson* itself. Piaf and Chevalier certainly played a part in this transfiguration and similarly became myths in death, Piaf particularly as she was only 48 when she died in 1963. Yet their mythic status is qualitatively different from that of the big three. Not being singer-songwriters (or only occasionally), they are more 'artistes' than artists, more urban folk-heroes: the archetypally tragic working-class French woman in Piaf's case, the archetypally roguish Parisian charmer in Chevalier's. What their cases suggest, along with Trenet's rejection by the *Académie*, is that full, *artistic* legitimacy is not conferred lightly. First, singers have to be writers; second, they have to be divested of the status of entertainer to reveal the solitary, disinterested poet beneath. *Chanson* has in fact to be cleansed of the commercialism associated with the *caf'conc'* or music hall if it is to become art,

---

[7]   Balen, N. (1992), *Charles Trenet: le fou chantant*, Monaco: Éditions du Rocher, 136.

for it is above all the literary skills – the lexical range, the allusiveness, the dexterity – of the big three, not their entertainment value, which are constantly underscored and reiterated in writing about them, as is the fact that they issued (professionally at least) from the same bohemian Left-Bank milieu as Camus, Prévert or Sartre. As the sociologist Paul Yonnet argues, this was the ultimate subtext of their lyrics being published by Seghers with no musical notation; of Ferré's and Brassens's settings of their favourite poets to music (Aragon, Baudelaire, Paul Fort, Villon); and conversely of Trenet's rejection by the Académie.[8]

Trenet's literary consecration did come eventually, however. In 1982, the year of his application to the Académie, he was adopted by the new Socialist government as a kind of national-cultural mascot: *Légion d'honneur* conferred by Mitterrand in May 1982, Commander of Arts and Letters awarded by Jack Lang (who had also supported his candidacy to the Académie) the following November, participation in Mitterrand's inauguration of the Zénith in 1984. And curiously, this marked a resurgence of his career and his public acclaim, even though in the 1970s he had produced some less than remarkable albums and had virtually retired from the stage. Hence his virtual beatification when he died. On public television, the leaders of the Right and Left, President Chirac and Prime Minister Jospin, spoke of their sadness and his greatness, while Jean-Marie Le Pen, Robert Hue (representing France's extreme Right and its Communist Party), and members of the public, young and old, sang snatches of *Douce France* [Sweet France], *Boum* [Boom], or *La Mer* [The Sea]. The symbolism of the editing here was perfectly transparent but for the discursively challenged it was spelt out by the voice-over: 'Today [Trenet] attains the status of a monument before which everyone bows.' Chirac described him as both 'an immense artist' and a 'symbol of a France that is smiling, imaginative', while Jack Lang and Catherine Tasca, past and present Ministers of Culture, stressed his cultural achievement which, tellingly, was to have made variety artistically respectable. His famous song *L'Ame des poètes* [The Souls of Poets] (1951), where he celebrates how the songs of 'the poets' live on in the popular memory, was often foregrounded in the coverage, making the point that in death Trenet himself had finally achieved a patrimonial eternity far above the vicissitudes of showbiz or the *Académie Française*. This kind of valedictory rhetoric is not, I suggest, idle oratory but an essential final stage in the legitimation of popular-cultural forms.

The first stage, where *chanson* is considered, came just as the *chanson* world was getting wise to the threat represented by Anglo-American pop; and it is possibly no coincidence that the Seghers volumes came out at precisely that time.[9] It is at this juncture, I believe, that the identity of text-song, and by

---

[8] Yonnet, P. (1985), *Jeux, modes et masses: la société française et le moderne 1945–1985*, Paris: Gallimard, 196.

[9] My suggestion of a connection between the consecration of song and the coming of pop is for the moment hypothetical, needing more research.

extension *chanson* generally, comes to be established in opposition to *pop* specifically, and that a defensive *chanson* rhetoric evolves. Hostility to pop is often, in fact, *shaped* by *chanson* rhetoric.[10] This can be seen particularly clearly in Marc Fumaroli's *L'Etat culturel* [The Cultural State], his vituperative attack on French cultural policy. Despite the high-culturalist premise of much of the essay, Fumaroli speaks warmly of Piaf and Chevalier, who express the great truths of the human condition. But he extends no such generosity to Americanized pop and its culture: 'France, before adopting social and moral stereotypes invented in Greenwich Village, before dressing in jeans and going deaf and dumb by dancing to a torrent of rock sound, had once been capable of dressing to suit its own taste and of understanding and feeling the words of its own songs as it sang them.'[11]

Fascinatingly, however, pop in France has steadily been undergoing a legitimation process similar to *chanson*'s, morphing from commercial pariah to national myth; though the process for pop has operated differently and proven more difficult, so that the parallels should not be overstated. Initially pop, both in its original form (Bill Haley, Elvis, Cliff Richard) and as adapted into French by lyricists like Pierre Delanoë or 'Jil et Jan' and singers like Hallyday and Eddy Mitchell, was viewed as fundamentally 'other' because of its alien, repetitive rhythm, its lyrical banalities and the social dangers it represented. Although rock'n'roll had been in France since 1956, 1961 was the year that the evolution of a youth music dramatically different from adult popular taste became a matter of national concern. In the course of that year, three rock 'festivals' were organized at Paris's Palais des Sports, leading to escalating violence and vandalism. Of the third, *Le Monde* reported that 'amidst an unbelievable racket, scenes of astonishing violence unfolded'; while *Paris Match* wrote: 'Now they are frightening us. The French people would like not to have to look at such haunting images of the sickness of youth again.'[12] But what particularly shocked the establishment (politicians and local authorities, teachers, intellectuals, parts of the press) was that such behaviour seemed woven into the very fabric of rock'n'roll, with its incomprehensible lyrics (whether in English or French) and the assorted hiccups and grunts of young male stars, sometimes dressed head to toe in black leather like Vince Taylor, who hurled themselves to their knees for no apparent purpose other than to attract attention to their pelvic girdle.

Initially associated with gangs of young men in black leather jackets (the feared *blousons noirs* from which stars like Johnny Hallyday sprang), and still at

---

[10] My argument here is developed in chapter 4 of Looseley, D. L. (2003), *Popular Music in Contemporary France: Authenticity, Politics, Debate*, Oxford and New York: Berg.

[11] Fumaroli, M. (1991), *L'État culturel: une religion moderne*, Paris: Editions de Fallois, 223.

[12] Both quoted in Victor, C., and Regoli, J. (1978), *20 Ans de rock français*, Paris: Albin Michel, 24–25.

this stage a predominantly working-class taste, rock'n'roll, rather like the nineteenth-century *goguettes*, gave a number of not very academic or well-off young men an opportunity for musical creativity which the French education system denied them due to inadequate music tuition in schools and the cost of training in municipal music schools. Consequently, rock, again like the music of the *goguettes*, was thought to be a seat of social dissidence and for a short time in 1961 there were moves in parliament to have it banned, as the *goguettes* had effectively been in 1852. This time, however, it was not the state which intervened but the music industry. Once the popularity of the new music proved to be more than a fad, record companies and promoters were quick to commercialize it beyond the relatively small niche audience of disaffected rockers, rerouting it into the innocuous comedy of the twist and thence into the anodyne French version of pop known as *le yéyé*. Johnny symbolically hung up the jeans and the leather redolent of gang warfare when he played at the Olympia in September 1961 wearing a midnight-blue, sequined tuxedo and introduced the nation to the twist. A succession of supposedly clean-living boys and demure girls appeared in the pages of the pop magazine *Salut les copains* [Hi, Gang] or its Catholic, Communist, or other imitators. In these publications, and in the first broadcasts for young people like *Salut les copains* on Europe 1 (started in 1959) or the TV show *Age tendre et tête de bois* [young and headstrong] (1961), the *copain* generation was represented as friendly, mutually supportive, and respectful of its elders though hurt at having its enthusiasm for music and parties misunderstood as rebellion. The reality of *copains* culture, however, was more complex, as Edgar Morin astutely recognized in two articles for *Le Monde* about the massive *yéyé* concert held at the Place de la Nation in June 1963. What he identified in it was a hidden ambivalence. In *yéyé*'s ludic passion for music, dancing and an eternal present lay two possible futures. It was a cathartic preparation for a life of docile consumption and at the same time a visceral refusal of that life. Five years later, the similarly ambivalent meanings of the May events were to reveal Morin to have been remarkably prescient.

Although pop did not play a direct role in the revolt of French youth in 1968, and certainly not *yéyé*, the events marked a vital turning point for it. Indeed, French pop only really took off in the wake of May, gradually ceasing to be a superimposed product and becoming the more complex, organic phenomenon it already was in America or Britain. It was not in fact until around 1970 that the term *la pop-music* (or *le pop, la pop, la musique pop*) even came into use, replacing both *le rock and roll* and *le yéyé*. This lexical shift attests to the fact that pop was becoming acclimatized, putting down roots which would continue to ramify throughout the 1970s. This process was visible in other ways too. By 1970, there was already more than one kind of music press: the unconditional fanzine on the one hand like *Salut les copains* and the growing ranks of its rivals; and a self-consciously cooler, more analytical type of magazine, starting with *Rock & Folk* in 1966 and *Best* in 1968. Secondly, pop's naturalization led to a process of market segmentation, which came about (in France as elsewhere) from the early 1970s, as pop tastes splintered and subdivided: rock, funk, disco, punk, and so on. Thirdly and most significantly, as this segmentation advanced, a new binary began to appear, just as it had with *chanson* after its commercialization. While pre-pop *chanson* continued to identify and authenticate itself by not being pop, pop itself was similarly subdividing into legitimate and illegitimate forms. Legitimate here does not mean mainstream. On the contrary, mainstream commercial music, such as disco, was deemed *illegitimate*, while *legitimacy* meant expressing oneself intensely and creatively through music, irrespective of commercial pressures, just as Brassens had mythically done.

This Bourdieusian 'distinction' process can be seen at work in two musical developments of the 1970s. One is the evolution of what became known as *la nouvelle chanson française*: a new generation of singer-songwriters who cited Brel, Brassens or Ferré as their models but who also worked happily in the pop idiom of electric instrumentation, American soft-rock or country rhythms and arrangements. This group includes Renaud, Bernard Lavilliers, Yves Simon, Francis Cabrel, Jean-Jacques Goldman and others. One might wish to argue, as Peter Hawkins does, that lyrically *la nouvelle chanson française* seldom meets the standard set by its founding fathers; or, as students today often do, that musically they sound very 1970s. Nevertheless, most of those listed are still major sellers in France today, almost 30 years later, and are critically acclaimed. This, I believe, is simultaneously an effect of the literacy and audibility of their lyrics and of their having been constantly represented – by the specialist media and by themselves – as being in the Brel–Brassens–Ferré tradition and therefore gilded by the myth.

The other 1970s development in which the distinction process can be seen is the growth of *le rock français*, followed in the 1980s by *le rock alternatif*. In the case of *le rock français* – meaning initially bands like Téléphone, Bijou, Trust and Starshooter – it is difficult to grasp precisely what makes it 'French' other than the use of the French language, since musically they owe much to Anglo-Saxon hard rock, heavy metal or punk. Because of this, though some applaud this development, music critics often have little time for it, preferring the Anglo-Saxon originals. There is, however, another level of meaning to the term *le rock français* in the 1970s, which is the burgeoning of a local – that is, non-Parisian – rock scene, product of a number of factors: the inevitable acclimatization of the pop idiom after almost 20 years and a consequent surge in the number of provincial amateur or semi-pro bands from the mid-1970s; the development of permanent regional festivals like the *Printemps de Bourges* (1977) or the *Transmusicales de Rennes* (1979); and the willingness of some municipalities in the 1970s, usually of the Left and peopled by ex-*gauchistes* (extreme-leftists), to recognize the local impact of rock and provide rehearsal and performance facilities accordingly.

The creativity and Frenchness of *le rock alternatif* are easier to identify, since here we are talking about the growth since punk of an independent French record sector and its promotion of a wide range of new acts fusing rock in various ways with French popular traditions (symbolized in the rediscovered accordion) or with sounds from elsewhere in the Francophone world. Hence the success of unclassifiable hybrids such as Les Rita Mitsouko, Les Garçons Bouchers, Les Négresses Vertes or La Mano Negra. Hence too those acts which directly recycle the urban tradition of the realist song: Pigalle, Têtes Raides, Casse-Pipe, and even to an extent the chart-topping Louise Attaque. From the same melting-pot also came the 'world music' (*la world music, musiques métissées*, or *la sono mondiale*) with which France has become especially identified, whose roots lie in North or sub-Saharan Africa (Khaled, Cheb Mammi, les Touré Kunda, Youssou N'Dour) or in the Caribbean (Kassav', Malavoi); and also French rap, which has similarly been hybridized to produce original French forms.

These four genres – French rock, alternative rock, world music and rap, and the last three especially – are all in some way distinguished from the commercial mainstream, to which they are clearly represented as superior. Why should this be so? There are, I suggest, three related reasons. One is simply that, after a period of direct imitation of a foreign, insufficiently understood form in the 1960s and 1970s, some French pop has lost its sense of inferiority, has become more confident, more experimental, and above all more aware of what its *own* roots and connections can bring to an increasingly standardized pop idiom, finding in *métissage* (cross-fertilization) new creative spaces alongside, but distinct from, global chart music. Some French music, then, has come of age. A second answer is that this evolution has been mediated through the French specialist press as something positive, though one has to stress here that the more self-consciously intellectual rock publications, like *Les Inrockuptibles* or the daily newspaper *Libération*'s music pages, have remained (at least until quite recently) obdurately dismissive of French product. It is in fact the *chanson* press which has mostly welcomed the new French sounds. Both the leading *chanson* magazine *Chorus* and a number of music journalists who have written books on French popular music now demonstrate a readiness to bring ever more diverse styles under the umbrella of *chanson*, including alternative rock, world music and rap, as long as it involves French lyrics.

The third and perhaps most unusual source of this distinction has been the Ministry of Culture. From 1982, shortly after Mitterrand's first presidential victory and the appointment of Jack Lang as Minister of Culture, popular music, including youth music, was adopted as part of the Culture Department's remit and a special unit within its *Direction de la musique et de la danse* was set up for the purpose. Developing a policy from scratch was no easy task and the Ministry clearly had to feel its way. What forms should the policy take and what kinds of music should be included in it? These were complex issues, particularly within the politico-electoral climate of government, and they were partly avoided for a time. Regarding the first question, Lang opted not to aid popular musicians directly as creative artists but to use pop instrumentally. This entailed a welfare policy for *amateur* music-making designed to tackle youth problems in the disaffected suburbs (helping rock groups as a way of channelling frustrated energies, for example); and measures to address *professional* pop as a set of economic and industrial parameters. As for which forms of music to assist, the Ministry initially chose caution. Jazz, already accepted as a 'legitimate' form, was an early beneficiary, as were 'traditional musics', a term covering both French regional folk musics and, increasingly, world music. By the same token, *chanson* too was adopted, as it had been broadly associated with the Left since 1968 and was to the taste of some of those close to Lang. But *chanson* was not what Lang's team was really looking for since, as the Ministry's own cultural practices survey in 1981 revealed, it did not particularly involve the new generation of young people, who were more committed to pop, or as it was increasingly becoming known generically, *le rock*.[13] Thus the policy switched in 1984 to rock in a fairly wide sense, despite the disapproval of cultural traditionalists and accusations of electoralism. Once this change had been negotiated, Lang set about supporting each new music fashion as publicly as possible: North-African raï, the Hispanic sound of the Gypsy Kings, world music, and later rap. When the Socialists were returned to power in 1997, a new Minister of Culture, Catherine Trautmann, took the Lang strategy a stage further by speaking up for techno, albeit with reservations concerning raves and ecstasy.

The recognition of popular music by the once rather po-faced Culture Administration was, I believe, a major turning point in the histories of both the Ministry and French popular music itself. Aside from any material benefits (which were not great since the budget devoted to such activities was small), what the Ministry's support mainly did for pop, just as it had for the traditional arts since its creation in 1959, was provide a stamp of legitimacy. Alternative rock, raï, world music and rap acquired a cloak of respectability while other forms did not; and the cloak was all the more sumptuous as Lang actively publicized his support in the media.

Whether government intervention has been a good thing or a bad is not within my scope here, but the response of the French music world over the last 20 years has been revealing. One might have expected to hear criticisms of popular elitism, an institutional disdain for that which is commercial and truly popular. In fact the opposite has happened, at least in so far as the views of the French music world were represented by a report on so-called 'present-day musics'

---

[13]   This latest lexical change complicates the understanding of French music terminology even further. In so far as one can isolate stable, agreed meanings for such shifting forms, *le rock* is now used in both the narrower English sense (bands, electric instruments, reduced importance of lyrics, and so on), or in a broader sense covering what used to be called *la pop*. I refer the reader to Looseley, *Popular Music in Contemporary France*, for fuller coverage of terminology.

(*musiques actuelles*) produced for Catherine Trautmann by a national music commission appointed in 1998, headed by Alex Dutilh.[14] The report is indeed critical; but its complaint is that the policy conducted since 1981 has not gone far enough in rejecting commercialism. Lang's 'mistake' as the Commission sees it was to justify support for popular culture by claiming that culture and the economy were 'the same struggle'. This has led to popular music's being singled out from the other subsidized arts and instrumentalized in terms of export revenue and employment opportunities, rather than supported for its own sake as a contemporary aesthetic. What the report therefore calls for is less emphasis on the economic and the social (the welfare policy for suburban youth) and more on popular music as a creative art. This means more direct aid to musicians, more efforts to widen access, and more interest in the popular-music heritage; more in fact of the very principles upon which the Ministry was founded 40 years before. The report's hobbyhorse, then, is parity of treatment with the other subsidized arts. Only then, it insists, will popular music achieve full cultural legitimacy alongside theatre and opera, rather than being the poor relation, only good for boosting national income and helping with urban regeneration.

A number of assumptions underpin the Dutilh report regarding national legitimacy. One is that words alone and symbolic gestures, be they funeral orations or Langian mateyness, are not enough. Another is that the only way of achieving parity with the traditional arts is to shield pop from the global domination and commercial imperatives of the majors (much French pop, like that of other countries, is distributed by multinational corporations like Universal or Virgin). The rationale here is ultimately French cultural exceptionalism, the idea that what distinguishes (or should distinguish) culture in France is that it is treated not just as a commodity but as an ineffable part of being human and being French, just like *chanson* is.

What my analysis of the evolution of both French *chanson* and French pop as cultural forms points to is their essential similarity. Stripping away the obvious differences, both have passed from being initially dissident forms to having that dissidence defused by commercialization. In each case, though, a subset has broken away from its commercial confinement and developed a more creative aesthetic. These subsets have then been taken up and eventually accredited as national art forms, by the press, parts of the cultural establishment and, crucially, the Ministry of Culture. These parallel evolutions shed light on both the process of legitimation in France and on the French cultural exception. They also perhaps point up the paradox of attempting to apply that exceptionalism to the new

---

[14]   The Dutilh report has not been published other than as a word-processed document in a spiral binding: see Commission nationale des musiques actuelles (1998), *Rapport de la Commission nationale des musiques actuelles à Catherine Trautmann, Ministre de la culture et de la communication*, September 1998; unpublished. For a fuller analysis, see Looseley, *Popular Music in Contemporary France*, chapters 8 and 9.

cultural forms thrown up by the global technological innovations of the twentieth century. Like cinema, contemporary popular music is a product of industrialization and cannot, as Simon Frith argues, be somehow divorced from its commercial and industrial dimensions: the electric guitar or synthesizer, the vinyl record or CD, the recording studio or the MIDI system.[15] France's chances of pursuing the cultural exception without taking stock of these realities are doubtless limited.

This is all the more true since the success of French techno, which the Ministry of Culture under Catherine Trautmann admittedly tried to adapt to and assist. But here, unfortunately, the cultural exception surely gets itself into a tangle. For French techno has largely been instrumental and performed by DJs or groups sporting very un-French names like Daft Punk and MotorBass, or non-specific ones like Air or Modjo. The French language, therefore, that authentic stamp of French exceptionalism, is virtually absent. Commercially successful bands like Daft Punk are thus free-floating in the great global marketplace, having carefully removed all visible signs of their local origins. It is true that techno too is currently undergoing the selfsame process of distinction-making I have traced, as a cleavage develops between its commercial and purist wings. But the problem for government is that the purist wing still comes as a package with raves (*teknivals, teufs, free parties*), for there has been no equivalent of the UK's Criminal Justice Bill of 1994 which banned them. Not until recently, that is. In 2001, the Mariani amendment (put forward by the Centre-Right politician of that name), which proposed a much harder line on illegal raves, was accepted by the then Socialist government and may well finish them off, particularly as the presidential majority to which Mariani belongs has since then returned to power for another five years. The amendment seems to contradict Trautmann's earlier support for techno; or else implies that the support should only go to the safe, commercial variety. But if this is so, how will it square with the required separation of the cultural and the commercial? Clearly, the place of techno in the cultural exception sets up a conundrum as yet unanswered but one on which the future of French cultural policy, and perhaps of French cultural values, ultimately depends.

---

[15]   Frith, Simon (1998), *Performing Rights: Evaluating Popular Music*, Oxford: Oxford University Press.

Chapter 3

The French music industry: structures, challenges and responses

Hugh Dauncey

Other chapters in this book touch on some of the economic and financial aspects of (popular) music in France. Here, we look at some of the structures of the 'music industry' and at some of the challenges it is facing.

The French music industry finds itself – in many ways – at the crossroads of most of the issues discussed in this survey of French (popular) music. It is the background to the development of *chanson* since the 1940s and throughout the 1950s and 1960s when Brel, Brassens and Ferré were in their heyday of political engagement and when Demy's musicals were interpreting France's relationship with the American 'other' in terms of musical and cinematographic forms and styles. Since the 1970s, it has accompanied – symbiotically – the development of other contemporary popular musics (*musiques actuelles*), and has increasingly been the site of struggles between France and the US in the commercial sphere as well as the cultural sphere, as multinational record companies have threatened France's perceptions of her own cultural-industrial sovereignty and as new imported forms of musical expression such as rap, house and trance have negotiated their acceptance into the mainstream of French musical culture. France's particular form of capitalism – described as an *économie mixte* (mixed economy) in which the private sector has always lived with a strong and often economically (as well as culturally) interventionist state – has meant that the music industry in France is not just another variant of the Western free-market culture business. The music industry in France – as with almost everything else – has been historically marked by unceasing state attempts to direct and regulate the development activities either to defend culture (variously defined) for culture's sake or to defend French business in the world economy.

This chapter examines the current state of the French music business and then looks at two examples of issues which characterize, firstly, France's reaction to the challenge to the world music industry posed by the internet, and, secondly, France's attempts to affirm her cultural and commercial identity in the global market for music. The French music industry is generally considered to be fragile and complex, but nevertheless possessing some strengths, notably linked to the

41

French state's support for France's cultural industries in general, and it is the concrete manifestation of this support for French music from government which is discussed in the analysis of the French Music Export Office below. The other issue currently challenging the music business worldwide, and to which France and French-owned companies such as the giant consortium Vivendi-Universal are contributing some questions and answers, is MP3 and whether the music majors should crush or colonize access to music through the e-economy.

The French music business: fragile or just French?

A 1996 survey undertaken for the Syndicat national de l'édition phonographique (SNEP) soon after the implementation of the quotas for French-language songs on radio revealed that music is a more important leisure pastime for the French than sport, television, travel, cinema- or theatre-going.[1] Whether buying records, going to concerts, listening to the radio or watching music on the television, musical 'consumption' of all kinds is thus unarguably a fundamental aspect of the everyday life of French people. This is perhaps a situation not dissimilar to patterns in other developed Western societies, even though it is intriguing to note that the French seem to prefer music to the cinema as a leisure activity, despite the strong reputation of French film-making and its traditional importance in French cultural life. However, in comparison with the US or the UK, the consumption of music in France – even in the most innocent of ways – is culturally, politically, and ultimately economically, more complicated a phenomenon. In a society which has traditionally claimed cultural leadership in literature, thought, fashion, art and music, the status of an everyday interest in music which is predominantly non-elite (only a quarter of those questioned in the survey professed an attachment to classical music) and disseminated through the democratic media of radio and television necessarily challenges both French people's own mental perceptions of French culture and the French state's discourses on the content of French culture and its claims to exceptionalism or superiority. Popular music consumption is *variétés* (favoured by 36 per cent), or rock and pop (favoured by 56 per cent of those aged 15 to 24), with all the questions that this raises for programming on state radio and TV (80 per cent suggested that TV should screen more music and 77 per cent accused radio of being too cautious in its coverage) in competition with commercial stations such as Skyrock and NRJ.

It is obviously simplistic to talk of a music business or music industry in the singular because of the fragmented nature of the different functions of

---

[1]   Mortaigne, Véronique (1996), 'La musique est le principal loisir des Français', *Le Monde*, 19 July, 21; and also Mortaigne, V. (1998), 'La musique occupe la première place dans les loisirs des jeunes', *Le Monde*, 22 July, 22.

composition, live performance, publishing, record production and distribution, income from rights and broadcasting. In France it can often seem that the music business is more fragmented than in other comparable countries. It is Mario d'Angelo's contention that the French music business is a 'vulnerable' system.[2] D'Angelo looks at music in France as a 'system' – by which he simply means taking an overall view of the range of activities concerning the production and consumption of music – in order better to reveal the complexities of relations between musicians, record companies, central and local government. His analysis is placed firmly within the context of a belief in French exceptionalism in music – the idea that France still possesses a tradition in music (Francophone rock, jazz, or varieties) which sets it apart from the rest of an increasingly globalized world. Thus the French music business (and 'system' as a whole) is vulnerable to the ever-growing threat of commercial and cultural globalization, despite the manifest strengths of music in France in terms of public interest in it as a leisure activity or government willingness (since the 1980s) to invest in it as an aspect of cultural policy. The technological changes affecting the music industry (from CDs, through mini-cassettes, mini-discs and MP3-players) are seen by d'Angelo as especially challenging to France because of the absence of French record companies of sufficient influence to direct these technological advances in ways that would suit France. Moreover, although France does possess media groups of some strength (although until very recently weak in comparison with those of the US or Japan – see the following discussion of Vivendi-Universal), these groups will not be able to steer the development of new products and services, both because of their dependence on the true sectoral leaders of the globalized music industry and because France has no leadership in the production of the actual technologies involved. These then are the features of France's music business which render it 'vulnerable' within a context of cultural and commercial globalization, but, as d'Angelo also points out, the French system is internally riven with conflicts and tensions.

'Music' in France is undoubtedly a complex system of interacting institutions in which the opportunities for conflict and tension are numerous. The usual oppositions between artists, recording companies, media groups, retailers and other agents of the music business occur within the context of state interest and intervention in the running of music as a cultural industry. The economic, political and legal structure of the contemporary French music industry is characterized by economic concentration, political competition and an idiosyncratically French legal approach to the collection and distribution of musical intellectual property rights.

Economic concentration is represented by the oligopoly of the major multinationals and their French subsidiaries: BMG France; EMI-Virgin France;

---

2   D'Angelo, Mario (1997), *Socio-économie de la musique en France: diagnostic d'un système vulnérable*, Paris: La Documentation française.

Polygram; Sony Music Entertainment; Warner Music France. The obvious lack of a French-owned major company has been a constant source of worry for the French music business 'system'. Against the backdrop of the major recording companies, France during the 1990s also boasted a number of independent record labels such as AB Productions, Auvidis, Disques Vogue, Erato Disques, Francis Dreyfus Music, Harmonia Mundi, Mélodie, Musidisc, Scorpio, Sonodisc and Tréma. A number of these independent record companies are occasionally fragile and threatened by take-over by the majors (in 1992 Disques Vogue was bought out by BMG and Erato was purchased by Warner) but they can play an important role in helping maintain the diversity of music available in retail outlets (particularly the smallest independent labels focusing on minority interest genres). Here, again, the system of relations between different agents of the music business is complex, since as has been suggested by analysts such as Negus, it is too simple to suggest a dichotomy between conglomerates and independents in which the former provide a kind of lowest-common-denominator music and the latter play the noble role of innovation.[3] However, in the context of French cultural concerns about the specificities of their musical tradition – *chanson, variétés, rock à la française* – the role of those French independents which are properly autonomous of the majors is surely particularly crucial.[4] The balance of influence between majors and independents can be estimated in various ways, but based on copyright figures a ratio of 60:40 seems probable, even if in financial terms the market shares may divide approaching 90:10.[5]

Political competition is represented by the often seemingly uncoordinated interests of institutions of central and local government (touched upon by Looseley and Teillet elsewhere in this volume), as the state, towns and regions attempt to integrate music into their strategies of cultural defence (protecting the exceptionalism of French music and culture) or policies of local development. Not strictly political, but of particular importance in terms of the definition and exploitation of the intellectual property rights of musicians and the elaboration of French law are the multitude of associations created to manage the collection of the rights of their members, such as the Société des auteurs, compositeurs et éditeurs de musique (SACEM), the Société des auteurs et compositeurs dramatiques (SACD), the Société pour l'administration du droit de reproduction mécanique (SDRM), the Société pour l'administration des droits des artistes et

3   Negus, Keith (1992), *Producing Pop: culture and conflict in the popular music industry.* London: Edward Arnold.
4   For an analysis of French independent labels, see D'Angelo, Mario, and Vesperini, P. (1993), *Avenir et devenir des indépendants français du disque*, 2 vols, Paris: IDEE Europe; and also Galinier, Pascal (1998), 'Du mouvement chez les indépendants du disque', *Le Monde*, 8 July, 24; Cornu, Francis (1997) 'La colère sourde d'un indépendant', *Le Monde*, 2 June, 3.
5   See D'Angelo, *Socio-économie de la musique en France*, 54.

musiciens interprètes (ADAMI) and the Société de perception et de répartition des droits des artistes-interprètes de la musique et de la danse (SPEDIDAM).[6]

These *sociétés civiles de gestion collective* ('non-trading collective management companies') are an example of France's idiosyncratic (or 'exceptional') approach to the question of intellectual property rights and their application in the music industry. The French *Code de la propriété intellectuelle* (Code of intellectual property – law 92-597) introduced in July 1992 defines the theoretical content of the property rights which are paid to French musicians and musical artists through the intermediaries of the SACEM, SACD, SDRN and ADAMI. Some of these associations have a long and glorious past – the SACEM and the SACD were originally founded in 1851 and 1777, respectively – and have gradually evolved with the development of technology, commerce and economics, whereas others such as the SDRM (1935), ADAMI (1955) and SPEDIDAM (1959) are relatively recent creations called into being as the complexity of the market in recorded music and 'mechanical reproduction' demanded ever more administration of the ways in which musical works were being used, sold and reproduced. In the 1980s, however (in anticipation of the challenges now being posed to the music industry by new technologies such as the internet and MP3) as the market in musical recordings expanded and French media freed themselves from the constraints of their state-led past, these existing bodies were completed by three further associations charged with collecting and redistributing the rights due to their members. These associations were the Société civile pour l'exercice des droits des producteurs phonographiques (SCPP), the Société civile des producteurs de phonogramme en France (SPPF) and the Société pour la perception de la rémunération équitable (SPRE).[7]

The legal peculiarity of these typically French organizations is that it is the musicians and other musical artists themselves who are themselves, through their membership of say, the SACEM, responsible for the collection and payment of rights incurred by the use of their intellectual property. Taking the SACEM as an example – it is the most important of these *sociétés de gestion collective*, both in terms of numbers of members and financially – its function is to collect the income from rights due to its members from the reproduction of their works by television, radio, nightclubs, concerts, record companies or any other forms of dissemination. In this way, in 1995, the SACEM received some three billion francs of rights concerning 900,000 musical works having been performed or reproduced in the form of records, cassettes or videos. These monies were then paid out to 60,000 members of the *société*.[8]

---

[6] The SACEM covers authors, composers and editors of music; the SACD covers authors of drama; the SDRM covers recording and reproduction; the ADAMI covers performing artists; and the SPEDIDAM covers performing artists in music and dance.
[7] SCPP, SPPF and SPRE cover record producers.
[8] See Cardona, J., and Lacroix, C. (1996), *Statistiques de la culture: chiffres clés 1996*, Paris: La Documentation française.

Distribution of musical products has followed a pattern of concentration similar to that experienced in the sphere of production as local independent record retail outlets (*points de vente de proximité*) have been replaced by chains of record shops, or by large-scale retail companies either specialized in the sale of cultural goods in general (*multispécialistes*) or companies whose retailing is entirely general and for whom the sale of music is simply accessory. In the mid-1990s, specialist independent retailing accounted for a mere 5 per cent of market share whereas chains of record shops such as Nuggets, Madison and Music Way (10 per cent) and the famous major *multispécialistes* Fnac and Virgin (30 per cent) claimed the remaining shares of the market not swallowed by super and hypermarkets (50 per cent), department stores (3 per cent) and mail order (2 per cent). The two principal *multispécialistes*, for whom music sales represent only part of their overall turnover of books, videos and cultural goods of all kinds exemplify two significant approaches to the retailing of recorded music: the Fédération nationale d'achat (des cadres) or Fnac was created in 1954 and acquired by the conglomerate Pinault–Printemps–Redoute in 1996; Virgin is naturally the French subsidiary of Virgin retail and since 1986 has challenged Fnac's domination of high-street city-centre record sales. Although Virgin (7 per cent) typically enjoyed only about a third of Fnac's market share (23 per cent) in the mid-1990s, the five French Megastores have been influential in helping redefine and modernize the ways in which music is sold in France through a lively, communicative and highly youth-friendly approach to the design of their outlets and sales policies. In contrast to Virgin's multicultural image, Fnac now appears stuffy and old-fashioned to many young people, especially compared to the rightly famous Virgin Megastore located on the Champs-Elysées in Paris, which alone takes a 5 per cent market share of record sales.

MP3 and e-music: a 'French touch' from Vivendi-Universal?

France has been at the forefront of debates and restructurings of the music industry provoked by new technologies of computerized music. The technology of recorded music has always been significant in fashioning its acceptance by and impact on society. The period under consideration in this book – the second half of the twentieth century – has of course seen all the technological changes which have developed the techniques of production and the patterns of distribution of recorded music in France. Another chapter touches upon the effects of the changes from 78s to long-playing records and to singles in the 1950s and 1960s and how these new product formats influenced – for example – the consumption of music at home and the demand for music journalism, and the analysis of French music and the media discusses the effects of the transistor radio in the 1960s and the music video in the 1980s. But here, the focus of our attention is no longer the material 'product' – packaged, handled and tangible – whose format has evolved so successfully from black bakelite 78 to glittering CD, but the immaterial, electronic, on-line music enabled by techniques of digital compression. The music industry has always managed to respond successfully to technological change in general, and in particular involving the technology of the music product itself (with some notable exceptions such as the mini-disc and mini-cassette) but the challenge of the 'new economy' has, since the late 1990s created considerable apprehension amongst the different stakeholders of the music business. The classic technological process involved in this reconsideration of the ways in which music is owned, possessed, distributed, copied and enjoyed is of course MP3, and for the music industry MP3 poses essentially two questions: firstly, how can the music business control and regulate the private, illicit use of MP3 by individuals to reproduce and redistribute copyrighted music; and secondly, how can the music business itself adopt and adapt the technology of MP3 and the advantages it offers in terms of 'net economy' distribution of musical products in order to serve its own commercial interests?

In France, attention has centred on a number of aspects of these questions, concerning primarily the difficulties raised for the traditional definitions of intellectual property rights and secondarily, the ways in which on-line music represents yet another challenge to the preservation of France's claimed 'cultural exception'. The French-owned international media conglomerate Vivendi has also – under the influence of its controversial French CEO Jean-Marie Messier – been instrumental in attempting to redraw the boundaries of the music industry to include MP3 music distribution within the normal structures of increasingly concentrated and integrated consortia.

France was arguably the first country properly to conceptualize – and rationalize within an institutional structure – the issue of intellectual property rights, at least in the field of music. The organization that was created in France in 1851 to organize the collection and payment of rights to its members was the famous Société des auteurs, compositeurs et éditeurs de musique (SACEM) which has constantly been in the vanguard of debates over the nature of rights and the fairest and most efficient ways of managing them.[9] As has been discussed in a previous section, the SACEM plays a pivotal role in the French music industry, as well as in the French model of financing the culture industries, since 25 per cent of the rights collected (directly or indirectly) by the SACEM and its partner associations are contributed to the funding of culture. The SACEM is pragmatically proactive in identifying and pursuing illegal exploitation of copyright music: it holds regular briefing sessions for the police and legal professions and even employs staff to surf the Web using specialist search engines to locate sites using music without authorization.[10] France's

---

[9] For information on the SACEM, see www.sacem.fr.
[10] See Zilbertin, Olivier (1999), 'Trois questions à Catherine Keer-Vignale, membre du directoire de la Sacem', *Le Monde*, 24 February, 2.

central role in stimulating debate on the ways in which traditional (musical) intellectual property rights may still be effectively protected in the 'new Far West' environment of the new web economy has also extended to the SACEM's alliance with the five main rights-collecting companies worldwide (40 per cent of total payments) in the association Fast-Track based in Paris and constituted under French law.[11] Fast-Track's brief is to centralize information on its members' rights in order to make it easier to identify illicit use of their works.

In 1985, the famously active Minister of Culture Jack Lang was the instigator of the law 85-660 (known as the Lang law) which instituted the payment of a contribution from the sale of every blank audio cassette, video cassette or writable CD to the organizations created to manage the redistribution of these monies to the creative authors whose works were likely to be copied by the users of these blank cassettes, videos and CDs. In 1999, this system of paying musicians from levies on the materials used by private copiers or by bootleg commercial copiers ('pirates' in the French terminology) gave rise to over 550 million francs. The success of such an approach (however complicated it is in institutional and accounting terms, concerning the varied associations of authors involved and the formulae required to redistribute the payments equitably) led the French government in 2000 to consider the extension of the notion of 'droits voisins' to cover the hardware necessary for the on-line copying, distribution and enjoyment of electronic music. In its fullest version, such a modification of the Lang law would have imposed levies on computer hard disks and MP3 players for example, in an attempt to regulate the spread of illegal commercial copying. In early 2001, a compromise position was reached in which MP3 players but not hard disks would be targeted by the modified law.[12] In effect, the ways in which MP3 technologies allow musical intellectual property rights to be evaded has led, in France, more to a reaffirmation of the traditional definitions of rights, accompanied by the amendment of existing legislation and institutional practice (Fast-Track etc.) than to a reconceptualization of intellectual property rights themselves.[13] France has been the EU member least impressed by arguments extolling the economic freedom of the Web, and is concerned to protect the traditional strengths of the French music industry and associated sectors by reinforcing standard procedures and stakeholders (SACEM and rights, French CD and disk producers, multimedia groups such as Thomson).

Just as France has been particularly active in defending musical property rights against the threats to them of the new economy, French companies have

---

[11]   See Siclier, Sylvain (2000), 'La Sacem s'allie à quatre sociétés d'auteurs pour protéger le droit des créateurs sur Internet', *Le Monde*, 28 December, 24.

[12]   See Mortaigne, Véronique, and Siclier, Sylvain (2001), 'Le financement de la culture mis à mal par l'Internet', *Le Monde*, 18 January, 17.

[13]   Although the focusing of attention on the SACEM has also raised some difficult questions about the overall transparency and fairness of its activities. See Mortaigne, Véronique (2001), 'Le droit d'auteur est-il dépassé?', *Le Monde*, 2 August, 1.

similarly been leading the way in attempting to direct the music industry's reaction to MP3 technology. It is perhaps the case that the approaches adopted by these French companies are essentially traditional, in that they derive from a rationale of incremental change rather than revolutionary transformation of the relationships between the music business and the internet. The most striking initiative in this respect (both in terms of scale and in terms of the issues that it raises) has been the take-over of the internet music company MP3.com by the media-music-film conglomerate Vivendi-Universal.

Vivendi-Universal concentrates Vivendi, Seagram and the French TV/media company Canal Plus according to a rationale that hopes to produce vertical integration between populations of subscribing customers (Vodafone, USA Network for mobile phones; Canal Plus for films), and portfolios of diversified cultural products, ranging from film and video (Universal Studio) through games to education (and health) to music (Universal Music Group).[14] Vivendi-Universal's involvement in mobile telephony, television, internet servers and the hardware in general required for access to the new cultural services of the e-economy means that it has an overall mastery of technology and services. During 2001, Vivendi-Universal became increasingly conscious that the extremely popular MP3.com business represented a potential threat to its vertically integrated provision of services and products, since, along with Napster's similar peer-to-peer internet exchange of music files, MP3.com allowed the music audience worldwide to consume music without paying either the original producers, distributors or artists. By taking over MP3.com – who similarly to Napster had been in damaging litigation with the record industry – Vivendi-Universal added the final element to its integration, mirroring the vertical integration and concentration of its competitor the German Bertelsmann-BMG, which had in 2000 signed an alliance with Napster. Through the buy-out of MP3.com, with whom it had refused to settle over alleged copyright infringement, Universal acquired a website hosting one million songs from over 150,000 artists with the intention of collaborating with Sony in an on-line music venture called Duet.

The Vivendi acquisition of MP3.com and projected collaboration with Sony, the Bertelsmann alliance with Napster and the MusicNet project supported by AOL–Time Warner, EMI, Bertelsmann and Real Networks all represented in 2000 and 2001 the attempts by the music majors and the media conglomerates of which they are now subsidiaries to 'colonize' e-music. It is too early to say what will be the eventual effects of these concentrations and vertical integrations either on the viability of the new independent peer-to-peer sites likely to replace Napster and MP3.com in the favours of internet music seekers or on the supply of musical production. Now that MP3.com and Napster have 'sold out', the

---

[14] See Musso, Pierre (2000), 'Vivendi-Universal: l'Amérique gagnante', *Le Monde*, 8 December, 17.

music they offer with their new partners may become increasingly homogenized by the promotion of the majors' own artists and those disaffected by such net-oligopoly may turn to the Web to create, produce and distribute independent music from independent websites. Such a vision of diversity is, almost paradoxically, shared by Vivendi-Universal's French CEO Jean-Marie Messier, who, in a provocative reformulation of France's traditional battle cry of cultural specificity has launched a debate on the 'cultural diversity' that he claims is his objective in the strategy he has planned for Vivendi-Universal.

Messier's views have enraged many in France, but they stem from a typically French interpretation of globalization and the need to preserve national cultural traditions and practices. Writing in the high-brow French newspaper of reference *Le Monde* (the site of much debate on the threats to French culture of globalizsation) in April 2001, Messier explained that Vivendi-Universal's objective was not 'to construct a "global" company' but 'to build a universal grouping – as its name suggests – in the cultural industries'.[15] For Messier, such a grouping is able to take 'local' cultural products and distribute them on a worldwide scale, thereby strengthening the diversity of cultural production: 'if global [culture] means standardized products that are imposed on all, universal [culture] means individual works, born somewhere, which then go around the world.' In a swipe against the cultural 'protectionism' of which France is sometimes accused, Messier goes on to explain how his view of 'cultural diversity' rather than 'exception' is superior: 'Defending cultural diversity means allowing everyone to enjoy their own culture and to access the culture of others. Cultural diversity is not the juxtaposition of hermetically-sealed claims to identity which are essentially nationalistic, but reflects the vitality of societies which are increasingly interbred, of cultural legacies revisited and creativity with many roots.' These views were guaranteed to enrage the French cultural establishment by their defence of globalized 'Anglo-Saxon' capitalism (the French state tradition has traditionally been wary of economic liberalism) and by their assertion that global companies in the culture industries (and film and music in particular) do not necessarily mean the Americanization/McDonaldization of French culture.

The French Music Export Office: the record label 'France'?

In January 2001, the then socialist Minister of Foreign Affairs (the very serious Hubert Védrine) stated that 'The music industries play an essential and growing role, via their audience – particularly young people and thus by their impact – in the image of France abroad'. In the context of the annual trade fair for the French music sector – the MIDEM – such a declaration was ringing proof of the French

---

15   Messier, Jean-Marie (2001), 'Vivre la diversité culturelle', *Le Monde*, 10 April, 1.

state's relatively new and increasingly serious interest in treating music in the same way as other cultural industries such as publishing and cinema, which have long been major elements of France's cultural self-presentation to the world. Védrine went on to suggest that France should concentrate – metaphorically and in some ways practically (through official websites, for example) – the supply of French music in a recording label 'France'.[16] This keynote declaration also took pains to recognize the commercial successes of the French music business in exporting French music – assisted by the parapublic French Music Export Office – 34 million albums sold abroad (22 per cent of total French record production) in 1999, and noted the continuing industrial importance of such efforts.[17] But the Minister of Foreign Affairs was also careful to locate all French efforts in the promotion of music abroad within the framework of *spécificité culturelle* [cultural specificity] and France's growing preoccupation with the modernization of intellectual property rights in the field of culture to take account of technological change and the challenge of the internet and MP3. Such are the major elements of French thinking on the exporting of French music.

The Bureau export de la musique française [French Music Export Office] was set up in 1993 as a result of agreement amongst a variety of major players in the French music 'system' that French music needed a proactive policy of defence against cultural globalization. The main instigators of the Music Export Office were the principal record companies, the Syndicat national de l'édition phonographique (SNEP), the Ministry of Culture, the Fonds pour la création musicale (FCM), SCPP and the SACEM and ADAMI. Thus the activities of the Music Export Office are supported by essentially the whole range of institutions in the French music industry who are keen to see French music exported, essentially to Europe, in an attempt to bolster the national industry economically, as well as to defend French music and culture itself against the 'Anglo-Saxons' and globalization in general. The Music Export Office collaborates very closely with the European Music Office – Jean-François Michel is director of both institutions – set up in Brussels in 1995 in order to lobby the EU Commission about the needs of the European music industry.[18]

The Music Export Office has essentially a dual objective: it aims to increase the presence of French music abroad and to raise its market share, particularly in Europe, and also to encourage the staging of concerts by French musicians. The

[16]   Hubert Védrine, 'Les industries musicales jouent un rôle essentiel et croissant, par leur audience – en particulier dans la jeunesse et donc par leur impact – pour l'image de la France à l'étranger'. See Mortaigne, Véronique (2001), 'L'idée est de réunir notre offre musicale autour d'un label "France"', *Le Monde*, 22 January, 24.
[17]   See Anon. (2001), 'Le Midem témoigne du succès à l'export de la musique française', *Le Monde*, 22 January, 24.
[18]   See Davet, Stéphane (1997), 'L'Europe supplante les Etats-Unis sur le marché de la musique populaire', *Le Monde*, 2 April, 2; and Davet, S. (1997), 'Jean-François Michel, secrétaire général du Bureau européen de la musique', *Le Monde*, 2 April, 22.

Export Office has branches in Holland (Amsterdam), Germany (Mainz) and, since May 1999 – in the form of the Bureau des musiques actuelles or 'French Music Bureau' – in the United Kingdom (London). The Office presents an intriguing case study of many features of the French music business, influenced – for once directly, overtly and explicitly – by what could be termed the 'contextual challenge' (globalization) that lies behind the 'vulnerability' of the French music system identified by d'Angelo in his analysis of the socioeconomics of French music and a traditional concern of the French state (at least in general cultural terms, if not always for music itself).[19] The Music Bureau is an organization supported by the usual complicated complex of institutions, commercial companies, trade unions, government ministries and their instruments which make the French music system such a fragile entity.

In the late 1970s the French state began to take an interest in the limited export activities of the French record industry and through the Ministry of Foreign Affairs, set up the Bureau de diffusion sonore du ministère des Affaires Etrangères (BDS) responsible for publicizing French records through the cultural services of embassies and the encouragement of air-play for French music on foreign radio stations. At this time, the underlying motive for such interventionism was arguably a somewhat confusing mix of linguistic defensiveness and cultural pride (for lack of a more neutral term) rather than a strong awareness of commercial and business considerations. And the musics concerned by the activities of the BDS were not yet those genres for which a significant commercial market would be possible, since before the 1980s and the Lang/Mitterrand innovations in cultural policy which transformed the French state's understanding of what should be considered as popular (and thus commercial) music, both the Ministry of Foreign Affairs and the Ministry of Culture were still marked very heavily by traditional considerations of elite culture.

To take Malraux's expression, the role of the Ministry of Culture was centred around the democratization of the 'plus hautes œuvres de l'esprit' [the greatest works of the mind], contextualized within the framework – as Teillet and others have discussed – of preserving and making accessible masterpieces, rather than encouraging (as would be the case after 1981) 'création par tous' [artistic creation by all]. The Ministry of Foreign Affairs was similarly incapable of understanding the possible economic interest of commercial music, so the music dealt with by the BDS was considerably removed from the Daft Punk, Air, Rita Mitsouko and other examples of properly 'popular', commercially successful

---

[19]   For discussion of two ways in which music still seems to slip from the French state's generally constant obsession with France's cultural exceptionalism, despite the great rise in government interest in music policy since the 1980s, see Mortaigne, Véronique (1996), 'Le complexe de la chanson française', *Le Monde*, 18 April 1996, 13, and (1999) 'La chanson, éternelle oubliée', *Le Monde*, 9 November, 16.

contemporary French music which has been the everyday fare of the French Music Export Office in the late 1990s and the early 2000s. Nevertheless, by the early 1980s, the BDS had contributed significantly to the putting into place of the twin supports of the French music industry's contemporary export drive, namely an international cultural presence through ministries and embassies abroad and their financial subsidies and the private sector's conventional actions to encourage the (difficult) success of Francophone music abroad. A further remark on the forerunner institutions and policies of the French Music Export Office is perhaps useful here, before we move on to discuss in more detail how it has functioned since 1993 in the context of an expanding European music market and rising interest for national repertoires. During the 1940s, 1950s and 1960s particularly (dramatically less so in the 1970s), France could still benefit from the general worldwide acceptance of French culture's special value and right to an automatic international presence, and the French music stars who achieved world reputations – Maurice Chevallier and Édith Piaf (discussed elsewhere in this volume), Jacques Brel (Belgian, but Francophone), Yves Montand, Charles Aznavour – did so through a combination of the appeal of their French 'style' and their awareness that they needed to adapt their talent to the demands of the Anglo-Saxon music public. Few have been the stars of French music in the 1970s and since who have been able to exploit any cachet of French culture's supposed superiority as traditional values of elite culture have been increasingly distanced from what makes the international commercial success of popular music. The only example of a French musician from the 1970s and 1980s who has achieved success similar to that of the stars of the decades after the Second World War is arguably Jean-Michel Jarre, whose electronic music (free of the linguistic handicap of lyrical French popular music) anticipates the international critical and commercial success of French 'electronica' (considered by Birgy later in this book) and 'French touch' bands such as Daft Punk in the 1990s.

The French Music Export Office's creation in 1993 coincided with a period when, as US domination of pop music lessened slightly, the European market gained in significance and Polygram and Virgin in France began to focus more on developing the repertoires of French musicians, particularly within the perspective of exporting French music beyond the confines of a national market whose growth would not be sufficient. The Export Office works in partnership with an extensive range of institutions covering all aspects of the French music business, but still essentially reflects the dual approach (state and industry, in the form of record companies) of the BDS of the late 1970s and 1980s. In addition to the state (represented at the highest level by the Ministry of Foreign Affairs and the Ministry of Culture) and industry (represented by the Syndicat national de l'édition phonographique – SNEP), it is important also to point out that the Bureau also collaborates with the SACEM, ADAMI and SPEDIDAM, as important stakeholders in the success of French music in the export market. The Export Office has ostensibly as its primary objective the promotion and the distribution of French records and videos overseas. This primary objective is to be attained through the promotion of live concerts, the dissemination of French music in all its forms and the participation of the Office in events encouraging the 'rayonnement' of French music. The use of the term 'rayonnement' (literally the 'radiating' or 'radiation' – as an expression characteristic of the heyday of French colonialism and cultural self-confidence, if not arrogance – betrays a secondary objective which is essentially political and cultural.

The activities of the Export Office inescapably possess a political dimension through the heavy state involvement in its creation and running. Equally, the Office uses the networks of contacts and infrastructures set up by the Ministries of Culture and Foreign Affairs abroad and is thus unavoidably perceived as a representative of France's political (and cultural) representation overseas. Politically and culturally, an intriguing feature of the Export Office's work is that although it uses the facilities of a French state still heavily marked by traditional perceptions of culture à la Malraux (despite the changes brought about since the 1980s) it has nevertheless come to represent the more modern, more popular and more commercial genres of contemporary French music. The Office's support for Francophone 'world music', rap and most recently techno – as expressions of *musiques actuelles* – is thus a crucial refocusing of the dissemination of French culture abroad. One of the partners of the Office is the SNEP (representing the French music industry) which in 1993 was controlled primarily (for technical reasons concerning the composition of its board of management) by the major recording companies, but as the work of the Office has developed, not only has the SNEP become more representative of the recording industry as a whole, but the Office has striven to represent the interests of major and independent record companies overall, with such success that the organization representing the French independent labels (the Société civile des producteurs de phonogramme en France – SPPF) has become a collaborator in the same way as the SNEP itself, thus further consolidating the Office's commitment to minority-interest *musiques actuelles* as well as the more mainstream artists more characteristic of the major labels.

The Bureau des musiques actuelles de Londres or French Music Bureau in London (FMBL) was set up in May 1999 by Marie-Agnès Beau, who had previously been one of the senior managers of the French Music Export Office in Paris. The experience of the FMBL can serve as an illuminating case study of the desire of the French state and of the French music business to increase the overseas market for French music. It is arguably the case that despite undoubted enthusiasm and competence and an energetically successful programme of information, publicity and promotions of all kinds, the FMBL is nevertheless still suffering from a certain lack of clarity in its brief – a lack which reflects the degree of confusion at the heart of the rationale of the French Music Export Office itself. Indeed, just as d'Angelo has suggested (in a very brief description of the activities of the Office) that export policy seems indecisive, without direction, short- or medium-term objectives or an overall rationale for planning, the FMBL displays a lack of focus in its aims and activities.[20]

The very title of the FBML betrays some of the – perhaps typically French – confusions over popular music created in France by the traditionally unforgiving distinction between elite and popular culture, the consequent reactions of hostility towards high culture (and those genres of music valued by it) of those convinced of the value of popular music, and the difficulties of the state since the 1980s and its attempts to 'democratize' musical culture to find terminologies acceptable to all to express the nature of popular music. The chapters by Le Guern and Teillet, in particular, in this current volume touch on these issues of classification and terminology, but here, it can immediately be seen that the English version of the French title of the FMBL is unable to translate either the form or the implications of 'musiques actuelles'.[21] Unlike the title of the parent 'Bureau export de la musique française' in Paris which remains masterfully vague and all-inclusive, the FBML in London specifically stresses that it is concerned with contemporary, modern musical forms, and in its definition of strategies and objectives, clearly states that its aim is 'to support and enhance the spread of French *popular musics* abroad'.[22] The music publicized by the FBML so successfully is indeed predominantly what an Anglo-Saxon audience would understand as contemporary French popular music – rap, techno, dance, hip hop etc – but these genres could also be seen as a somewhat restrictive interpretation of the overall brief of the Bureau to export all French music, and thus, as an indication of a tension, if not a confusion, within the aims of the overall 'export drive' itself.

The physical siting of the FMBL is similarly indicative of the difficulties of the objective of exporting French music connected with the issue of language, inextricably linked, as it is, to that of French culture and its 'rayonnement'. The FMBL is housed by the French Institute in London, placing it firmly within the sphere of language and culture and the traditional institutions set up by France to disseminate culture and foster the understanding of the French language. The documentation of the FMBL attempts to make the best of the somewhat precarious position of 'music export' by laying claim to the possibility of creating synergy between the linguistic, cultural and commercial aspects of its activities.[23]

---

[20]   D'Angelo, Mario (1997), *Socio-économie de la musique*, 138–39.

[21]   For some analysis of the cultural and political implications of such terminological choices, see Mortaigne, Véronique (1998), 'La Commission nationale des musiques actuelles vient de rendre son rapport', *Le Monde*, 18 September, 29.

[22]   Information sheet, *Objectifs et stratégies*, French Music Bureau, London: 30 June 1999, 1.

[23]   Ibid.

Conclusion

Writing in 1981, Antoine Hennion was already qualifying the traditional belief that the French music industry was totally dominated by the 'Anglo-Saxon' oligopoly of the music majors.[24] Since the early 1980s the debate on who controls the world music business has obviously increasingly been coloured by arguments over globalization, and the French state's attempts to encourage France's music producers and distributors have been more and more informed by theories of cultural exception and the defence of the French language and culture (including music). The French music industry's 'vulnerability' is the result of both the threat of the major US-dominated music and media conglomerates and of its own complexities and archaisms, but these complexities and archaisms are also sources of strength and innovative strategies for the defence of French music and culture. The role of the state, for example and the French approach to the management of music rights and the funding of culture provide France with structures and principles (the Music Export Bureau, the SACEM, the belief in France's cultural specificity) which both strengthen France's music business and allow France to play a leading role in discussions at EU level on how Europe can protect itself against US cultural and commercial hegemony. French-led consortia such as Vivendi-Universal are also, paradoxically, appearing to show the way forward in the worldwide music industry's reactions to the e-economy in cultural products and a redefinition of traditional ideas about cultural globalization and the protection of national cultural identities.

---

[24]   Hennion, Antoine (1981), *Les professionnels du disque. Une sociologie des varietes*, Paris: Metaile.

Chapter 4

Popular music on French radio and television

Geoff Hare

Music, both popular and 'serious', has of course been present on French radio and television since the very earliest days of both media. Entertainment, musical or otherwise, alongside news and information, and the educational functions of the transmission of culture, has been an important mission associated with both broadcasting media in France as in other Western countries. And a major element of the Western entertainment tradition is of course *popular* music. While the technology associated with broadcasting has been commonly available in the developed economies of Western Europe and North America at more or less the same time, French society and politics have developed *differently* from their neighbours. A major distinction between France and Britain for instance has been, firstly, the role of the state within society, in this context in controlling, restricting and regulating broadcasting systems, and, secondly, governmental attitudes to an independent commercial sector providing competition to the public service tradition. Recently, as globalization has tended to erode national autonomy in broadcasting systems and to threaten national cultural identity, and since global culture has been purveyed mainly by English-speaking cultural phenomena and multinational businesses whose ideological home is often perceived as being in the United States of America, a further French 'exception' has been a concern to protect the position of the French language within France and the world. This concern has taken political form in the shape of a protectionist policy towards French cultural productions and the national media that transmit them. Hence, the French film and cinema industry and the French popular music industry and the broadcasting of French popular song, for instance, have, in the one case, been the subject of international trade negotiations to prevent the import of cultural productions being treated like cars or bars of soap, and in the other, subject to legally enforced quotas to limit competition from American or British popular music. While some of these themes are relevant to both media and the ways in which popular music is treated by them, this chapter will deal separately with radio and then television, looking first at the chronologically earlier medium, that of radio.

Radio

To understand the relationship of radio and music in France today, some attention needs to be paid to the period when television was not a competitor, that is, well into the 1960s, and to the key period of change in the 1980s. The main factors that have affected the changing profile of popular music programming on French radio in these periods, and thus popular music's contribution to France's exceptionalism (the ways in which France has defined itself as different from other European nations), have been as follows: firstly, the relative paucity of radio stations in the period up to 1981, and their concentration on programming for a mass, generalist audience; secondly the creation of a new independent and commercial radio sector, following legislation in 1981, that led to a rapid multiplication of outlets for music programming, and a segmentation of the audience initially by age and later also by musical genre; and, finally, the imposition of strict linguistic quotas on music radio in the mid-1990s – as part of a long French tradition of linguistic and cultural protectionism – that effectively restricted the amount of British and American popular music that could be played by French stations, thus giving a promotional boost to the domestic French music industry. There are thus three periods that define popular music programming on French radio, periods articulated by legislative change.

Pre-1981: limited radio outlets for popular music

In the inter-war period, when radio was becoming a mass medium, competition between publicly owned radio stations and, from 1923, a private sector, allowed a situation to develop where contrasting tones and functions distinguished commercial radios such as Radio Cité from state-controlled radio. Where the latter was serious and concentrated on information and the transmission of mainly high culture to the gradually increasing audiences that had access to a radio set, the other concentrated on entertainment radio and the popular audience. Commercial radio programmed popular music, initially live from the French music-hall tradition and later recorded, from the stock of French phonographic productions. The music-hall tradition grew in the inter-war period. The most famous Parisian music halls were the Casino de Paris and the Folies Bergère, and post-war Bobino and the Olympia. Marc argues that they created all-round stars, like Maurice Chevalier and Mistinguett, able to perform onstage, in the cinema and then of course on radio, and that they brought in new types of music, from America, with Bechet and Josephine Baker. The staple show of the later music hall, for example produced by the best-known post-war music-hall impresario Bruno Coquatrix (1910–79) who ran the Olympia, was a series of evenings devoted to a single performer, or where the star performed throughout the second half. Stars like Bécaud and Jacques Brel were created by their performances at the Olympia; they made their names in their first appearances in

1954 and 1958 respectively. When Johnny Hallyday had his first success at the Olympia in 1961 he had already had a hit record and radio shows like *Salut les copains* had already begun to promote records.[1] The 1992 *Quid* encyclopaedia records 27 music halls still operating in Paris. The linked success of the music hall and the recording industry was bound to feed radio music programming.

The post-war 'state radio monopoly'

In the period from the end of the Second World War to the arrival of the Mitterrand presidency in 1981, the development of French popular music was affected by the relative paucity of licensed radio stations in France. Those that did exist were closely controlled by government, and a particular cultural ideology dominated. The paternalistic attachment of French public service radio to a programming policy of privileging elite culture restricted outlets for French popular music. France Culture and France Musique, high culture and low audience stations, were popular music deserts. The one general audience station where popular music was to be heard at different times of the day was France Inter. Music programming, however, then as now, also had to share air time with all the other types of programming (news and current affairs, drama, game shows, humour etc.) that had to be provided by the one general audience station. The explanation for this situation was political. As French society and government came back to some normality after the Second World War German Occupation, the collaborationist Vichy regime, and the gradual Liberation of the territory from June 1944 onwards, the left-wing-dominated progressive government that emerged from the Resistance Movement was unhappy to allow any broadcasting to be handed back to the 'powers of money and big business'. What was subsequently called the state broadcasting monopoly was put in place and refined by successive governments of both the Fourth and Fifth Republics. In particular, President de Gaulle, from 1958 onwards, was conscious of the importance of communicating directly to the mass of French citizens in his new presidential style of regime, the Fifth Republic. Bypassing parliamentary and party politics meant using the mass media to communicate directly to the French people. A firm believer in strong central state power, de Gaulle and his conservative successors were reluctant to give up the public service monopoly of broadcasting. Ironically, it was not until the election of the first left-wing President of the Republic in 1981 and the installation of a Socialist-dominated government (including four Communist ministers indeed) that the state monopoly was to be broken, and large numbers of independent radio stations were to be authorized.

The feature of radio broadcasting that had the biggest influence on the development and promotion of popular music in this period was broadcasting from across frontiers. The post-war state radio monopoly was in this sense a

---

[1]   Marc, Edmond (1972), *La Chanson française*, Paris: Hatier, 50, 62, 77–78.

myth. French is spoken in countries bordering France and commercial radio operators saw a French-speaking market to exploit inside France by broadcasting entertainment radio with a strong music content into France from transmitters situated just over the border. From Luxembourg, from 1933 onwards, from Monaco since 1943, from the Saarland in Germany from 1955, and from Andorra since 1958, the east, the south-east, Paris and the north, and the south-west – indeed most of France – had good long-wave reception of commercial radio and an alternative and more popular diet of radio news and entertainment. Such was the competition felt by state-controlled radio, and its masters, from these *périphériques* stations, that the French state bought a controlling interest in some of these 'independent' radios and a partial interest in others. The tolerance of the existence of these *périphériques* was such that they were soon allowed to set up studios in Paris, and use dedicated lines owned by the state telephone company to contact their transmitters. RTL, Radio Monte Carlo, Europe 1, and Sud-Radio each, however, ran only one generalist station and so, while pop music did have an outlet for young French listeners, the *périphériques* too felt commercial pressures to broadcast to the whole of the French audience – in order, as commercial stations, to attract revenue from advertisers wishing to sell to those who, in the 1950s, 1960s and into the 1970s still held the family purse strings. Music radio was not yet therefore a 'genre' in its own right.

Those programmes of popular music that remain in the French communal memory promoted music that was either on the edge of or central to that particularly French genre of 'chanson'. Its exponents from Trenet and Piaf, through Aznavour and Montand, to Brel and Brassens appealed to a very wide audience, both in terms of age and in terms of cultural background, in just the same way that broadcasting did not differentiate, yet, in segmenting the mass audience.

Nonetheless, in the 1960s it became impossible for French radio to ignore rock and pop music since, for one thing, the French recorded music industry and a nascent music press were producing French-language cover versions of British and American hits, a top-twenty sales chart, and promoting French stars such as Johnny Hallyday, Sylvie Vartan, Eddy Mitchell, Dick Rivers, Claude François, Sheila, and others. Indeed, Europe 1, from 1959 with the programme *Salut les copains*, was quick to win a huge youth audience with programming of chart hits. The success of Europe 1's new youth music programming has to be put in the context of the new portability of radio through the growth of the transistor precisely at this time, which allowed the new youth audience to take radio and music out of the family sitting room or kitchen and into their own space, including into the street.

The 1980s and 1990s: new radio outlets and more musical specialization

Social demand for a more diversified pattern of specialized radio provision to cater for regions or smaller localities, and for particular musical tastes, was recognized too late by Radio France, the public service radio network, although it created in 1980 three experimental local radios, and a Parisian pop music station Radio 7. The latter had not enough time to establish itself (unlike Britain's Radio 1) before independent pop radio took over. Radio 7 was to lose most of its audience within seven years and be closed down. That a social need for more music radio outlets existed may be seen in the experience of pirate radio in the 1970s. For a few years the Giscard d'Estaing government had taken a hard line with a handful of operators of pirate radio stations attempting to break the state monopoly by playing pop music that was not getting much air time on the existing stations. It took political change in the shape of a left-wing victory in the presidential and parliamentary elections of 1981 to bring the promise of sweeping changes in broadcasting as in many other sectors of French social and economic life.

The main push behind these new radios was musical. With the promise of legislation to come, the Mitterrand government tolerated 'free local radios' for a year before the initial anarchistic situation was gradually regulated by the new broadcasting licensing body that emerged from legislation of July 1982 on 'the freedom of communication'. Independent radio meant initially non-commercial, local FM radio, but by 1984 advertising had been allowed and by 1986, the grouping together of local stations into national commercial networks.[2] It was not only the stations of Radio France that felt the competitive pinch in terms of audience. The old *périphériques* stations RTL, Europe 1 and RMC, lost income and market share and quickly applied for FM licences to set up networks under the new legislation.

Independent radio in the 1980s and 1990s: the Anglo-American invasion

While some of the new commercial stations used the new liberty of communication in the shape of talk radio, many interested in radio for commercial reasons found that the format that most easily found an audience was 'music and news', mostly music aimed at a youth and young adult audience, along the model of American radio. Initially French radio was formatted by audience age alone: under 25, 25–45, and over 45. Jean-Paul Baudecroux's NRJ network, aimed at the youth audience, became the most successful both in terms of number of listeners and commercial growth. A process of commercial concentration led to the construction of about eight major national networks emerging out of an initial 1500 or so locally approved stations. NRJ, Skyrock and Fun were in competition for the youth audience; young adult stations included Chérie FM, and networks taken over by the *périphériques* and called Europe 2

---

[2]   See Hare, Geoff (1992), 'The law of the jingle: a decade of change in French radio', in R. Chapman and N. Hewitt (eds), *Popular Culture and Mass Communication in Twentieth Century France*, Lampeter: Edwin Mellen Press, 27–46.

and RTL 2. The older segment was served by Nostalgie and after various changes of format in search of an audience, by RFM. It took until the 1990s for French commercial formats to become more musically specialized and differentiated within each age group. This followed a second wave of concentrations and take-overs that has left the French commercial radio sector in the hands of three major media groups, each controlling a major network within each age range: Europe Communications group owns Europe 1 (news and sport), Skyrock (youth); Europe 2 (young adult), RFM (adult, 'gold'), the CLT–UFA group owns the generalist RTL, the young adult network RTL2, and the youth audience Fun Radio; the relative newcomer to radio, the Baudecroux group, owns NRJ (youth audience), Chérie FM (young adult), Nostalgie (adult music), and a music and humour network Rire et Chansons.

This period of increasing concentration of ownership and competition for listeners led to a situation where the three major national commercial youth music networks gave less and less air time to French popular music (June 1992 figures showed 13 per cent of plays for French music on NRJ, 8 per cent on Skyrock, 7 per cent on Fun). For reasons of commercial competitiveness, the networks were wary of offering their listeners new and relatively unknown French artists, and preferred an overwhelming diet of already successful British and American music. On 8 February 1996 the conservative daily *Le Figaro*, for example, published an article by Claude Duneton under the title 'Dix menaces qui pèsent sur la langue française' [Ten threats to the French language], where he says: 'une nation où les enfants n'entendraient plus chanter en français serait une nation culturellement en voie de disparition' [a nation where children no longer heard people singing in French would be a culturally endangered nation]. News of the loss of French popular music from youth radio was sufficient for a reaction of 'moral panic' within the French cultural establishment, of commercial panic within the French music industry, and a hurried resort to a traditional remedy – political control, in the form of a law enforcing linguistic quotas on popular song programmed on French radio.

Linguistic quotas and the defence of French musical culture

The legislation itself, the so-called 'Pelchat amendment', passed into French law as part of a wider Broadcasting Reform Act on 1 February 1994. It imposed on all French radio stations a compulsory minimum of 40 per cent of French-language songs in their popular music programming at times of day where there is a significant listening audience (6.30 a.m. to 10.30 p.m.). Within this 40 per cent minimum of French songs, there was a further requirement for radios to give air time, for at least half of the quota, to new talent ('nouveaux talents') or newly issued recordings ('nouvelles productions').

The result was that by September 1998 the French Broadcasting Regulator (le Conseil Supérieur de l'Audiovisuel or CSA) had banned a regional radio from broadcasting for a day following persistent flouting of the conditions of its licence, by playing too many songs in English. In the same year ten final warnings were given to other national and regional networks. In 1999 the CSA issued further final warnings to French commercial radios. Nonetheless, in the two years between the passing of the bill and the full implementation of its provisions, 1300 independent radios had their licensing agreements either simply renewed by the CSA, where they already respected the quota, or modified through negotiation, so that they would progressively come into line with the new law before it came into force.

It should be pointed out, however, that in addition to the highly publicized cultural and linguistic motivation behind this legislation, there was also a commercial and economic motivation to do with the protection of the French music industry. The economic and commercial concerns that put radio quotas on the political agenda show how much the music industry is seen to depend on radio. In the 1990s France was the fifth largest market for recorded music sales (behind USA, Japan, Germany and UK). The French market grew strongly in the 1980s under the influence of the arrival of CDs, of access by music industry to TV advertising, and of the halving of the rate of VAT applied to records. However in the early to mid-1990s the market saw very moderate growth, even stagnation.[3] At the committee stage of the 1994 Broadcasting Reform Act evidence was given by the French Performing Rights Association (SACEM) and by the French record production industry on the link between radio plays and record sales, which had recently dipped. A key fact was that between 1988 and 1992 sales of French-produced music recordings had fallen behind non-French sales on the internal French market (imports of recorded music – excluding classical music – out-sold French discs by 10 percentage points, whereas the situation had been the reverse a few years earlier). The international music industry was of course dominated by Anglo-American music. At the same time as sales were falling, French pop music (as seen above) was getting less air time on youth radio. Independent French record producers in particular were suffering. Since there was an accepted correlation between sales and radio play-lists, the music industry favoured regulation of radio, to save the French national music industry from following those of Belgium, Holland, Scandinavia and Germany, which were all but extinct. The example of linguistic quotas in Quebec was cited.

These economic concerns coincided with much more potent and long-standing cultural concerns that gave them political legitimacy. The existence of linguistic legislation is perhaps only understood with any immediacy from a culture where English is not the native tongue. The solution of quotas fitted long-standing and wider cultural protectionism related to concerns about the status of

---

3   SNEP (1997), *L'Economie du disque*, Paris: SNEP (Syndicat national de l'édition phonographique), 2.

the French language in the modern world and its links to national identity. Language is for France much more of a symbol of national sovereignty than is the French currency. In the year of the Maastricht Treaty when France signed up to losing the Franc and adopting the Euro, parliament accepted a constitutional amendment stating: 'The language of the Republic is French.'[4] The ultimate fear was that French might be relegated to the status of a second-class language, and with it French culture and France itself.

The key cultural area where Anglo-American influences were apparently taking over from French was in popular music, and this was seen as important, since popular music in the traditional French form of 'chanson' sits quite happily within the French establishment's definition of culture. Brassens was awarded the poetry prize by the Académie française in 1967; Trenet was decorated with the Légion d'honneur. Unlike post-war American popular music where rhythm and beat have been the most important feature, French song has been characterized by the importance of the lyric, the text, and has been seen therefore as closer to the high cultural literary genres. Song has not been seen as divorced from high culture (unlike Britain), and has been a very productive area of French artistic creativity ever since the birth of radio and the record industry. Therefore new concerns about the dwindling influence of the French language within youth music radio and the concomitant deleterious effect on creativity in French popular music put French song on the agenda of traditional French cultural protectionism.

From the point of view of the radio stations themselves, youth radio had the most problems with the regulation. The most popular national networks targeting the 15 to 25 year olds, such as NRJ, Skyrock or Fun Radio, had built their audiences on a diet of music containing a high proportion of American rock and pop. Stations finding it difficult to reach the quota generally claimed in their defence that there were not enough French records being produced for their particular target audience, or at least not enough of sufficient quality. NRJ claimed that whereas the French repertoire for an *adult* audience is very rich, the youth radios were stuck between rap and boy bands and there was very little to play.[5] Fun Radio reacted by introducing more phone-ins at evening prime times, partly as a way of stretching the limited amount of playable French music to the 40 per cent of remaining programming.[6]

One of Fun's main competitors, the network Skyrock, seeing the difficulty it would have in reaching the 40 per cent quota, changed its format radically in 1995, banking its future on French rap music. Its percentage of rap went from 35

---

[4]   Brulard, Inès (1997), 'Linguistic policies' in Sheila Perry (ed.), *Aspects of Contemporary France*, London: Routledge, 191–207, 195, 199.

[5]   Bara, Guillaume (1998), 'Cocoriquotas ou quotallergie', *Télérama* (2516), 1 April.

[6]   Dauncey, Hugh, and Hare, Geoff (1999), 'French youth talk radio: the free market and free speech', *Media, Culture and Society*, **21** (1), 93–108.

per cent in 1995 to 50 per cent in 1996, and to 75 per cent in the late 1990s. Its audience increased and it contributed to a remarkable flowering of French rap.[7]

The music industry saw the quotas as a boost to new music. French rap and hip-hop were in a phase of development that coincided with the quotas. After one year of quotas, sales went up from 45 per cent to 52 per cent of total music sales.[8] Singles benefited most. The verdict of the SNEP (the association representing major French record producers) was that the quotas seemed to have given new impetus to the 'virtuous circle' of 'production – diffusion – sales'. The SNEP claimed quotas had helped French music producers to quadruple their investment in new French talent.[9] One complaint was that certain artists working in France, such as Khaled, and representing the North African communities and singing in Arabic or Berber, were not counted as part of the national repertoire. This complaint took on a particular resonance in 1998, the year when the 'black, blanc, beur' multicoloured national football team were winning the World Cup and being touted by Left and Right as representing the new France.[10]

Over the initial two-year period of monitoring, the law seemed effective in that there was an increase in the proportion of French songs broadcast. Overall French-language recordings went up from 1995 – 41 per cent, to 1997 – 45 per cent of total music played. One unforeseen consequence was the increasing uniformity in the French music being played. The same French singers or bands and the same songs were being heard. Hence, over-exposure of new rap stars like MC Solaar. However French artists as a percentage of the whole went up from 1995 – 21 per cent, to 1997 – 24 per cent.[11] New talents like Tribal Jam and Mad in Paris, Doc Gynéco, and Pascal Obispo broke through, but overall the number of plays of new talents went down – since the new talents of 1995–96 (MC Solaar, Axelle Red, Native, Iam) were subsequently counted in the category of established talents.[12] As time went on, therefore, there was not the hoped-for on-going expansion of records by new talents. However most radios had more or less fallen in line, more French songs were being heard on radio and more records were being sold. Furthermore, 83 per cent of the French public were in favour of quotas on radio, according to a poll commissioned by the music industry.[13]

In the late 1990s, discord between the music industry and the radio sector led to an amendment to the law in the direction of flexibility. Increasing differentiation of formats turned the quotas into a blunt instrument. The

---

[7]   Bara, 'Cocoriquotas ou quotallergie'.
[8]   Briet, Sylvie (1997), 'Chanson française: les quotas radio font moins de couacs', *Libération*, 21 January, 26.
[9]   Bara, 'Cocoriquotas ou quotallergie'.
[10]   Ibid.
[11]   IPSOS (1997), *Bilan Radio Aircheck 1997*, IPSOS Music, 1.
[12]   Suquet, Patrick (1998), 'Moins de titres francophones à la radio en 1997', *Ecran Total*, 11 February.
[13]   SNEP (1997), *L'Economie du disque*, 27.

uniformity of the quotas became less and less appropriate to an increasingly diversified radio landscape, where the number of different formats has multiplied. Greater specialization of radios led to formats being differentiated both by age of listeners and by musical style – dictated by highly competitive conditions. Specialization in certain types of music, like dance, for example, meant it was difficult to find sufficient numbers or sufficiently good French records.[14] The problem was illustrated by one of the most serious cases of breaking the law, that of the regional network Vibration (based in Orléans), which in order to conform to the law initially changed its format to more French rap, lost half its audience, and came back to its original wide-ranging pop and rock format with 60 per cent of new releases, but without reaching the 40 per cent target for French recordings. It claimed it needed to retain its distinctiveness in order not to lose its audience and disappear, and that the law needed to recognize this.

In order to take account of the diversification of French radio, and to avoid the risk of standardization of radio in general through more and more uniform play lists,[15] the CSA floated the idea of 'modulated' quotas. In June 2000 parliament accepted an amendment to the law that was designed to favour the exposure of new performers on radio, but not to penalize radios that concentrate on the musical heritage ('adult' radios). For specific formats the CSA may now grant a 'derogation' to allow a radio either to drop to 35 per cent of French records provided the percentage of new talent reaches 25 per cent of the total, or to play only 10 per cent of new talent where a radio reaches 60 per cent of French song overall.[16]

Music radio in the twenty-first century

The differentiation of French music radio has settled down as the inevitable economic concentration of capital and competition for audiences within the sector reached a state of equilibrium as the new century dawned. Youth music radio (NRJ, Skyrock, Fun) is still able to support the French music industry in its new productions. Adult radio stations have tried to differentiate their formats between younger and older adults, that is, between a mix of new and older songs, both French and Anglo-American, and one or two stations such as RFM playing 'gold' rock and pop from the 1960s onwards. There remain one or two stations aiming at an over-50s audience, such as MFM or Chante France or the state

---

[14]   Mauboussin, Elisabeth (1999), 'Quel avenir pour les quotas de diffusion de chansons d'expression française?', *Légipresse* (162), June, 77.

[15]   Labarde, Philippe (1998), 'Interview: Les quotas encore en question', *Vive la Radio*, March.

[16]   Aaron, Didier (2001), 'L'évolution de la programmation musicale en radio', *Dossiers de l'audiovisuel* (97), 11.

network France Bleue, that have a higher percentage of French song and indeed a higher percentage of traditional 'chanson'.

The quotas issue tells us that France has a diverse and flourishing radio industry. It tells us that while the interests of the music industry and of radio are symbiotically interlinked, they are not identical. They show too that cultural imperialism theories and models are alive and well in France, and that this may reflect the dominance of an older generation of French decision-makers rather than the mass of the younger generation of listeners. Radio quotas are part of a much wider anxiety among French elites about national identity and merely one of a number of policy instruments putting into effect a defence of the French language and ultimately of national identity. However, whereas French elites readily apply notions of cultural imperialism to the relations of the USA to Western Europe, French youth has been fascinated by American culture in the post-war era.

Finally, the affair reminds us that, while national identity may be a much more explicit concern in France than in most other modern states, issues of identity are central to popular music, and to radio and the mass media in general.

Television

Television is often assumed to have taken over from sound radio as the key entertainment medium of the late twentieth century. In terms of popular music the relationship is not so simple. As will be seen, television's programming of popular music has in some ways imitated and followed trends set on radio. Like radio, television's programming of popular music suffered for a long time from a dearth of channels and therefore of air time. Two other main factors affecting French television's changing relationship to popular music as content have been, firstly, the late commercialization of television with the creation of independent terrestrial channels in the middle 1980s and the privatization of the top audience channel TF1 in 1987, which created a strong independent sector entirely dependent on income from advertising and therefore needing to attract large audiences; and secondly, European legislation on quotas of French and European-produced programmes, imposed on television from 1990 onwards, that have had a restrictive effect on music programming. Within the commercial and legal contexts created by these factors, two major television phenomena have structured music television, the French television tradition of the variety show, and the long wait for a dedicated French music channel.

Popular music and the 'variety show' in the public service television era

The genre called 'Variétés' has been, at least until the expansion of television channels from the mid-1980s, a key vehicle for the televising of popular music in France. The genre was taken from the radio format which itself was a borrowing from the music hall. Initially television simply filmed such performances, even radio shows. Titles such as *Radio Parade* and *Music hall à la TV* leave no room for doubt about the lack of creativity in the early use of television medium.[17] There is a strong tradition of shows being televised from music-hall theatres, such as the Olympia. From 1956 onwards the Eurovision Song Contest was a major annual showcase. Talent competitions were popular in the 1960s, for example Mireille's *Petit Conservatoire* (also inspired from radio). Johnny Hallyday, Mireille Matthieu, and Thierry Le Luron first came to a national audience in this way. The harmonica player Albert Raisner was a popular presenter in the 1960s. A variation on the variety-show format in the 1960s was the live special devoted to a single star, or the hybrid Sunday-afternoon family show *Dimanche Martin*, in the 1970s and 1980s, recorded in front of a live audience in a theatre. It involved the traditional elements of the music hall (song; dance, humour and speciality acts), but also game show and children's talent competition held together by the star host Jacques Martin. The variety show later turned into part talk show, part variety show, such as Jacques Chancel's *Le Grand Echiquier* and Michel Drucker's *Champs Elysées* in the 1980s and two decades later Drucker's *Vivement Dimanche*. These shows also revolve around star host interviewer or compère, who has his own guests, his own team and his own style; thus giving continuity to the shows, and are recorded in front of a live audience, two of them a small audience in the studio.

The variety show is essentially family television and it is no coincidence that its peak popularity was at the time when there were only one or two channels, and limited broadcasting time, so little opportunity for narrow-casting to a niche audience. Stars such as Henri Salvador and Gilbert Bécaud could be regarded as appealing to a family audience. The mid-1960s onwards saw a major leap in the number of television sets in French homes: from 6 million in 1965 to 16 million in the late 1970s. The second channel came on stream in 1964 and a third channel (with some regional programming in 1972). It was not until the mid-1980s that France saw a huge expansion of supply of programming with the deregulation of its state-controlled television system. The state-controlled public service monopoly was broken with the creation in 1984 of the subscription channel Canal Plus, and in 1986 of a fifth and sixth commercial privately owned channel (the fifth channel was to go bankrupt and cease transmission in 1992). This period also saw the extension of hours of broadcasting. The major break with tradition however was the privatization and commercialization of the biggest audience channel, the first channel, TF1, in 1987 that brought far more money and competition into terrestrial television.

---

[17]   Achard, Pierre (1995), '50 ans de paillettes', *Notes: le journal de la SACEM* (144), January, rep. in *Dossiers de l'audiovisuel* (97), 2001, 14–17.

Popular music and the 'variety show' in the era of commercial TV

The traditional TV variety show genre did not die overnight. It received a boost by the creation of commercial television. Letailleur has traced the history of the genre through the 1980s and 1990s. In the 1980s, more international music, especially American and British, and a greater range of music in general, was heard in France following the changes discussed above in the radio scene. This was bound to affect television programming. Whereas the typical Saturday-night family variety show, such those hosted by Sacha Distel (*Sacha Show*), on American lines, but using mainly French talent such as Brassens and Montand, along with guests such as Duke Ellington, were replaced by new faces and a new tone. A new era was heralded, in 1982, on the second channel, by the programme *Les Enfants du rock*, that gave a showcase for punk, hard rock and new wave, and set a new tone that was built on by Antoine de Caunes (among others) on Canal Plus and certain commercial channels. This was the beginning of a division of the audience by age in television music programming. The variety show could no longer be used to attract all age groups. In the era of the star presenter as the key to audiences, the main commercial channel TF1 'bought' key figures from the public service channels, and programmed more variety shows in the key audience period following the main (8 p.m.) evening news, in the hope of keeping the audience all evening. Regulation allowed two advertising breaks in such shows, whereas one was the maximum for a cinema film. In 1990 42 per cent of variety shows were at this time of the evening.[18] A new structure of show was introduced to reduce the risk of losing an audience through changing channels through the newly available remote control: stars announced at the start to appear later, often at the end of the show. The key name here is Michel Drucker with *Champs-Elysées*.

The first showing of Michael Jackson's video *Thriller* in 1983 on *Champs-Elysées* was another landmark in French music television. It brought back a certain number of young viewers to the variety show as it programmed youth music, and also foreshadowed a new genre and a new type of television that is picked up by the commercial channel M6 (see below). Initially it brought a reliance by television on stars that emerged from the programming of the major music radios, and the accusation by the music industry that TV was merely using established music stars and not taking risks on new talent. The situation was further complicated by the arrival of legislation imposing minimum quotas of French and European 'audiovisual works'.

---

[18]   Letailleur, Laurent (2001), 'Les variétés à la télévision', *Dossiers de l'audiovisuel* (97), 19.

Effects of television quotas on the variety show genre

The Uruguay round of GATT talks (1986–93) culminated in a French-inspired European-Union defence of cinema film and television programmes as artistic products and not as ordinary consumer products. This successful negotiation enabled cultural products to be treated as a 'cultural exception' to free-trade rules and therefore potentially subject to quotas or other forms of protectionism. Under French pressure, this notion of cultural quotas has been applied to European Union audiovisual policy through the 'Télévision sans frontières' directive of 1989 and in its revision in 1997, at least in the form of a political aspiration expressed as 'where practicable'. This has enabled France legally to maintain its own quotas of European-produced television programmes.[19]

By a decree of 17 January 1990 television channels, both public service and private/commercial, were obliged to programme a certain annual volume of European-produced and French-language material. As regards popular music, the variety show did not count among these home-grown quotas. 15 per cent of the previous year's turnover had to be put into the creation of new French works. Each channel had to programme 120 hours of French or European programming beginning in the peak time of 8–9 p.m. This meant in effect 60 to 80 evenings reserved for telefilms or magazine programmes. As Letailleur points out, once one adds cinema films and sports events, there is precious little time left for entertainment shows such as variety shows at this time of the evening on the main audience channels.[20]

Furthermore, a new television genre became popular and further shrunk the prime-time televising of popular music on the big channels: the reality show, whether crime-related, the search for missing people, or psycho-therapy for exhibitionists.[21] The effect of the above changes on variety programming may be seen by figures showing how many of the genre appeared in the 50 top audience shows in 1992 (2) compared to 1990 (19).[22]

Radio killed the variety star

As regards the relation of radio to TV (as seen above), the 1990s saw a move to much narrower formatting by age, a segmentation of musical tastes, and a reduction in the range of French song played. The variety show had been based predominantly on French song and on a diversity or range of types and genres of

---

[19]   Strode, Louise (1999), 'Language, Cultural Policy and National Identity in France, 1989–1997', unpublished PhD thesis, University of Loughborough, 155–63.

[20]   Letailleur, 'Les variétés à la télévision', 20.

[21]   For a discussion of French reality programming see Dauncey, Hugh (1994), 'Reality shows on French television: Télé-vérité, Télé-service, Télé-civisme or Télé-flicaille?', *French Cultural Studies*, 5, 85–98.

[22]   Letailleur, 'Les variétés à la télévision'.

song. Letailleur argues that the narrower musical range and exclusivity of taste being promoted by the commercial radio sector helped kill off the variety show as the main vehicle for French popular music, as audiences withered for those shows that were left. Two music shows worth recalling differ from the standard variety show format: TF1's daily weekday afternoon show *La chance aux chansons*, from 1984 onwards on TF1, a long-standing show based on traditional French song (that no self-respecting young person would admit to watching), and *Taratata*, from 1993 on the second channel, a late night contemporary music show, where all the acts played live and aimed precisely at a young audience. Both depended to a great extent for their (very different) styles on their presenters Pascal Sevran and Nagui. The former is very *vieille France*, and the latter, of North African origins, much more trendy in dress and language.

Music and 'post-television'

The variety show has not traditionally been a recyclable genre in the sense that, unlike cinema films or series, it has not been broadcast in the form of repeats. The public-service educational (fifth) channel, (la Cinquième) has distributed two series of half-hour musical documentaries, each one devoted to music-hall or *chanson* stars from Mistinguett to Pierre Perret (*Les Lumières du Music-Hall*) that are a valuable resource for study of French popular music, and which uses archive footage from early and more recent television to what they claim to be (the beginnings of) an encyclopaedia of French song.[23] Neo-television or post-(modern) television, which one might define as self-referential television – programming that talks about itself in a self-celebratory mode – has found a way of recycling the variety show genre as a form of nostalgia. Archives formed the basis of *Les rendez-vous du dimanche soir* on France 3, *Dansez maintenant* on France 2 (stars of bygone eras) and TV archives plus a round table of guests to reminisce about extracts in *Telle est la télé* (TF1). These programmes have however been short-lived.

Dedicated music channels: France versus America

From the mid-1980s there was much talk of creating a television channel dedicated to music, especially French music, and indeed linked in to the French music industry in the same way that Canal Plus was linked to the French cinema industry. It was seen as a response to an audience demand, but also as a way of protecting and promoting another French cultural industry. It was achieved in part in terms of French free-to-air television. The creation of the American global music channel MTV for distribution on satellite and cable was a further spur to create a French competitor.

---

[23] See the channel's website: www.lacinquieme.fr.

The search for a commercial music channel on terrestrial television

In the 1990s, partly as a response to the quotas problem, the amount of contemporary popular music programmed on free terrestrial television went down by 16 per cent over the decade. Two commercial channels showing dramatic falls were particularly to blame: the main audience channel TF1 dropped from 197 hours to 77, and Canal Plus from 329 to 26 hours. Public service TV on the other hand increased its programming to 480 hours from 302, particularly on its popular audience channel France 2.[24] The proportion of music programming on terrestrial channels is low, 6.9 per cent of total air time (of which 1 per cent is devoted to classical music). This compares to 12.1 per cent devoted to cinema, 4.7 per cent to sport, and 9.5 per cent to news and current affairs.[25] This situation highlights the continuing importance of the minority audience terrestrial commercial channel M6, whose music programming certainly fell in the 1990s, marginally, but from 2614 hours in 1990 to 2400 hours in 2000. M6 is not, however, the dedicated music channel that some hoped it might be.

When the first free-to-air commercial channels were created in March 1986, the sixth channel franchise was awarded to a consortium including the advertising agency Publicis and the radio broadcaster NRJ. The franchise stipulated that it was to be aimed at the under-25s (who watched little TV) and was to programme half of its time to music, to publish 100 music videos per year and devote 50 per cent of its programming to French-made programmes. This long-argued for link between the popular music industry and television was however short-lived. A change of government within three months of the channel's opening allowed the new Prime Minister Chirac, as a part of changes to the media landscape created by the outgoing socialist governments, to reallocate the franchises for the new commercial channels to more politically acceptable partners. The replacement channel was to be less exclusively musical.

M6 and the youth music audience

The new franchise was won by Metropole TV (M6), run by the Luxembourg company CLT and the French utility company Lyonnaise des Eaux, and presided over by Jean Drucker. It agreed to maintain a young target audience (15 to 35 years) and to devote 40 per cent of its programme time to popular music, half of which should be French. Its audience grew to about 16 per cent in terms of audience share (20 per cent of the under-50s), and it reached its all-time record

---

[24]   Lebœuf, D., and Samyn, C. (2001), 'Dix ans de musique en télévision: 1990–2000', *Dossiers de l'audiovisuel* (97), 22.
[25]   Ibid.

with the French version of *Big Brother*, *Loft Story*, in 2001 (up to 38 per cent on certain evenings) – a programme that appealed particularly to the youth audience.[26]

The broadcasting licensing authority saw M6 as a way of offering musical programming to the French youth audience, as competition to English-language music channels on cable and satellite. M6 initially broadcast 25 hours per week of popular music, produced 100 music videos per year and organized concerts to be later broadcast.[27] Its requirement to devote 40 per cent of its programming to contemporary music was reduced to 30 per cent in the reallocation of its franchise in 1996. It was gradually trying to reduce its image as merely a video jukebox created by programmes such as *Boulevard des clips*, and to promote its image as a generalist channel. But its specificity is indeed the air space given to music videos and its investment in their production: in 1999 it broadcast 1700 hours of *vidéo clips* and co-produced 150. It concentrates its music programming into morning, afternoon and late-night slots, with a prime-time music magazine on Saturday evening.[28] M6 also has an important stake in music publishing and sponsors pop concerts and festivals. It is not the television equivalent of youth music radios, but youth is its target audience when it comes to music.

New pay-TV channels and niche broadcasting

Cable and satellite channels have followed the fragmentation of public taste in popular music that has been seen above. The late 1990s saw a jump in the number of pay-TV channels, once the digital satellite suppliers CanalSatellite (owned by Canal Plus) and TPS (a consortium dominated by TF1, but also including public service TV and M6) began broadcasting in 1996. Practically all such channels are thematic and seek niche audiences. Of the 83 thematic channels approved by the Broadcasting Licensing Authority at the start of the new century, nine were devoted to music – six of them to popular music. RFM TV and Fun TV are channels emerging from radio stations; M6 Musique is an extension of the commercial TV channel that is most active in pop music; MTV is the European version of the American all-music channel; MCM is its French equivalent; and a sixth is Zik. They have each sought their own niche market. Fun and RFM seek the 15 to 25 year olds and the 'golden-oldie' markets respectively, as their radio identity would suggest. M6 Musique is looking to cater for the increasing specialization of musical taste in the 18 to 35 years market, and concentrates this channel exclusively on music videos. The hourly volume of popular music now

---

[26]   Jeanneney, Jean-Noël (2001), *L'Echo du siècle. Dictionnaire historique de la radio et de la télévision en France*, Paris: Hachette Littératures/ARTE Editions (1st edn 1999), 207.

[27]   Mussou, Claude (2001), 'M6 gardera-t-elle le tempo', *Dossiers de l'audiovisuel* (97), 38.

[28]   Ibid., 38–39.

available on these channels now makes up for the loss of hours on terrestrial TV, but not in terms of loss of audience.[29]

MCM

MCM was one of the first pop music channels on cable and satellite, and in 1995 became the top audience channel in this niche. It has tried to position itself first of all in the French market, but seeks to expand internationally. Its target is the 15 to 24 year olds and their lifestyle: in addition to music, it programmes magazines on new fun sports (rollergliding, snowboarding, etc.) and on video games. It aims to use digital technology to allow more interactivity in choice of music videos. Along with M6 it claims to be the only French channel that seeks to promote new musical talent, whereas other channels take fewer risks. Its main competitor is MTV, with 1.5 million subscribers compared to 2.5 million for MCM. MTV banks on stars and broadcasts only 1% of French songs.[30]

'Le video-clip'

The French music video, as seen above, is an important genre on French music television. It may have Anglo-American origins – Queen's *Bohemian Rhapsody* in 1975 usually being regarded as creating the genre – and it may have been Michael Jackson's *Thriller* that imposed it as a necessity for promoting pop songs, but, in France, it is now state-subsidized. Culture Ministers F. Léotard and J. Lang in 1987 and 1990 created a National Fund for 'vidéomusiques', managed jointly by the national Fund for Cinematography and the Fund for Musical Creation. Also at the state's behest, the sixth TV channel and its successor M6 have invested in music video production. As in many other cultural and artistic niches, the French state is keen to see France and the French language represented alongside the dominant Anglo-American producers and artists. If commercial forces are insufficient to guarantee the maintenance of a French presence, then the state will step in – in this case in a new domain of popular culture.

Conclusion

Music programming on radio and television has moved from offering, pre-1981, a relatively standardized diet of popular music to a mass audience to offering a wide range of musical formats to segmented audiences on distinct, dedicated

---

[29]   Lebœuf and Samyn, 'Dix ans de musique en télévision: 1990–2000', 23–24.
[30]   Aaron, D., Lebœuf, D., and Samyn, C. (2001), 'MCM: nouvelles gammes', *Dossiers de l'audiovisuel* (97), 36–37.

musical stations or channels. Radio has led this trend and has had more influence than television on the ways that French musical tastes and the French music industry have developed. From the pre- and post-war days when the French were listening to Charles Trenet and Édith Piaf on their valve radios, through the 1960s when radio was taking the lead in introducing French youth to rock and pop via French cover versions of American hits, to the 1990s when Skyrock helped create a French form of rap, radio has been the key medium of creation of French musical taste. Television has merely tried to follow in the wake of its more flexible and older sibling. The variety show, long the staple musical format offered to a 'family audience', has been superseded by more segmented offerings to a more fragmented audience, as musical tastes have diversified, initially by age group.

The case of popular music on French radio and television illustrates various paradoxes within French exceptionalism. If the role of the French state within French society is exemplified in the way it kept control of broadcasting long after Britain, for example, had introduced independent television, one of the effects of this statism was to restrict the number and range of outlets for popular music on radio and television. Did this restrict the development of more diverse forms of French popular music beyond the traditional 'chanson' that was for so long the staple diet of the variety show, and that spanned the generations and the social classes in its appeal? Or was it an early form of protectionism against the feared influence of Anglo-American culture on indigenous French culture, a protectionism that has later been pursued quite overtly, since the 1990s in the form of linguistic quotas? French responses to globalization (which is often equated with Americanization) may also be seen as paradoxical. At different times American pop culture has been rejected as the carrier of a threat to national cultural identity. There was suspicion among decision makers about the *yéyé* phenomenon of the 1960s, a French adaptation of British and American pop songs, as given wide exposure on Radio Europe No. 1, and to an extent on French television. This suspicion has been recurrent at different historical moments, for example in the case of certain American-influenced rap groups such as NTM and more generally in the amount of American song that began to appear on the new independent radio sector on the 1990s. What is indisputable is the fascination of French youth for aspects of American musical culture, from rock and pop music, through Michael Jackson's videos to gangster rap. More recently, the state has attempted to encourage and indeed to subsidize the production of certain Anglo-American-born genres of pop culture within a French context – as a kind of cultural 'glocalization'. A prime example is the video clip, whether as a form of television support for music or as an art form in itself. Since the Jack Lang era of French cultural policy, certain aspects of youth culture (rock, rap, techno, or video clips) can be seen as respectable forms of expression of aspects of French culture.

Chapter 5

The popular music press

Mat Pires

From its very beginnings in France, in the mid-1950s, rock and roll gave rise to critical reaction in the press. Some was negative, and oblivious to the music: tut-tutting accounts of Johnny Hallyday's car crashes, or of violent incidents at Vince Taylor's concerts. However, reaction to the music itself was also in evidence. This was nothing more than dribs and drabs in the 1950s, but by the early 1960s it had become a flood, with dedicated magazines and a readership of millions. Rock was thus the first popular music to sustain (and be sustained by) mass-circulation journalism. Indeed, it is striking how little press coverage there was of pre-1950s popular musics. The musically simplistic sheet-music of the early twentieth century, reproducible with a piano in the home, offered little purchase for analysis or assessment. The advent of analogic reproduction – 78 rpm discs in the 1920s – benefited essentially jazz music, which amateur pianists found difficult, and the new, stabler commodification did lead to some journalistic activity: the British *Melody Maker* was launched in 1926 as a trade paper for the jazz community, and French periodicals such as *Jazz Hot* emerged after the war, but readerships were discreet: 78s remained expensive and fragile, and their reproductive hardware cumbersome.

In the aftermath of the Second World War popular music consumption underwent a sea change. The baby boom ensured there was a large number of relatively well-off teenagers in the late 1950s and early 1960s. The transistor, invented in 1947 and incorporated into miniaturized radios and record players from the mid-1950s, allowed youngsters to develop a personal musical taste distinct from their parents', whose previous sway over the living-room radiogram had curtailed such a process. Finally, the sturdier microgroove records, which also emerged at this time, improved sound reproduction, and brought records within teenagers' means at the beginning of the 1960s.

This chapter looks at the emergence of popular music journalism in the period since the mid-1950s, and concentrates on the links between the music, its celebrities, and the press.

The place of music in the press

The mediation of post-rock popular music went through several phases, which corresponded to the emerging independence of the field. The earliest examples

77

of coverage appeared in the 'Presse des Jeunes', youth-interest titles with a very wide remit, ranging from news to science and technology, history, and culture. Their overall feel was boyish and very educationally inflected (girls had titles of their own, which ignored the emerging musical culture). *Top Réalités Jeunesse* (successor to *Benjamin*) was one of these titles. It was produced by an independent publisher, but the Presse des Jeunes also included publications produced by specific organizations. The principal title here is the Catholic *Rallye–Jeunesse*, but the French Communist Party's *Nous les garçons et les filles* was a similar attempt to harness a burgeoning youth culture. From 1961 we find titles devoted uniquely to the singing scene, the 'Presse des Idoles' [magazines about the stars]: *Disco Revue*, then the hugely successful *Salut les copains*. This type of publication, as its name suggests, was more interested in personalities than music itself, and it was only with the launch of *Rock & Folk* in 1966 that the 'Presse Musicale' [music press] came into being in France. The chapter considers developments in music mediation through these different titles, from the mid-1950s to the present day.

Top Réalités Jeunesse

There is some disagreement about the exact date of the beginning of rock and roll, though agreement that it is somewhere in the middle of the 1950s.[1] The absence of such a cultural form before this period is clearly reflected in the press. For instance, *Benjamin*, a leading Presse des Jeunes title, could devote a 1953 article to the innovation of microgroove records (29 Nov.), without any suggestion that readers might themselves buy any. With no genre to call their own at this time, music afforded youngsters no identity as such.

The earliest example of music coverage in *Benjamin* was a discreet rubric entitled 'C'est à entendre' [Things to listen to], and frequently given over to classical, latin, or jazz music, or even narrated stories. Its first foray into the new musical idiom, appropriately, concerned what is generally considered the earliest French rock recording, the spoof e.p. 'Rock and roll', by 'Henry Cording' (aka Henri Salvador) (30 Dec. 1956). The text, which is friendly and amusing, is however essentially a rewrite of the record's sleeve notes, signed 'Jack K. Netty', and 'translated' by Boris Vian, but in fact *by* Vian, who was also the lyricist 'Vernon Sinclair'. Several aspects of this text anticipated the tone and content of early music reviews, notably references to classical music (a legitimating factor for a highly marginal cultural form), and references to a social rather than individual consumption of music, notably in dancing.

---

[1]   Peterson, R. A. (1991), 'Mais pourquoi donc en 1955? Comment expliquer la naissance du rock', in P. Mignon and A. Hennion (eds), *Rock: de l'histoire au mythe*, Paris: Anthropos, 9–39.

This social element was a common approach. It is clear in many reviews that the principal 'use' of recordings was social, with reviewed records promising you 'a fantastic evening among friends' (2 June 1957), or else 'a perfect rhythm for dancing to'[2] (3 Feb. 1957). The value, or possible interpretation, of the lyrics per se is never entered into. Evaluations of singers' voices revolve around voice *strength*, a leftover from the days before the invention of the microphone, diction, and institutional recognition: one singer, Simone Langlois, is praised for picking up the Académie Charles Cros's 'grand prix du disque' (12 Oct. 1958). The language used is nondescript; there is no sense of music meriting any special treatment.

Alongside reviews, *Benjamin* published occasional features on singers. Articles such as 'Annie Fratellini' (10 Nov. 1957) or 'Zizi Jeanmaire' (4 May 1958) prefigure the way pop mediation was to develop in the 1960s. The article on 'Roi du calypso Harry Belafonte' (14 Sept. 1958) even, for the first time, featured the singer on the cover of the publication, a slot which was to become a basic shop window for the pop field.

Benjamin, an educationally inflected paper for 'older children', yielded in 1958 to a new-look publication. This was *Top Réalités Jeunesse*, the first youth-interest title to appeal to 'adolescent' boys,[3] indeed the first, really, to define, by its content, such a category. Its outlook is well illustrated by 'preparation for adulthood'-type articles, for instance on organizing a dinner party (19 Jan. 1964), where readers are advised not to 'stuff the guests with food', or 'overdo the alcohol'. *Top* also adopted a new appearance (which distinguished it clearly from the tabloid newspaper *Benjamin*): a pocket-size, staple-bound format, with a lightly glossed cover. In other words, in all but size, a *magazine*. This in itself represented a social promotion for the readership, and circulation rose tangibly.[4]

Music remained a side issue, covering just 16.1 per cent of the publication, though this proportion was greater than for cinema, or literature and art.[5] A regular 'stars' page was shared by singers and film actors, and one review column, 'Disques au Top', covered pop, jazz, and classical music: still a far cry from the musical hegemony of the later youth press. Moreover, with time, classical music came to dominate this review section, although singers as personalities occupied more and more of the star features. This shift from music to personalities within pop coverage, which was to continue into the mid-1960s, saw interviews appear with some of the early stars of the French rock scene: Johnny Hallyday (2 Oct. 1960), Sylvie Vartan (1 Apr. 1962), and Ray Charles (a

---

[2] All translations of French material are my own.
[3] Fourment, A. (1987), *Histoire de la presse des jeunes et des journaux d'enfants (1768–1988)*, Paris: Eole, 334, 337.
[4] The title's 1965 print run is quoted variously at 94,748 (Fourment, *Histoire*, 412) and over 200,000 (Pluvinage-Paternostre, A. (1971), *L'adolescent et sa presse*, Brussels: Editions de l'Institut de sociologie de l'Université libre, 5).
[5] Ibid., 94.

cover feature on 29 Jan. 1961). Old habits die hard, though; the types of question asked of these young stars frequently led to a mediation firmly positioned within an older type of musical appreciation. Thus we learn how Johnny Hallyday's love for music has led him to 'practise the piano two hours a day', while the young Michel Paje, who refuses to sing the 'yéyé' songs (of the young French rockers), 'adores classical music, especially Chopin and Tchaikovsky' (19 Jan. 1964).

Rallye–Jeunesse

Presse des Jeunes titles like *Top* had no agenda other than that of selling copies and making a profit; if coverage of popular music was likely to favour such an end then it was pursued. However, we shall see in the next two sections that the burgeoning interest in music and its stars among the adolescent community was perceived as a potential entry point for at least two ideological movements. The first of these was the Catholic Church.

Rallye–Jeunesse was launched in January 1958 as a cooperative venture between the well-established publishing arm of the French Catholic Church, the Maison de la Bonne Presse, and four Catholic youth movements.[6] It was distributed within schools and on church piety stalls, and outside church circles was practically unknown, and unobtainable.[7] Nonetheless, *Rallye–Jeunesse* was the first youth publication to respond to the musical craze in certain sections of the teenage community;[8] as such it prefigured the explosion a few years later of the 'Presse des Idoles'.

Rallye–Jeunesse was, however, a general-interest publication, with a balanced output: in 1965 popular song accounted for 12.4 per cent of the title, literature and art 13.5 per cent, politics and social issues 20 per cent, and cinema 4.3 per cent.[9] Its unambiguously Christian, and educational outlook brought problems in its mediation of pop music – as one writer put it, *Rallye* 'could not cover Johnny Hallyday like other magazines'.[10] This necessarily led to a double-edged discourse, both laudatory and dismissive. A second particularity of *Rallye* was the involvement of its readership, via a network of 4,000 'Rallye-correspondants' across France. These youngsters sent in some 1,000 letters a week to the editorial office, reacting to features in the magazine and relaying the opinions of their friends, and those from the Paris area also frequently participated in debates and

---

[6]   Godfrin, J. and P. (1965), *Une Centrale de presse catholique: la Maison de la Bonne Presse et ses publications*, Paris: PUF, 103.
[7]   Ibid., 102; Marny, J. (1965), *Les adolescents d'aujourd'hui*, Paris: Le Centurion, 108.
[8]   Fourment, *Histoire*, 374–75; Le Gall, Y. (1966), 'La presse à grand tirage et les magazines', in *Mass media 1. La Presse d'aujourd'hui*, Paris: Bloud & Gay, 19–63, 47.
[9]   Pluvinage-Paternostre, *L'adolescent*, 94.
[10]   Godfrin, *Une Centrale*, 105.

round tables.[11] This then was a first step towards eliminating the age-lag between the popular music's producers and consumers on one hand, and its mediators on the other.

Like *Benjamin* and *Top*, *Rallye–Jeunesse* went through two series. Its first (Jan. 1958 to Apr. 1959), as a fortnightly tabloid, carried only two articles on popular music, an anecdotal piece about Django Reinhardt's son (Jan. 1959), and one real review, of *Vous êtes formidable!*, a record by a young Swiss singer, Yves Sandrier (Mar. 1958). This is essentially an interview – suggesting the unclear boundaries of these text-types at this time – accompanied by captioned photos of the artist performing in a school play, and of a reporter from the radio station Europe 1, in the singer's bedroom, announcing good record sales to him and his mother. The transcription of Sandrier's responses to the interviewer's questions is highly artificial, with the *passé simple*, a tense no longer used in spoken French, and syntax improved to a written norm. Moreover, biographical and anecdotal information forms the bulk of the text; the actual record review occupies one phrase, above the reproduced lyrics, which describes the song as 'optimistic' and 'pleasant to sing', again associating the record closely with a cultural utility.

Rallye–Jeunesse's relaunch as a glossy monthly magazine came in April 1959, and circulation, in this new guise, rose to an impressive 295,000.[12] Popular music coverage became a regular feature, though in the form of differently formatted columns and features. Review features included the unengagingly titled 'Les opinions de J.-C. de Thandt' [The opinions of J.-C. T.], or André Sève's 'Qui veut du rock?' [Anyone for rock?]. Both attempt to adopt an appropriate language for the music they are reviewing, using for instance puns, alliteration and metaphor. However, Sève nonetheless describes as 'vulgar' a song entitled '24 000 baisers' ('24,000 kisses'), and ends by appealing to the readership to help him to follow the 'rockmen' by sending him the titles of their favourite records (July–Aug. 1961).

In longer reviews a paternalistic attitude, notably towards adolescent sexuality, is present, a reflection of *Rallye*'s Catholic identity. The adjective 'sensual' marks a song as inappropriate for young, suggestible minds (Aug. 1959), in a discourse apparently addressing the moral concerns of the readers' *parents*. Again though, in this review the author is 'looking forward to hearing your opinions about this'. The moral presence also underpinned a veritable campaign waged over several months against Johnny Hallyday's onstage 'contorsions' – in other words hip-swinging and generally moving to the beat. Interestingly, readers' letters (Apr. 1961) are supportive of Hallyday, asserting that such movements are an integral part of his appeal and of the musical culture generally. Despite this, *Rallye–Jeunesse* continued its campaign, drawing both

---

[11] Ibid., 104.
[12] Fourment, *Histoire*, 412.

Elvis Presley and Eddy Mitchell (June, July–Aug. 1961) into the ranks of the contortionists.

A longer review shows an even stronger gulf between author and reader. André Sève (Nov. 1960) takes issue at length with the ending of Charles Aznavour's song 'Tu t'laisses aller' (about a man unhappy at his wife's slovenly appearance), which suggests the middle-aged woman should not try to imitate the 'little girl' of bygone days, but should try to appeal differently. Noble sentiments, to be sure, but wholly irrelevant to a target readership aged between 15 and 18.[13]

The bio-narrative angle, seen in the article on Yves Sandrier, remained present in the new series. Some articles used a fairy-tale environment, incorporating direct speech to tell, for instance, how young Lucette Raillat abandoned shorthand typing for the world of song (Mar. 1960), or how Maria Candido struggled with uncooperative parents, bought a piano with the help of a friendly antique dealer, and went on to become an opera singer at an early age (Jan. 1961). Such child-orientated discursive frameworks were a leftover from the 'older children' outlook, but they nonetheless made the star both accessible to the reader, and yet enviable, successful, and impressive. Again, we see the appeal to a legitimating, 'high' culture, in Candido's apprenticeship in classical music, with an arty antique dealer as first teacher.

A final text-type essayed in *Rallye*, entitled 'Dialogue' (Jan. 1961), transcribes a short conversation between André Sève and 'Roger', a 16-year-old 'Rallye-correspondant' from Grenoble. Despite the structural equal footing, this forum does not preclude an element of paternalistic authority, with Roger's mild enthusiasm interrupted and trumped by Sève's connoisseurial disdain. This 'dialogue' is naturally written in an oralized manner, a trend which was to become increasingly prevalent.

In keeping with its educational bent, and its general-interest profile, *Rallye* commissioned two general articles on rock music from grown-up 'specialists'. Despite a generally positive tone, 'Rock and roll' (June 1961) describes its subject as 'a ravenous monster that gobbles up its victims in one season'; concerts are 'riots', where audiences make 'more noise than the poor singer stuck on the stage', and musicians are given to 'shamelessly overusing technical gadgetry'. In 'Point de vue sur le twist' ['Viewpoint on the twist'], (Sept. 1962), rock fans are 'a bunch of ne'er-do-wells unfortunately given to smashing up the seats rather than sitting on them'; musicians are rich 'not because of their talent, for they have none', and are 'practically all incapable of sustaining their fame through a normal artistic activity' (*sic*). The article, which is superimposed on sketches of dancing couples and decorated gaily with record sleeves and photos of beaming singers, ends with the words 'Ultimately, one has to consider the twist, both rhythmically and musically, as rather impoverished'.

---

[13]   Godfrin, *Une Centrale*, 102.

The discursive uncertainty of *Rallye–Jeunesse*'s journalists in fact mirrored that of its readers. In its letters, complaints about 'paganisation', and requests for 'comprehensive information about a religion, a commentary of *Pacem in terris*', rub shoulders with assertions that 'you are not devoting enough space to today's modern singing stars, of whom I am, if one may use the term, a *fan*'.[14] The polarization reflects the way pop music was reinventing young people and their cultural practices, rendering untenable an intrinsically adult discourse.

Although its moral agenda prevented it from becoming the mouthpiece for the *yéyé* generation, *Rallye–Jeunesse* was a pioneer of the printed mediation of popular song and rock. Its success, moreover, inspired a similar, though far less successful, attempt to tap into the new youth culture by the French Communist Party, which launched *Nous les garçons et les filles* in 1963.

Nous les garçons et les filles

Compared with *Rallye–Jeunesse*, *Nous les garçons et les filles* is of little significance in the evolution of the music press. Launched one year after the resounding debut of *Salut les copains* (see below), it sought to capitalize on the new music magazine market, typographically imitating the *Salut les copains* masthead, and taking its name from a hit by *yéyé* singer Françoise Hardy. However *Nous les garçons et les filles* reflected the breadth of interests of the Presse des Jeunes, and came up against discursive difficulties very similar to those of *Rallye*. The difference was that it was backed not by a church but by a political organization, the French Communist Party.

If the pleasure afforded youngsters by *yéyé* culture represented a threat to the Catholic *Rallye*, which attempted containment via appeals to morality (deploring 'contorsions', for example), *Nous les garçons et les filles* sought to *politicize* pleasure: 'Youth, in this upside-down society, is full of enthusiasm, of derision and laughter. Youngsters want to learn through struggle, to sing as they fight' (May 1963). In the opening editorial, pleasure (into which singing is incorporated) is portrayed as a conscious political reaction to oppression.

Curiously the only mention of music in this editorial is a single reference to jazz – there is no sign at all of rock or the *yéyés*. However, singing stars occupied practically all its covers, and music 35 per cent of the inside pages, far ahead of politics and social issues, with a mere 7.9 per cent.[15] The reaction to this content is tangible from the second-issue editorial, where after acknowledging the support of some readers, the editors note that:

---

14   Quoted Marny, *Les adolescents*, 111–12.
15   Pluvinage-Paternostre, *L'adolescent*, 94.

[o]thers ... were expecting yet another of those countless publications given over to the cult of the star, because, so they said, 'that's all we're interested in'. Now, now! You misrepresent yourselves. Honestly, you're not like that. You're interested in everything, like everyone else. You have worries, like your friends ... And anyway, you can talk about songs without saying a thing. We could be a gossip column, with chit-chat about so-and-so's engagement. We don't want to do that. You deserve better. (June 1963, p. 35)

This paternalism is almost plaintive: readers' optimism and obsession are both resistant to political mobilization, and accordingly the editors appeal to their 'worries', and condemn an exclusive interest in music. But catering to music-fan teenagers brought opprobrium from the militant readership: 'only the bourgeois can afford guitars, have you ever considered that?'; 'Aren't you ashamed of talking about Sylvie Vartan when you could be writing sensational pieces about Hitler's war-time atrocities.'[16] *Nous les garçons et les filles* did try to politicize its music coverage, but this turned out to be a difficult undertaking. A remark about Ray Charles receiving an injection from a doctor as he leaves the stage, shows how he is 'the victim of commercial exploitation, his entourage colluding in his drug-taking to help him cope with loneliness, continue singing, and thus remain "profitable"', according to one commentator.[17]

Though *Nous les garçons et les filles* could not ignore the singing stars of the 1960s, its review section continued to present their records alongside jazz and classical discs in a disingenuously asserted equality. While it seems reasonable to assert that theme music in films had brought classical music its share of 'hits' (Nov. 1964), the glossing of *La musique d'église à Salzbourg* [Church music in Salzburg] as 'an important record' (Apr. 1964) is surprising in terms not only of youth culture, but of politics, too – one can easily imagine classical music being condemned as 'bourgeois' in a publication prepared to print a letter describing guitar ownership as such. A desire to 'contain' pop as nothing special is in evidence, a reactionary comparativism which shows how young people's *idols*, and the notion of *copains* – 'pals', but also a buzzword encapsulating youthful togetherness – threatened established authorities, whether political or religious.

Nous les garçons et les filles tried to be a youth-interest paper in a market which had turned to an overwhelming interest in music and pop stars. Although its initial circulation of 300,000 (distribution via news-stands and by activists), was similar to that of the Catholic *Rallye*, by 1966 it had dropped to 80,000, unable like all the Presse des Jeunes titles to compete with the explosive growth in the Presse des Idoles, magazines whose exclusive passion was pop stars. It is to these publications that we now turn.

---

[16] Letters, Mar. 1960, quoted Marny, *Les adolescents*, 136–37.
[17] Marny, *Les adolescents*, 139. Marny prefers an account of Charles in *Salut les copains*, although it too uses the singer's blindness and childhood to promote its own *rags to riches* myth (Pires, M. (1997), 'Les stars noires et *Salut les copains*, 1962–1968', *Communication et langages*, **111**, 59–71, 60–61).

Disco Revue

Music journalism in the 1950s had consisted of individual articles in Presse des Jeunes titles. The ever-increasing interest in popular music among their readerships, though, pointed inevitably to the emergence of specialist publications. It was not, however, a music press which emerged, but the Presse des Idoles: journalism not about music, but about singing stars.

Disco Revue, which appeared on 28 September 1961, was the first of these titles. It was the brainchild of 19-year-old Jean-Claude Berthon, who had been inspired by the British music press while on holiday. In the words of Henri Leproux, the influential owner of the Golf Drouot, venue of many of the early rock concerts in Paris, Berthon's was the first publication in France 'to cover the rock and "yéyé" crazes – the associated gossip, the pop idols' romances, the musicians' equipment, and all the little rumours ... the rest of the press never touched on'.[18] Berthon was a highly visible editor, penning lengthy replies to readers in 'Courrier de Jean-Claude' (Letters to J.-C.), a forum for comment on the rock scene.

The range of features in *Disco Revue* reflected clearly the format which was to become standard in the pop press. Alongside articles on specific singers or on aspects of the world of rock and roll, some bought in and translated ('Le phénomène Presley', Jan.–Oct. 1963), there was a gossip column, and a record review section, though this was absent from some issues. Readers were involved not only in the extensive letters pages, but in the charts they helped to produce, by sending in their ten records of the month, information which the editors compiled into hit parades for French singers, female singers, groups and so on. In some issues there is also a chart based on the record sales of certain record dealers, the format which would become standard; at this time uncertainty still surrounded the measurement of success.

Unlike its predecessors *Disco Revue* was almost entirely devoted to the singing stars; the only exceptions were cover features on James Dean and Brigitte Bardot. Inside pages featured full-page photos, and even free posters and centrefolds, the stock-in-trade of later pop publications. However, financial constraints meant the major part of *Disco Revue* – including its covers before May 1962 – remained black and white.

Berthon not only replied to readers' letters, he also penned articles and record reviews. His reviews of substandard records could be acerbic – this was no hagiographer – though a consciousness of possible in-group cultural legitimation no longer led to the far-fetched analogies with classical music of *Benjamin* and *Rallye–Jeunesse*, and there is more self-assurance about the music and its attendant culture; gone the appeals for information from the readership, and gone the condemnations of 'contorsions': listen to Ray Charles's 'Hit the road Jack',

---

[18]   Quoted Jouffa, F. (1978), *Idoles Story*, Neuilly: Alain Mathieu, 37.

asserts Berthon, and 'you won't be able to stop your hips from swaying' (26 Oct. 1961).

While France's first professional pop critic could be enthusiastically jejune, as here, reflecting the age parity he was also the first to enjoy with his readers, his prose could also be rather austere. On the incessant screaming at a Beatles concert, Berthon straight-facedly explains that 'that is the English way of letting your hair down and showing your satisfaction in public' (June 1963). This stuffy style perhaps slightly missed the point of a youth culture in which music was a catalyst for profound shifts in society, notably the emergence of the new age of the teenager, rather than an art form to be assessed, detachedly, as such. Despite an undeniable passion, Berthon lacked a natural flair for writing; one of his *Disco Revue* colleagues describes his articles on one hand as 'enthusiastic, though a bit naïve, a bit *teeny*', on the other as earnest and rather didactic.[19]

Disco Revue attracted in its short life an enthusiastic, though insufficient, following.[20] Its appearances were irregular, and financial problems were considerable, with little advertising income: apart from a few full-page record-company ads, the only faithful advertiser was 'Jacques, le coiffeur des rock'n rollers' [the rock'n'rollers' hairdresser], self-proclaimed inventor of the 'bouffant' hair-do. This difficulty was compounded by the editor's conflicting commitments. After June 1963, his military service left the magazine helmless, although, doubtless with Elvis Presley's much publicized army stint in 1958 in mind, Berthon kept his readers informed of how he was faring, and even posed in uniform (Oct. 1963). Further to this, Berthon had musical ambitions of his own, releasing 'Le soleil de l'été', a version of 'Summertime love', in September 1963, to apparent indifference: even in *Disco Revue*'s own hit parade of French rockers (1 Feb. 1964), 'Jean-Claude' only managed 17th place.

The principal problem, though, was *Disco Revue*'s principal competitor. In 1962 Berthon was invited to talk about the title on a rock radio programme whose presenter, Daniel Filipacchi, subsequently offered to take over its management. Berthon refused, and Filipacchi decided to launch a magazine of his own, in close association with his radio show.[21] Its success only worsened *Disco Revue*'s situation. In October 1963 Berthon admitted, in reply to a puzzled reader, that he hadn't reviewed Petula Clark's last record because the record company hadn't sent him a copy, and he couldn't afford to buy one. In another sign of strain *Disco Revue* started exaggerating its age, claiming in January 1963 to have been 'published since 1 June 1960'. To no avail; even a glossy relaunch in February

---

[19]   Achard, M. (1996), 'Avant Rock&Folk', *Rock & Folk*, hors-série **12**, November 8–12, 12.

[20]   *Disco Revue* claims a print run of 80,000 in its June 1964 issue.

[21]   Filipacchi had experience of this, as he and his co-presenter Frank Ténot also hosted 'Pour ceux qui aiment le jazz' (For jazz-lovers) on Europe 1, and had launched *Jazz magazine* in association with it.

1964 only delayed its disappearance in September of that year. Filipacchi's radio access to his readership really was a decisive commercial advantage.

Salut les copains

July 1962 was a key moment for the music press: the launch of *Salut les copains*, the best-selling music title ever seen in France. In less than a year monthly sales topped a million copies,[22] and the concert to celebrate this historic threshold became a mythical event in the early history of French rock, the 'Nuit de la Nation' (Night at Place de la Nation) of 22 June 1963.

Salut les copains emerged out of an eponymous radio show, which was itself a cultural landmark by 1962. The show started broadcasting in 1959 on Europe 1, an independent radio station set up in 1955, whose relaxed approach created a perceptible linguistic novelty, one commentator crediting it with being the 'true creator of a new "tone" in radio language. Because of its peripheral character and its commercial status linked to advertising, this station was not held to the same "seriousness" as the national stations and was free to seek a more direct language with which to reach its audience'.[23] Such a shift corresponded to the general abandonment of the the the text-reading 'speaker' for the spontaneous speech of the 'DJ'. This was not to everyone's taste: 'sentences trail off, words are drawled or droned, the whole thing is coarsely pretentious and unbelievably vulgar', blustered one journalist in the conservative newspaper *L'aurore*.[24] The unapologetic use of a highly informal, oral idiom on the radio, was a new departure, since such channels of communication had previously been inaccessible to marginalized groups. Technological improvements and relative teenage wealth not only opened them up to youngsters, they also allowed those external to the culture – adults – to examine and assess the metalanguage which they disseminated.

'Salut, les copains' was presented by two 'DJs', Daniel Filipacchi and Frank Ténot, on weekdays from five till seven. Its success among transistor-carrying adolescents after school rang alarm bells in some quarters: President Pompidou worried it might prevent youngsters from working;[25] while a *Figaro* journalist complained that 'the adult world is dismissed with insolence and stupidity'.[26]

The launch of *Salut les copains* as a magazine benefited hugely from the reputation of the show.[27] Indeed its original remit was simply to provide

---

[22]   Fourment, *Histoire*, 412–13.
[23]   Deramat, J. M. (1964), *Pourquoi tous ces copains?*, Paris: Librairie Charpentier, 83–84.
[24]   Guérin, A. (1963), 'Le yéyé tel qu'on le parle', *L'Aurore*, 9 December.
[25]   Mentioned in *Télérama*, 3 July 1996, 125.
[26]   13 July 1964; quoted Girod, F. (1966), *Manuel de la pensée yéyé*, Paris: Julliard, 14.
[27]   Such interdependence was at the heart of many early music papers. Pascal, R. (1964), 'Les journaux des fans', *Esprit*, 2 (NS), 247–52) mentions *Bonjour les amis*, from a Radio

supplementary information on the stars whose music featured on Europe 1; it thus sidelined *music* to concentrate on the personalities of the *singers*. With time this obsession with singers became still more accentuated: singers occupied 85 per cent of the title in 1964, 88.6 per cent in 1968,[28] a shift away from the last vestiges of a Presse des Jeunes outlook which had manifested itself in the early inclusion of short stories, or articles on professions, issues of the day, sports, and so on.

SLC's particular musical fascination was the *yéyés*, French rock singers who recorded rock and roll songs in French for a French audience, and found fame in the early 1960s as the interest in rock and roll *groups* (Les Chaussettes Noires, Les Vautours...) gave way to personality cults. Their undisputed leader was Johnny Hallyday, seconded on the female side by Sylvie Vartan, Françoise Hardy and Sheila, and on the male side by Eddy Mitchell, Richard Anthony, and Claude François, as well as numerous also-rans such as Frank Alamo, Dick Rivers or Lucky Blondo.[29] As an adjective, 'yéyé' was frequently used to encompass the whole culture of stardom, music and fans.

The new magazine furnished endless information about the private lives of these singers – everything from holidays and love-affairs to favourite food – as a complement to the songs broadcast on Europe 1. Articles bore titles such as 'Tout, tout, tout sur Françoise' [Absolutely everything about Françoise], and the February 1965 issue featured 85 photos of the singer. The title moreover eschewed any political or moral position: the same Françoise Hardy, reporting on a visit to South Africa, spent most of her time on the surgical prowess of Christian Barnard; the question of apartheid was dispatched in a couple of lines.[30]

The physical appearance of the magazine was a crucial asset: glossy paper, numerous colour photos, and a varied and inventive layout. The emphasis on iconographic content was partly due to technical improvements such as heliogravure, and partly to the participation of top photographers, notably Jean-Marie Périer. Indeed, in photographic terms, *SLC* had nothing to envy today's pop press. Singers were photographed from every angle: in foreign lands, in contrived circumstances ('an anguishing situation', July 1967), in designer clothes ... The result was pure personality cult.

The language used in *SLC* represented a departure too. As an offshoot of a radio programme noted for its linguistic novelty (DJ spiel, informal idiom), the

---

Andorre programme, *Nous les jeunes*, from Radio Lausanne, and the TV offshoot *Age tendre, tête de bois*. Even in the 1980s, *Les Inrockuptibles* had a close relationship with a France Inter programme, which, conversely, adopted a form of the magazine's title, 'L'inrockuptible'.

[28]   Rositi, F. (1969), 'Studio sull'ambivalenza culturale – Il caso della cultura giovanile', *Ikon*, **19** (71), 9–38, 17.

[29]   Hermelin, C. (1965), 'L'interprète-modèle et "Salut les Copains"', *Communications*, **6**, 43–53, 47.

[30]   Pires, 'Les stars noires', 66–67.

magazine naturally adopted a relaxed discourse, a fact noted at the time: 'just like on the radio (at least on Europe 1), the *tu* form is used to address the readers, the tone is youthful, colourful and expressive.'[31]

This is particularly in evidence is in *Salut les copains*'s one review column, 'La lettre de Johnny', written by Johnny Hallyday (or ghosted for him). Hallyday had been an occasional record reviewer on the radio show 'Salut, les copains',[32] and was thus an obvious choice, but the leader of the *yéyés* had a very different standpoint from his record-reviewer predecessors, whose credentials came of a certain respect for pre-existing models of review journalism. Hallyday's came from his unassailable position within musical production, one which swept aside normal journalistic practice, to the point where Hallyday could even review one of his own records in the first issue. The language tends strongly towards an oral standard, in both syntax (dislocated sentences), and in the use of colloquialisms and puns, a deliberate undermining of the definitiveness of writing. On one level this created a sense of equality between the reviewer and the readership – an informal, chatty, atmosphere – although Hallyday's privileged position is often pointed up in photos of him with the stars, and in anecdotes about what he has got up to with them. Nevertheless, the column brought new releases a more uniform, unitary structure than they had enjoyed previously, and the letter format (with its manuscript 'Salut' and signature) created an intimate, complicitous presence, rather than a critical distance.

One intriguing aspect of these letters is the way only seven of them, all in the magazine's first year of existence, actually reviewed records.[33] Their original aim, according to Hallyday, was twofold, 'a few commentaries on newly released records, and some news of my activities' (July 1963). Within a year, the letters slip away from records to concentrate on Hallyday's activities, circumstances and opinions. As early as December 1962, the column is devoted to photos of a Hallyday concert; a list of records is given as an afterthought, with the remark that since they are all good, no commentaries are necessary. Subsequent letters concern his military service (following in the footsteps of Elvis and Jean-Claude Berthon), his taste for art, mathematical brain-teasers, and his relationship with Sylvie Vartan. Despite rather hollow comments about how he would rather talk about music than his private life (May 1963), his abandonment reflects clearly the prioritizing of stars over music in the Presse des Idoles.

A partial explanation lies in the domination of the record market of 1962–63 by singles and e.p.s. As all the tracks on these soundcarriers were likely to be broadcast on radio, the readership did not *need* descriptions of the music to

---

31 Deramat, *Pourquoi*, 91.
32 See 'Votre émission préférée: *Salut, les copains*', *Rallye–Jeunesse*, July–Aug. 1962.
33 Issues 1 (26–27) (entitled '9 Galettes dans ma valise'); 2 (34, 39); 3 (38–39); 4 (35); 6 (33); 8 (68); and 11 (69), between July 1962 and June 1963.

inform their buying choices; they wanted to know about the exploits of the singers behind the music, information more difficult to convey by radio. The *album*, which encouraged an individualistic, non-radio-mediated music consumption, would only become the dominant soundcarrier around 1967.[34] Hallyday's abandoning of his record-reviewer's clothes, contingent with this desire, left the French music press with no review carrier. This gap was only filled satisfactorily (and definitively this time) by the launch of a new music title, *Rock & Folk*, in 1966.

Rock & Folk

In November 1966, a year before the celebrated American *Rolling Stone* (1967), the appearance of *Rock & Folk*, and with it the Presse Musicale, finally gave French popular music coverage a stable editorial home. The launch of *Best* in October 1968[35] completed a duo which dominated the following 20 years of French popular music journalism.

Originally an offshoot of the magazine *Jazz Hot*, *Rock & Folk* sought to tap into the readership which the million-copy *Salut les copains* had uncovered. *SLC*'s love-affair with the French *yéyés* had left Anglo-American currents under-represented; rumour even had it that sales went down when English groups adorned its cover.[36] With the appearance of *Rock & Folk* a music-press polarization was quickly established: *SLC* concentrated on home-grown talent, while the new title followed Anglo-American rock.[37] The 'folk' of its title soon became nothing more than a historical accident, to which lip-service was paid in a one-page feature, 'Les Fous de Folk' [Folk addicts]; even this was finally abandoned in 1985.

The title brought in a tripartite division into gossip columns (*échos*), articles and interviews, and reviews (*chroniques*), and balanced its coverage between stars and music; a good deal of its advertising was for musical equipment or instruments. Like *Disco Revue*, it took practically no interest in non-musical subjects.

---

[34] Buxton, D. (1985), *Le rock: star-système et société de consommation*, Grenoble: La Pensée sauvage, 142.

[35] For reasons of space I have not considered this title, which imitated the *Rock & Folk* formula, albeit highly successfully (it slightly outsold *Rock & Folk* throughout the 1970s). It closed in 1995; two attempts to relaunch it (1995, 1999) were short-lived.

[36] 'La première une de "Rock & Folk"', *Libération* (*Le Magazine de Libération* supplement), 26 Nov. 1994, 63.

[37] Mignon, P. (1988), 'La production sociale du rock', *Cahiers 'Jeunesses et sociétés'*, **10**, 3–32, 19–20. Bonzom, M.-C. (1987), "Rock & Folk: L'idéologie rock sous presse" (DEA thesis, Université de Rennes, 14–15), following Jamet, Michel (1983), *La presse périodique en France*, Paris: Armand Colin, 26, situates the two magazines' contrasting fortunes within rock's gradual replacement of *variété* as the leading popular music.

Within its articles and reviews, *Rock & Folk* developed an account of rock music orientated to an apparently overwhelmingly young, male readership.[38] Marie-Christine Bonzom[39] has shown convincingly how the construction of this rock fan type depended on the construction of correspondingly excluded types: an in-group and an out-group. The in-group, male, white and urban, was counterbalanced by the exclusion of, among others, blacks, women, and rural 'rednecks'. Black people in *Rock & Folk* have inbred rhythm, sensuality, are partial to spicy food, tend to laziness, and so on: 'gay minstrel' stereotypes, which had also been present in *Salut les copains*.[40] Women, when they are not sexual adjuncts of men, appear as monstrous figures, typefied by rockers such as Lene Lovitch. On the rare occasions before 1987 when a woman made the cover of *Rock & Folk*, those portrayed were frequently male rockers' partners such as Jerry Hall, rather than actual female musicians. As Bonzom notes, the appearance of a woman on stage in France was at this time generally greeted with cries of 'À poil!' [Get your clothes off]; this situation was amply reflected by an issue of *Rock & Folk* on whose cover the 'page 3' model and singing one-hit wonder, Samantha Fox, posed topless (Nov. 1986). One could hardly have been further from the anti-Thatcher stance of British music titles such as *New Musical Express*. The third type to suffer the contempt of this metropolitan elite was the rural 'redneck', with a taste for country music, presumed far-right political views, and general lack of culture.

Along with the construction of this in-group, the title's language was a key part of its appeal.[41] Although in 1966 its rhetoric was very similar to previous youth magazines (excepting the 'Lettres de Johnny'), with time, *Rock & Folk* undeniably carved out a reputation for a discourse which clashed with preconceived ideas of journalistic discourse, notably in terms of detachment and objectivity. This provoked both admiration and vituperation.[42]

Perhaps the area where the new discourse could display to the full its rhetorical powers was the review section. Record reviews, up till this point, had had an uneven career. Irregular in both frequency and format in the Presse des Jeunes, they found a relatively stable place in *Disco Revue* (although several

---

[38]   *Rock & Folk*'s readership is difficult to profile, but one point of general agreement is that it is mainly under 25 (Jamet, *La presse*, 27; Bonzom, *Rock & Folk*, 54; Sotinel, T. (1990), 'Le blues de la presse rock', *Le Monde*, 1 August, 6, with nonetheless a sizeable older minority (Buxton, quoted Bonzom, *Rock & Folk*, 260).

[39]   Bonzom, M.-C. (1991), 'Le Noir, la Femme, et le Sudiste. Une mythologie du rock sous presse', in: Mignon and Hennion (eds), *Rock: de l'histoire au mythe*, 65–74.

[40]   Pires, 'Les stars noires'.

[41]   See Gatfield, C. M. (1975), 'La formation du vocabulaire de la musique pop: Étude morpho-sémantique d'une langue de spécialité' (thesis, Universities of Toulouse II – Le Mirail and London Ontario Canada.

[42]   Vincent, F. (1986), 'Rock & Folk, du pareil au même ...', *La Revue des revues*, **2**, November, 55), is admirative, while Hirsch, J.-F. (ed.) (1971), 'La pop music' (dossier in: *Musique en jeu* **2**, 66–110), 105, is more critical.

early issues had none), and a very short-lived slot in *Salut les copains*, before being ignominiously ousted by Johnny Hallyday's burgeoning autobiography. As I have said, this reflects the market domination of the single and e.p. over the album. *Rock & Folk* emerged quite logically at the moment – 1967 – when the album finally eclipsed these seven-inch formats. With a high potential for individualistic, connoisseurial consumption, the album was tailor-made for journalistic mediation. No longer was dancing a *sine qua non* of musical assessment; the record collection was now a key to one's personality and inner temperament, rather than a collection of tunes liable to ensure a decent evening's entertainment for one's guests. Reviews at *Rock & Folk* initially (trial issue) took the form of mini-interviews with *yéyé* star Eddy Mitchell, a format reminiscent of the 'Lettre de Johnny', but the first issue proper dispensed with this and introduced a section very similar to that of today: a series of shortish texts (generally 300–500 words) penned by staff and freelance journalists.

How, then, did the language of *Rock & Folk* change? For one thing, it became funnier. Seriousness was a problematic area for pop and rock critics. On one hand, they took their subject seriously, sought to assert the field, and gain respect for it. However, while this was a logical solution in the 1960s and early 1970s, as time wore on, and pop began to emerge into the mainstream, a humorous mediation became possible, indeed logical; such an approach could articulate not only the historical marginality of a cultural form still widely despised, it could also demonstrate self-assurance in evoking other cultural practices, and comparing itself to them. Identity derived from a carnivalesque portrayal of the cultural gap.

This portrayal was taken to its logical conclusion in what Bonzom calls the 'scenario-review':[43] a review dominated by an extended metaphor. Marginality was articulated in humorously symbolic scenarios, with a lexically daring, culturally iconoclastic text. Hence Ziggy Marley is compared to a pharmaceutical product in order to evoke cannabis smoking among Rastafarians (Aug. 1993), or a pastiche of a Racinian drama serves as the basis for a review of The Police's *Outlandos d'Amour* (Feb. 1979), creating a meaningful opposition between 'legitimate', school-syllabus culture and the marginality of pop.[44] Such use of complex *mises-en-scène* corresponded to a cultural form gaining in confidence, needing to define itself socially and culturally: as pop music existed within a wide variety of meanings and cultural practices, such associations made perfect sense. In a way, music journalism was detaching itself from the music, asserting its independence; the 'scenario-review' asserted the personality of the journalist, whose authorial prestige was now premised not only on knowledge of music and milieu, but on rhetorical prowess.

---

[43]   Bonzom, *Rock & Folk*, 67.
[44]   Pires, M. (1998), 'Popular music reviewing in the French press, 1956–1996' (PhD thesis, University of Surrey), 207, 313.

Throughout the 1970s, *Rock & Folk* built up an undeniable reputation, as well as a growing public: sales of around 50,000 in 1974 rose to 143,000 in 1980–81. However, by 1993 they were back around the 50,000 mark.[45] This collapse may have been due to editorial choices, but one perhaps more plausible account is that its readers simply started to get pop coverage elsewhere. *Libération* and *Nouvel Observateur* started covering popular music in 1982, and the habit spread quickly to other publications. This inevitably 'poached' some music press readers, for whom a specialist title became superfluous. Strikingly, the years of *Rock & Folk*'s decline, 1981–88, are exactly those of the rise of *Libération*'s successful second series, launched after the election of François Mitterrand.

Les Inrockuptibles, and beyond

Rock & Folk and *Best*'s domination of the French music press market lasted until the turn of the 1980s. The relative marginality of popular music and its coverage had until then brought the specialist titles a highly loyal readership. The 1980s, though, saw a sea change in attitudes to popular music. Coverage in print expanded, but also on television. Pop programmes had existed since state broadcaster ORTF's 'Age tendre et tête de bois' in the 1960s, but the 1980s saw the launch not only of the highly successful terrestrial TV magazine *Les Enfants du Rock*, but of entire satellite channels devoted to music. As pop lost any pretention to marginality, and the range of pop journalism on offer continued to widen, so *Rock & Folk*'s circulation plummeted. But increasing competition was not the only reason behind the decline of the established music press; a too-cosy relationship with the music industry had also been under scrutiny for some time, with charges in some quarters that the magazines did little more than relay press releases supplied by the major record companies.[46]

This situation did not however signal the demise of the music magazine. In 1986 a group of university students, tired of seeing their own articles refused by *Rock & Folk* and *Best*, and particularly vexed by the ignoring of the so-called 'indie' current (and of its flagship band, The Smiths), set up a magazine of their own, *Les Inrockuptibles*. Conscientiously distinguishing itself from its rivals by a sober, spacious layout and black and white photography, it played to a more cerebral pop consumer, displaying contempt for rock superstars such as Tina Turner or Bruce Springsteen – the mainstay of the established titles. *Les Inrockuptibles* was the one conspicuous success of the French music press in the 1990s. It became a weekly in 1995, increasing its coverage of cinema and literature, and even straying into areas such as politics, with a noticeably more

---

[45] See Bonzom, *Rock & Folk*, 15; *Annuaire de la presse et de la publicité*, 1986, 165; 1987, 174; 1991, 169; 1995, 334.
[46] Dister, A. (1990), 'Les enfants de la passion', *Nouvel observateur*, 18 October, 76.

left-leaning viewpoint than any of its predecessors. The incorporation of related cultural practices served on one hand to legitimize rock and pop, but also, as Andrews[47] points out, to define a new position in the cultural field, in opposition to cultural consumers variously defined as 'beaufs', 'bœufs', or 'béotiens' (nerds, dumbos, philistines). As to its language, Andrews talks of 'a highly metaphoric and allusive style, wearing its literary credentials prominently while flouting the rules of fine writing'.[48] While the metaphorical element, as we have seen, was far from new, allusions to classically 'legitimate' cultures were undeniably more marked than elsewhere. The reviews of one 1993 issue of *Les Inrockuptibles* contain references to *Bouvard et Pécuchet*, *Ubu Roi*, *Gargantua* (all in one review), *Lolita*, *The Maltese Falcon*, *The Portrait of Dorian Gray*, Rilke, Apollinaire, Burroughs, and Rimbaud. The contemporaneous *Rock & Folk* manages one reference to Goethe and one to the *Série Noire* collection of detective novels.[49] It is more than an echo of the classical-music-based legitimation of the early rock reviewers.

Since it became a general culture weekly, though, *Les Inrockuptibles* is more likely to compete with *Nouvel observateur* and the highbrow TV guide *Télérama* than with *Rock & Folk*. Of the more recent arrivals, *L'affiche* is perhaps the most significant, launched in 1993 and particularly attuned to the rap currents. As for the electronic music which emerged in the 1980s (techno, house), the established music press has been largely uncomprehending, thrown off course no doubt by the absence of the mainstays of rock and pop culture: clearly definable stars, albums, and concerts. The best echo given to these genres, outside the very small-circulation specialist press, has been in the daily newspaper *Libération*. Indeed, *Libération*'s music coverage in general has gained itself a solid reputation over the past two decades.[50] Rock has for many years been covered by the well-known English critic Nick Kent, while a determined musical open-mindedness has seen forays into everything from techno to rai, afro-beat, and country. Such a scattershot approach has been absent from the magazines – perhaps inevitably, given their need to define and defend the tastes of a reader-type.

Conclusion

Since its beginnings, the popular music press has had something of a circular trajectory. In the 1950s cultural insecurity led to comparisons with classical

---

[47]   Andrews, C. (2000), 'The social ageing of *Les Inrockuptibles*', *French Cultural Studies*, **11**, 235–48.

[48]   Ibid., 246.

[49]   Pires, 'Popular music reviewing', 227.

[50]   Chocron, C. (1994), 'La perception du rock dans la presse quotidienne: L'exemple de "Libération"', in A.-M. Gourdon (ed.), *Le Rock: aspects esthétiques, culturels et sociaux*, Paris: CNRS Editions, 213–22.

music, and reassuring asides about how long pop stars practised their instruments, or reminders of their affection for the great composers. This was a simple legitimation strategy, an assertion of respectability by analogy with another, more respectable field. The star system which emerged in the 1960s, and which was measurably greater than in previous decades (in terms of record sales, concert attendances, and of pop-induced hysteria generally) dispensed with this rather craven attitude. The pop field had gained in self-assurance – one article in *Salut les copains* talked of 'a generation so extraordinary in both size and quality that it will bring about a real revolution in the history of society' (Dec. 1963). However, this new independence led to an obsessively self-celebratory press account of a dehistoricized, decontextualized musical culture. The advent of the Music Press proper, later in the 1960s, saw music re-established alongside the singing stars. Its new intellectual pretensions, contingent with changes in music consumption, resulted in considerable historicizing, with the establishment of greats, influences, genres and counter-genres, and so on. As such, this new discourse inevitably referred to comparable emergent fields such as television, cinema, or comic-strips. It also sought to renew its association with highly established fields such as literature, and even classical music.

Through all this change, one constant in the popular music press has been the involvement of the reader. *Letters* have frequently had a key importance. The extent of the letters pages was considerable in both *Disco Revue*, whose editor frequently penned lengthy replies to his correspondents, and in *Rock & Folk*;[51] *Salut les copains* not only published readers' letters, but provided a monthly missive from the *yéyé*'s foremost star. In *Rallye–Jeunesse*, readers also contributed to decisions about editorial policy, via a network of correspondents, and one reader even participated in a dialogue-based record review. A second strategy for involving the readership concerns pronoun use. A study of a corpus of record reviews published in 1993[52] found that the specialist magazine *Rock & Folk* used considerably more tokens of *vous* (you) in addressing (or haranguing) its readers, and journalists implicated themselves much more in *je* (I) or *on/nous* (we) tokens. These were almost completely avoided by the daily newspaper *Le Monde*, which preferred an objective, detached account of the music under review. These very disparate elements both reflect the importance, for a discourse directed at a highly culturally active readership, of avoiding any sense of a gulf between producers and consumers, whether it be due to age or social differences, or to the very nature of the written text.

The recent downward swing of the music press has apparently mirrored the waning capacity of music to create an identity:[53] in 2002 Britain's largest-selling

---

51 Hirsch, 'La pop-music'.
52 Pires, 'Popular music reviewing', 252–63.
53 The point is touched on by Ellen, M. (1994), 'Getting my mojo working', *Guardian*, 20 June.

weekly music title was *Kerrang!*, a heavy metal specialist with a tightly knit community of fans, which overtook the broader *New Musical Express*.[54] At the same time the ubiquity of music coverage, and of pop music itself, has led to a general devaluation. On-line music retailers such as amazon.com post consumers' own reviews and ratings for no charge, and though most are banal, the 150-odd reviews of crooner David Hasselhoff's *Looking For ... The Best* compilation album, all seek to outdo one another in finely honed, outwardly appreciative sarcasm. When the readers vie for supremacy in parodying the producers, the wheel really has come full circle.

---

[54]   Gibson, O. (2002), 'Kerrang! rocks its way to the top', *Guardian*, 15 February.

Chapter 6

The disintegration of community: popular music in French cinema 1945–present

Phil Powrie[1]

This chapter will sketch a history of popular music in the French cinema from the beginning of the sound era to the present, focusing largely on the post-war period. It will show how popular music in film is an index of social change, notably in negotiations around the issue of community. It is a preliminary mapping, since a broad history of this type has not yet appeared either in English or in French.[2] The definition of popular music used is inclusive, covering classical music as well as jazz and pop, and is determined principally by box-office success.[3]

The chapter is structured around a broad historicization of musical typologies, which will also include categories usually treated separately, singers and composers.[4] The reason for these three categories of popular music in the cinema

---

[1]   For my piano teacher Annick Saxton, who taught me to love Chopin's lyric flights.

[2]   The work of Michel Chion, the most important French theorist of music in the cinema, is not French-specific; see Chion, M. (1985), *Le Son au cinéma*, Paris: Cahiers du cinéma, 1985; and Chion (1995), *La Musique au cinéma*, Paris: Fayard. Lacombe's work is in one case a relatively superficial celebration of a particular form, the *chanson* (Lacombe, A. (1984), *La Chanson dans le cinéma français*, Paris: Import Diffusion Music), or in the other, tends to dwell on composers (Lacombe, A., and Porcile, F. (1995), *Les Musiques du cinéma français*, Paris: Bordas, 1995). Both Chion, and Lacombe and Porcile are more interested in innovation than in standard commercial practices which dominate the popular cinema; as the latter say baldly, 'you have to look for musical innovation elsewhere than commercial cinema' (Lacombe and Porcile, *Les Musiques*, 221).

[3]   There is a full list of all films mentioned in the Appendix which has the following information for each film: the date, the director, the main singer/composer, and, for post-1945 films, the audience figures. Films with one asterisk denote that the film was in the top 20 in France that year; two asterisks denote that the film was the top-selling French film that year. Post-1945 information is taken from Simsi, S. (2000), *Ciné-Passions: 7ᵉ art et industrie de 1945–2000*, Paris: Editions Dixit, which is based on extensive research in the archives of the *Centre National de la Cinématographie*.

[4]   A further type to be mentioned only in passing because it is statistically insignificant, is the film about a famous composer, such as *Un grand amour de Beethoven*, *La Symphonie fantastique* with Jean-Louis Barrault in the role of Berlioz, *La Belle meunière* with Tino Rossi as Schubert, or, much later, *La Note bleue* concerning the Chopin–Sand relationship.

97

(popular music, singer-songwriters as actors, orchestral scores by well-known composers) is first that they overlap, and second that they all have a part to play in what one might understand by popular French cinema music. We can identify several broad stages in a history of popular music in the French cinema. The dates are as symbolic as the stages are broad, and the stages overlap in more complex ways than there is space to develop here.

1. The popular song or *chanson* (1930–1945).
2. Operetta and French swing (1935–1955).
3. Jazz and *yéyé* (1955–1970).
4. The compilation score (1980–).

The point underlying this chapter is that all of the categories outlined, whether the three manifestations of music (popular music, singer-songwriters as actors, orchestral scores by well-known composers), or the four typologies within popular music listed above, demonstrate the fluctuations and tensions in that most special of relationships, between French and American culture. Popular music in French cinema is at the heart of negotiations over French national identity, and evidences the slow disintegration of specifically French cultural forms.

Chanson (1930–1945) and French community

It is important to understand something of the tradition of the *chanson* so as to be able to situate what follows, since *chanson* was an important feature of films in the 1930s, but disappeared post-war. This is all the more striking because, paradoxically, there was a resurgence of the *chanson* tradition elsewhere in popular culture during the period 1945–1980.

During the 1930s, the cinema (and the radio) gradually absorbed the popular singers whose singing had, prior to the expansion of these new technologies, been confined to the *café-concert* and the music hall. This shift included the music revue stars such as Mistinguett, Josephine Baker, Maurice Chevalier and Florelle, as well as realist singers, such as Fréhel and Damia.

Music in these films is either *extensive*, because the film narrative revolves around a singer, so story and songs are intertwined; or *intensive*, when songs merely punctuate a more realist narrative. The films specifically about singers usually recount their rise to fame. This is the case for Josephine Baker's two sound films, *Zouzou*, where she stars alongside Jean Gabin, and *Princesse Tam-Tam*, as it is too for Tino Rossi, one of the great popular singers of the latter half of the 1930s. In *Marinella*, whose music was composed by Vincent Scotto (as was the case for many Rossi films), he plays a painter with singing talent who becomes a star. In *Naples au baiser de feu* he plays a Neapolitan restaurant singer. One of the great singer-songwriters, Charles Trenet, wrote the script and the songs for *La Route enchantée*, in which he plays a scatterbrain who rises to fame through his singing. But films can also be about the loss of voice, such as *La Ronde des heures*, a melodramatic musical comedy which served as a vehicle for the immensely popular singer André Baugé,[5] in which he plays a singer who marries a rich heiress, is forced to give up his singing, and ends up as a clown.

Where intensive music is concerned, popular songs punctuate the narratives of both musical films and non-musical films. The musical film is best represented by the films of René Clair, such as *Sous les toits de Paris*, where the popular songs of music-sheet sellers bring people together at street level. Clair is indeed the best example, along with Jacques Demy, of the genre of the French musical, his other great films in this vein being *A nous la liberté* and *Quatorze Juillet*. More frequently, however, popular songs serve as punctuation in films where the narrative has little or no connection with a musical environment. The most obvious genre here is the comedy, such as the films of Fernandel. In *Ignace*, for example, the first musical number of the same name shows Fernandel as an army recruit explaining why his name is so beautiful, and ends with him dissolving into laughter with a close-up on his toothy grin; other numbers, such as the duo 'Pour être ordonnance' ['To be an orderly'] similarly have no connection with a musical environment, even if later in the film a musical show is put on which motivates a couple of the musical numbers. In other words, then, the musical numbers serve as intermezzos, pauses in the action which allow spectators, both within the film if motivated by the narrative, and in the film theatre if disconnected from the narrative, to focus on the star performing. What is performed is an excessive version of ordinariness mediated through the star's body, in this case through Fernandel's grimaces. Such songs allow spectators to celebrate not just emotion, but a *community of emotion*; Fernandel's *joie de vivre* is a celebration of the community's *joie de vivre*.

There are examples of the punctuating song too in the more realist films of the period, where issues of community also play a major role: Florelle's comment on loneliness to Lange in *Le Crime de Monsieur Lange*; Fréhel's rendition of a popular 1925 song, 'Où est-il donc?', in *Pépé le Moko*; Gabin's celebration of community in 'Quand on se promène au bord de l'eau' in *La Belle Equipe*. In the realist films, the songs bring into focus the overall narrative, which is a celebration of community. The popular song quite literally brings people together in a specifically French community.[6] In such films, the song therefore plays a key role in microcosmically defining issues which circulate through the narrative as

---

[5]   Baugé appeared in some ten films during the 1930s, including *Pour un sou d'amour* and *Le Roman d'un jeune homme pauvre*.

[6]   See O'Shaughnessy, M. (2001), 'The Parisian popular as reactionary modernisation', *Studies in French Cinema*, 1 (2), 80–88 for a more extended discussion of this point in *Sous les toits de Paris* and *Pépé le Moko*, amongst other films (*La Nuit du carrefour*; *Le Grand jeu*).

a whole, supporting Lacombe's otherwise odd contention that in 1930s films, 'chanson had ... the same function as the actors'.[7]

The swansong of this type of *chanson* can be characterized by *Les Portes de la nuit*. The latter's 'Les feuilles mortes' was written specifically for the film by Jacques Prévert, the scriptwriter, and the composer Joseph Kosma. It was sung by Yves Montand in what was his second film. The lyrics, which speak of the regrets of lost love, could just as well apply to the separation of the *chanson* from the film, leaving only the mute body of the singer-songwriter, as we shall see in a later section:

> En ce temps-là, la vie était plus belle
> Et le soleil plus brûlant qu'aujourd'hui.
> Tu étais ma plus douce amie
> Mais je n'ai que faire des regrets
> Et la chanson que tu chantais,
> Toujours, toujours je l'entendrai!

> [In those times life was better
> And the sun shone more brightly than today.
> You were my sweetest friend
> But I would prefer to have no regrets
> And the song you sang,
> I will always always hear!]

Operetta and French swing (1935–1955): carrying on the good times

As Lacombe and Porcile point out, in the post-war period, with some exceptions, the stars of song and the stars of the screen did not mix. Trenet and Piaf, for example, appeared in very few films; and film stars who felt capable of singing ended up not doing so in film. Arletty made records; Michel Simon complained bitterly that directors refused to acquiesce when he would suggest that some things might be better sung than spoken.[8] There were songs in films, but the films have their roots in pre-war French forms; and, contrary to the frequently tragic mode of the *chanson*, the music in these films was resolutely upbeat, and associated with utopian genres such as comedy, or musical films such as the operetta or big-band film.

First, there is the popular comic song with its music-hall roots, typified by Fernandel, or Bourvil, his frequent co-star. Bourvil bursts into song in *Blanc comme neige* in 1948. His song 'La Tactique du gendarme' in the sixth best-selling French film of 1950, *Le Roi Pandore*, ensured his popularity.

Apart from the comic song, the other popular musical form in the post-war period was operetta, 'popular spectacle *par excellence*',[9] as it had also been in

---

[7]   Lacombe, *La Chanson*, 2.
[8]   Lacombe and Porcile, *Les Musiques*, 96–98.
[9]   Ibid., 107.

1930s Hollywood with the Maurice Chevalier–Jeannette MacDonald series (1932–34) and the Jeannette MacDonald–Nelson Eddy series (1935–42). Tino Rossi, who had already been a pre-war star, regularly had films in the top ten French films with three to four million spectators through to the early 1950s (*Sérénade aux nuages*, 1945; *L'Ile d'amour*, 1945; *Destins*, 1946; *Le Gardian*, 1946; *Le chanteur inconnu*, 1947; *Deux amours*, 1949; *Paris chante toujours*, 1952). He overshadowed Egyptian-born singer Georges Guétary, who, before going to Hollywood and starring alongside Gene Kelly in *An American in Paris*, had four major successes in France, all directed by Gilles Grangier, and all with two to four million spectators (*Le Cavalier noir*, 1945; *Trente et quarante*, 1945; *Jo la romance*, 1948; *Amour et compagnie*, 1949).

Arguably more popular than both Rossi and Guétary was the Spanish tenor Luis Mariano, who specialized in the film adaptations of his popular stage operettas. He rose as Rossi waned, with a string of very successful films in the early 1950s. *Andalousie* was the best-selling French film of 1951; *Violettes impériales* the second best-selling film of 1952, with *Rendez-vous à Grenade* doing well in the same year. *La Belle de Cadix* was the fourth best-selling French film of 1953, as was *Le Chanteur de Mexico* in 1956. His following late 1950s films, *A la Jamaïque* and *Sérénade au Téxas*, although less popular, remained in the first 20 French films of their year. Mariano appealed to the thirst for the exotic, as the titles of his films suggest, albeit tempered by familiar musical and melodramatic forms.

Operetta films, even in their American variant, had a European flavour, as they were often based on music by European composers, usually set in European locations, often with European directors, such as Lubitsch, and, finally, in the first series mentioned above, with the quintessentially (and stereotypically) French Maurice Chevalier. The other major musical form to come to prominence in the post-war period, jazz in its swing variant, was much more attuned to American music. The Ray Ventura Orchestra, for example, did well on screen because they echoed the US musicals of the 1930s, and were clearly an antidote to the tragic realism of the cinema of Carné, whose films, with embattled proletarian heroes, reflected perhaps too starkly the political realities of the time. In their first pre-war success, *Feux de joie*, a group of musicians decide to work together in a hotel on the Côte d'Azur; in *Tourbillon de Paris*, impoverished students play to make a living and end up turning professional. Ray Ventura's successes carried on after the war in a series of films with the director Jean Boyer, notably in *Mademoiselle s'amuse*, and *Nous irons à Paris*, the story of a pirate radio patronized by Ray Ventura amongst other musical stars of the time, and the best-selling French film of 1950. It was followed by *Nous irons à Monte-Carlo*, now lagging well behind Mariano's *Violettes impériales* as the ninth French film of the year.

Ventura's work stretches right back to the Popular Front period in the 1930s, and in that sense his films suggest the slow shift which underlies this section, from a very French community with its indigenous cultural forms, such as *chanson*, or European-inflected forms such as operetta, to forms overlaid with American influences, in his case the big-band swing jazz familiar in American musicals. His was not the only work which took its cue from American musicals; one of the hits of 1941 had been the very American *Mademoiselle Swing*, starring Irène de Trébert as the star of the Swing-Club d'Angoulême; she, like the American musical stars, was at home with tap dance as well as singing.

Whether French or American in flavour, though, or a combination of both, what all of these films have in common is a utopian ideology of community, even if the music generally suggests hybridity, and the jazz soundtracks in particular suggest a more obvious fissuring of the utopia by Americanization.

Jazz and *yéyé* (1955–1970): the ghost of the *chanson* and the disintegration of community

The year 1945 is a far too convenient date in French history, and musical forms bring out its artificiality for conceptualizing cultural activity. Forms of community, whether the nostalgic *chanson*, or the more utopian operetta and swing music, all began well before the war, and, in the case of the latter two, went well beyond it. This implies, if the permanence of popular forms is taken as the criterion, that the notion of a French community, although no doubt severely shaken by the war, has already begun disintegrating in the 1930s. The war was merely a fallow period for Americanization, which resurfaced and gradually accelerated during France's post-war recovery.

Given the encroachment of American culture post-war, it is all the more surprising that *chanson* should have a post-war revival in French popular culture more generally, while disappearing from the soundtracks of French films during the same period. Its resurgence was due to a variety of factors: the nightclub culture of Saint-Germain-des-Prés; the arrival of the LP which gave singer-songwriters more space for experimentation; the political instability generated by the Occupation, decolonization, and the events of May 1968.[10] *Chanson*'s demise in film was no doubt partly due to the increased distribution of US films in the post-war period.[11] This led at one and the same time to the disappearance in film

---

[10]   See Hawkins, P. (2000), *Chanson: The French Singer-Songwriter from Aristide Bruant to the Present Day*, Aldershot: Ashgate, 215–16.

[11]   More spectators went to see French films than American films (a situation which was to change only in 1986–87), and there were normally more than twice or three times as many French films than American films in the top 20 films until the mid-1980s. These statistics would seem to suggest the hegemony of French films; however, in the period 1945–60, American films were nevertheless the best-selling films for 11 of those 16 years.

of what was too parochial a cultural form in the *chanson*, and the gradual increase in the use of American-inflected forms, such as jazz and pop.

Singer-songwriters still appeared in films, however, even if they did not sing. Some appeared only in a few films (Gilbert Bécaud, Jean Ferrat, Georges Moustaki, Charles Trenet). Amongst those who appeared regularly, some - Jacques Dutronc, Yves Montand – became better known as actors than as the singers they were early in their careers; while others – Charles Aznavour, Jacques Brel, Serge Gainsbourg – maintained both careers. The body (and non-singing voice) of the singer-songwriter therefore supplements his (since all of the more obvious examples are men) extra-filmic song. It is almost as if popular forms such as the *chanson* were, literally, silenced, to make way for more Americanized forms, such as jazz, and American-influenced rock.

French *chanson* may have died on screen, but it was rapidly replaced during the late 1950s and 1960s by the new youth music phenomenon, heavily influenced by American rock and roll, the *yéyé* singers, as they were known. Many of these (Adamo, Françoise Hardy and Sylvie Vartan being amongst the better known) appeared in only a few films. Unquestionably, though, the king of *yéyé* was Johnny Hallyday, and like Elvis Presley, his mid-1960s films, which represent the high point of this popular form, were little more than a pretext for show-stopping musical numbers. *D'où viens-tu Johnny?* was the fifth best-selling French film of 1963, followed by the less successful *Cherchez l'idole* the following year. The original English titles of Hallyday's early LPs suggest only too clearly the American influence: *Twistin' the rock* (1961), *Sings America's rocking hits* (1962).

Chanson in film was replaced by American-style rock; French operetta and swing jazz, both associated with the 1930s, were overtaken from the mid-1950s by more modern jazz, linked to the police thriller, after comedy the most popular film genre in France. There are several reasons for this. First, the spread of jazz on radio; second, the use of jazz in American films from the early 1950s; third, the spread of a different kind of hard-boiled crime fiction through Marcel Duhamel's popular 'série noire' from 1947, which published many American authors in translation; and finally, at least where non-orchestral jazz is concerned, the fact that it was cheaper. There were relatively few films which used scores in the way in which jazz might have been heard in the jazz clubs of New York or Paris, however. Roger Vadim asked jazzmen to score some of his films (the Modern Jazz Quartet for *Sait-on jamais*, Thelonius Monk and Art Blakey for *Les Liaisons dangereuses*), and Miles Davis's score for *Ascenseur pour l'échafaud* is one of the best known. Most films, whether American or French, merely incorporated jazz elements in their background scores to create what Chion calls a 'jazz ambiance'[12] appropriate to the increasingly Americanized police thriller, with privileged jazz instruments (such as the muted trumpet or the saxophone), and characteristic jazz chords.

---

[12]   Chion, *La musique*, 133.

In *Voulez-vous danser avec moi?*, a comedy with Brigitte Bardot, and the eleventh best-selling film of 1959, André Hodeir set the tunes of Henri Crolla, a jazz guitarist with whom he frequently collaborated, to a jazz arrangement. Martial Solal, whose music Lacombe and Porcile characterize as 'modern jazz à la française',[13] is perhaps best known for his work with Godard on *À bout de souffle*, and the bursts of jazz in echoing spaces of Melville's New York-based *Deux hommes à Manhattan*. Both of these films are in a complex relationship with the USA, the latter by its location. *À bout de souffle* can be seen partly as a pastiche of the American crime thriller, as the combination of strident jazz and Michel/Belmondo's excessively long death throes suggests. Other jazz musicians brought jazz inflexions to their scores for Melville's thrillers. Paul Misraki, one-time collaborator of Ray Ventura, was the composer for Melville's thriller *Le Doulos*, and his music for the popular Lemmy Caution crime series, starring Eddie Constantine (*Comment qu'elle est!, Lemmy pour les dames, A toi de faire, mignonne*), has a resolutely American feel to it.

The two major post-war jazz-oriented composers were Claude Bolling and Michel Legrand, both accomplished jazz musicians. Bolling was a jazz pianist, a friend of Duke Ellington, and creator of 'crossover' jazz-classical pieces (his gold-disc Suite for Flute and Jazz Piano stayed in the US charts for ten years). His greatest success where film music is concerned was his jaunty honky-tonk piano score for *Borsalino* in 1969, which combined a 1930s sound, the period in which the film is set, with a more distinctly dance-like (rather than blues-like) tune; Bolling's film work veers rather more towards the kind of music the French call *variétés* – middle-of-road entertainment music – than jazz. He went on to score a number of Deray's thrillers and noirish dramas in following years, including the sequel *Borsalino et Cie, Flic Story*, and *Trois hommes à abattre*. Similarly, the experimental composer Michel Magne, whose recording studios at Hérouville played host to both *yéyé* singers like Adamo, but also mainstream rock stars like Pink Floyd and David Bowie, used big-band jazz styles amongst many others for his film work. In *Les Tontons flingueurs*, for example, the theme tune is a blues, and the blues are even used for the organ piece at a church wedding; Magne's scores for the immensely popular *Fantômas* films of the mid-1960s, with about four million spectators each, were Mancini-style big-band jazz.

More obviously jazz-oriented in some of his film music, Legrand made records with Miles Davis and John Coltrane amongst others early in his career, and has carried on as a flourishing jazz artist. Where French cinema is concerned, Legrand is best known for the jazz scores he wrote for two key films of the 1960s, Demy's musicals, *Les Parapluies de Cherbourg*, and *Les Demoiselles de Rochefort*, both starring Catherine Deneuve. These films are addressed in considerable detail elsewhere in this volume; suffice to say that the tension

---

13   Lacombe and Porcile, *Les Musiques*, 109.

between American and French jazz, characterized in *Les Demoiselles de Rochefort* by the appearance of Gene Kelly, shows once more how the relationship between the two countries is mediated through film music, in this case variants of jazz.

The other major film composers of this period were less affected by jazz. Georges Delerue used jazz occasionally, but, like Maurice Jarre, basically remained within the French tradition. Delerue, who with the pre-war Jaubert is the only French film composer to figure in Chion's list of film composers in his encyclopedic 1995 volume, was often seen by Americans as typically French, according to Chion,[14] because of his classicism. Minor mode writing, with solo woodwinds over sweeping strings, a predilection for the dulcimer and the harpsichord, all suggest the Baroque, a far cry from the jazz-inspired work of Michel Legrand, or from the work of Francis Lai, often associated with the films of Claude Lelouch, and who had emerged from the *chanson* tradition with songs written for Mireille Mathieu, Yves Montand, and Édith Piaf.

What brings all of these composers together, however, is that the only realistic gauge of the popularity of their music (as opposed to the success of the films in which that music can be heard) is not whether their music has jazz or classical inflexions, but the catchy tunes for which they (and the films) are often remembered: the theme tunes to *Borsalino* (Bolling) and *Un homme et une femme* (Lai); 'Lara's Song' in *Doctor Zhivago*, and the waltz in *Paris brûle-t-il?* (Jarre), 'The Windmills of my mind' in *The Thomas Crown Affair* and the theme for *Summer of '42* (Legrand). These popular tunes are no more American in flavour than French. It is difficult to know whether certain soundtracks were popular in their own right, or became popular as the result of their combination with the image-track. However, one index of popularity is the anthologization of orchestral theme tunes. For example, a recent CD of so-called 'European' film music contains mostly orchestral scores composed specifically for the films concerned (rather than classical or pop numbers), and of the 33 films featured, no fewer than 23 are normally considered to be 'French' films.[15]

Modern jazz tracks, as opposed to composed orchestral scores, could also be heard in films. These are usually motivated diegetically, as is the case for *Le*

---

[14]   Chion, *La Musique*, 314.

[15]   *Cinema Café: The European Film Music Album*. The City of Prague Philharmonic with instrumentalists soloists and singers; conductors: Nic Raine and Paul Bateman (Silva Screen filmxcd 302, 2CDs, 155: 41 mins). The films featured are as follows; they are given in chronological order with their original title (which is not always that given on the CD): *Mon Oncle, Orfeu negro, La Dolce Vita, Jules et Jim, Phaedra, Un Homme et Une Femme, Playtime, Z, Morte a Venezia, Ultimo tango a Parigi, La Nuit américaine, Emmanuelle, Amarcord, Bilitis, Providence, Die Blechtrommel, Opera sauvage, Diva, Fort Saganne, Subway, Jean de Florette, 37∞ 2 le matin, Camille Claudel, Le Grand Bleu, Cinema Paradiso, Cyrano de Bergerac, Le Mari de la coiffeuse, Nikita, Atlantis, La Double vie de Véronique, La Reine Margot, Il Postino, Antonia.*

Souffle au Cœur, the sixth most popular French film of 1971. This opens with a frantic Charlie Parker track and a discussion of the relative merits of trad and modern jazz by two boys, who then go into a record shop and steal the latest Charlie Parker; the soundtrack also includes material by the trad jazz saxophonist Sidney Bechet, and French bebop pianist Henri Renaud. The soundtrack of this film approaches a particular type of compilation score, what we could call the diegetically motivated compilation score, where what we hear is something played or something alluded to within the diegesis. This type of jazz, much more than softer jazz, 'came to signify personal expression – a character's secret and internal voice',[16] in stark contrast to the shared emotion of the *chanson*, and its intimations of community. Jazz in films signalled the confirmation of the alienated individual who had started appearing in the doomed proletarian heroes of the films of Marcel Carné; the difference, however, is that in those films, the music is not so obviously tied to individual expression and emotion.

To conclude this section, from the mid- to late 1950s, *chansonniers* in film no longer sang; the operetta and the big-band film died out, replaced by youth idols who mimicked American rock and roll singers. Where background scoring is concerned, distinctly French composers such as the pre-war Maurice Jaubert were replaced by 'professional' composers, who were just as likely to come from a jazz background as from a classically trained background, and who in popular genres such as the police thriller tended to use recognizably American inflexions in their jazz scores; and audiences were as likely to hear the new bebop jazz as they were jazz scores. When assembled, these features together suggest the disintegration of a specifically French community defined by distinctly French cultural forms (however much that sense of community might well have been no more than a utopian dream in the 1930s), fragmentation, loss of clear identity, in both music and in society. This is even more the case, arguably, with the compilation score which we shall consider in the following section.

The compilation score (1980–)

With some exceptions it is only since the mid-1990s that films regularly have pure compilation scores. In this category, we find the following types:

- 1985 onwards, scores based on well-known classical pieces, associated since the mid-1980s with the popular heritage films;
- 1980 onwards, scores based on a 'postmodern' mixture of classical and/or pop and/or *chanson*;

---

[16]   Lack, R. (1997), *Twenty Four Frames Under: A Buried History of Film Music*, London: Quartet, 203.

- 1995 onwards, scores based mostly or exclusively on pop songs defined very broadly (so it would include, for example, the kind of hip hop music found in *Taxi*).

a) Classical music

Paradoxically, classical music in the heritage films of the 1980s and beyond could be seen as more popular than the more obviously popular jazz, if we take as an index of popularity the audience figures for the films concerned rather than the type of music. So, for example, films with jazz scores, either compilations, as in *Les Tricheurs*, or composed specifically for the films, such as Miles Davis's score for *Ascenseur pour l'échafaud* or Legrand's Franco-American jazz score for *Les Demoiselles de Rochefort*, were less popular at the box office than some of the key heritage films using classical music during the 1980s and 1990s, such as the Baroque compilation of *Tous les matins du monde*, or the (partly) Baroque-inspired orchestral score[17] of *Cyrano de Bergerac* by Jean-Claude Petit, for which Petit won a César (and a BAFTA), or indeed his earlier reworking of Verdi for *Jean de Florette*.

Of the three types of compilation score listed, classical music is the category which has shifted most in its usage. Art-house films had used classical music from the 1950s,[18] although spectator numbers for such films tended to stay below one and a half million. Given that the average score for the top 20 films in each year was three million, neither the films nor the music could really be called popular. During the 1980s, however, classical music, despite its high-cultural associations, became a feature of two popular film genres which emerged in that decade.

The first was the opera film, which enjoyed a vogue in the 1980s. In some ways, given the spectator numbers of a million or slightly less for the films concerned, it would be wrong to call the genre popular; but then, given the high-cultural associations of opera more generally, it is surprising that opera films managed to attract even these numbers. In this group we can include filmed opera, the more popular being *Don Giovanni* and *La Traviata* with around a

---

17   The overture, for example, is structured slow–fast–slow, like Lully's overtures in the sixteenth century, and Cyrano's theme is in sarabande style with a solo trumpet.

18   In the 1950s there was Vivaldi and Bach in Melville's *Les Enfants terribles*, Brahms's sextet in Malle's *Les Amants*, Mozart's Requiem in Bresson's *Un condamné à mort s'est échappé*, Mozart (as well as Martial Solal's jazz score) could be heard in Godard's *À bout de souffle*, and 'The Ride of the Valkyries' in Chabrol's *Les Cousins*. In the 1960s, Demy used the *allegretto* from Beethoven's Seventh Symphony in *Lola*, Malle used Erik Satie's piano music in *Le Feu follet*. In the 1970s, Truffaut used Vivaldi in *L'Enfant sauvage*; in the 1980s, Blier's *Notre Histoire* used Martinu, Leconte used Brahms's piano quintet in *Monsieur Hire*, Deville used Schubert in *Péril en la demeure*, and Schubert also featured in Blier's *Trop belle pour toi*.

million spectators, and *Carmen* with two million.[19] Two of these three were part of a dozen produced by Daniel Toscan du Plantier, who wanted to take opera out of its specialist arena. Opera seems in fact to have been 'in the air' during this period, as suggested by the immense popularity of the 'three tenors', and the incorporation of opera in other types of film, such as the considerably more popular *Diva*, as well as the Italian *La Luna*, and the German *Fitzcarraldo* (both with about half a million French spectators).[20]

This genre, which appeared early in the decade, was less popular than the heritage film, which in France is often seen as starting with *Jean de Florette* and *Manon des sources* in 1986. Classical music in the heritage film can be heard in various forms. First, the original can be played without modification: *Tous les matins du monde* uses Baroque composers (Marin Marais, Lully, Rameau); *Le Colonel Chabert* uses Scarlatti, Mozart, Beethoven, Schubert, Schumann. Second, the music can also be arranged, as with Jean-Louis Petit's arrangement of Verdi's *La Forza del destino* in *Jean de Florette*, where the bombastic melodramatic theme is played on an essentially popular instrument, the harmonica, no doubt accounting for its subsequent popularity (it features on the above-mentioned CD). The type furthest from the compilation score is probably the most frequent, the pastiche, usually to suggest period, as in Jean-Claude Petit's clever pastiche of early Romantic music in *Le Hussard sur le toit*, or Gabriel Yared's music for *Camille Claudel*, a pastiche of late Romantic music.

Classical music in these films signifies loss. It does not much seem to matter whether the music is Baroque, Romantic, or modern (as Hans Werner Henze's modernist version of Vinteuil's 'petite phrase' in *Un Amour de Swann*, or Delerue's elegiac violin piece which opens and closes *Dien Bien Phu*). The music is nearly always associated with loss for a character in the narrative: loss of innocence in *Tous les matins du monde*, and *Le Colonel Chabert*; loss of creative independence in *Camille Claudel*; loss of a person when Papet fails to recognize Jean de Florette as his son; loss of a colony in *Dien Bien Phu*); or, finally, loss of home or roots, as when a lone clarinet plays a Mozart dance in *Le Hussard sur le toit*, whose music helps the inmates of the quarantine prison sleep at night. That, and the fact that the heritage film is clearly set in the past, suggests that the music in these films expresses loss of community. The music is frequently melancholic and nostalgic. Nostalgia is, etymologically, pining for the

---

[19]   It is worth noting that there were no less than six French *Carmen* adaptations during the mid-1980s, occasioned partly by the release of copyright for the Leilhac-Halévy dialogue of Bizet's opera. Godard's *Prénom: Carmen* deconstructed the story, using Beethoven's late quartets rather than Bizet; in the same year, 1983, Peter Brooks offered three films of the three stage versions; and there was a soft-porn hippy version, *Carmen nue*, in the following year.

[20]   See Lack, *Twenty Four Frames*, 246–55, for a general overview of the genre.

lost homeland.[21] Just as jazz comes to signify a combination of 'Americanness' and individuality, the breakdown of community, classical music in these popular films is an attempt to recover that community.

b) Postmodern mix

If classical music scores help spectators to fantasize community through the celebration of heritage, it could be argued that the postmodern score, in keeping with postmodernism more generally, whose defining characteristic is a playful dislocation, articulates rootlessness, a disengagement from community, in its mix of high and low cultural forms. The musically mixed score is most in evidence in these films.

Jameson called *Diva*, the first film by the directors of the *cinéma du look*, the first French postmodern film.[22] The film's score earned Vladimir Cosma a *César* (the French equivalent of the Oscars). It opens with images of the Paris Opera set to classical music, which the audience would no doubt assume is background non-diegetic scoring until the postman turns off the cassette machine fitted onto his *mobylette*. He enters the Opera, and we see a performance of a then little-known aria by the Black-American diva of the title, 'Ebben? Ne andro lontano', taken from Alfredo Catalani's opera, *La Wally*, popularized since then by the film. The following sequence takes place in a different public space, a train station, and is set to an insistent techno-rock score more usually associated with the police thrillers which *Diva* is reworking. The contrast between these two types of music, associated with very different spaces, and indeed with very different colour-schemes (blue and yellow respectively), serves as the basic contrast between two different types of plot, themselves represented by two different tapes which become confused during the film's narrative, the high-cultural opera plot and the popular-cultural thriller plot.[23] Different music is associated with different spaces throughout the film: an airy floating synthesizer piece with Gorodish's vast loft and the disused hangar in which he does the deal with the corrupt police chief; 'Promenade sentimentale', a Sati-esque piano piece with the Jardins du Luxembourg in which the postman and the diva wander during the night.[24] A final type of music is the popular accordion-playing on the

---

[21] See Powrie, P. (1997), *French Cinema in the 1980s: Nostalgia and the Crisis of Masculinity*, Oxford: Clarendon Press, 16–20.

[22] Jameson, F. (1990), '*Diva* and French Socialism', in *Signatures of the Visible,* New York and London: Routledge, 55–62, 55.

[23] See Powrie, P. (2001), *Jean-Jacques Beineix*, Manchester: Manchester University Press, 56–64 for an elaboration of these points.

[24] A much-anthologized piece. It is one of the two pieces from *Diva* (the other being the aria from *La Wally*) on the *Cinéma Café* album mentioned above. It can also be found, amongst others, alongside 25 other film pieces (none of them French) on Roger Woodward's *The Essential Piano Album* (CD AW015); on *Promenade sentimentale* (CBS/SONY 32 DP 411), where it figures amongst other pieces by Cosma; on a jazz album, *Chet Baker Plays Vladimir Cosma* (Carrere 66251/96251).

thug's Walkman (when we might have expected punk, given his appearance); this rather more specifically French and popular music is, unlike the other types of music, contained, and unheard in the small space of the thug's Walkman until his death, when it echoes eerily in Jules's loft. It is as if popular French music had been repressed by the remainder of the score, and principally by the combination of classical music and American singer.

A decade later, in Carax's *Les Amants du Pont-Neuf*, the score again combines different types of music. The most exemplary sequence is the night of the 1989 Bicentennial celebrations as down-and-outs Michèle and Alex dance on the Pont-Neuf to a background of fireworks. The score, which oscillates between diegetic and non-diegetic, combines accordion music by Jo Privat, one of the great musette players of the 1940s and 1950s, Maghrebi music, Iggy Pop's 'Strong Girl', Public Enemy's 'You're gonna get yours', and a Strauss waltz, each seguing into the other, as well as being overlaid in some cases, suggesting the multi-culturalism which the Bicentennial celebrations strove to stress. However, this is ironic because Michèle and Alex, who are, we assume as spectators, able to 'hear' these different musics emanating from different parts of Paris, and who signify both the bringing together of the musics and of the groups they represent by being on a space which links borders, the bridge, are themselves separated from the celebrations by that same space, as well as by their marginality as drop-outs.

The points which these scores have in common is their playfulness (diegetic or non-diegetic?), and their refusal to hierarchize different types of music. Music in the 1980s films is used pleonastically. It supports location, so we have techno-rock for a train, or echoing electronic sounds for a loft. It can also support character attitude or emotion, so we have the same echoing electronic sounds supporting Alba's previously heard statement that her boyfriend Gorodish is 'going through his cool phase', and 'trying to stop the waves'. In the early 1990s, however, Carax is using the music to make ironic 'political' statements about the marginality of French youth in relation to the French state.

c) Pop songs

At about the same time as the *cinéma du look* emerged, with its classical/pop/other compilations, so too did more pop-oriented compilation scores. As in the USA, where they emerged at the same time,[25] these scores could

---

[25]   Anahid Kassabian suggests that 'the phenomenal possibilities' of this type of score 'were not much exploited until, perhaps, *American Graffiti* (1973) and *Saturday Night Fever* (1977)' (Kassabian, A. (2001), *Hearing Film: Tracking Identifications in Contemporary Hollywood Film Music*, New York and London: Routledge, 50) in the USA, 1977 also being the date for *Diabolo Menthe* which will be discussed below as an example of this type in France.

be found in films aimed at or dealing with younger generations. Songs in this type of compilation score are there largely to suggest period, whether nostalgia for a past period, or to help audiences locate themselves in a contemporary ambience.

An early example is *Diabolo menthe*, a semi- autobiographical coming-of-age drama set in the early 1960s which was the third best-selling French film of 1977. The film opens with Cliff Richard's 1959 hit 'Living Doll' (a piece by The Shadows, from the same year, 'Sleep Walk', occurs later in the film), and is made up of a compilation of mostly French songs from the early 1960s by *yéyé* singers (Vartan, Adamo) and more established singers such as Aznavour and Claude Nougaro.

A more interesting use of music can be found in a considerably less complex film *La Boum 2*, another coming-of-age film, centring on parties and music (*boum* means party in teenage French), and the fifth best-selling French film of 1982 (its predecessor *La Boum* was the best-selling film of 1980). The music is by Vladimir Cosma, but the songs are performed (in English) by the Liverpool 'clean pop' band Cook da Books, who perform on stage in the film. Whereas *Diabolo Menthe*'s score compiled pre-existing music, *La Boum 2* created pop music for the film, which then became a hit (the slow 'Your eyes' by Cosma, sung by Cook da Books, was a big hit in France in 1983). More interesting still in this film is the use of types of music to categorize the actors. Vic/Sophie Marceau's younger lover is a fan of Cook da Books, while the older 25-year-old rival plays a slightly jazzy *variétés* piano piece to impress Vic, suggesting a difference in age and in culture. Vic is the film's major protagonist, and she, unlike the men, is associated with a number of types of music. We see her listening to a classical music concert in the film's opening sequences (although irreverently eating as she listens). Having grounded Vic in class terms by the use of classical music, but also suggested her rebellious streak, the film goes on to associate her with a range of other types. As her mother gazes at her as she practises disco dancing in a class, there is a curious flashback which begins with still pictures of Vic as a child. This segues into three action sequences (which we assume are still part of the flashback), where we see Vic perform three sequences from *Singin' in the Rain*, appearing as both Debbie Reynolds and Cyd Charisse. Vic, in other words, is less monolithically stereotyped by the music than her boyfriends. The wider range of music allows her to perform several different stereotypes. This suggests, in a film full of stereotypes, that the American connection allows her to *out-perform* the others, and thereby gives her just the kind of maturity required for younger audiences to see her as a more rounded character, poised on the cusp between childhood and womanhood. (The film is at pains to emphasize the childishness of the pursuits during the various parties, such as innocuous card-games, while also giving Vic the possibility of sexual independence in a rather confused dialogue between Vic and her mother where Vic makes it clear that she knows all about contraception.) The film's music is interesting then, because it negotiates a transition between childhood and adulthood, but also between what we might consider to be a fairly naive use of music to define character *type*, and a more sophisticated use of music to define character *transition*.

During the 1990s a new musical type, hip hop, gradually replaced other types of pop in the compilation score. Imported from America, hip hop had emerged as a popular form in France in the late 1980s.[26] The most iconic youth film of the mid-1990s, one of a group of films which form the subgenre of *cinéma de banlieue*, is *La Haine*.[27] It has very little music on its soundtrack (although a CD of music by a variety of French rappers 'inspired' by the film was released and became a hit). The sequence where music plays a significant part, however, and which shows 'hip hop's vitality in the context of the banlieue'[28] is 'DJ Skeud Interlude'. In this sequence the DJ Cut Killer mixes an iconic *chanson*, Edith Piaf's 'Je ne regrette rien' and the hard rap group Suprême NTM's 'Nique la police' (literally, 'fuck the police'). The nostalgia attached to the Piaf element of the mix functions in two ways. First, it articulates a sense of loss, which we could argue is loss of community; and second, that nostalgia, which is a looking backwards to what has been lost, even if the words of the song say otherwise, articulates less a clash than a distancing from the present, an alienated violent present articulated by NTM.

By the end of the 1990s, the Besson-produced *Taxi*, the third best-selling French film of 1998, showed the shift to hip hop with a score compiled of songs by the Marseille-based hip hop group IAM. The film opens to the same music as Tarantino's *Pulp Fiction*, however, 'Pumpkin And Honey Bunny/Misirlou', by Dick Dale and His Del-tones. The tension between American and French popular music forms is still present, then, both by the opening appeal to a popular American film, as by the hip hop which follows, since it is an essentially American musical form, even if it has over the years been tempered, as Cannon suggests, to accommodate the French language.[29] Indeed, Besson's own films have all been scored by Eric Serra, whose music has shown a gradual shift from what could be called a Euro-rock riff style to a more Americanized and more heavily orchestrated score. Like the example of *La Boum 2* given above,

---

[26]   See Cannon, S. (2000), '"Let's film to the sound of the underground?" The uses of hip hop and reggae in recent French films', in Bill Marshall and Robynn Stilwell (eds), *Musicals: Hollywood and Beyond*, Exeter: Intellect, 163–70, and the chapter by Cannon in this volume.

[27]   See Konstantarakos, M. (1999), 'Which Mapping of the City?: *La Haine* (Kassovitz, 1995) and the "Cinéma de banlieue"', in Phil Powrie (ed.), *Contemporary French Cinema: Continuity and Difference*, Oxford: Oxford University Press, 152–61; and Tarr, C., 'Ethnicity and identity in the "Cinéma de banlieue"', in Phil Powrie (ed.), *Contemporary French Cinema: Continuity and Difference*, Oxford: Oxford University Press, 162–73.

[28]   Cannon, 'Let's film', 165.

[29]   Ibid., 164; see also the chapter by Cannon in this volume.

however, Serra normally includes a pop song somewhere, either as part of the diegesis (the final performance in *Subway*), or over the credits.[30]

d) USA/France

'Je ne regrette rien' also appears in a recent very popular film, *Le Goût des autres*, a study in the segregation of different classes anchored in questions of taste, as the title of the film suggests. It is a film which is not necessarily aimed at the youth market, like those of Besson, and in which we find a more characteristic mix of musical forms. This final case study will show how the music in the film suggests a final recent development focusing once more on the American connection.

The classes represented in the film cover a wide range, but exclude the manual working class, suggesting a microcosm of French society: a poorly educated businessman, his highly educated administrator, his chauffeur and bodyguard, a coterie of actors and artists, and a barmaid (played by the film's director, Agnès Jaoui), who mediates between the two main groups (businessman and actors/artists). Individuals within these groups persist in misunderstanding each other and their motives. Music in the film plays a key role in helping the groups to move closer together for the audience.

The two main characters, the businessman Castella (Jean-Louis Bacri, who co-wrote the script with Jaoui), and the actress who has been giving him English lessons, and with whom he falls in love, Clara (Anne Alvaro), both have specific music associated with them at the beginning of the film. For Clara, it is classical music, indeed a specific set of recordings made by the pianist Gerald Moore with the singers Kathleen Ferrier and Isobel Baillie. The tracks chosen are all in English to echo the fact that she has been teaching him English,[31] and the most prominent voice is that of the contralto Kathleen Ferrier, Clara's voice also being contralto. Castella's music is the moody 'Au lait' by American jazz-rock guitarist Pat Metheny, taken from the album *Offramp* (1982). The two types of music are worlds apart, as are the characters. The music functions referentially to establish these separate worlds (well before we understand what is at issue); and indeed this is foregrounded at one point of the film when Castella thinks he has heard the beginning of Henri Salvador's 1966 hit 'Juanita Banana' in the tea-room, to the consternation of Clara, since it is in fact part of a Schubert piano sonata.

During the film, the characters have to confront their prejudices. Clara, who had initially despised Castella, develops affection for him. As the film progresses, the music swaps allegiance. Classical music follows a despondent Castella as he leaves the group of artists; and the jazz-rock, which had previously

---

[30]   I am grateful to Mark Brownrigg for these points.

[31]   'I would that my love' by Mendelssohn; 'Let us wander, not unseen', from Purcell's *The Indian Queen*; 'Spring is coming', from Handel's *Ottone*.

been used to suggest Castella's despondency, is heard over a series of shots whose ostensible purpose is to show Clara and Castella in their separate places of work, as Clara rehearses her new play, and Castella discusses the design he has commissioned from Clara's friends in his office. Because we hear the music insistently over the shots (dialogue is in the background), the effect is to bring them together, as is emphasized in the following scene when, as the same music is picked up after a pause, Clara tells her friend that she has invited Castella to the first night of the play, thus signalling her acceptance of his love for her.

The music in this film is particularly interesting, then, because through it we hear a fragmented community imagining integration before we see it articulated narratively. The final scene of the film shows the jilted chauffeur, who has been seen practising the flute on a number of occasions, leading a brass band into a rendering of Piaf's 'Je ne regrette rien'. Whereas in *La Haine*, the song might have suggested fragmentation as much as resistance, as we saw above, in *Le Goût des autres*, it signals not just closure, that is resolution of the many conflicts in the film, but also, most crucially, the coming together of a community reworking a traditional French song. 'Je ne regrette rien' carries on into the credits, but it is not the final music of the film. Halfway through the credits, the music changes to 'Au lait', associated in the film first with Castella, then with the bridging of the gap between Castella and Clara. It too then signals resolution and togetherness; French and American musical forms seem evenly balanced.

However, it is worth reflecting on the main musical contrast in the film: both the classical music and the jazz-rock are respectively English and American. The resolution of conflict is achieved with a traditional French song, but in most of the film the negotiation between conflicting classes in French society has been managed through Anglo-American music. We can contrast this structure with that of *On connaît la chanson*, also written by Bacri and Jaoui, and the sixth most popular French film of 1997. This was a homage to Dennis Potter, where the characters, again a microcosm of French society, occasionally mime specifically French songs ranging from the 1930s to the 1970s. Crucially, however, those songs are never sung in their entirety, remaining remembered snatches of song functioning as brief illustrations of the characters' inner feelings; and they do not work with the narrative in the same way as *Le Goût des autres*. Like Ozon's *8 Femmes*, where French pop songs from the 1960s onwards are sung in their entirety in a film more obviously presented as a musical, the songs are affectionate and nostalgic choruses, in the sense of the chorus in a Greek tragedy.

Conclusion

The study of *Le Goût des autres* suggests (although this remains to be confirmed by more empirical work), that, despite the success of *On connaît la chanson* and *8 Femmes,* many recent French films have been moving to an Anglo-American-dominated compilation score, and that this constitutes a new trend. This would be in the logic of the developments charted in this chapter, from an imagined French community brought together in epiphanic *chanson*, to the slow infiltration of American music which has occurred at the same time as French community has deteriorated (broadly since the early 1950s). The stages in that development, then, would be:

- an imagined French community in the period 1930–1945, dominated by *chanson* and French popular songs;
- the beginning of a period of tension between French and American musical forms in the period 1935–1985 as different forms of jazz, and then rock began to permeate scores;
- a momentary reaction to this musical trend of gradual Americanization in the1980s heritage film, with its emphasis on classical musical heritage;
- a renewal of the trend towards Americanization as hip hop was imported from the USA during the 1990s.

That said, all of the musical types discussed have to some extent Gallicized Anglo-American forms (as Cannon explains in the case of IAM in this volume), or 'contained' them, for example by inserting American-style pop songs (often sung in English) within an orchestral score by a French composer. Although such Gallicization is less the case for the modern jazz score (but then this type is statistically less important than the others), it is more the case for operetta, French swing, *yéyé*, postmodern compilations, and hip hop.

There are obviously dangers in the kind of broad sweep history sketched out here; after all, there may be so many exceptions as to invalidate the trends outlined. Nevertheless, it will be interesting to see in the next decade whether compilation scores show an increase in American or highly Americanized components at the expense of French popular forms.

Table 6.1   Appendix of films mentioned in Chapter 6

Title of film	Year	Director	Singer/composer	Audience figures
37° 2 le matin*	1986	Jean-Jacques Beineix	Gabriel Yared	3 632 326
8 Femmes	2002	François Ozon	Various pop	—
À bout de souffle	1959	Jean-Luc Godard	Martial Solal, Mozart	2 082 760
À la Jamaïque	1957	André Berthomieu	Luis Mariano, Francis López	2 661 091
À nous la liberté	1931	René Clair	Georges Auric	—
À toi de faire, mignonne	1963	Bernard Borderie	Paul Misraki	1 637 349
Amants du Pont-Neuf, Les	1991	Léos Carax	Various classical/rock	867 197
Amants, Les*	1958	Louis Malle	Alain de Rosnay, Brahms	2 594 452
Amarcord	1974	Federico Fellini	Nino Rota	1 104 520
American Graffiti	1974	George Lucas	Various (pop)	1 248 919
Amour et compagnie	1949	Gilles Grangier	Georges Guétary, Marius Coste, Johnny Heste	1 909 945
An American in Paris	1952	Vincent Minnelli	Georges Guétary, George Gershwin	3 027 240
Andalousie**	1951	Robert Vernay	Luis Mariano, Francis López	5 734 973
Antonia	1995	Marleen Gorris	Ilona Sekacz	—
Ascenseur pour l'echafaud	1958	Louis Malle	Miles Davis	1 902 036
Atlantis	1991	Luc Besson	Eric Serra	1 068 772
Belle de Cadix, La*	1953	Raymond Bernard	Luis Mariano, Francis López	4 328 273
Belle Equipe, La	1936	Julien Duvivier	Maurice Yvain	—
Belle meunière, La	1948	Marcel Pagnol	Tino Rossi, Vincent Scotto	1 696 120
Bilitis*	1977	David Hamilton	Francis Lai	1 437 155
Blanc comme neige*	1948	André Berthomieu	Etienne Lorin, Georges Van Parys	3 666 283
Blechtrommel, Die*	1979	Volker Schlöndorff	Maurice Jarre	1 959 414
Borsalino et Cie	1974	Jacques Deray	Claude Bolling	1 698 380
Borsalino*	1970	Jacques Deray	Claude Bolling	4 710 381
Boum, La**	1980	Claude Pinoteau	Vladimir Cosma	4 378 430
Boum 2, La*	1982	Claude Pinoteau	Vladimir Cosma	4 071 585
Camille Claudel*	1988	Bruno Nuttyens	Gabriel Yared	2 717 136

Table 6.1 (cont.)

Title of film	Year	Director	Singer/composer	Audience figures
Carmen	1983	Francesco Rosi	Georges Bizet	868 251
Carmen nue	1983	Albert Lopez	Georges Bizet	—
Cavalier noir, Le*	1945	Gilles Grangier	Georges Guétary, Francis López	3 672 572
Chanteur de Mexico, Le*	1956	Richard Pottier	Luis Mariano, Francis López	4 779 435
Chanteur inconnu, Le*	1947	André Cayatte	Tino Rossi, Vincent Scotto	3 623 739
Cherchez l'idole	1964	Michel Boisrond	Johnny Hallyday, Georges Garvarentz	1 602 426
Cinema Paradiso*	1989	Giuseppe Tornatore	Ennio Morricone	2 052 787
Colonel Chabert, Le*	1994	Yves Angelo	Various (all classical)	1 694 670
Comment qu'elle est!	1960	Bernard Borderie	Paul Misraki	2 104 417
Cousins, Les	1959	Claude Chabrol	Paul Misraki, Wagner	1 816 407
Crime de Monsieur Lange, Le	1936	Jean Renoir	Florelle, Jean Weiner	—
Cyrano de Bergerac*	1990	Jean-Paul Rappeneau	Jean-Claude Petit	4 732 136
D'où viens-tu Johnny?*	1963	Noël Howard	Johnny Hallyday, Eddie Vartan	2 785 185
Demoiselles de Rochefort, Les	1967	Jacques Demy	Legrand	1 319 432
Destins*	1946	Richard Pottier	Tino Rossi, Vincent Scotto	4 664 583
Deux amours*	1949	Richard Pottier	Tino Rossi, Vincent Scotto	2 668 955
Deux hommes à Manhattan	1959	Jean-Pierre Melville	Christian Chevalier, Martial Solal	308 524
Diabolo menthe*	1977	Diane Kurys	Various (pop)	3 013 638
Dien Bien Phu	1992	Pierre Schoendorffer	Georges Delerue	—
Diva*	1981	Jean-Jacques Beineix	Vladimir Cosma, Catalani	2 281 569
Doctor Zhivago*	1966	David Lean	Maurice Jarre	9 816 054
Dolce Vita, La*	1960	Federico Fellini	Nino Rota	2 934 425
Don Giovanni	1979	Joseph Losey	Mozart	1 055 012
Double vie de Véronique, La	1991	Krysztof Kieslowski	Preisner	592 241
Doulos, Le	1963	Jean-Pierre Melville	Martial Solal	1 475 391
Emmanuelle**	1974	Just Jaeckin Pierre	Bachelet, Francis Lai	8 893 996
Enfant sauvage, L'	1970	François Truffaut	Vivaldi	1 458 164
Enfants terribles, Les	1950	Jean-Pierre Melville	Vivaldi, Bach	719 844

Table 6.1 (cont.)

Title of film	Year	Director	Singer/composer	Audience figures
Feu follet, Le	1963	Louis Malle	Various jazz, Satie	495 431
Feux de joie	1938	Jacques Houssin	Paul Misraki, Ray Ventura	—
Fitzcarraldo	1982	Werner Herzog	Various operas, Popol Vuh	448 284
Flic Story*	1975	Jacques Deray	Claude Bolling	1 970 875
Fort Saganne*	1984	Alain Corneau	Philippe Sarde	2 157 767
Gardian, Le*	1946	Jean de Marguenat	Tino Rossi, Vincent Scotto	3 482 619
Goût des autres, Le*	1999	Agnès Jaoui	Various classical, Pat Metheny	3 800 000
Grand Bleu, Le**	1988	Luc Besson	Eric Serra	9 192 732
Grand jeu, Le	1933	Jacques Feyder	Hans Eisler	—
Haine, La*	1995	Mathieu Kassovitz	Édith Piaf, NTM	2 042 070
Ignace	1937	Pierre Colombier	Roger Dumas	—
Île d'amour, L'*	1945	Maurice Cam	Tino Rossi, Vincent Scotto	3 142 290
Jean de Florette**	1986	Claude Berri	Jean-Claude Petit, Verdi	7 223 657
Jo la romance	1948	Gilles Grangier	Georges Guétary	2 275 122
Jules et Jim	1962	François Truffaut	Georges Delerue	1 567 176
Lemmy pour les dames	1962	Bernard Borderie	Paul Misraki	1 655 548
Liaisons dangereuses, Les	1960	Roger Vadim	Thelonius Monk/Art Blakey	—
Lola	1961	Jacques Demy	Michel Legrand, Beethoven	616 114
Luna, La	1979	Bernardo Bertolucci	Verdi, Ennio Morricone	646 970
Mademoiselle s'amuse*	1948	Jean Boyer	Ray Ventura, Paul Misraki	2 994 210
Mademoiselle Swing	1941	Richard Pottier	Irène de Trébert, Raymond Legrand, Marc Lanjean	—
Manon des sources*	1986	Claude Berri	Jean-Claude Petit, Verdi	6 645 177
Mari de la coiffeuse, Le	1990	Patrice Leconte	Michael Nyman	356 980
Marinella	1935	Pierre Caron	Tino Rossi, Vincent Scotto	—
Mauvais sang	1986	Leos Carax	Various classical/rock	504 803
Mon Oncle*	1958	Jacques Tati	Barcellini, Romand	4 576 928
Monsieur Hire	1989	Patrice Leconte	Brahms	608 468

Table 6.1 (*cont.*)

Title of film	Year	Director	Singer/composer	Audience figures
Morte a Venezia	1971	Luchino Visconti	Mahler	1 427 833
Naples au baiser de feu	1936	Augusto Genina	Tino Rossi, Vincent Scotto	—
Nikita*	1990	Luc Besson	Eric Serra	3 787 845
Note bleue, La	1984	Andrzej Zulawski	Chopin, Bellini	—
Notre histoire	1984	Bertrand Blier	Martinu, Laurent Rossi	881 592
Nous irons à Monte-Carlo*	1952	Jean Boyer	Ray Ventura, Paul Misraki	3 348 795
Nous irons à Paris**	1950	Jean Boyer	Ray Ventura, Paul Misraki	6 658 693
Nuit américaine, La	1973	François Truffaut	Georges Delerue	827 665
Nuit du carrefour, La	1932	Jean Renoir	—	—
On connaît la chanson*	1997	Alain Resnais	Various pop	2 638 765
Opera sauvage	1979	—	Vangelis	—
Orfeu negro*	1959	Marcel Camus	Luiz Bonfa	3 690 517
Paris brule-t-il?*	1966	René Clément	Maurice Jarre	4 946 274
Paris chante toujours*	1952	Pierre Montazel	Tino Rossi, Vincent Scotto	3 144 242
Pépé le Moko	1937	Julien Duvivier	Vincent Scotto	—
Péril en la demeure	1985	Michel Deville	Schubert, Granados, Brahms	1 648 467
Phaedra	1962	Jules Dassin	Mikis Theodorakis	1 596 714
Playtime	1967	Jacques Tati	Francis Lemarque, James Campbell	1 227 699
Portes de la nuit, Les	1946	Marcel Carné	Jospeh Kosma	2 559 337
Postino, Il	1996	Radford Luis	Enriquez Bacalov	1 488 517
Pour un sou d'amour	1931	Jean Grémillon	André Baugé	—
Prénom: Carmen	1983	Jean-Luc Godard	Beethoven	395 462
Princesse Tam-Tam	1935	Edmond Gréville	Alain Romans	—
Providence	1977	Alain Resnais	Miklós Rózsa	652 985
Pulp Fiction*	1994	Quentin Tarantino	Various	2 820 011
Quatorze Juillet	1933	René Clair	Maurice Jaubert	—
Reine Margot, La*	1994	Patrice Chéreau	Goran Bregovic	1 979 412
Rendez-vous à Grenade	1952	Richard Pottier	Luis Mariano, Francis López	2 348 593

Table 6.1 (*cont.*)

Title of film	Year	Director	Singer/composer	Audience figures
Roi Pandore, Le	1949	André Berthomieu	Bruno Coquatrix, Etienne Lorin	—
Roman d'un jeune homme pauvre, Le	1935	Abel Gance	André Baugé	—
Ronde des heures, La	1930	Alexandre Ryder	André Baugé	—
Route enchantée, La	1938	Pierre Caron	Charles Trenet	—
Sait-on jamais	1957	Roger Vadim	Modern Jazz Quartet	1 510 505
Samouraï, Le*	1967	Jean-Pierre Melville	Martial Solal	1 932 372
Saturday Night Fever*	1978	John Badham	Various (pop)	4 361 587
Sérénade au Texas	1958	Richard Pottier	Luis Mariano, Franci López	2 555 768
Sérénade aux nuages*	1945	André Cayatte	Tino Rossi, Vincent Scotto	3 498 968
Singin' in the Rain	1953	Gene Kelly, Stanley Donen	Nacio Herb Brown, Lenny Hayton	1 448 145
Sous les toits de Paris	1930	René Clair	Raoul Moretti, R.Nazelles (songs)	—
Subway*	1985	Luc Besson	Eric Serra	2 920 588
Summer of '42	1971	Robert Mulligan	Michel Legrand	1 490 718
Symphonie fantastique, La	1942	Christian-Jaque	Berlioz	—
Taxi*	1998	Gérard Pirès	IAM	6 464 411
Thomas Crown Affair, The	1968	Norman Jewison	Legrand	802 633
Tontons flingueurs, Les*	1963	Georges Lautner	Michel Magne	3 321 121
Tourbillon de Paris	1939	Henri Diamant-Berger	Ray Ventura, Paul Misraki	—
Tous les matins du monde**	1991	Alain Corneau	Various Baroque	2 152 966
Traviata, La	1983	Franco Zeffirelli	Verdi	973 555
Trente et quarante	1945	Gilles Grangier	Georges Guétary	2 172 386
Tricheurs, Les*	1958	Marcel Carné	Various modern jazz	4 953 600
Trois hommes à abattre*	1980	Jacques Deray	Claude Bolling	2 194 795
Trop belle pour toi	1989	Bertrand Blier	Schubert, Francis Lai	2 031 131
Ultimo tango a Parigi*	1972	Bernardo Bertolucci	Gato Barbieri	5 150 995
Un amour de Swann	1984	Volker Schlöndorff	Hans Werner Henze	807 611

Table 6.1 (cont.)

Title of film	Year	Director	Singer/composer	Audience figures
Un condamné à mort s'est échappé	1956	Robert Bresson	Mozart	2 747 434
Un grand amour de Beethoven	1936	Abel Gance	Beethoven, Louis Masson	—
Un homme et une femme*	1966	Claude Lelouch	Michel Legrand	4 269 209
La Vie et rien d'autre	1989	Bertrand Tavernier	Oswald d'Andrea	1 507 708
Violettes impériales**	1952	Richard Pottier	Luis Mariano, Francis López	8 125 766
Voulez-vous danser avec moi?**	1959	Michel Boisrond	André Hodeir, Henri Crolla	3 196 005
Z*	1969	Constantin Costa-Gavras	Mikis Theodorakis	3 952 913
Zouzou	1934	Marc Allégret	Josephine Baker, Jean Gabin, Alain Romans, Vincent Scotto, George Van Parys	—

* Included in the top 20 films in France that year.

** The top-selling film in France for that year.

Chapter 7

Le Demy-monde:
the bewitched, betwixt and
between French musical

Robynn J. Stilwell

The pun is ubiquitous, almost obligatory, in the French literature on director Jacques Demy. 'Demy-monde' is so easy, yet more than just a catchphrase, for Demy created a style that, despite all his obvious influences, was distinctly his. He was of the Nouvelle Vague generation, yet never quite one of them. He, like them, admired Hollywood film-making, but his fascination with the highly artificial film musical also linked with his admiration of older European directors like Jean Cocteau and Max Ophüls to create a world of magic and opulence often in direct opposition to the studied realist-cool of the New Wave. The discourse of 'magic' and 'dream' surrounding Demy is as pervasive as the pun.[1]

'Demy-monde' carries with it connotations of twilight and shade, of alluring sin, of the hard, real exchange of sex and money that still does not preclude romance and love. But 'half' also implies a splitting that finds a profound resonance in Demy's work. Dualities scattered throughout the literature typically juxtapose beauty (magic/lyricism/love, accentuating their cinematic metonymy) with cruelty,[2] or the exotic with the everyday (sometimes making an implicit connection between beauty and the exotic, between the cruel and the everyday). Taboulay observes, 'Et le plus troublant c'est que le monde de Demy est à la fois en rupture et en continuité avec le nôtre' [Most worryingly, Demy's world is both divorced from and co-terminus with our own],[3] returning us to the concept of the Demy-monde, even with its internal contradictions, as something apart: his

---

[1]   See, for instance, the titles of the books by Berthomé, Jean-Pierre (1982), *Les Racines du Rêve* [The Roots of Dreams], Nantes: L'Atalante; and Taboulay, Camille (1996), *Le cinéma enchanté de Jacques Demy* [The Magic Cinema of Jacques Demy], Paris: Cahiers du cinéma – as the only two books on Demy, powerful determinants and/or reflections of such discourse – and the article by Toubiana, Serge (1982), 'Jacques Demy ou le retour au pays des rêves' [Jacques Demy and the return to the land of dreams], *Cahiers du Cinema*, 341, 5–13; they are far from the only examples, however – almost every French source in the bibliography contains at least one reference to magic or dream.

[2]   Less commonly, blood or perversion, particularly Demy's fascination with incest which appears in *Peau d'âne* (1970) and *Trois Places pour le 26* (1988).

[3]   Taboulay, *Le cinéma enchanté*, 50.

films 'étaient – et sont encore – autre chose, d'abord' [were – and are still – first of all, something else].[4]

Other dualities that emerge freqently include provincial/urban (Parisian), nostalgic/new, and particularly French/American. These concerns are not exclusive to Demy's films in mid-century France, but they are particularly pointed in his work, especially his two best-known films, *Les Parapluies de Cherbourg* (1964) and *Les Demoiselles de Rochefort* (1967). In this chapter, we will examine these two films in the contexts of their time – and their pasts – and the way that they highlight the close yet ambivalent ties between French and American musical and cinematic culture during the first half of the twentieth century.

A musical digression: French style with an American accent (and vice versa)

Michel Legrand was one of Jacques Demy's close coterie of collaborators, and his musical contributions are a significant marker of Demy's cinematic style. Legrand's musical style was distinctly French, but by mid-twentieth century, French musical language was deeply inflected with an American accent.

Throughout the century, France and America engaged in a musical dance characterized by advance and retreat, resistance and submission, parallel lines and occasional backtracks and crossovers. This tango helped define each nation musically, tracing its steps through all levels of musical life. Art music, jazz, and popular musics all participated, in an intricate interweaving pattern that crossed not only the Atlantic but stylistic and cultural borders (no matter how tightly these may have been policed).

At the turn of the twentieth century, French composers like Claude Debussy and Maurice Ravel were associated with the Impressionist painters because they were experimenting with timbre (tone colour) and rhythm, rather than line and form. This intersected with a vogue for exoticism that began with the World Exposition in Paris in 1889 and was further fuelled by the importation of the Ballets Russes beginning in 1909.

The impact of this Russian ballet troupe-in-exile is probably difficult to overestimate in the development of twentieth century music, dance, and even musicals (a topic to which we will return). Composers, artists, choreographers, and dancers of the highest rank collaborated on an unprecedented level of equality. The lush exoticism of the 1910s – encompassing orientalism, archaism, and primitivism, often in an indiscriminate mixture – gave way to the austere neo-classicism and the vivacious jazz-age chic of the 1920s.

During this period, America was just finding an international voice as a musical culture. After two generations educated in Germany, young art-music

---

[4]   Toubiana, 'Jacques Demy ou le retour au pays des rêves', 4.

composers began to go to Paris to study, drawn by the exciting atmosphere surrounding the Ballets Russes. Among them were Aaron Copland, Virgil Thomson, and Roy Harris, who would go on to establish a new, identifiable 'American' sound, one heavily influenced by the Franco-Russian style. But also during the 1920s, American popular music, from 'hot jazz' to dance band music to the Tin Pan Alley songwriters like Irving Berlin and George Gershwin, became exceedingly popular in France, in part because of its perceived links to the 'exotic' and 'primitive' already so popular. Jazz clarinettist/saxophonist Sidney Bechet spent a great deal of the 1920s in Paris, and a number of other African-American ex-patriates found France more welcoming than the US.[5] Beginning in 1925, Josephine Baker became the star of La Revue nègre and Les Folies Bergère, dancing nearly naked in a girdle of bananas, and with her unusual blend of the erotic and the eccentric, she would be one of the most popular performers in France for well over a decade. Songwriters Cole Porter and George Gershwin spent significant amounts of time in Paris, with Porter contributing *Within the Quota* to the Ballets Suédois (a company modelled on the Ballets Russes, which also premiered Darius Milhaud's jazz-inflected *Le Bœuf sur le toit* and *La Création du monde*) and Gershwin producing the tone poem *An American in Paris* only a few years after *Rhapsody in Blue* premiered at Carnegie Hall in New York – the first symphonic work recognized as incorporating jazz elements. Although music critics, then and now, hasten to point out the structural and orchestrational deficits of Gershwin's orchestral works, or the rhythmic stiffness of Milhaud's 'jazz', popular and art music were blending with unprecedented thoroughness and success; and at least among the French and Americans, there was an openness and respect for each other that transcended the erstwhile art/popular split.[6]

In post-war America, jazz began a transition from popular to art music. It moved away from dance-oriented swing to bebop and cool – jazz to be listened to, a music to be understood by the mind rather than the body, a music asserting itself as an art. Cool jazz in particular drew inspiration from the innovations of the French Impressionists: experiments in tone colour, use of extended chords, reliance on modes rather than traditional scales, with a dash of Igor Stravinsky's

[5]   Many of these artists found less racism in France, although when one looks at the depictions and descriptions, it becomes clear that the racism was simply of a different sort, perhaps less physically and emotionally violent but just as demeaning in many ways.

[6]   Legend has it that George Gershwin approached Maurice Ravel for composition lessons, but was turned down with the most gracious of refusals: 'You would just learn to write bad Ravel instead of good Gershwin.' Ravel's Piano Concerto in G of 1929 has distinct echoes of Gershwin (as does Aaron Copland's Piano Concerto of 1926, written while in Paris and pre-dating *An American in Paris* by only a year). Marjory Irvin cogently explored the extent to which George Gershwin's own personal voice (a blend of Yiddish and African-American traits) was equated with 'jazz' during this period. See Irvin, Marjory (1973), 'It's George, Not Jazz: Gershwin's Influence in Piano Music', *American Music Teacher*, 23, November–December, 31–34.

asymmetrical rhythms first introduced by the Ballets Russes. Darius Milhaud took a position teaching in the US, and among his students were cool jazz pianist Dave Brubeck and pop songwriter Burt Bacharach.

In post-war France, jazz was integrated into the popular chanson through gently swung and slightly syncopated rhythms (it was never as strikingly rhythmic as the American style), and also became part of the 'academic' line of art music. As American jazz incorporated impressionistic elements, rehybridizing became even easier. France is really the first country outside America in which jazz becomes an art music. Composers like Georges Delerue, Claude Bolling, and – importantly for our present task – Michel Legrand were educated at the Paris Conservatoire during the 1940s and 1950s, and the flowing, Gallic, 'chanson' jazz was part of their formal training, which they then carried to the genres of popular song, nightclub jazz, 'third-stream' art music,[7] and film scores.

So the relationship between music, dance, film music, and film musicals was particularly convoluted and interdependent between American and France. Boundaries between art music and jazz, even self-consciously 'arty' jazz and popular song were increasingly permeable and the national styles of each country were heavily marked by stylistic influences from the other.

Film musicals and national cinema

The musical was an internationally popular genre from the 1930s through the 1950s, and although almost all countries produced musicals, it was a genre that was seen as distinctly American, rivalled perhaps only by the Western in its iconic 'Americanness' – or perhaps more specifically, its 'Hollywoodness'. In the development of a national style of cinema outside Hollywood, the musical was always struggling to negotiate between the glamorous, technically proficient Hollywood model and the always distinct musical style of the home culture, a negotiation that seems especially loaded because of the double impact of cinematic style and musical style.[8]

The French musicals starring Josephine Baker in the 1930s, for instance, are an intriguing intermingling of American and French styles. *Princess Tam-Tam* (1935) is particularly convoluted. It demonstrates the strong influence of the most avant-garde American musicals of the time, the Warner Brothers musicals directed by Busby Berkeley (though one could also argue a French line from Berkeley back through the Ziegfeld Follies to the Folies Bergère). *Princess*

---

[7] 'Third-stream' music was a term coined by composer Gunther Schuller in the late 1950s to describe music which was neither 'art' nor 'jazz' but a combination of the two.
[8] See e.g. the section on European musical forms in Marshall, Bill, and Stilwell, Robynn (eds) (2000), *Musicals: Hollywood and Beyond*, Exeter: Intellect Books, particularly chapters by Bergfelder, Claus and Jäckel, and Papadimitriou.

Tam-Tam also exhibits the indiscriminate exoticism of the early Ballets Russes which had never quite disappeared in France: Tam-Tam (an Indonesian name) is really named Alwina (a name which could be Welsh or German); she is discovered in a backlot Africa that is part northern Arabic and part savannah; but the musical representation is Near Eastern; and her tartan dress with its oversized brooch looks suspiciously Caledonian.

In post-war Hollywood – at the same time jazz is becoming an art music and the great generation of Tin Pan Alley composers are reaching their crest and decline – the American film musical was reaching its peak with the famous Freed unit. The Freed unit musicals are usually seen as a subgenre within the musical, and even within the MGM musical, but there are really *two* quite distinct strains within the Freed unit – something that has perhaps been under-appreciated in the literature because of two tendencies: (1) to look at the Freed unit as a whole, particularly as collaborators continually recombine, and (2) to approach Vincente Minnelli as one of the prime 'auteurs' of the classical Hollywood era. This has blurred the distinction between the lush Romantic productions of Vincente Minnelli and the more neo-classical/modernist musicals made by the team of Donen and Kelly (who, as a team, do not fit neatly into the auteur paradigm).

Minnelli's aesthetic was clearly shaped, at least in part, by the ornate exoticist fantasies of the Ballets Russes' early years. This painterly eye was something Minnelli shared with Demy, who once commented 'Dans un musical il n'y a pas seulement les gens qui chantent, il y a aussi les couleurs' [In a musical there is colour, as well as just people singing].[9] Possibly the apotheosis of the American musical was the famous finale of *An American in Paris*, a 17-minute ballet which could easily have been a Ballets Russes production in tone and content.[10]

Most importantly, perhaps, for the musical as a genre, the idea of collaboration was respected and even celebrated. When asked later in his career, Gene Kelly was particularly adamant that the studio system was fundamental to the production of something as complicated as a musical.[11] Another way of seeing this collaborative infrastructure is as a production line, something which was infiltrating French culture during the 1950s and 1960s with a cachet of 'modernness' conflated with 'Americanness'.

The convoluted relationship between America and France is undoubtedly part of the reason that Minnelli and Kelly (and Donen) were so popular in France,

9   de Bechade, Chantal (1982), 'Éveiller le sentiment amoureux … Entretien avec Jacques Demy', *La Revue du cinéma*, 377, 26–27, 27.

10   Kelly even auditioned for and was accepted into the corps of the Ballets Russes de Monte Carlo (the remnants of the original company which relocated to Monte Carlo after Diaghilev's death in 1929). He decided, however, that he preferred dancing to Tin Pan Alley tunes and developing his own style of dancing. See Hirschhorn, Clive (1974), *Gene Kelly: A Biography*, London: W. H. Allen, 60.

11   Knox, Donald (1973), *The Magic Factory: How MGM Made* An American in Paris, New York: Praeger Publishers, 32, 205, *passim*; a sentiment echoed by others throughout.

even revered by the critics of *Cahiers du Cinema* and the directors of the French New Wave. The American musical was coming to an ignominious end by the time these directors were really beginning to make their mark, but the directors showed their admiration through homages which almost border on the postmodern in their referentiality – *Singin' in the Rain* in Truffaut's *Day for Night*; *An American in Paris* in Godard's *Une Femme est une Femme*.[12] But Jacques Demy goes deeper.

Demy's two films reflect the aesthetic dualities of the Freed-unit musicals: *Les Parapluies de Cherbourg* represents the Baroque[13] intensity of Vincente Minnelli (right down to the frenetic wallpaper), whereas *Les Demoiselles de Rochefort* has the chic neo-classical energy of a Kelly–Donen musical. These dualities can be seen as oppositions which not only delineate different priorities but accentuate the concessions that must be made in collaboration to allow artists with aesthetics so diametrically opposed as Kelly and Minnelli nevertheless to create imaginative musicals like *The Pirate* and *An American in Paris*.

Table 7.1   A comparison of aesthetic dualities

Minnelli	Kelly–Donen
Interior	Exterior
Singing	Dancing
Composition (stillness)	Energy (movement)
Ornate	Minimal
Deep, saturated colours	Pastels
Period	Modern
Les Parapluies de Cherbourg	*Les Demoiselles de Rochefort*

Briefly, let us look at the implications of these dualities. The most overriding of these is the interior/exterior split, which orders all the others, not just physically but psychologically. Kelly and Donen's insistence upon shooting on location in *On the Town* is perhaps the most famous manifestation, but Kelly–Donen films have a much larger proportion of 'exteriors' even on the backlot, best represented in the typical Kelly street dance. One of the main points of tension between Kelly and Minnelli in the production of *Brigadoon* (1954) was whether they should shoot on location (Kelly's position) or on a soundstage

---

[12]   Godard even wanted to collaborate with Kelly on a musical, but his improvisational style did not mesh with the kind of preparation Kelly knew was important for a musical. See Hirschhorn, *Gene Kelly: A Biography*, 269.

[13]   Johnson, William (1996), 'More Demy: In Praise of The Young Girls of Rochefort,' *Film Comment*, **32** (5), September–October, 72–76, 72, proposes that the move from Cherbourg to Rochefort was 'classical' to 'Baroque', but in terms of musical and visual style, the opposite certainly holds true.

(Minnelli's). With the studio's backing, and the pressure of a cheaper shoot when musicals were not performing well at the box office, Minnelli won. *Brigadoon*, with its central juxtaposition of the magical and the modern/ordinary was, not surprisingly, Demy's favourite.

If one examines Minnelli's musicals *without* Kelly or Fred Astaire in the lead, they are strikingly lacking in dance sequences. The party scene in *Meet Me in St Louis* is one of the few exceptions, and that is relatively contained. Most surprisingly (shockingly?), even with Leslie Caron in the lead, there are no dance scenes in *Gigi* (1957). This difference can also be seen more subtly in expression; singing is often more introspection (an 'internal' process) than dancing, which is demonstrative and external.[14]

Likewise relating to the interior/exterior, introspection/expression dichotomy, Minnelli's mise-en-scène is – not surprisingly for a designer – often and obviously highly constructed and artificial, whereas Kelly–Donen's is light and sketchy – compare the famously parallel introductions of Ivy in *On the Town* with Lise in *An American in Paris*. Lise is literally framed in ornate gilt frames and performs on almost full sets with distinct costumes delineating her character; Ivy is in cream shorts and sweater (later a bronze evening gown/tutu) against a pale yellow cyclorama, with only minimal props to establish locations (the ironing board, the easel, the barre). This disparity gives the eye something to do when singing is to the fore; or it clears space when movement is the primary attraction.

The time aspect flows from this. A period film is a look back to a moment preserved in time, still, enclosed. A modern film is one in movement towards an unknown future.

Demy's two films play out these dualities.

Les Parapluies de Cherbourg

Les Parapluies de Cherbourg holds quite a particular position in French film culture. One of the most well-known musicals of the 1960s, it is the only French musical to be internationally successful to such a degree, and probably the only non-English-language musical that could be considered part of the generic canon. It also became the springboard for Michel Legrand's emergence as an international film composer. It is therefore important as an export item; but it also has significance as an internal representation of French culture.

Lindeperg and Marshall have analysed the ways in which *Parapluies* embodies – and to some extent critiques – Kristin Ross's influential analysis of changing French culture at mid-century, particularly the emphasis on the

---

14   Possible exceptions would be Kelly's 'Alter Ego' dance in *Cover Girl* (1944) or 'Once Upon a Time (Up in Smoke)' from *It's Always Fair Weather* (1955), both of which use extraordinary technical innovation to externalize internal conflict.

formation of the heterosexual couple as a site of consumerism, the shift from family mercantile to 'Americanized' corporate structures, and the prioritization of the car as a site of both liberation and 'immobile time'.[15] Time is the focus of Lindeperg and Marshall's analysis, and without contradicting them, I would like to accentuate some elements of Ross's theory slightly differently to explain why the choice of the musical genre – at a time when it was dying out in America – became suddenly so pertinent in commenting on French society.

The production line that produces the prized commodity of the car also produces Hollywood films, as Ross briefly alludes: 'in the late 1950s young French film directors and moviegoers alike tended to prefer the American product, produced and distributed with assembly-line regularity in tight little genres.'[16] And no genre was so dependent upon the studio's production-line resources as the very American musical. Perhaps not coincidently, Donald Knox's industrial oral history of the studio system tracing the production of *An American in Paris* was entitled *The Magic Factory*, juxtaposing the fantastic world of the musical with the prosaic, repetitive world of the assembly line.

Narratively, the musical deeply enshrined another prominent element of Ross's cultural critique – the formation of the heterosexual couple. Rick Altman's seminal genre study *The American Film Musical* takes that as the central determining factor for the organization of all other generic features. Therefore no other genre was as well placed to comment upon the issue of coupling.

Parapluies takes these modernizing, Americanizing elements and fuses them into the framework of a retrospective French one, Bizet's *Carmen*.[17] Like the musical, *Carmen* is a 'breakout' French opera, the only one to hold such a significant place in the canon and yet something which is not wholly 'French'.

Demy tips his hand to *Carmen* in the opening scene, when Guy announces to his fellow mechanics that he and Geneviève are going to see the opera that evening; his friend expresses his preference for the movies not once, but twice, implicitly setting up some sort of parallel (or competition) between the two forms. But *Carmen* is more than just a bit of local colour; the plot of *Parapluies* can be seen as an updating – somewhat de-sensationalized[18] – of this most

---

[15]   Lindeperg, Sylvie, and Marshall, Bill (2000), 'Time, History and Memory in *Les Parapluies de Cherbourg*', in Marshall and Stilwell (eds), *Musicals: Hollywood and Beyond*, 98–106; Ross, Kristin (1995), *Fast Cars, Clean Bodies: Decolonization and the Reordering of French Culture*, London: October Books.

[16]   Ibid., 46.

[17]   Taboulay, *Le cinéma enchanté de Jacques Demy*, 19, notes that Carlo Ponti had approached Demy in 1960 to produce a modern *Carmen*, although she does not make the connection between *Carmen* and *Les Parapluies de Cherbourg*. The brief sketch of Ponti's proposed modernization does not, however, resemble the future film.

[18]   Ross, *Fast Cars*, discusses the ambiguity towards coupling in the novels of the period, both a desire for and a fear of the 'levelling' effect of becoming a consuming couple.

popular of French operas. Guy and José are both young men torn between love and military service (José has a harder time fulfilling his national duty, but then *Carmen* is set in a time without a specific military threat, whereas Guy is clearly situated within the context of the Algerian conflict); both Carmen and Geneviève have jobs outside the home and are sexually active (Geneviève is certainly not as sexually predatory as Carmen, but in the context of the time, the fact that she does 'go all the way' is scandalous); both Carmen and Geneviève go off with a wealthier beau in their lovers' absence (though Geneviève does it more for security, they are both drawn primarily by the promise of money); and the character who clinches the parallel, Micaela/Madeleine, the sweet, wholesome young woman who tends the hero's ailing mother-figure and who figures as José/Guy's marriageable mate.

Why refer to *Carmen*? Historically, the idea of a young man torn away from love by military duty was certainly apt. But culturally, it was also a means for Demy to make connections both with French musical culture and the Hollywood musical through Minnelli's extravagant stylization. *Carmen* was a product of a similar impulse towards the exotic and the flamboyant, and there is more than a little irony in this most successful of French operas actually being about Spain – albeit a colourful imagination of Spain rather than the real thing.

Ross's concept of 'immobile' time features, too, in the contiguity of these two tales frozen in time, for *Parapluies* was always a period piece, wedded to its historical moment even when time moved on. This immobility is reflected in space as well.

For a genre so associated with spectacle as the musical, *Les Parapluies de Cherbourg* – like Minnelli's *Meet Me in St Louis* or *Gigi* – is a remarkably static and interior spectacle, intensified by the prevalence of interior shots and the through-sung score.[19] The visual spectacle is constructed from the deeply saturated colour scheme, and the ornate artificiality of the shot composition. Both of these are well demonstrated by the shot when Guy takes Geneviève home and they kiss at the wrought-iron gate, which divides the screen in half; one side is violet the other pea-green, the walls and doorways creating strong diagonals. The stifling quality of these hectic compositions is nowhere better represented than when a tired, sad, and heavily pregnant Geneviève takes off her coat to reveal that her dress exactly matches her wallpaper – she literally blends into the wall. Her trip on the moving sidewalk with Guy is perhaps the only example of freedom of movement in the entire film, though even that is tinged with regret. Another rare exterior – and, one would have thought, an excellent opportunity for spectacle – is the carnival scene, but it is brief, contained in the narrow street and seen mostly through the windows; it is another example of

---

[19] Ironically, Bizet's *Carmen* was an *opéra-comique*, with spoken dialogue like a musical; some months after its 1875 debut it was 'retrofitted' with recitatives to make it more saleable to other nations whose expectations were for operas sung in their entirety.

Geneviève being trapped or stifled as she struggles 'upstream', escaping once more into the confines of the shop.

This claustrophobic visual composition is complemented admirably by Legrand's flowing, narrow-gauge melodies, well suited to the cadences of spoken French and making the sung dialogue possibly less obtrusive than it would seem in an English or German-language film (and to a foreign-language audience dependent upon subtitles would probably seem even less artificial). The overwhelming pressure of recitative-like melody, brilliant colour, and interior stillness highlights the emotional centrepiece, the classic 'Hollywood' goodbye at the train station. Suddenly we are outside under an overcast sky, almost all colour drained away, and the melody breaks free of its constraints.

'J'attendrai' (known in English as 'If it takes forever') is the most famous song from the score, and the most melodically distinctive. Legrand's expansive tune ranges over a far wider span than any other tune in the score (indeed most popular tunes) and is based on appoggiaturas intensified by altered tones.[20] This gives immediacy to the relationship between Guy and Geneviève (echoing later in the film when Guy returns to the platform café and when they meet in the epilogue at his petrol station). It exemplifies what Michel Chion terms 'added value'[21] − it gives an epic sweep to a relationship which, if one were only observing the action onscreen, could be seen as little more than an adolescent infatuation.

The melodic intensity of 'J'attendrai' musically underscores the narrative ambivalence of *Les Parapluies de Cherbourg*. Is Guy and Geneviève's passion as grand as the music suggests? Unlike the lovers in a Hollywood musical, where a happy ending is a foregone conclusion, or a tragic opera, in which one or both of the lovers is destined to die, they are adolescents and they fancy themselves in love, but when the reality of military duty and motherhood intrude, they have to make practical decisions. Geneviève regrets not marrying Guy, but she is not

---

[20]   The appoggiatura – a dissonant note that resolves downward – has a very long association in Western music with longing (the main theme of Tchaikovsky's *Romeo and Juliet Overture* is another good example), and Legrand has heightened the effect by leading to the appoggiatura with a sharpened escape-note figure – what this means is that the dissonant note is initially raised (a move that increases anxiety), released upward (the wrong direction) and then flattened (we're back to the original note, but it 'feels' even more depressed than it normally would) before being resolved. The appoggiatura is exaggerated by the cross-relation of the sharp version, and the melody continues with a drop that then leads to a repetition of the opening figure at a higher pitch. All of this means that the emotive association of the appoggiatura is greatly intensified.

[21]   'Added value: the expressive and informative value with which a sound enriches a given image so as to create the definite impression, in the immediate or remembered experience one has of it, that this information or expression 'naturally' comes from what is seen, and is already contained in the image itself. Added value is what gives the (eminently incorrect) impression that sound is unnecessary, that sound merely duplicates a meaning which in reality it brings about, either all on its own or by discrepancies between it and the image.' (Chion, Michel (1994), *Audio+ Vision: Sound on Screen*, ed. and trans. Claudia Gorbman, New York: Columbia University Press, 5.)

noticeably distraught about it, and seems more embarrassed than agonized at their later meeting; Guy seems positively happy with Madeleine and their son. Even as a bittersweet ending, it seems to question the dramatic conventions of doomed lovers *or* a happy coupling.

Dance interlude: Paris/New York/Hollywood/Rochefort

While *Parapluies* appropriately marries a Minnelli aesthetic to a sung source, *Les Demoiselles de Rochefort* has an even more intimate connection to the Kelly–Donen dance aesthetic. The line starts in 1925 with a Ballets Russes production, *Les Matelots*, about three sailors on leave on the Côte d'Azur. It was one of the fleet, chic ballets of the late period, with music by Georges Auric, one of the bright young things of jazzy French academic music, who would later be most prominent as a film composer. In 1944, Jerome Robbins combined classical ballet with Latin dance and street-wise behaviour in the Ballet Theatre production, *Fancy Free*, about three sailors on leave in New York City. Leonard Bernstein's score blended the astringent Franco-Russian neo-classical style, which had fused with American hymnody and Irish folk song (among other influences) to create the new Americana style, and Bernstein added a new infusion of hot swing. The success of this ballet was so great that Bernstein and Robbins, along with writers Betty Comden and Adolph Green,[22] transformed it into a hit Broadway musical *On the Town* (1945). In 1949, Gene Kelly and Stanley Donen took the show to the streets of New York for their seminal film musical version. MGM did not like Bernstein's music and jettisoned most of the songs – but significantly retained the ballet music for the dances by Kelly. Comden and Green, Kelly and Donen would also produce *It's Always Fair Weather* (1955), a semi-sequel with music by French-American composer André Previn (a classical conductor with 'serious jazz chops'). Robbins and Bernstein also collaborated on *West Side Story* (Broadway production (1957) and film (1961)), the latter of which showed the clear influence of the Kelly–Donen shooting style in the dance sequences and featured a star-making performance by George Chakiris. In 1960, Kelly staged a ballet, *Pas de Dieux*, for the Paris Opéra-Ballet. The ballet, set to the Gershwin Piano Concerto in F (also used in *An American in Paris*) blended war chariots descending from the heavens (emblematic of the theatrical machinery of the Baroque French ballet tradition[23]) and modern street lights, perhaps the visual equivalent of the musical car horns

---

[22] Comden and Green also wrote the screenplays for *Singin' in the Rain* (1952) and *The Band Wagon* (1953).

[23] This iconic image was also exploited in the Ballets Russes's neo-classical *Apollo* (1928), with score by Igor Stravinsky and choreography by George Balanchine, who would later create the lean, athletic American style of classical ballet that formed the basis of Robbins's style.

in Gershwin's score of *An American in Paris*. The line is unbroken, if highly convoluted.

Les Demoiselles de Rochefort

Demoiselles is even more emphatic than *Parapluies* as an homage to the Hollywood musical, clearly in the dance lineage outlined above, thematically, stylistically, and even in casting. A film starring Gene Kelly and George Chakiris with a tight timeline (a weekend), a sailor on leave, and a touring company of players overdetermines the association with the energetic, movement-oriented Kelly–Donen musical. The pastel colour scheme (Demy had the town repainted in ice-cream colours for the shoot), the concentration on exteriors shot in the clean lines and open square of the town's architecture, and the three intertwining plots resemble no Hollywood musical more than *On the Town*.[24]

But Demy is not merely copying the Hollywood format; he comments upon the generic traits of couple-formation – what Rick Altman (two decades later, in 1987) termed the 'dual-focus narrative': non-linear, it alternates between the two leads, showing them in gender-defined scenes that nonetheless demonstrate how they are destined to be together without a traditional chain of cause and effect. Demy took this idea, tripled it, and deployed it along the timeline, perhaps reflecting another aspect of Ross's 'immobile time'.

We are given three couples. Yvonne (Danielle Darrieux) and Simon (Michel Piccoli) are middle-aged, experienced, without illusion but also with tenderness and an appreciation of what love can offer. Delphine (Catherine Deneuve) and Maxence (Jacques Perrin) are youthful, pretty, and wildly romantic (even a little superficial). Solange (Françoise Dorleac) and Andy (Gene Kelly) balance the sensitive older man with the passionate younger woman. Only this last couple is played out on a normal time line, with their meeting occuring halfway through, brought together by a child (the twins' little brother Boubou) to echo many a Gene Kelly film associating him with children; they do not realize just how fated they are until the end, however. Yvonne and Simon's coupling is retrospective: they have already met, fallen in love, produced a child, and parted – over a silly prejudice against his surname (either contrived or fairy-tale-like, depending upon your view). We see them separately describing their affair, knowing that each is talking about the other with regret and longing but we know that *they* do not yet know they are living in the same town; again, their actual remeeting occurs at the end. Delphine and Maxence's pairing is *pro*spective: they too are introduced in dual-focus fashion

---

[24]   This is not the only 1960s musical which bears more than a passing resemblance to *On the Town*, as the 24-hour timeline, the breaking up and reformation of the core group, and the headlong rush to the final show with the police in hot pursuit is also found in *A Hard Day's Night* (Richard Lester, 1964).

(he has painted a portrait of his 'ideal' which looks just like her although they have never met; she describes her ideal, which fits him exactly), but they do not actually *ever* meet within the film. We know that their meeting is inevitable as Maxence climbs into the lorry at the end, not only because Delphine is there but because the dual-focus narrative has so emphatically conditioned us to expect it.

Each of the couples is musically reinforced. Each has a tune, sung individually, separately, about each other – this musical pairing is most clear in the Yvonne/Simon and Delphine/Maxence pairings (the ones we do not really see on screen together). The Andy/Solange pairing is less parallel but more musically meaningful: they are represented by the tune of her 'concerto', which she plays for Simon Dame and then drops at the scene of her meeting with Andy like Cinderella's slipper. Andy picks it up and reads it, internalizing it to the point that when he sings his song to Simon – relating his life, how he has changed since they first met, and what he is looking for in life – it is all to Solange's tune (even though Dame does not recognize it until Andy plays it in full concerto mode at the piano – not very perceptive for a musician!).

Yet as satisfying as this structure might be for the three couples, it quite prominently leaves out two of the leads, Etienne (George Chakiris) and Bill (Grover Dale), the leaders of the travelling motor show – young, handsome, brilliant dancers who are the first characters introduced, woven throughout the entire film, perform a significant dance routine with the twins, and ask them to be in their show – in classical musical terms, usually a clear sign of Romantic destiny. Indeed, after the show, Etienne and Bill express their love (or at least desire) for the twins, who refuse them, even though they have not yet been united with their destined mates. In the complicated structure of the film, Demy sets up conflicting narrative drives – the dual-focus and the 'let's put on a show', and in the end, the dual-focus wins out.

The intertwining of the various strands also gives the film the distinctly French flavour of farce, particularly in the last section, with all the near-miss meetings of Delphine and Maxence, the mixed meetings (Andy with Delphine, Maxence with Solange), and the contrived final meetings of Yvonne and Simon (at Boubou's school) and Andy and Solange (at the music shop). The gruesome ax-murder is narratively the result of a pairing that won't fall into place (she kept refusing him), but stylistically perhaps a nod towards the very French grand guignol. Some of the traits of *Demoiselles* (particularly the exaggerated 'romantic' touches in the Andy/Solange relationship) teeter on the verge of parody – as indeed, they may well be. At times, the references have an almost postmodern, de-centring quality.[25]

In *Les Demoiselles de Rochefort*, the dominance of exteriors is as important as the interiors are to *Les Parapluies de Cherbourg*. Even the 'interiors' in the

---

[25] Several authors, most notably Mesnil, Michel (1991), 'Demy ou le génie du lieu', *Esprit*, 1, 31–36, speak of Demy's detachment.

film – the chip shop, the dance studio, the music store – are light, open spaces with large windows, bringing the outdoors inside. This homage to the street dances of the Kelly–Robbins line includes some direct quotations: the opening gestures of Andy and Solange's pas de deux in the music shop are lifted from 'Our Love is Here to Stay' on the banks of the Seine in *An American in Paris* (the earlier film's teasing attitude towards modern art is also echoed in *Demoiselles*); Kelly dances briefly with two American sailors who appear on the street; and the montage near the end, interweaving all the major characters singing their own 'signature' tunes, clearly harks back to the 'Quintet' in *West Side Story*. But this homage to the dancing musical also results in a cultural/stylistic dissonance. Legrand's melodies are more 'song-like' than in *Parapluies* (less recitative-like), but they are still very 'French' – flowing rhythms with only the most localized and gentle of syncopations, and conjunct, narrow motion. None of the songs has the kind of reaching melodic leaps that 'J'attendrai' does, and in those that do, the leaps are 'easy' leaps for singers: they are within the chord (so none of the dissonant intervals that can be found in Leonard Bernstein's songs like 'Cool'[26]) and fall in parallel lines, rather than chaining upward (as in 'New York, New York'). While these features make the songs easy to sing, it also robs them of the particular energy that comes from extended syncopations, asymmetrical rhythms, and dissonant intervals. Yet these latter features are those which energize – and indeed, engender – the expansive choreographic styles of Kelly and Robbins.

Demoiselles was choreographed by an obscure young choreographer Norman Maen,[27] whose only other credit appears to be a 1970 Val Doonican television series in Britain. He borrows from the Kelly/Robbins style, though, unimaginatively, and the dancers, other than the leads, were imported from England. The dance style does not sit particularly well on them: their rhythmic sense is fairly 'square' and they do not fill up space in the same way as the American leads.

This dissonance has not gone unnoticed by critics, even if they cannot quite put a finger on the problem. American William Johnson termed the dancing 'energetic but generally uninspired',[28] and Frenchman Jean-Pierre Berthomé says the choreography 'désappointent nos espérances'.[29] It is unusual that the only references to the dancing in a musical are politely derogatory; it is almost as if the criticism couldn't *not* be said. Both writers also exempt Kelly, who choreographed his own dances. Even at 55 years old, Kelly is still a graceful,

---

[26]   The songs of *West Side Story* are fiendishly difficult to sing. Almost every song features a nasty upward interval, including the tritone ('Maria', 'Cool') and the minor 7th ('Somewhere').

[27]   This name would seem to be a pseudonym, a kind of 'camp' respelling of Norman Main, the male lead of *A Star is Born*.

[28]   Johnson, 'More Demy', 76.

[29]   Berthomé, Jean-Pierre (1982), *Les Racines du Rêve*, Nantes: L'Atalante, 84.

powerful dancer (Johnson bemusedly notes 'he looks too old for the energy he displays'). Just as prominently, the other two Americans, Dale and Chakiris (technically and musically, one of the best dancers in the entire history of Hollywood musicals), continually threaten to overpower their 'disappointing' choreography and Legrand's narrow-gauge flowing music.

Les Demoiselles de Rochefort, despite its popularity within France and despite its obvious homage to American musicals, was never as successful outside France as *Les Parapluies de Cherbourg*. In a tribute to the later film, Johnson remarks that its 'hybrid nature, part French, part American, may have cost it popularity on both sides of the Atlantic'.[30] As he also points out, its American release in April 1968 was hardly the best timing for such a confection. Something else the French and Americans had in common – Vietnam – was at the top of the national agenda.

Conclusion

Demy's musicals are distinctly French, and his regionalistic spotlighting of cities and regions outside Paris certainly would have helped widen the horizons of foreign audiences – the depiction of Rochefort is particularly appealing (although, to be fair, all we really see of Cherbourg is a petrol station in the snow). Yet the films are also quite clearly reminiscent of Hollywood musicals. They are not imitations, the way, say, *Princess Tam-Tam* can seem; Demy is knowing about his borrowings, to the point of making distinctions between the Minnelli and Kelly–Donen subgenres of the MGM musical – something which is not always distinct even in scholarship today – and making sophisticated play of the dual-focus narrative. In the schematic way in which Demy plays the Minnelli aesthetic against the Kelly–Donen one, it is even possible to see the two films as a dual-focus commentary on the Hollywood musical.

But the key relationship between France and America, the nostalgic and the new, is a fraught one, even in these two films. The ambivalent narrative of coupling in *Parapluies* is bolstered by an equally ambivalent subtext about the commercial change and modernization (Americanization) going on in the film, where the specialized umbrella shop is taken over by a modern appliance store, yet Guy's freedom from the tyranny of the local garage-owner is found in the proud ownership of a shiny new Esso franchise. And what of the peculiar marginalization of Etienne and Bill in *Demoiselles*? Is it coincidental that they are the most American, in their manners and movement, in their association with the traveling motor show? The appeal of modernization and movement is youthful and vigorous: for all the joyousness of Rochefort, it is to Paris that all the younger characters follow their dreams. Only the older generation, Yvonne

---

[30]　Johnson (1996), 'More Demy', 76.

and Simon, stay in Rochefort. Once again, Andy and Solange represent a conflicted middle ground. Andy is of the older generation, coded as more European than Etienne or Bill by virtue of his French education and his old-world career as a concert pianist (he most emphatically *isn't* a rock star); but despite his age, he is filled with the youthful vigour and romantic passion associated with America.

Britain's Gilbert Adair sighs, 'Alas, Demy does not travel well'.[31] Conversely, Michel Mesnil says Demy has a

certain exotisme culturel mal cerné par nous Français, mais immédiatement sensible pour l'étranger qui aime en nous, avant les traces d'un éventuel génie, le fait que nous lui paraissons tellement et si délicieusement *autres*. Un tel charme venu d'ailleurs n'est toutefois pas accessible seulement à l'extérieur des frontières. Il suffit, pour le percevoir, de se mettre un instant à distance de cette mère patrie.

[kind of cultural exoticism grasped badly by we French, but immediately noticeable by foreigners who love us, not for any possible genius, but for the fact that we seem quite and so deliciously *other*. Such charm from elsewhere is however not solely to be perceived from beyond national frontiers. All that's needed to be aware of it is to distance oneself for an instant from the mother country.][32]

Ironically, the Demy-monde is ambivalent enough that both are true.

---

[31]   Adair, Gilbert (1983), 'Racine of Dreams (review)', *Sight and Sound*, **52** (2), 144.
[32]   Mesnil, 'Demy ou le génie du lieu', 36; italics original.

Chapter 8

Chanson engagée and political activism in the 1950s and 1960s: Léo Ferré and Georges Brassens

Chris Tinker

One of the defining qualities of French *chanson* throughout its long history has been its capacity to explore a multiplicity of social as well as personal identities. Léo Ferré and Georges Brassens, two major *auteurs-compositeurs-interprètes* (singer-songwriters) who epitomized the golden era of French popular song during the 1950s and 1960s, added to growing oppositional discourses in France, both through the medium of song and in their various media appearances. Following broadly in the tradition of the *chansonnier*, the cabaret artist specializing in political and social satire, they expressed resistance to bourgeois power and domination, particularly the Catholic Church and the French state. Ferré and Brassens also took an overtly anti-nationalist stance in their songwriting, making a significant contribution to continuing debates around French national identities. They were indeed writing during a period which saw France's economic and social reconstruction, following her crushing defeat at the hands of Nazi Germany, as well as her post-war decline as a colonial power, brought sharply into focus by the Algerian war. Using Ferré and Brassens as key examples, this chapter will provide an overview of the main social and political issues explored in post-war French *chanson*. Moreover, it will situate their work within the context of intellectual and political debates taking place in France at the time, asking how far their social commitment extends, and whether it is at all possible, or even desirable, to follow words with actions.

For the intellectual and artistic left in France, the bourgeoisie have long represented the 'archetypal demon'.[1] Ferré in particular continued a well-established French tradition of undermining the middle classes,[2] providing unflattering, satirical portraits of individual characters or social groups, a technique reminiscent of that practised in the nineteenth century by realist

---

[1]   See Forbes, J., and Kelly, M. (eds), *French Cultural Studies: an introduction*, Oxford: Oxford University Press, 1995, 3–4.
[2]   The nearest Brassens comes to a critique of the bourgeoisie is the unsympathetic representation in 'Les Croquants' (1956), a song which asserts aphoristically that money is the root of all evil.

novelists such as Balzac and Flaubert, naturalists such as Zola, or earlier singer-songwriters such as Gustave Nadaud.[3] Ferré's 'Les Rupins' [The well-off][4] (1960) characterizes the contemporary bourgeoisie by its obsession with money, highlighting the empty values of materialism, consumerism, triviality, and frivolity. The narrator is so disillusioned and pessimistic that he questions the validity, power and efficacy of the French Republican ideals of *liberté, égalité and fraternité*, which have lost their original meaning and substance. Ferré's satirical critique of the bourgeoisie additionally takes on a specifically Parisian dimension. Although fascinated with Paris, he regards the Parisian middle classes as ignorant, dismissing them in 'Les Parisiens' [The Parisians] (1961) as 'pharisiens'.[5] They may lead cosmopolitan lifestyles, but are nonetheless represented as short-sighted, self-centred, and parochial, if not xenophobic. While these 'others' – individuals and groups – are identified as partially responsible for maintaining bourgeois values and aspirations, Ferré also singles out for criticism many of the social institutions which exercise power over the individual through ideological and/or physical force.

As traditional bourgeois notions of the family and the authority of the Catholic Church became increasingly challenged in the post-war period, particularly during the growing secularization and liberalization of the 1960s, it is appropriate that these two institutions are identified by the singer-songwriters as repressive forces. Ferré's narrator focuses in 'Monsieur Tout-blanc' [Mister Whiter-than-white] (1950) on the Catholic Church and Pope Pius XII at a time when they came under increasing scrutiny for their role during the Occupation. 'Monsieur Tout-blanc' proves indeed how the Church can elicit strong feelings from an idealistic and relatively young singer-songwriter such as Ferré.[6] Although such anti-clericalism expressed in popular music could be considered audacious, the Catholic Church was a relatively safe target since it had undergone a steady decline in influence, particularly since the end of the Second World War. Moreover, the secular state had usurped and sapped much of the power and dominance once maintained by the Catholic Church, particularly since its separation from the French state in 1905. It is for this reason that any challenge to the authority of the Gaullist state was potentially much more

---

[3]   For further discusssion of Nadaud, see Robine, M. (1994), *Anthologie de la chanson française: Des trouvères aux grands auteurs du dix-neuvième siècle*, Paris: Albin Michel, 757–830.

[4]   Wherever possible in this chapter, I have used the English translations of song titles provided in Hawkins, P. (2000), *Chanson: the French Singer-Songwriter from Aristide Bruant to the Present Day*, Aldershot: Ashgate. Otherwise, the translation provided is my own.

[5]   An example is to be found in the live recording in *Thank you Satan en public à l'Alhambra 1961*, Barclay 841-262-2.

[6]   For further examples of anti-clericalism in post-war *chanson*, see Brassens's 'Le Mécréant' (1960) and 'Les Quatre bacheliers' (1966), and Jacques Brel's 'Grand Jacques' (1955), 'Les Flamandes' (1959) and 'Ces gens-là' (1966).

subversive, particularly during the social upheaval of the 1960s. Representing the French political system in scatological terms, Ferré's 'Salut Beatnik!' [Hi beatnik!] (1967) views politicians of all political hues as insincere and ineffectual. Furthermore, the French trade unions are dismissed simply as a joke. Their ineffectual brand of Marxism is not derived from the father of communism, Karl Marx, but rather from the comic film stars, the Marx Brothers.

Ferré also focused on the institutions of the Gaullist state around which many areas of French life were organized. Written in the aftermath of the 'events' of May 1968, 'Paris je ne t'aime plus' [Paris I love you no more] (1970) laments the state of the French universities which had become overcrowded and antiquated. Another state-run source of education and information targeted by Ferré is French radio and television. The *paysage audiovisuel français* is found wanting in several respects, not least of all because Ferré and his songs were the victims of censorship. The performance of songs on radio and television was just one of several areas of cultural and artistic production in France which were subject to heavy-handed, Gaullist state censorship during the 1950s and 1960s.[7] The national broadcasting authority, the RTF (Radiodiffusion-Télévision Française), and its successor, the ORTF (Office de Radiodiffusion-Télévision Française), along with Ministry of Information and the *Enarques*, high-ranking civil servants, would ultimately determine the amount of air time granted to potential enemies of the state. Almost half of Brassens's songs between 1952 and 1964 were banned from the airwaves by the RTF for their content, either because they attacked the police and the judiciary, or because they were considered indecent. Although state-run television, which took off in France during the 1960s after a relatively slow start, was initially dismissed by the intellectual elite, De Gaulle in particular recognized the potential of television for forming public opinion. Any *chansons de contestation* [protest songs] were perceived at best as a thorn in the side of the state, at worst as a potential focus for social discontent. The ORTF urged programme makers to avoid playing songs of a political nature, claiming that such sensitive issues could be dealt with much more responsibly by established current affairs programmes. Jean Ferrat, who belonged to the same generation of singer-songwriters as Ferré and Brassens, was a notable victim of political censorship in 1969, following an appearance on the French television programme, *Invité du Dimanche*. The director of programmes, annoyed that Ferrat had been allowed to speak as well

---

[7] Other notable victims of censorship include Paul Carpita, whose film, *Le Rendez-vous des quais*, was banned from 1955 until 1980 for representing dockers from Marseille who refused to dispatch military supplies for use in the Indochina war. *La Question*, written by Henri Alleg, which contained accusations of torture during the Algerian war, was censored in 1958. Such was the level of media censorship during the period under discussion that journalist Maurice Clavel, in a famous outburst, stormed out of a television interview in 1970. See Boyer, J.-A. (1991), *J'ai rendez-vous avec vous*, Cinétévé/INA Entreprises/La Sept.

as sing, sacked the production crew, and Ferrat was effectively banned from appearing on French television for two years.

As for Ferré, his exclusion from the airwaves during the 1960s is made all too apparent by the lack of archive footage of his performances. Ferré's particularly outspoken and controversial views, such as his opposition to the Algerian war, aroused hostility not only from the Gaullist state, but also from the music industry and the intellectual community. Ferré recalled how TV controller Jean-Pierre Elkabbach banned him from performing live on television.[8] Ferré became a casualty of music industry self-censorship when his song 'Mon Général', a critique of De Gaulle originally written in 1947, could only finally be published by Seghers after the Algerian war.[9] In order to avoid direct state intervention in its affairs, the French music industry, dominated and controlled by a small group of powerful figures including the record mogul Eddie Barclay, the impresario Jacques Canetti, and the music-hall proprietor Bruno Cocatrix, had to exercise its own form of in-house censorship, particularly where sensitive political issues were concerned. Despite being subjected to this gagging order, Ferré affirmed his commitment to free expression through his own songs. One particular example which illustrates Ferré's antagonistic relationship with the medium is the satirical 'Complainte de la Télé' [The television's lament] (1966). Personifying French television as a prostitute touting for business, the narrator attacks the controllers of the medium from which he is excluded, and opposes the creation of a '*télécratie*', that is, a government by television.

In sum, Ferré's anti-bourgeois critique is particularly contemporary, realistic, and hard-hitting, as his social satire is firmly grounded in the cultural and political landscape of 1960s France. He felt compelled to address the real problems affecting his contemporaries, and was particularly aware of the social stagnation from which France, a blocked society,[10] was suffering, especially in the run-up to 1968, and constructed a critique of specific French institutions, particularly the Gaullist state.

Brassens, in contrast, refused to involve himself in such contemporary political debates. Rather than discuss politicians whose presence is, in a sense, ephemeral, he instead focused on the institutions which he perceived as permanent, and of which he had direct, personal experience; namely the forces

---

[8] See Bravo, C. (8 Nov. 1991), *Merci et encore Bravo*, Antenne 2 (television programme).

[9] The case of Boris Vian's 'Le Déserteur' (1954), originally sung by Mouloudji, illustrates how original author's work may be distorted out of recognition. Richard Anthony's upbeat cover version of a song which was initially intended as a denunciation of the Algerian war, was reworked so as to be politically acceptable and commercially profitable, to the extent that the final product was positively innocuous and uncontroversial. See Dillaz, S. (1973), *La Chanson française de contestation*, Paris: Seghers, 124–25. Jean Ferrat's 'Pauvre Boris' (1967) expresses his disgust at the changes made to Vian's 'Le Déserteur'.

[10] See Crozier, M. (1968), *La Société bloquée*, Paris: Points Seuil.

of law and order. The humorous narrative song, 'Le Gorille', opposes capital punishment, which was not abolished in France until 1981 when François Mitterrand was elected President of the Republic. While Brassens opposed the death penalty, the relatively 'conservative' *auteur-compositeur-interprète* Michel Sardou sang in favour of capital punishment for child murderers such as the notorious Patrick Henry in 'Je suis pour' [I'm in favour] (1976). This controversial song led to an anti-Sardou campaign, and he had to cut short his concert tour for fear of violent reprisals. Brassens also targets the police force, as the agents of law enforcement, in 'Le Mauvais sujet repenti' [The repentant delinquent] (1952) and 'Hécatombe' [Massacre] (1952). The narrator of 'Le Mauvais sujet repenti', exploiting and inverting traditional moral values for his own satirical ends, judges that any prostitute who is actually willing to sleep with a policeman must be feeling very desperate indeed. In another comic jibe against the police, the narrator of Brassens's 'Hécatombe' represents the massacre of the police by a crowd of burly women. Perhaps it was partly Brassens's own brush with the police during his youth which made him take up a personal vendetta against the defenders of law and order. In 1939, Brassens and a group of friends became involved in a series of burglaries which led to their arrest and a short term in prison, an episode which is recounted in 'Les Quatre Bacheliers' [The four holders of the baccalaureate] (1966).[11]

Although Brassens tended to stick to general targets in the field of politics and society, his anti-nationalist critique was much more focused. 'Corne d'Aurochs' (1955)[12] highlights the irrational fears of a small-minded, myopic character who refuses to use a medicine, simply because it was discovered by a German. Such an ironic song relies heavily on the audience understanding that Corne d'Aurochs is the target of the satire, and that the implied author does not share his bigoted, racist views. What is unusual about the song, 'Corne d'Aurochs', is the narrator's specific reference to the historical antipathy between France and Germany. Although Brassens was highly conscious of a popular vein of French anti-German feeling, particularly since the Occupation, the narrator refuses to adopt such a mentality, unable to hold the individual citizens of Germany collectively responsible for the crimes committed by the Nazi regime.

The nation-state, be it German or British, is rejected effectively in favour of the interests of the individual in 'Les Deux Oncles' [The two uncles] (1965). The narrator is unwilling to become locked into the kind of tribalism represented in this song, whereby the two uncles pledge their unquestioning allegiance either to the German or the British side. The narrator underlines the essentially subjective and arbitrary nature of such choices, and so decides to steer his own individual,

---

11 See Calvet, L.-J. (1981/1993), *Georges Brassens*, Paris: Lieu Commun, 30–32.
12 'Corne d'Aurochs' (Bull's horn) was the nickname coined by Brassens by one of his old friends, Emile Miramont. 'Corne' signifies 'horn'. 'Aurochs' is a type of wild bullock, which is an endangered species. See Calvet, *Georges Brassens*, 321, and also Rochard, L. (1996), *Brassens: orfèvre des mots*, Pont-Scorff: 'Imprim'art', 21.

neutral course. Because the individual is of sole importance, any discussion concerning the collective merits of either the Germans or the British is ultimately meaningless and irrelevant to the narrator. However, such an idealistic position ignores the reality of war in which loyalty to the nation effectively took priority over the interests of the individual. While it is all very well for the narrator to pass judgement with hindsight, he fails to recognize that the choice facing individuals such as Martin, the resistance fighter, and Gaston, the collaborator, was inescapably real during the Occupation. Such uncompromising expressions of idealism serve, however, more positively to suggest an alternative to the xenophobia represented in 'Les Deux Oncles'. Indeed, the song was written at a time when France was commemorating the twentieth anniversary of the end of the Occupation, a period which also saw an increasing *rapprochement* between France and West Germany within the context of the newly evolving European Community.[13] Moreover, 'Les Deux Oncles' questions the myth of Resistance which was elaborated in France during the 1950s and 1960s by intellectuals such as Henri Michel and Lucien Febvre.[14]

In a similar vein to 'Les Deux Oncles', Brassens's 'La Tondue' (1964) argues effectively against the supremacy of collective national identity over individual identity. This song questions the *épuration* [purge] which took place in the aftermath of Second World War, when collaborators or Nazi sympathizers, many in the artistic and literary world, were publicly tried and executed, partly in an attempt to relieve the collective French conscience of its collaboration with the Nazis during the Occupation. Brassens's narrator sees little point in seeking revenge against women who slept with German soldiers in what was dubbed the *collaboration horizontale*. These women had their heads shaved in public, hence the term 'tondue'. Although the narrator wishes to let bygones be bygones, he is aware that, in showing sympathy for these victims of the *épuration*, he is liable to be regarded as a collaborator himself. Brassens's direct reference to the historical conflict between France and Germany is, in a sense, remarkable, given that Brassens's songs tend generally not to discuss issues and events which were so close to home, sticking rather to timeless, universal themes such as love, friendship, death and the passing of time. If Brassens wrote

---

[13] A series of songs were released as France commemorated the twentieth anniversary of the Second World War. Along with Brassens's 'La Tondue' and 'Les Deux oncles', came Ferrat's 'Nuit et Brouillard', and Pierre Louki's *Ça fera vingt ans* and Claude Vinci's album, *20 ans déjà*. See Bellaïche, R. (1994), 'Jean Ferrat', *Je chante*, Paris: Chelles, 44.

[14] De Gaulle further advanced the myth and boosted his own Resistance credentials symbolically by transferring the remains of the resistance hero and martyr, Jean Moulin, to the Panthéon. The myth of Resistance which insisted on the unity and heroism of the French would eventually be shattered in the 1970s following De Gaulle's death. The film, *Le Chagrin et la pitié* (1971), directed by Marcel Ophuls, epitomized the shift in emphasis towards the guilt and divisions of the French during the Occupation. The extent to which songs urge engagement for or against collaboration or resistance is developed further in the following chapter by Chris Lloyd.

about the Occupation, then he must have regarded it as a subject of paramount importance.

Ferré focused on French attitudes towards the 'other' in his own songs which oppose nationalism through specific reference to Algeria which, although three fully integrated French *départements*, eventually became the site of a struggle for independence (1954–62) from what was, in effect, French colonial rule. His risqué humour includes reference in 'Les Temps difficiles' [Hard times] to the torture committed by French soldiers against Algerians. Ferré also expressed his sympathy with the signatories of the *Manifeste des 121*, a petition which asserted that France behaved immorally during the Algerian war. In September 1960, 121 writers, university lecturers and artists published a text which encouraged soldiers to disobedience, rather than serve in an unjust war. Ferré's attitude towards the Algerian question aroused opposition, particularly from the OAS, L'Organisation de l'Armée Secrète [The Secret Army Organization], staunch defenders of l'*Algérie française* [French Algeria] during the decolonization of the 1950s and 1960s, which bombed the Parisian *Alhambra* music hall in 1961, shortly before he was due to go on stage. Situating himself within a long tradition of writing songs which oppose nationalism and militarism, and which promote pacifism,[15] Ferré was indeed courageous enough to tackle the Algerian war, which, along with the Occupation, remains to this day something of a taboo subject in France. The Algerian war provided inspiration for a number of songs by other artists, notably 'Le Déserteur' [The deserter] (1954), written by the anti-conformist writer, singer and jazz musician, Boris Vian. The song, in which the narrator refuses to take part in war, was recorded and performed in 1956 by Mouloudji, a strong pacifist whose career received a temporary setback when the song was banned from the airwaves.

Despite Ferré's broad anti-nationalist stance, certain songs betrayed a tendency towards protectionism and chauvinism, given his ambivalent attitude towards the growing influence of American popular culture in France. Songs such as 'Epique époque' [Great era] (1964) reflected growing fears in France of American cultural imperialism, and expressed concern at the proliferation of American mass culture and certain forms of popular music, notably *la chanson yéyé*. This was the French equivalent of American rock 'n' roll music which became popular in France during the 1960s, exemplified by Johnny Hallyday, Eddie Mitchell and Sylvie Vartan. While there was indeed widespread anti-American sentiment from all corners during the Vietnam war, be it from left or right, a more appreciative attitude towards the Americans was, however, to be found in French song, notably in Michel Sardou's 'Les Ricains' [The Yanks] (1967).

---

[15] For further discusssion, see Robine, A. (1994), *Anthologie de la chanson française: Des trouvères aux grands auteurs du dix-neuvième siècle*, Paris: Alban Michel, 267, of how *chanson populaire* has variously dealt with war and the military.

As the foregoing discussion illustrates, Ferré and Brassens broadly opposed bourgeois and nationalist ideologies. However, they did little to question the patriarchal order in France which went largely unchallenged until the emergence of feminist movements during the late 1960s and early 1970s. Their songs often insisted on the stereotypes of *l'homme viril* [virile man] and *la femme féminine* [feminine woman],[16] fetishized the male-female couple, and served generally to uphold *le pouvoir marital* [marital power].[17] Nevertheless, Ferré and Brassens continued a long tradition within French popular song of social and political *engagement*. For Sartre, whose own existentialist philosophy was in wide circulation during this particular period, it is the duty of the writer not only to describe and explain the ills which afflict society, but also to incite the reader to take remedial action.[18] Existentialism flourished, albeit in a diluted or commercialized form, in the Parisian artistic world during the 1950s and 1960s, particularly in the fashionable district of Saint-Germain-des-Prés on the Left Bank of Paris, with its cafés, restaurants, nightclubs, and a thriving jazz scene, where many writers and performers such as Juliette Gréco and Boris Vian launched their careers. Although Sartre takes the literary writer as his model, his views on the role of the artist are applicable to our discussion, relating to the singer-songwriter. It is in the light of this particular post-war, existentialist reading of *engagement,* that the remainder of this chapter considers whether Ferré and Brassens were able or willing to put forward a specific plan of positive social action.

Valuing the freedom of the individual above all else, Ferré identifies his narrator in explicitly political terms as an anarchist from early on in his career, in songs such as 'Graine d'ananar' [Seed of anarchy] (1953). Appropriating the traditional rhetorical discourse of the anarchist movement, the narrator adopts the slogan 'Ni Dieu ni maître' [Neither God nor master] (1964) in the rousing song of the same name.[19] Not only does the narrator seek social equality, but also advocates fierce reprisals and vengeance. Ferré's 'Les Anarchistes' [The anarchists] (1966) is a passionate hymn, dedicated to Maurice Joyeux (1910–91), a celebrated anarchist who spent much time in prison, and who helped to rebuild the Fédération Anarchiste [Anarchist Federation] and its journal, *Le Libertaire* [The Libertarian], to which Brassens (covertly) and Ferré contributed.

Although Ferré's narrator situates the anarchist movement in a French context, he also adopts an international perspective, drawing his inspiration from the Spanish anarchists, fighting for freedom under the dictatorship of General

---

[16]   Terms used by Badinter, E. (1986), *L'Un est l'autre*, Paris: Odile Jacob, 315.

[17]   See Hawkins, *Chanson*, 35–50 for further discussion of gender issues in *chanson* and the work of female singer-songwriters.

[18]   Forbes and Kelly, *French Cultural Studies: an introduction*, 118.

[19]   A newspaper entitled 'Ni Dieu ni maître' was founded after the Paris Commune by the French revolutionary and communist sympathizer Maxime d'Auguste Blanqui (1805–81). The slogan was later used by André Breton in 'Arcane 17', 1947.

Franco. The Spanish anarchists are represented as oppressed, marginalized figures; fighters who are prepared to sacrifice their own blood for their cause, inspired not only by a sense of despair, but also by optimism. Ferré's narrator opposes the authoritarianism of fascist dictators such as Franco who envisaged the eventual spread of Nazism throughout Europe, prior to the Second World War. Ferré's 'Franco la muerte' [Franco, death] (1964), a vitriolic attack upon the Spanish dictator, was indeed a song written in reaction to the execution of Julian Grimau, leader of the secret Spanish Communist Party, in 1963.[20] Although civil war represents a huge tragedy for Spain,[21] it is regarded ultimately as a justifiable means of achieving justice and liberty for the individual.

Such a romanticized representation of anarchists united together appears in contradiction to the freedom of the individual, so fiercely pursued. The narrator, however, regards some degree of cooperation between like-minded people as a necessary and constructive step towards liberty.[22] Nevertheless, sensitive to charges of collectivism and authoritarianism, Ferré decided to remove 'Les Anarchistes' from his concert programme following its release. He feared that if the song became an anthem around which to rally the troops, this would in effect both promote collectivist 'anarchism', and undermine the whole individualistic notion of 'anarchy'. Apart from a celebrated concert at *La Mutualité* in Paris, Ferré remained absent from the demonstrations of 1968, for which he was much criticized by anarchists. Neither did he sign the *Manifeste des 121*, the petition which called for Algerian independence. There were even violent protests at his concerts, due to his perceived non-participation.[23] For Ferré, it should be enough for him to incite others to action and protest. The way in which he could be most effective was within his role as a singer-songwriter: 'Moi ma seule façon de signer, c'est de chanter' [My only way of signing, is to sing].[24] Singing is Ferré's means of *engagement*: 'L'engagement? je suis né engagé quand je suis sorti du ventre de ma mère' [Commitment? I was born committed when I appeared from my mother's womb].[25] Ferré was particularly repelled by what he regarded as

---

[20]   Belleret, R. (1996), *Léo Ferré: une vie d'artiste,* Arles: Actes sud., 347. Jean Ferrat, who belonged to the same generation of singer-songwriters as Ferré, was particularly inspired by Hispanic poet rebels such as Federico Garcia Lorca ('Federico Garcia Lorca', 1964) and Pablo Neruda ('Complainte de Pablo Neruda', 1994, a musical setting of an Aragon poem). Ferrat could, however, be accused of exoticizing and glamorizing the communist revolution, particularly the Cuban dictatorship of Fidel Castro in 'Cuba Si' (1967), and also in 'A Santiago de Cuba' (1967).
[21]   See Dillaz, S. (1973), *La Chanson française de contestation*, Paris: Seghers, 152, with reference to Ferrat's 'Les Belles étrangères' (Senlis, 1965) and Ferré's 'Le Flamenco de Paris' (1946).
[22]   Belleret, *Léo Ferré: une vie d'artiste*, 443–50, 464.
[23]   Legras, M. (1994), 'Léo, Come on, Boy ...', *Chorus: Les Cahiers de la chanson,* Bréziolles: Les Editions du Verbe, 113–14.
[24]   Ibid., 139.
[25]   Ibid.

dogmatic ideologies such as communism, whereby personal freedom subordinates itself to greater collective concerns.[26] The Marxist communist tradition became the dominant ideological framework amongst intellectuals in post-war France, and the Parti Communiste Français (PCF) [French Communist Party] exercised considerable influence in all areas of artistic production including *la chanson*. Jean Ferrat's 'En groupe en ligue en procession' [In a group, in league, in procession] (1966) constitutes a rally to the communist cause. Although the communist solution was to become widely discredited following Khrushchev's disclosure of Stalin's atrocities, Ferrat held on to his pure reading of communism in 'Camarade' [Comrade] (1970) and later in 'Le Bilan' [The assessment] (1980), taking a stance against all forms of injustice, especially in the light of the the the Soviet seizure of power in East Germany (1953), Hungary (1956) and Czechoslovakia (1968).

Although Ferré did not share Ferrat's communist sympathies, this did not mean to say that Ferré rejected a loose arrangement between individual anarchists within the *Fédération Anarchiste*. Anarchy ultimately enables the individual to become closer to other like-minded people who share the common belief in the freedom of the individual, and an opposition to any form of authority which seeks to limit or repress such freedom. As Ferré explains, 'Anarchy is frightening and shocking, but, in my view, it's extraordinary. It's love of and respect for others ... and, of course, this is possible to achieve.'[27] Although Ferré sought to adhere strictly to a theoretical, dictionary-like definition of anarchy ('the negation of all authority'),[28] he ultimately regards it as an expression of love for his fellow humans: 'the negation of all authority ... is love'.[29]

While forming a close association with anarchists, Ferré also enlisted the help of disaffected French youth. Ferré showed how he could bridge the generation gap through music in 1968 rock recordings he made with the rock group, *Zoo*. The narrator sees the beatniks, like himself, as following in a long tradition of social outcasts and rebels. 'Salut Beatnik!' (1967) represents a repeated call for solidarity across the generation gap. Ferré's desire to guide younger generations, expressed in 'Salut Beatnik!', while well meaning, may smack of paternalism and proselytism.[30] His own early adulthood illustrates how easy it is to be

---

[26]   Layani, Jacques (1987), *Léo Ferré – la Mémoire et le temps*, Collection Paroles et musiques, Paris: Seghers, 51. See also Fléouter, C. (1996), *Léo*, Paris: Laffont, 60, who recalls Ferré's outrage and disgust when he was prevented from speaking at a Parti Communiste Français (PCF) meeting.

[27]   'L'Anarchie ça fait peur. Tout ça c'est la bombe alors que pour moi c'est extraordinaire. C'est l'amour, et l'amour de l'autre et le respect de l'autre ... et ça c'est possible évidemment.' See *Journal Télévisé de 20h*, TF1 26 Sept. 1989.

[28]   'la négation de toute autorité d'où qu'elle vienne'.

[29]   'la négation de toute autorité d'où qu'elle vienne ... c'est l'amour'. See Bravo, C. (8 Nov. 1991) *Merci et encore Bravo*, Antenne 2 (television programme).

[30]   Legras, 'Léo, Come on, Boy ...', 139.

seduced by radical ideologies, be they on the far right or left of the political spectrum. Although Ferré became an anarchist by the time he achieved fame, he had actually flirted with monarchism as a *lycée* and university student. Ferré, along with François Mitterrand, who was to become the first socialist President of France, joined the militant royalist group, Les Camelots du Roi while studying for his law degree. However, by the time the Second World War broke out, Ferré was already frequenting the bohemian world of Saint-Germain-des-Prés, and by the end of the 1940s was both performing at galas for the Fédération Anarchiste, and writing for the anarchist journal, *Le Libertaire*.[31] With the benefit of hindsight, Ferré advises the youth of 1968 to resist authority, and to live by the hippy slogan: 'make love not war'.[32] He recommends young people to experience what he regards as the two most important pleasures in life: 'I tell young people that drugs are terrible, but I also tell them that there are two fantastic drugs: love and music. Make love and make music!'[33]

Ferré's case highlights a distinction between the views of the implied author who urges collective resistance and the real author who plays down his role as an instigator of social revolution. In Brassens's case, there is a much clearer identification between the real and implied author, as both refuse to make the kind of concessions towards collectivism found in Ferré's songs. Brassens himself comments:

> I've never believed in collective solutions ... it's a very personal and debatable opinion ... I don't want to provide explanations or a moral code, or say in which direction we should be heading ... songs provide 4 or 5 minutes of enjoyment ... if I could be effective, I would write these kind of songs, but it's not in my character. I work discreetly. I had taken the side of all the Vietnamese in 'Bad Reputation', and 'Corne d'Aurochs' ... I can't write songs about such subjects ... it wouldn't work. I'm unable to change the world ... I don't know what should be done ...[34]

---

[31] See Fléouter, *Léo*, 1996, 26; and Robine, M. (1994), 'Ni Dieu ni maître' *Chorus: Les Cahiers de la chanson*, Bréziolles: Les Editions du Verbe, 95.

[32] See also Fléouter, *Léo*, 190; and Layani, *Léo Ferré*, 131, for discussion of Ferré's popularity with the youth.

[33] 'Je dis aux jeunes qu'il y a quelque chose d'abominable: c'est la drogue; je leur dis mais il y a deux drogues les plus extras: c'est l'amour et la musique: faites l'amour et la musique'. See *Le Journal télévisé de 20 heures*, TF1, 26 Sept. 1989.

[34] 'Je n'ai jamais cru aux solutions collectives ... c'est une opinion très personnelle et très discutable ... je ne tiens pas à donner des explications, une morale, à indiquer les voies ... qu'il faut suivre ... une chanson donne 4, 5 minutes de la joie ... si je croyais à l'efficacité, j'en ferais ... C'est pas mon tempérament. Je le fais discrètement. J'avais pris parti par avance pour tous les Vietnamiens dans "Mauvaise Réputation", "Corne d'Aurochs" ... Je ne peux pas faire des chansons avec ça ... ça ne marcherait pas ... Je ne suis pas capable de refaire la société ... je ne sais pas ce qu'il faut faire ...'. See Boyer, J.-A., *J'ai rendez-vous avec vous*, 1991 (television studio performance) on Brassens's opposition to collective social action in 'Le Pluriel'. See also Sève, A. (1975), *Toute une vie pour la chanson*, Paris: Editions du centurion, 138–39.

Brassens refuses to be enslaved by any artificial social order, and reserves the right to opt out, a stance expressed in 'Mourir pour des idées' [To die for ideas] (1972).[35] He objects not only to the traditional enemy, the state, but also to any collective force which, no matter how well intentioned, defines itself as oppositional. Brassens fears that the word of the majority still rules to the extent that 'we're still at the tribal stage where the uniformity of thoughts and morals prevails'.[36] Brassens refused therefore to become involved in the protests against the continuation of the Vietnam war. He was also unwilling to take part in the debate surrounding the events of May 1968 in France, and when questioned as to what he did during the period, he replied flippantly, 'des calculs' [gallstones].[37] Brassens, a fierce opponent of the authoritarian, totalitarian stance of the French Communist Party, opposed collectivism in 'La Tondue' (1964) and in 'Les Deux oncles' (1965), as well as in 'Le Pluriel' (1966).[38] Brassens maintained a generally individualistic rather than collectivist approach to life. He would rather formulate his own moral code than adopt a preordained set of repressive ideological values.[39] Brassens believed that in anarchy 'there is no real dogma or morality'.[40] However, as he admitted, 'I find it difficult to be friends with people who try to assert their will upon others'.[41] Such a refusal to discuss differences of opinion with, or to be influenced by, others itself betrays a somewhat inflexible and dogmatic attitude.

If Brassens undertook any form of committed social action, it was not through the medium of song, but rather the written word. Before he achieved fame he wrote for an anarchist newspaper, *Le Libertaire,* under various pseudonyms. Earlier, Brassens asserted his personal freedom by refusing to work in the German work camps (Service du Travail Obligatoire) during the Second World War.[42] Not only is Brassens's opposition to collectivism ideological, but also pragmatic. Brassens argued that *chanson* is ultimately an ineffective medium for promoting social change.[43] Although Ferré felt able to write socially committed songs, Brassens considered himself personally incapable. Both modest and sceptical, he insisted that neither he nor his songs served any useful social

---

[35]   See Boyer, *J'ai rendez-vous avec vous*, and *Top Club*, INA 1979, in Letellier, D., *Georges Brassens: 15 chansons mythiques*, Polygram/INA Entreprises 1996 (video cassette 043 820 3).
[36]   'Nous sommes encore à l'état tribal où règne l'uniformité des pensées et des mœurs'. Bonnafé, A. (1963/1988), *Georges Brassens – l'anar ... bon enfant*, Paris: Seghers, 16, 36.
[37]   See Boyer, *J'ai rendez-vous avec vous*, for further discussion of Brassens's illnesses.
[38]   Calvet, *Georges Brassens*, 90–91, 195.
[39]   Bonnafé, *Georges Brassens*, 70.
[40]   'Il y a pas de véritable dogme: une morale'. Sève, *Toute une vie pour la chanson*, 46–47.
[41]   'Je peux difficilement devenir ami avec un être qui essaie d'imposer sa volonté aux autres'. Ibid., 46–47.
[42]   Calvet, *Georges Brassens*, 85–87.
[43]   See *Affaire Chesman*, Antenne 2, 16 Feb. 1960.

purpose, and so refused to deal with topical issues. At most, he alluded indirectly to contemporary events in songs which were primarily concerned with the discussion of universal themes.[44]

In his pure reading of anarchy, Brassens refused to encroach upon the personal liberty of the individual which is to be guarded and cherished at all costs. This visceral attachment to, and fetishization of, freedom is expressed in 'Heureux qui comme Ulysse' [As happy as Ulysees] (1970). Rather than comply with the wishes of the majority, Brassens pursued his own course, right from the start of his songwriting career, even at the risk of making enemies.[45] Referring to himself as 'la mauvaise herbe' [the weed], Brassens's narrator is aware that what he will say could cause offence in both 'La Mauvaise Réputation' [The bad reputation] (1952) and 'La Mauvaise Herbe' [The weed] (1954).[46] Resolving to stave off any attack upon his personal freedom, Brassens's narrator resists and rejects the very rules and conventions which govern society. He even sometimes resorts to provocation for its own sake, identifying himself as 'le polisson de la chanson' [the bad boy of song] 'Le Pornographe' [The pornographer] (1958).

Although Brassens asserted his individuality and non-conformity, his freedom was ultimately illusory. Having situated himself on the margins of society, Brassens was, in turn, ironically expected by the sensational end of the popular press, 'les gazetiers fouille-merde',[47] to live up to his 'mauvaise réputation' [bad reputation], as his narrator complains in 'Les Trompettes de la renommée' [The trumpets of fame] (1962).[48] While the state-controlled audio-visual media felt threatened enough by Brassens to censor his songs, the popular press regarded Brassens as a star who had the potential to shock, generate eye-catching headlines, and ultimately sell newspapers.

Brassens and his narrative voices emphasize the right of the individual to personal freedom and autonomy, following the tradition of libertines such as the Marquis de Sade whose main goal was to expand human freedom.[49] Brassens's rejection of collective social action is absolute, to the extent that contemporary society is virtually erased from his songs. It is up to the contemporary listener to deduce a social stance in Brassens's songs from the universal messages they

---

[44]   See Sève, *Toute une vie pour la chanson*, 68.

[45]   René Fallet's article, 'Allez Georges Brassens', a review of one of Brassens's early concert performances, recognizes his potential to create controversy. See Cottet, J.-P. (1990), *Georges Brassens: Histoire de copains et de copines*, Collection les Grands, FR3, and Sermonte, J.-P. (1988), *Brassens: le prince et le croque-note*, Paris: Editions du rocher, 36–37.

[46]   See *Dimanche Illustre*, INA 1975, in Letellier, D. (1996), *Georges Brassens: 15 chansons mythiques*, Polygram/INA Entreprises (043 820 3).

[47]   Sallée, A. (1991), *Brassens*, Paris: Solar, 119–20.

[48]   For a performance of this song, see Averty, J.-C. (1979), *Georges Brassens: Unique*, Bondy: DEC 1979 (no catalogue number).

[49]   Marshall, P. (1993), *Demanding the Impossible: A History of Anarchism*, London: Fontana, 143.

carry. Ferré's position is more problematic: while some of his songs urge social revolution, the real author adopts a more reticent position in practice.

By identifying themselves as anarchists, and cultivating the kind of marginal persona established earlier by Aristide Bruant at the turn of the nineteenth and twentieth centuries,[50] both Ferré and Brassens conform to a specifically French construction of the artist within post-revolutionary, secular modernity. The contrasting approaches to the question of social action outlined in this chapter are evidence of the vigorous contribution which they made towards contemporary political and philosophical debates in their songs, and in their media appearances. Such a contribution serves ultimately to reinforce their intellectual credentials as well as the special status accorded to the singer-songwriter within French culture.

Discography

Brassens, *J'ai rendez-vous avec vous* (intégrale), Philips/Universal, 1988, complete boxed set of 11 CDs No. 836 309-2.
Ferré, *Les Années Odéon* (1953–58), Sony, 1993, boxed set of CDs No. 475655/2.
Ferré, *Avec le temps* (1960–74), Barclay, 1989, boxed set of 11 CDs No. 8412602.

---

[50]   For further discussion of Bruant, see Hawkins, *Chanson*, 67–73.

Chapter 9

Divided loyalties:
singing in the Occupation

Christopher Lloyd

To what extent do popular songs and their performers shape and reflect national identity at a time of political crisis and social disarray, such as the occupation of France by the Germans from 1940 to 1944? Songs are a somewhat neglected source of cultural and historical information, particularly for the study of changing emotions, attitudes and daily behaviour. Even if one samples only the comparatively small corpus of songs that survive in recordings, one discovers a wide variety: certain songs clearly put a case in favour of various ideological positions, while others comment on the problems of daily life. A representative selection thus covers topics as diverse as *maréchalisme* (that is, the cult of Marshal Pétain), the Resistance and rationing. At the same time, star performers clearly possess symbolic power over mass audiences, even if they use a different form of discourse from political leaders. Their popularity and durability, apart from the content or aesthetic interest of their songs, suggest it is perfectly reasonable to see singers as vehicles expressing forms of national identity (albeit an identity which, in the context of the occupation, is fragmented and conflicting). After examining the issues raised by the expression of overt ideological commitment in the well-known and more obscure anthems of opposing groups, we will turn to the equally problematic question of songs which are usually perceived as forms of entertainment or escapism, paying particular attention to the career of Maurice Chevalier, since he is in many ways exemplary.

The authors of the *Mémoire de la chanson française* assert that 'De tous temps, la chanson a accompagné les gestes les plus quotidiens de la vie, elle a appelé au combat, célébré la rencontre des corps, provoqué le rire, tenté d'apprivoiser la mort' [Throughout the ages, songs have accompanied the most basic actions of life: they have called to battle, celebrated the encounter of bodies, provoked laughter, attempted to tame death].[1] Songs, in other words, are central to the defining factors of life, rather than simply incidental entertainments. Or should one argue rather that such apparent distractions can be as significant as the grander abstractions of ideologies and politics? Montherlant

---

[1] Duverney, A.-M., and d'Horrer, O. (1979), *Mémoire de la chanson française depuis 1900*, Paris: Musique et Promotion, 7.

wrote of the Munich agreement (whereby France and Great Britain avoided war by abandoning Czechoslovakia to the Germans in 1938) that 'La France est rendue à la belote et à Tino Rossi' [France has gone back to belote and Tino Rossi]:[2] a contemptuous reference from a right-wing authoritarian admirer of the Nazis to the fact that his compatriots preferred the distractions of card-playing or the famous Corsican tenor to the harsher realities of European power politics. For such commentators, Rossi's popularity (he recorded far more songs during the Second World War than any other French performer) signalled a woeful perversion of national identity and patriotic energy. While the schoolgirl Micheline Bood (whose family were Anglophile Gaullists) rhapsodizes adoringly in her Occupation diary over 'ce cher Tino Rossi' and his voice 'combien suave et mélodieuse' [so mellifluous and melodious],[3] Alfred Fabre-Luce, a proponent of Vichy's programme of moral and social regeneration known as the National Revolution, complained that 'Un eunuque fait rêver les Françaises', as opposed to 'un chant viril de travailleur devant une terre en friche' [A eunuch is making French women dream; the virile song of a worker ploughing a fallow field].[4] Mass singing of this healthier variety was incorporated into Vichy's ideological programme of national purification. The Chantiers de jeunesse [youth work camps] were created in summer 1940 as a substitute for military service with the slogan 'Chanter c'est s'unir' [to sing is to be united], with collective discipline overriding musical talent; the authors of a manual for trainees noted that 'Le fait n'est pas de savoir mais de vouloir chanter' [What matters is not being able to sing but wanting to].[5]

In practice, however, songs may well seek to promote the unity of groups (from the paramilitary collaborators of the Milice to the provocative sartorial eccentricities of swing and *zazous*), but such affirmation of group identity also exposes the profound division and antagonism between the groups which claim to speak for the nation. This can be illustrated by the two most famous songs of the occupation, which are respectively hymns to Pétain and to the resistance: 'Maréchal, nous voilà!' and 'Le Chant des partisans' [Marshal, here we are; The Song of the partisans]. The first song was written by Montagard and Courtioux in 1941, with its most celebrated interpreter being the tenor André Dassary. In her excellent account of Vichy's exploitation of music, *Vichy à travers chants* (1996), Nathalie Dompnier observes that Pétain's public appearances in the unoccupied southern zone controlled by Vichy were carefully orchestrated spectacles, 'l'occasion de mises en scène musicales minutieuses qui doivent participer à l'élaboration de l'image de Pétain et au bon déroulement de ses visites' [the occasion for detailed musical productions intended to help promote Pétain's

---

2   Quoted in Cannavo, R. (1993), *Monsieur Trenet*, Paris: Lieu Commun, 290.
3   Bood, M. (1974), *Les Années doubles: journal d'une lycéenne*, Paris: Laffont, 69.
4   Quoted in Miller, G. (1988), *Les Pousse-au-jouir du Maréchal Pétain*, Paris: Livre de poche, 150.
5   Quoted in ibid., 145.

image and the smooth running of his visits], verging on religious ceremonies.[6] The parallel with the elaborate staging of Hitler's public manifestations is also worth noting, what the historian of the Third Reich Michael Burleigh has called 'exercises in mass bathos … in which a man assumed mythic dimensions'.[7] Such spectacles may strike us retrospectively as tawdry and meretricious, for their instigators have lost both their emotional potency and political credibility, but this is not a reason to ignore or underestimate their impact on audiences whose limited knowledge and deprived material and social circumstances made such figures far more appealing.

Democratic pluralism, peace and prosperity, as well as the rise of the mass media have attenuated the power of the dictatorial demagogue who in such public displays is presented both as statesman controlling the destiny of nations and live performer seducing the masses. As Dompnier further notes, the mass reproduction of songs through the recording industry is largely a post-war phenomenon which weakened the collective, oral function which they still retained in the early 1940s (a period when sales of sheet-music to be performed at home or in public were larger than those of records to be listened to more passively). As the cult of Pétain was elaborated, the jaunty march 'Maréchal, nous voilà!' effectively became the régime's unofficial anthem.

Une flamme sacrée
Monte du sol natal
Et la France enivrée
Te salue Maréchal
Tous les enfants qui t'aiment
Et vénèrent tes ans
Et ton appel suprême
Ont répondu: «présent».

Maréchal, nous voilà!
Devant toi, le sauveur de la France
Nous jurons, nous tes gars
De servir et de suivre tes pas.
Maréchal, nous voilà!
Tu nous as redonné l'espérance
La Patrie renaîtra
Maréchal, Maréchal, nous voilà![8]

---

6   Dompnier, N., *Vichy à travers chants*, Paris: Nathan, 1996, 114.

7   Burleigh, M. (2000), *The Third Reich*, New York: Hill & Wang, 266.

8   A literal translation has the unfortunate effect of accentuating the crashing banality of this ditty: 'A sacred flame rises from the native soil and France, intoxicated, salutes you, Marshal. All your children who love you and venerate your age have answered 'present' to your supreme call. Marshal, here we are before you, the saviour of France. We your lads swear to serve and follow your footsteps. Marshal, here we are, you have given hope back to us. The motherland will be reborn. Marshal, here we are, here we are.'

It also spawned many imitations whose trite idolizing of Pétain seems ludicrously blasphemous and grotesquely at odds with historical and biographical reality to anyone who studies their texts 60 years on. Hence Hervé Le Boterf's observation that André Dassary exploited his popularity to interpret 'une kyrielle de marches dans le style soldat-laboureur propres à discréditer, par leur niaiserie, la politique du retour à la terre' [a string of marches in the soldier-ploughman style liable to discredit through their idiocy the policy of the return to the soil].[9] This ironic effect was, obviously, not intended. Thus Pétain in 'Maréchal, nous voilà!' appears as sacred flame, patriarchal guardian, military saviour and unifier of the nation, offering work and hope in place of the ravages of war, although retrospectively we know that most of such promises were broken (Pétain was a childless roué who sank into senility as his régime became a police state which abandoned much of its territory, economy and citizens to the Germans). Nevertheless, to counteract such propaganda, with its infantilization of the nation and equation of Pétain with France, required a powerful counterblast. The Resistance attempted to appropriate some of the musical charm of 'Maréchal, nous voilà!' by producing parodic versions, either reversing its idolatrous terms to make Pétain an enemy (thus 'Malgré toi, nous sauverons la France,/Nous jurons qu'un beau jour/L'ennemi partira pour toujours' [In spite of you, we will save France. We swear that one fine day the enemy will go away][10]) or transferring his virtues to de Gaulle as 'Général, nous voilà!'

In this respect, it is worth recalling that although the Germans banned performances of 'La Marseillaise' in the occupied northern zone, Vichy was determined to retain the national anthem, despite its unpopularity with past authoritarian regimes owing to its revolutionary and anti-German origins as the 'Chant de guerre pour l'armée du Rhin' [war song for the Rhine army] (composed by Joseph Rouget de Lisle in 1792[11]). Versions published by Vichy suppressed references to 'cohortes étrangères' and 'vils despotes', but its bellicose, bloodthirsty stanzas still remain closer to the spirit of resistance than to collaboration (the final stanza 'Amour sacré de la Patrie', which usually remained uncensored, still celebrates the triumph of Liberty over 'tes ennemis expirants'). This paradox is partly explained by the celebrity of 'La Marseillaise', an essential patriotic commodity, and partly by a long-standing tradition. Dompnier argues that 'l'hymne est une représentation sociale que la population d'un pays s'approprie, qui fonde son identité et la définit non seulement par rapport à elle-même mais aussi aux yeux de l'extérieur' [the national anthem is a social representation adopted by the population of a country, which founds its

---

[9]   Le Boterf, H. (1997), *La Vie parisienne sous l'Occupation*, Paris: Editions France-Empire, 263.
[10]   Quoted by Dompnier, *Vichy à travers chants*, 46.
[11]   For details, see Vovelle, M. (1998), 'La Marseillaise: War or Peace', in P. Nora (ed.), *Realms of Memory*, vol. 3, *Symbols*, English edn ed. L.R. Kritzmann, trans. A. Goldhammer, New York: Columbia University Press.

identity and defines it not only in relation to itself but also in the eyes of outsiders].[12] Louis-Jean Calvet has shown that recycling famous songs like 'La Marseillaise' for diverse ideological purposes was common practice throughout the nineteenth century (one might note in passing the existence of numerous variants of the British national anthem, which likewise attempt to universalize the aspirations of conflicting political groupings). One early nineteenth-century reference source in fact enumerates 2350 'timbres', that is 'des airs destinés à la parodie' ('parodie' here meaning the use of existing music with new words, without necessarily implying satirical distortion).

Whereas 'Maréchal, nous voilà!' in its original form as a jaunty rallying call avoids the divisions and betrayals of Pétain's régime, the song which encapsulates resistance, on the other hand, 'Le Chant des partisans', co-authored by the Gaullists Joseph Kessel and Maurice Druon in 1943, with music composed by Anna Marly, is a much more sombre and solemn evocation of 'L'Armée des ombres' (The army in the shadows: the title of the novel on resistance which Kessel published in the same year).

Ami, entends-tu le vol noir des corbeaux sur nos plaines?
Ami, entends-tu les cris sourds du pays qu'on enchaîne?
Ohé! Partisans, ouvriers et paysans, c'est l'alarme!
Ce soir l'ennemi connaîtra le prix du sang et des larmes.

Montez de la mine, descendez des collines, camarades.
Sortez de la paille, les fusils, la mitraille, les grenades.
Ohé! Les tueurs, à la balle ou au couteau, tuez vite!
Ohé! saboteur, attention à ton fardeau, dynamite!

C'est nous qui brisons les barreaux des prisons pour nos frères.
La haine à nos trousses et la faim qui nous pousse, la misère.
Il y a des pays où les gens au creux du lit font des rêves.
Ici, nous, vois-tu, nous on marche et nous on tue, nous on crève.[13]

Compared with the facile, jaunty optimism of 'Maréchal, nous voilà!', what is most striking about this song (reinforced by its sombre, dirge-like music) is the brutal directness with which it evokes the business of resistance, the action of killing or being killed (by bullet, knife, or dynamite). The partisans being called

---

[12] Dompnier, *Vichy à travers chants.*
[13] 'Friend, can you hear the black flight of the crows over our plains? Friend, can you hear the muffled cries of the land in chains? Ahoy, partisans, workers and peasants, sound the alarm. Tonight the enemy will learn the price of blood and tears. Come up from the mines and come down from the hills, comrades. Bring out the guns, bullets and grenades. Killers, kill quickly with bullet or knife. Saboteur, watch out for your burden, dynamite. We will break the prison bars for our brothers, pursued by hatred and driven by hunger and misery. There are countries where people dream asleep in their beds. But we are on the march, killing and dying.'

to action are ordinary men (workers, peasants, miners), for whom survival remains uncertain. Whether the appeal was actually answered or even heard is another matter: Richard Raskin has shown that 'Le Chant des partisans' was little known even by maquisards in France before the liberation in 1944; its initial function was to promote a positive image of the Resistance for doubters abroad.[14] The song was adopted as the theme tune for the Free French programme 'Honneur et Patrie' broadcast from London by the BBC from May 1943 to May 1944 and has acquired a quasi-sacred status as the anthem of Resistance, in spite or because of the stereotyped images it conveys and its elision of the complexities of resistance. Thus the ceremony marking the consecration of Jean Moulin as the supreme martyr of the Resistance with the transfer of his supposed ashes to the Pantheon in 1964 concluded with a choir singing 'Le Chant des partisans' (though Moulin's activities as an administrator and coordinator, the political rivalries which he encountered, and his probable betrayal to the Gestapo by a senior member of the rival resistance movement Combat, naturally all fall outside the compass of this song). In a somewhat pious anthology entitled *Les Chansons de notre histoire*, André Gauthier concludes unsurprisingly of this 'Musique obsédante et profonde' that 'on pouvait entendre en elle l'invincible accent de la liberté en marche ... par le jeu de ses dernières notes en suspens, l'impression de menace signifiait la lutte à poursuivre et l'ultime effort vers la victoire!' [Haunting, profound music, in which one hears the invincible sound of liberty on the march. ... Its final, unresolved notes convey the menacing impression of the ongoing struggle and the final effort to achieve victory].[15]

Such an interpretation also suggests how inevitably songs tend to be fitted retrospectively into an ideological agenda as much dependent on subsequent historical and political developments as their actual music and text. In fact the two songs 'Maréchal, nous voilà!' and 'Le Chant des partisans', with their explicit commitment either to *pétainisme* or violent resistance, are only the best-known survivors of many ideologically committed songs, most of which have been consigned to oblivion. This applies particularly to the anthems of disgraced collaborationist organisms like the Milice, the Legion of Volunteers against Bolshevism (the LVF) or the French Division Charlemagne of the Waffen SS. While the song of the LVF is a bland appeal for Franco-German reconciliation ('Nous apportons avec nous l'espérance / Que nos deux pays enfin réconciliés / Ecarteront à jamais la souffrance / Qu'ils ont connue dans les annés passées' [We bring with us hope that our two countries, reconciled at last, will shake off for ever the suffering which they have endured in past years]), SS songs celebrate death and destruction ('Là où nous passons / Que tout tremble / Et le diable rit avec nous' [When we pass by, let everything tremble, and the devil laughs with

---

[14]   Raskin, R. (1991), 'Le Chant des partisans', *Folklore*, 102, 62–76.
[15]   Gauthier, A. (1967), *Les Chansons de notre histoire*, Paris: Pierre Waleffe, 204.

us]).[16] An anthology published in 1945 entitled *La France nouvelle: chansons de la Résistance* celebrates, in the words of its anonymous editor, 'des voix qui chantent pour rythmer l'effort, chasser les craintes et consoler les souffrances, pour clamer l'espoir, l'enthousiasme, la joie de la libération, la foi en l'avenir de la patrie et de l'humanité!' [voices singing to give rhythm to their efforts, to dispel their fears, to offer consolation for suffering, to proclaim hope, enthusiasm and joy in liberation, faith in the future of the motherland and humanity!].[17] The hundred or so texts in this collection (the music had to be purchased separately) embrace many aspects of allied and French victory, from celebrations of the maquis, such as 'Ceux du maquis' (another song made famous by the BBC) and 'Le Chant des FFI', to endless patriotic marches and ditties, and the national anthems and most popular hits of the victorious nations, done into French (such as 'Dieu sauve le roi!' and 'Oui nous n'avons pas de bananes'). While songs which welcome the departure of the Germans and their Vichy acolytes and the return of prisoners predominate (so that Vichy is present only as a purely negative interlude) certain songs which found favour during the Occupation survive, despite their rather equivocal messages (e.g. Maurice Chevalier's numbers 'Ça fait d'excellents Français' and 'Notre espoir', which will be discussed below, and Charles Trenet's 'Douce France'), just as other songs which evoke occupation fashions (wooden soles and painted legs) are retained. Offering a Liberation variant on a well-known song is a further possibility: thus Trenet's 'La Romance de Paris' is given with a 'Version 44' and as 'La Romance du maquis'.

These ready adaptations indicate how untypical explicit ideological commitment is in popular songs, which generally aim to be all-embracing rather than limited to narrow sectional interests. Indeed, most songs produced during the Occupation fall into a fairly neutral category, of entertainment or what might be called oblique commentary on issues of daily life. Nonetheless, certain songs, despite their apparent neutrality or blandness, can evoke attitudes and feelings which produce a surprisingly hostile response in commentators for whom they represent symbolic but negative values. Thus while most listeners today probably find the comic songs of the phoney war period at best anodyne exercises in nostalgia, or at worst vainglorious expressions of optimism in an allied victory over the Germans, which the defeat of 1940 was to render nugatory, the anthologist André Gauthier is enraged by the French version of 'On ira pendre notre linge sur la ligne Siegfried' (1939: adapted by Paul Misraki from Jimmy Kennedy and performed by Ray Ventura and his band, who were celebrated for their comic numbers, until their bandleader's Jewish origins drove them into exile in South America for the course of the Occupation): 'ce refrain qui eut son heure de célébrité nous semble aujourd'hui l'un des meilleurs exemples de

---

[16] Quoted by Giolitto, P. (1999), *Volontaire français sous l'uniforme allemand*, Paris: Perrin, 76, 398.
[17] *La France nouvelle: chansons de la Résistance*, Paris: Editions Salabert, 1945, 1.

bourrage de crânes et de crétinisation de la masse!' [this refrain had its moment of fame but seems to us today a perfect example of brainwashing and cretinization of the masses!].[18]

Criticism of the Germans or collaboration was impossible in songs performed or recorded in occupied France, given the rigorous censorship imposed on publications and the entertainment industry. Occasionally, satirical references escaped notice, by accident or design. For example, Radio Montpellier was suspended for a week in May 1941 for playing Chevalier's 'Prenez le temps d'aimer', which contains a spoken, veiled criticism of Hitler – typically, the career-minded Chevalier complained about the broadcast rather than the ban.[19] In her unpublished study of 406 songs produced from 1941 to 1943, Sophie Dransart has found only one critical reference to Pétain (in Georges Milton's 'Nous les Français', 1942).[20] That being said, however, more indirect criticism of the living conditions produced by Occupation (such as shortages, the black market, bureaucracy) is in fact a common feature in many songs, the best of which are often memorably inventive in a humorous or *fantaisiste* fashion, 'sur le mode grotesque, de l'exagération, des jeux de mots ou du ridicule' [using the grotesque, exaggeration, word-play or ridicule].[21] Andrex's 'Monsieur Jo' (1943) recounts the exploits of a notorious profiteer until his final downfall (the parallel with the infamous scrap metal dealer Joanovici seems inescapable, although the latter escaped retribution till well after the Liberation). Georgius, dubbed by one admirer the 'Daumier de la chanson'),[22] in 'Elle a un stock' (1941), recounts the hoarding and bartering exploits of a *femme de ménage* in an increasingly surreal inventory. Such insistence on essentially domestic woes is seen by many commentators as a form of avoidance of wider and harsher political and military realities. As Dransart says, 'La chanson, de par sa nature, est un moyen d'évasion' [song by its nature is a means of escape],[23] a point reinforced by the significant rise in attendance at cinemas and other public shows during the occupation. But the pejorative notion of escapism overlooks the rather obvious fact that songs and their performers are hardly able to provide practical solutions to social and economic problems; what they offer instead through music and verse, in other words through an aestheticized commentary on shared experience, is a sense of solace and solidarity. Here again, words and music are

---

[18] Gauthier, *Les Chansons de notre histoire*, 200.

[19] See Eck, H. (ed.) (1985), *La Guerre des ondes*, Paris: Armand Colin/Lausanne Payot, 32.

[20] Dransart, S. (1994), 'La Chanson de variété en France sous l'Occupation', mémoire de maîtrise (Université de Paris I).

[21] Ibid., 91.

[22] Chollet, J.-J. (1997), *Georgius, l'amuseur public no 1*, Paris: Christian Pirot, 7. See Lloyd, C. (2001), 'Comic Songs in the Occupation', *Journal of European Studies*, 31, 379–93, for a fuller discussion.

[23] Dransart, 'La Chanson de variété en France sous l'Occupation', 137.

less important than performance, particularly in front of a live audience: 'Par la seule force de communication, la chanson [est] devenue un moment d'émotion collective, un instant artistique' [By the sheer force of communication, song has become a moment embodying collective emotion, an artistic instant].[24] Hence Peter Hawkins's more persuasive argument that popular 'songs fulfil a very basic need for the stylisation of our everyday experience'.[25]

In many respects, the career of a singer like Maurice Chevalier is typical of entertainers during the occupation and therefore merits attention.[26] Self-serving opportunism and a reluctance to quit the spotlight of public attention, even when temporary invisibility might be a better survival tactic, could be seen as his main characteristics. This is to ignore the fact, however, that at least for French audiences, immensely popular singers like Chevalier do have a genuine consolatory function; they encapsulate and express feelings and attitudes which are widely shared by their public. Can we recapture and explain some of this lost glory, over half a century after the event? Does the popular artist fulfil a civic mission, especially in moments of crisis? And did Chevalier betray this mission by collaborating with the Vichy government and the Germans between 1940 and 1944? Such questions are central to understanding popular songs during the occupation.

In May 1944, Josephine Baker (one of the very few artistes to engage in resistance activities) condemned Chevalier as a 'collaborationniste nazi' who merited severe punishment; and within a few months, after being detained by maquisards in the Dordogne, he learned that a court in Algiers had sentenced him to death. What had he done during the Occupation to call down such an exemplary judgement? In November 1941, he had accepted an invitation to perform in Germany, without payment, for French prisoners of war at Alten Grabow (the camp where he had himself been a prisoner in the First World War). In addition, he had appeared onstage on frequent occasions between 1941 and early 1943, mainly in the unoccupied south zone, but also for several months at the Casino de Paris and in Belgium; he had also made a series of eleven broadcasts for Radio-Paris, the station controlled by the German Propagandastaffel. On the other hand, he spent the last 18 months of the occupation in virtual retreat, first in Cannes and then in the Dordogne, passing the time by writing his autobiography. Unfortunately, he took up this literary pursuit too late to escape the hostile attention of critics who began accusing him of collaboration from 1942; envy and spite may have motivated his detractors as much as authentic patriotism.

---

[24]   Dillaz, S. (1991), *La Chanson sous la Troisième République*, Paris: Tallandier, 114.

[25]   Hawkins, P. (2000), *Chanson: the French Singer-Songwriter from Aristide Bruant to the Present Day*, Aldershot: Ashgate, 57.

[26]   For a fuller discussion, see Lloyd, C. (1997), 'Maurice Chevalier et l'Occupation', in *La Culture populaire en France*, ed. P. Whyte and C. Lloyd, Durham Modern Languages Series, 79–92, and Charman, T. (1991), '*Chantons sous l'occupation*: Maurice Chevalier and Collaboration in Occupied France', *Imperial War Museum Review*, 6, 96–108.

Chevalier describes these tumultuous events in the third volume of his autobiography, *Tempes grises*, published in 1948. Between 1946 and 1969 he would tirelessly produce ten volumes altogether. In fact he was rapidly cleared of all charges (thanks in part to support from the Communist Party) and was able to add a new career as a writer to his activities as a singer and actor. To understand Chevalier's enormous popularity and his subsequent behaviour during the Occupation (which seems both representative and reprehensible), it is useful to recall his origins in the poorest classes of Parisian society in the late nineteenth century. In the words of the historian Serge Dillaz:

> Le personnage de Maurice Chevalier fait de distinction et de gouaille synthétise à lui seul le formidable brassage social occasionné par la Grande Guerre. A ce titre, il est plus qu'un simple interprète. Il est miroir. Il se reconnaît dans le public et ce dernier se reconnaît en lui.

> [The character created by Maurice Chevalier, mixing refinement and lowbrow humour, encapsulates the tremendous social intermingling caused by the Great War. In this respect, he is more than just a simple performer. He recognizes himself in the public, and the public recognizes itself in him.][27]

In September 1939, he heard the news of the invasion of Poland while on a Riviera golf course, in the company of the Duke of Windsor (no doubt Chevalier thought that this disgraced monarch, who was on friendly terms with Nazi leaders, was a good connection). In fact, he was fond of admitting his ignorance of political issues with a rather complacent disingenuousness which overlooks the influence exerted by popular entertainers:

> Qu'on nous laisse tranquillement ... faire nos métiers de distrayeurs. Que ceux qui font œuvre politique, que ceux dont c'est la raison de vivre, l'idée ou l'intérêt prennent leurs responsabilités et que ceux qui ne peuvent être que de simples artistes soient laissés à leur industrie de sourire et de grâce. ... Deux denrées bien nécessaires à la Santé française.

> [Just leave us alone to do our job as entertainers. Let those who are in politics, for whom politics is their main reason for living, idea or interest, accept their responsibilities, while those who can only be simple artists are left to pursue their industry of smiles and graces. Two products which are certainly necessary for French health.][28]

However, as this last reference to the nation's well-being suggests, Chevalier considers singing to be more than a frivolous or superfluous distraction:

> C'est à travers les chansons que chantent et qu'ont chanté les peuples, que se retrouvent les sentiments et les émotions du pays, aussi bien dans le malheur qu'aux époques ensoleillées.

---

[27]   Dillaz, *La Chanson sous la Troisième République*, 114, 177.
[28]   Chevalier, M. (1948), *Tempes grises*, Paris: Julliard, 51.

[It is through songs that peoples sing and have sung, that the sentiments and emotions of nations are given form, both in times of unhappiness and in sunny periods.][29]

He clearly sees that popular art can have a therapeutic function and the star performer can act as a vehicle which expresses and comments on the feelings of his audience.

Maurice Chevalier certainly had no hesitation in continuing his national mission through the first three years of the occupation. Unfortunately, in so doing he displayed a somewhat blinkered conformism and opportunism; after the event, his attempts to exculpate himself by references to unavoidable pressures and obligations which forced him to carry on performing also sound unconvincing. The issue is not so much one of overt commitment to either resistance or collaboration, as one of the moral responsibility of the celebrity who can choose to exert influence in a positive or negative sense, to appear courageous or craven. Like the great majority of French people, he tells us, 'je croyais à Pétain au début de son règne' [I believed in Pétain at the beginning of his reign].[30] Just before his performance at the Casino de Paris, in September 1941 the widely read newspaper *Le Petit Parisien* printed an interview headed 'Maurice Chevalier, le populaire artiste, prône la collaboration entre les peuples français et allemand' [Maurice Chevalier, the popular artist, is promoting collaboration between the French and German peoples]. In his memoirs, Chevalier claims that this interview is an 'abominable fausseté' [abominable falsehood],[31] although his enthusiastic remarks about Marshal Pétain were repeated a fortnight later in *Comœdia* and probably during his subsequent broadcasts on Radio Paris.[32] As for the notorious visit to Alten Grabow, Chevalier claims that he had merely acceded to the entreaties of French POWs who 'réclament leur chanteur national' [demanded their national singer]; again the French and international press distorted this event by alleging that 'Maurice Chevalier vient de faire une tournée dans les villes d'Allemagne' [Maurice Chevalier has just gone on tour in German cities].[33]

Eight months later, the American magazine *Life* published in its issue dated 24 August 1942 a blacklist of 'some of the Frenchmen condemned by the Underground for collaborating with the Germans: some to be assassinated, others to be tried when France is free'.[34] Next to politicians like Déat, Pétain, Laval,

---

[29]   Ibid., 10.
[30]   Ibid., 108.
[31]   Ibid., 63.
[32]   See Behr, E. (1993), *Thank Heaven for Little Girls: the True Story of Maurice Chevalier's Life and Times*, London: Hutchinson, 229.
[33]   Chevalier, *Tempes grises*, 66–67.
[34]   Reproduced in Guitry, S. (1947), *Quatre ans d'occupations*, Paris: Editions de l'Elan, 409.

Darlan and Doriot, one finds the names of Mistinguett, Marcel Pagnol, Sacha Guitry and Maurice Chevalier. The actress Françoise Rosay had denounced Chevalier and Guitry to the British press before settling in Hollywood (though she herself had appeared in a film made in Berlin in 1938); possibly she gave the names of her more successful colleagues to *Life* as well. However, despite such warnings, Chevalier returned to the occupied zone to perform again for six weeks at the Casino de Paris from September 1942. Seeing himself 'entouré de trappes et d'embûches' [surrounded by traps and pitfalls],[35] he finally abandoned performing. Nevertheless, he was denounced over the airwaves of Radio Londres by the satirical singer Pierre Dac in February 1944. At the Liberation, his execution by agents of the Resistance was announced by the international press. *New York Times* reported on 27 August 1944, for instance: 'French report Chevalier slain for collaborating with Germans' (in the event, the victim proved to be a namesake, the pro-Vichy mayor of a provincial town).

There is little doubt that Maurice Chevalier behaved with ostentatious indiscretion during the Occupation. The chronicler Galtier-Boissière noted in his journal the caustic rejoinder given by the 'perroquet pro-hitlérien de Radio-Paris', [pro-Hitler parrot on Radio Paris] Jean Hérold-Paquis, at his trial for treason in September 1945: 'Je gagnais 30 000 francs par mois, donc en deux mois, ce que Maurice Chevalier touchait, au même micro, pour une seule émission' [I used to earn 30,000 francs a month, that is in two months what Maurice Chevalier earned for a single broadcast on the same station].[36] Whereas Hérold-Paquis was condemned to death and shot on 11 October 1945, Chevalier was rapidly cleared of all blame (like the majority of entertainers briefly detained at the Liberation). But whatever the huge sums earned by stars and their rather unappealing mercenary zeal (Édith Piaf, who also toured French prison camps in Germany, could command the equivalent of a clerk's annual salary for a single performance), their performances of songs or works of art can hardly be equated with the political pronouncements of Nazi propagandists, unless one can find an explicitly pro-collaborationist message or ideological bias in these songs. Hérold-Paquis's lawyer claimed at his trial that his client too, when all was said and done, was no more than an entertainer; the court saw a clear distinction.[37]

As for Chevalier, he went on to claim, in the English version of his autobiography published in 1960, that he had helped the Resistance in 1943 by acting as a clandestine *boîte aux lettres*; he also made much of the help which he gave to the Jewish parents of his female companion Nita Raya. Like many Frenchmen, in other words, Chevalier was happy to contribute retrospectively to the glorious myth of resistance, or *résistancialisme*, by eliding the less honourable aspects of his wartime record and stressing unverifiable deeds of

---

35   Chevalier, *Tempes grises*, 80.
36   Galtier-Boissière, J. (1992), *Journal 1940–1950*, Paris: Quai Voltaire, 508.
37   For more details, see Anon. (1947) *Les Procès de la radio*, Paris: Albin Michel.

patriotism. However, this hardly merits severe condemnation, still less the accusation of collaboration, given his apparent lack of ideological commitment (his position of opportunistic *attentisme* or time-serving is characteristic of most entertainers). How should one interpret the commentary on defeat, occupation and liberation which one finds in several of Chevalier's best-known songs from the period? He observed correctly that 'Il n'a jamais été question pour moi de messages obscurs ou de rébellion contre quoi que ce soit' [There was never any question of my preaching obscure messages or rebellion against anything].[38] Nonetheless, while the message may be clear enough (and part of his songs' charm stems from their luminous simplicity), the interpretation which it invites can vary according to the exact circumstances in which it is heard.

Three well-known songs provide effective illustration: 'Ça fait d'excellents Français' (Boyer and Van Parys, 1939), 'Notre espoir' (Chevalier and Betti, 1941) and 'La Chanson du maçon' (Vandair/Chevalier and Betti, 1941). The first song offers an amusing and perceptive satirical account of the failings of the French army during the first months of the war, the so-called phoney war or *drôle de guerre*. Although the documentary value of such a comic piece should not be exaggerated, the picture it paints goes a long way towards explaining the *débâcle* of May 1940, in the obvious defeatism of its final lines, for example.[39] 'Ça fait d'excellents Français' merits a parenthetical detour, or rather a return to the issue of songs being used for overt propaganda purposes. This is because its popularity made it a prime target in 'La Guerre des ondes' [the war of the airwaves], that is the use of music for propaganda purposes in radio broadcasts. About half of the daily output of Radio Paris (the German-controlled station which broadcast over the whole of occupied France) was devoted to music, including a programme called 'Au rythme des temps' which adopted famous songs for propaganda. Their adversaries, the team who produced the celebrated 'Les Français parlent aux Français' for the French section of the BBC in London also 'font assaut d'esprit «chansonnier» pour ridiculiser l'adversaire' [launched an assault using satirical songs to ridicule their adversary], their main innovation being 'd'organiser une émission politique comme un spectacle' [to organize a poltical broadcast like a variety show].[40] The humorists Pierre Dac and Maurice Van Moppès produced a stream of parodic songs deriding collaborators and the Nazis, including Dac's version of 'Ça fait d'excellents Français', which targets the greed for fame and lucre of stars like Maurice Chevalier, who were happy to accept large sums to perform on Radio Paris and to ignore the propaganda benefits which they thereby offered to the Germans.

Dac's willingness to commit himself to resistance showed that the entertainer could if he wished join in the propaganda battle: in fact in the closing weeks of

---

38   Chevalier, M. (1970), *Les Pensées de Momo*, Paris: Presses de la cité, 96.
39   See Lloyd, 'Comic Songs' for more detailed discussion.
40   See Eck, *La Guerre des ondes*, 9, 67.

the Occupation, he engaged in a virulent war of words with Vichy's Minister of Propaganda, Philippe Henriot, cut short by the latter's assassination. Hence his closing words that 'Henriot est mort pour Hitler, fusillé par les Français' [Henriot died for Hitler, shot by the French].[41] After the Liberation, he claimed that he helped save Chevalier from further persecution, seeing him as a 'victime de sa célébrité',[42] though Chevalier counted Dac as one of his main persecutors. But despite the undoubted personal courage of a satirist like Dac, which distinguishes him radically from so many other entertainers, and despite the propaganda value of his texts, the problem with such parodic songs is their ephemeral and parasitic nature. Not only do they require their audience to have a good knowledge of the original version which they distort, but also they seem rather crude in comparison. Thus Dac's simple contrast between bad and excellent Frenchmen is much less subtle than the ironic awareness of social and ideological divisions revealed in Chevalier's original version. Similarly Van Moppès's reworking of standard numbers like 'Prosper' or 'Tout va très bien, madame la marquise' show none of the wit and inventiveness of the original versions, limited as they are simply to poking fun at Hitler. The 'Couplet 1944' added by an unknown author to 'Ça fait d'excellents Français', in the anthology of resistance songs discussed earlier, again does no more than offer sycophantic praise of the FFIs, completely losing the tone of affectionate derision that makes the original so telling. At best, all that distinguishes such songs is their overt commitment to the cause of resistance.

If we return to Chevalier's two other songs, it is no surprise to discover that the singer was much more cautious in offering any but the blandest of opinions. In the case of 'Notre espoir' (where he wrote the words himself), ironically the German censor was suspicious of the phrase 'Zim ba boum ba la', 'craignant quelque sens caché' [fearing there was some hidden meaning], according to the composer Henri Betti,[43] though the absence of meaning was meant to be the point. Indeed, we are to understand that the best policy is not to express controversial views but to feign joyful feelings, 'sans grande joie pourtant' [with little real joy, however]:

L'important c'était de recommencer
Qu'importe l'expression
L'essentiel était de pouvoir dispenser du rêve en chanson.[44]

This urge for quiet renewal is expressed again in 'La Chanson du maçon', which is often interpreted as a pro-Vichy song. There is a further appeal for unity and reconstruction:

[41]   Dac, P. (1972), *Un Français libre à Londres en guerre*, Paris: Editions France-Empire, 232.
[42]   Ibid., 282.
[43]   Quoted by Kirgener, C. (1988), *Maurice Chevalier*, Paris: Vernal/Lebaud, 139–40.
[44]   'The main thing was to start again, whatever the expression. The essential thing was to be able to give out dreams in song.'

Si tout le monde chantait comme les maçons
Si chacun apportait son moellon
Nous rebâtirions notre maison ...[45]

As Henri Betti remarked, had it appeared three years later, this song would have been understood not as a 'hymne pétainiste' but as a celebration of *la France combattante* (the lyricist Maurice Vandair was in fact a member of the French Communist Party).[46] The fact remains that propaganda in favour of Vichy's National Revolution did exploit images close to those evoked by this song, such as the well-known drawing of a ruined house, representing the Third Republic sapped by Jewry and the leftist reforms of the pre-war Popular Front, set against a splendid new house representing the virile values of Vichy's Etat français. On the other hand, as Laurent Gervereau notes, in the nationalist domain, Vichy and Resistance propaganda often overlaps, since both claim to speak for the nation and its eternal values; and the observation extends to cultural representations, so that a famous song like Charles Trenet's 'Douce France' 'reprend une terminologie pétainiste alors que certains y voient une allusion à la Résistance' [adopts Pétainist terminology, though others see in it an allusion to Resistance].[47] In any event, three years later, Chevalier exchanged the 'églogue vichyssoise' of 'Ça sent si bon la France' (Larue and Louiguy, 1941) for the 'patriotisme viril et résistant' of 'Fleur de Paris' (Bourtayre and Vandair, 1944).[48]

Such ambiguities show that Chevalier cannot be accused of actively promoting the Vichy regime in his songs, unless their content is wilfully distorted. In this context, it is interesting to recall that the film director Marcel Ophuls exploited Chevalier's music and personality in his demystifying documentary film *Le Chagrin et la pitié* (1971), not only in order to suggest the cultural climate of the occupation but also rather more tendentiously to suggest troubling affinities between culture and politics. For example, towards the middle of the first part of the film, entitled 'L'effondrement' [the collapse], we are shown a newsreel extract about 'La Visite du Maréchal'. The director replaces the original commentary by Chevalier's song 'Ça sent si bon la France', which has the effect of creating a series of derisive equivalents. As we see Marshal Pétain meeting his subjects, we hear the national singer Maurice Chevalier extolling the virtues of *la France profonde*. The satirical intention seems fairly obvious: by promoting a pro-Vichy message, Chevalier is exposed as a collaborator who is assisting the senile dictator and his regime as they dupe the French nation. Culturally, in other words, Chevalier is supposed to be the equivalent of Pétain in

---

[45] 'If everyone sang like builders, if everyone brought along his breeze block, we'd soon rebuild our house.'
[46] See Kirgener, *Maurice Chevalier*, 144–45.
[47] Gervereau, L., and Peeschanski, D. (1990), *La Propagande sous Vichy*, Paris: BDIC, 143.
[48] See Perrault, G. (1987), *Paris sous l'Occupation*, Paris, 190.

the field of politics, although this rather crude interpretation may not actually be the one Ophuls wants to provoke.

In any case, it seems unlikely Ophuls intended to slander Maurice Chevalier, whose music has a simple, plebeian appeal that is remote from Vichy's reactionary, exclusive elitism. A more persuasive interpretation is that Chevalier is meant to be emblematic of the average Frenchman, overtaken and humiliated by events and wanting above all to be left in peace. Chevalier's music is heard four times in *Le Chagrin et la pitié*. 'Ça fait d'excellents Français' and 'Notre espoir' accompany the credits at the beginning and end of the first part. The penultimate sequence of the second part (entitled 'Le choix' [the choice]) shows the interview in English which Chevalier gave to Paramount in 1944 when he was seeking to exculpate himself. By recalling the rumours of his death (or liquidation), the singer presents himself as a victim and survivor of the chaos of liberation. Since this impression of dishonesty and discomfort is characteristic of many other interviews in *Le Chagrin et la pitié*, Maurice Chevalier's exercise in self-justification makes him a typical sample of the discreditable behaviour which the film exposes with cruel satisfaction. Finally, this last song is used, now in an orchestrated version, to accompany the last sequence which shows General de Gaulle's triumphal visit to Clermont-Ferrand. This invites the conclusion that Maurice Chevalier and the Gallic spirit which he embodies have in effect survived the transition between two interchangeable political regimes, that songs and popular culture actually have a more durable legitimacy than political leaders. If a derisory equivalence was established between Chevalier and Pétain at the beginning of the film, at the end the director establishes a correspondence between Pétain and de Gaulle, as the latter takes on the provincial tour of inspection of his disgraced predecessor. Monarchs come and go, but Maurice Chevalier lasts for ever, it would seem.

Given that 'La chance de Maurice Chevalier est de s'être trouvé en harmonie parfaite avec l'air du temps' [Maurice Chevalier had the luck to be in perfect harmony with the spirit of his time][49] the fact that he supported Pétain in 1941–42 is hardly astonishing. Is this a reason to condemn him or accuse him and other singers of betraying their mission as representatives of French culture? The authors of a history of French song observe rightly that:

> Chevalier s'est toujours inscrit dans le cadre des idées, des normes dominantes. ... Socialement, il était lui-même une réussite du système et, par son personnage ... et par l'idéologie de ses chansons, il servait de caution populaire à l'ordre établi.
>
> [Chevalier always followed the stream of dominant ideas and norms. Socially, he was himself a successful product of the system and through his character and the ideology of his songs provided a popular guarantee for the establishment.][50]

---

[49]   Brunschwig, C., Calvet, L.-J. and Klein, J.C. (1981), *Cent ans de chanson française*, Paris: Seuil, 94.

[50]   Ibid., 94–95.

In other words, a Chevalier prepared to protest against or resist the system would not have been Chevalier. Nonetheless, does this explain or justify the accusations of collaboration or moral weakness levelled against the singer and other entertainers who continued their careers during the Occupation? The egotism and weakness displayed by celebrities like Chevalier or Guitry (who ultimately did little harm to anyone or anything beyond their own reputation with posterity) should not be confused with deliberate acts of criminal treason, which can be defined in a literal, juridical sense, of surrendering the country, its people and resources to the enemy. Such a definition is illustrated unequivocally by acts of political, industrial, bureaucratic, paramilitary or intellectual collaboration committed respectively by such individuals as Laval, Renault, Bousquet, Darnand and Brasillach.

But would not silence have been preferable, to avoid any suspicion of complicity? This is essentially the thesis put forward by André Halimi in his book *Chantons sous l'Occupation*, one of the few studies devoted to popular culture during the period (the documentary film with the same title also directed by Halimi is incidentally much more informative and less biased than his book). As his copious documentation shows, 'A ne lire que les pages-spectacles des journaux, on pourrait ignorer totalement que la France est occupée' [If you only read the variety pages of the newspapers, you might never realize that France was an occupied country]. Hence his observation that 'Pendant quatre années, sous l'Occupation, des millions d'hommes en France ont ri, joué la comédie, bu et mangé. Il faut le dire avec force: des millions de Français ont chanté sous l'Occupation. ... Le dossier est accablant.' [For four years during the Occupation, millions of Frenchmen laughed, played, drank and ate. It needs to be stated firmly that millions of French people sang during the Occupation. The case is damning.][51] Since eating, drinking and laughter are basic human needs, Halimi's sententious, moralizing tone and his facile juxtapositions are difficult to understand. Pointing out that the Gestapo was committing atrocities when theatres were packed out does not really demonstrate the guilt and decadence of the French nation, but rather the paradoxical coexistence of areas of oppression and liberty during the Occupation. The fact that three times as many French people went to music hall shows in 1943 than in 1938 mainly reveals an urge to 'Quitter l'horreur du monde réel pour les rivages de l'imaginaire' [Leave the horror of the real world for the shores of the imaginary], however ephemeral this escape may be, to quote Serge Added.[52] And the reader who has any sense of historical objectivity should heed Todorov's warning in *Les Abus de la mémoire*, that pious denunciations of the iniquities tolerated by French citizens under Vichy merely expose the accusers to charges of complacent hypocrisy for ignoring the iniquities of their own age.[53]

---

[51]   Halimi, A. (1976), *Chantons sous l'Occupation*, Paris: Olivier Orban, 136, 9.
[52]   Quoted in Rioux, J.-P. (ed.) (1990), *La Vie culturelle sous Vichy*, Paris: Editions Complexe, 342.
[53]   Todorov, T. (1995), *Les Abus de la mémoire*, Paris: Arléa, 54.

Our present-day cult of stars and celebrities makes us forget that it is foolish to expect entertainers, whose success depends on inventing and selling a largely fictional, fantasized personality to a paying audience, to behave like real heroes, leaders or guardians of moral values. The last word is best given to a performer celebrated for his provocations. In two post-war songs, Georges Brassens attempted to confront the betrayals and failings caused by occupation (he himself was a conscript worker in Germany, even if his musical fame belongs to a later generation). 'Les Deux Oncles' (1964) equates resistance and collaboration as interchangeable postures, both outmoded and forgotten: 'De vos épurations, vos collaborations, / Vos abominations et vos désolations, / De vos plats de choucroute et vos tasses de thé, / Tout le monde s'en fiche à l'unanimité.' But this dismissal and lines like 'Maintenant que vos controverses se sont tues'[54] ignore the obsession with the occupation which post-war generations have inherited from those who lived through it (witness the belated trials of collaborators like Touvier and Papon or damaging accusations against members of the Resistance throughout the 1990s, not to mention the controversy created from the 1950s to the 1970s by successive films which sought to anatomize the painful truths of collaboration or deportation). The battle for truth and legitimacy continues to be fought. In another song, 'Honte à qui peut chanter' [shame on you for singing], Brassens appears to excoriate those who sing while Rome burns: 'A l'heure de Pétain, à l'heure de Laval, Que faisiez-vous mon cher en plein dans la rafale? / Je chantais, et les autres ne s'en privaient pas ...'. Yet, as he concludes: 'Si Dieu veut l'incendie, il veut les ritournelles. / A qui fera-t-on croire que le bon populo, / Quand il chante quand même, est un parfait salaud?'[55] The distractions of song are more than egocentric frivolity; by creating a parallel universe (which comments indirectly on the real one and contains its horrors), the singer undertakes a form of cultural resistance in which his or her audience participates and achieves a brief moment of liberty.

---

[54] 'As for your purges, your collaborations, your abominations and your devastations, your plates of sauerkraut and cups of tea, nobody cares a toss about them'. 'Now your controversies have fallen silent.'

[55] 'In the time of Pétain, in the time of Laval, what were you doing, my dear fellow, when the storm was raging? I was singing, and others didn't hold back either.' 'If God wants fire and brimstone, he also wants ditties. No one really thinks that when people sing despite their troubles that makes them callous bastards.'

Chapter 10

Rock and culture in France: ways, processes and conditions of integration

Philippe Teillet

In April 2002 the weekly magazine *Les Inrockuptibles* published a supplement (entitled 'Chroniques lycéennes' – Secondary School Reviews) giving an account of a project conducted with the national education and culture ministries. It revealed that 6000 secondary-school pupils (70 per cent of whom were in vocational training) had worked with their teachers on writing reviews of 10 CDs (albums by Daft Punk, Miossec, Manu Chao, Marvin Gaye, Rachid Taha, Air, Noir Désir, Yann Tiersen, Saïan Supa Crew, Björk) chosen by the magazine staff. If in his article Jean-Daniel Beauvallet, in charge of this project for *Les Inrockuptibles*, pointed out the remarkable contrast between what he had just taken part in and his own secondary-school experience, it may be noted that this project provoked no hostile reaction at all and that instead it was presented as an obvious thing to do both by the music critics ('we therefore immediately agreed to take part') and by the official in charge of 'current music'[1] at the Ministry of Education (virtually the alter ego of the counsellor with responsibility for the same sector at the Ministry of Culture since 1998). The official at the Ministry of Education who had initiated the project reminded us that first of all it was part of a five-year joint plan between the two Ministries to organize a range of activities promoting the arts and culture at school, and secondly, that 'rock, rap, *chanson*, and electronic music occupy an unrivalled place in adolescents' imagination and in their artistic practices. Moreover these styles of music with their 50 years of history represent a major cultural phenomenon of the twentieth century.[2] The

---

[1]   The term 'musiques actuelles' in French, coined by State services, groups under a common title, without any real coherence, musical genres whose only link is the lack of interest traditionally shown in them by the authorities. Here we are referring to jazz, *chanson* (French song), traditional music, 'amplified music', rock, rap, techno, etc. For an analysis of this term we refer you to the comments in the annex of Teillet, Philippe (2002), 'Eléments pour une histoire des politiques publiques en faveur des musiques amplifiées', in Poirrier, Philippe (ed.), *Les collectivités locales et la culture*, Paris: Comité d'Histoire du Ministère de la culture, La Documentation française, 361–93.

[2]   *Les Inrockuptibles*, 'Chroniques lycéennes', April 2002, 2.

ideas seemed to be perfectly suited to both sides, that is, the heads of *Les Inrockuptibles* and the two main state cultural services. In other words, seen from the point of view of these decision makers, such a project emerged quite logically from their respective roles.

While we must be wary of claiming that such a project is unique to France, it appears to us, however, to possess remarkable characteristics and to be in a position to surprise foreign observers of the cultural life of France. If we have put it at the beginning of this article, it is because it conveys perfectly the position that rock and, more widely, 'current music' occupy in what may be defined as the French cultural field. Therefore we are not proposing here to outline the history of rock in France, but to present some reflections and observations, allowing the reader to understand how rock integrates into the French cultural field, that is, the admission of its representatives to a network of social positions that have been historically organized around cultural activities.

Originally rock and its actors (in the sociological sense) have occupied a clearly dominated position, notably compared to jazz and its own actors who, a few years earlier, indeed a few decades earlier, found themselves in the same situation as importers of a new musical genre into France. But the 'representatives' of rock seem to have possessed less social and cultural resources than the artists and musicians who became infatuated with jazz from the inter-war period onwards. This admission to the cultural field has at least two aspects. On the one hand it means occupying a position on a scale of cultural values or more precisely within a socially constructed representation of their hierarchy. On the other hand, since France has been characterized since the beginning of the 1960s by strong government voluntarism in cultural matters, we must examine the place that has been granted to artists within the rock field in this sector of public policy.

To ascertain this we shall consider the remark by Guy Saez,[3] who observed a kind of split in intellectual circles due to the development of cultural policies. The latter prompted the appearance of new institutions, new distribution networks and new financing of work outside the media and culture industries. Saez suggested that traditional elites (in our case the 'academic' world, both that of actual 'Academies' and in part that of universities, notably 'intellectuals' intervening simultaneously in the fields of university research and the media) might find themselves situated 'on the sidelines of cultural dynamics' because of this. This hypothesis proposes a sociological analysis of the critiques and controversies which regularly feature cultural policy, since those whom it marginalizes are more particularly prompted to challenge it. The hypothesis also considers the cultural policy sector (the agents and institutions who depend on it and compete more or less strongly to maximize the rewards it can bring them) as

---

[3]   Saez, Guy (1995), 'Villes et culture: un gouvernement par la coopération', *Pouvoirs*, 73, 115.

a relatively autonomous, 'separate' space, within the cultural field. It is argued therefore that there are at least two poles in this field: one covered by public cultural interventions (the cultural pole) and another, not contributing or contributing only marginally to artistic production and distribution, which is essentially concerned with constructing representations of society in its economic, political, social, cultural or artistic dimensions (the intellectual pole). Further, it will be noted that these two poles (cultural and intellectual) are supported by the existence of two government ministries (culture and education) whose areas of intervention cover approximately the people and institutions making up each pole. The French cultural field, it is argued, is thus partially defined as the sum of the relations between and within these two poles. A third pole then complements the other two. It is an economic and media pole comprising businesses and activities in the cultural industries and media sector.

This argument, doubtless a fragile, debatable and perfectible one, which represents the cultural field in a polarized manner, will allow us, by initially excluding questions relating to the economic and media pole, to concern ourselves with the place of rock (etc.) in the intellectual pole, before we turn to the place rock occupies within the cultural pole. In the first case, the degree of integration of rock essentially depends on its ability to be recognized as having or being granted an intellectual dimension. In other words we come up against a process within discourse working on existing representations of itself. In the second case, the existence of a public intervention sector that has created institutions, professionals and financial support mechanisms leads us to see the integration of rock as the effect of a transformation (or development) of public cultural policies.

The intellectualization of rock

The choice of *Les Inrockuptibles* as a partner in the project mentioned in the introduction is symptomatic of the position currently occupied by this magazine in the French cultural field. More than any other publication dedicated to 'current music', it represents so far the most complete form of intellectualization of rock. Its participation also indicates that it is within the press, and more precisely via musical criticism, that this process has occurred. Universities and scholarly institutions more generally in France have taken little or no interest in these types of music and have in no way contributed to awarding them an intellectual dimension.[4] In this respect the situation of rock (etc.)[5] is markedly different

---

4   The recent creation (May 2002) of a review (*Volume*) dedicated to a university research approach to current music and the plastic arts appears to want to end this situation following the failure of *Vibration* (a journal of popular music studies, published by éditions Privat in the mid-1980s).

5   That is to say amplified music (rap, techno, electronic music, 'world music' etc.).

from that of theatre and cinema – film studies developed in part in the university world – different even from the situation of jazz and strip cartoons which have, to an extent, found a place in teaching institutions in the arts). Intellectualization can be defined as a distinctive process of mediation between producers and receivers of works of art, a process of mediation comprising a form of 'reciprocal co-construction ... of the objective properties of creative works and of the representations which allow them to exist as such'.[6] In this case the specific contribution of intellectualization is shown by the changes in the representation of certain works by the introduction of scholarly elements that were originally absent. It goes without saying that this process cannot concern the entirety of musical productions in the world of rock (etc.). The only musical productions concerned are those that have been the object of this process of mediation constructing in part their representation. Thus the claim can never be made that rock (etc.) as a whole has achieved an intellectual dimension. However this process of music criticism has happened in France in conditions and forms that must be looked at in more detail.

A process of music criticism

Created in 1986, a magazine appearing six times a year, *Les Inrockuptibles*, became monthly and then weekly, and for a long time contained only interviews, in a sober format. Today it is a comprehensive cultural magazine[7] in which music is just one of the artistic fields tackled. It brings together a readership embodying the same properties of other cultural magazines' readers, but in more exaggerated form.[8] Besides this, the paper is at the cutting edge in its coverage not only of record production and current media issues, but also of political and ideological debate, and of different fields of artistic creation. In terms of its place in the intellectual pole of the cultural field, one of its assistant editors, Sylvain Bourmeau, is founder of a political science magazine (*Politix*), where he has remained a member of the editorial board. He also produces and presents a weekly programme on *France-Culture* (the national public service radio that is a more intellectual version of BBC Radio 4 in Britain). Stéphane Davet, a former journalist of the magazine, is now responsible for rock, rap and electronic music at the daily newspaper *Le Monde*. The cinema columnists of *Les Inrockuptibles* have become some of the most perceptive critics (and are recognized as such) of the more innovative or demanding cinema productions. From an ideological

---

6   Heinich, Nathalie (2002), *La sociologie de l'art*, Paris: La Découverte, 67.
7   With a website, www.lesinrocks.com, sub-titled 'le guide culturel'.
8   Mainly young, belonging to the socioeconomic class category of executives and higher intellectual professions, city dwellers, indeed Parisian and endowed with a higher education qualification. See Donnat, Olivier (1998), *Les pratiques culturelles des Français, Enquête 1997*, Paris: La Documentation française, 179.

point of view the magazine is situated somewhere between the critical Left and the social democratic Left. This position in French political space is exemplified by its selection of interviews with personalities like Pierre Bourdieu, Jacques Bouveresse, Anthony Giddens, Michel Rocard and Jeremy Rifkin as well as by stances taken or at least sympathy shown in favour of anti-globalization movements. In terms of the cultural pole, by becoming weekly, the paper has reinforced its multidisciplinary dimension. In this way it gives increasing attention to contemporary art, both the plastic arts and the performing arts. Finally it has no inhibitions about displaying its links with the audio-visual media and the record and entertainment industries, by publicizing (without abandoning its critical function) new record releases or by supporting tours by French or foreign artists in France. Also, in a recent new format, it devotes much attention to television programmes on mainstream channels, and cable and satellite alike. This complex definition as a magazine of opinion and debate, a television weekly, rock newspaper and artistic magazine represents a doubly oppositional position. The writers of *Les Inrockuptibles* are in fact regularly driven to contest traditional cultural hierarchies, not only by continuing to comment on the news in different spheres of 'current music' whose legitimacy remains fragile, but also, for example, by agreeing to discuss the most demanding literature alongside television series, or by supporting the actions of young contemporary artists who are generally very critical towards the main cultural institutions and their policies. This questioning of norms and cultural values is accompanied moreover by a desire not to leave it up to the market alone to decide the value of musical or other productions (for example by working on the recognition or rediscovery of rare or difficult works that consequently have a restricted audience, or, on the other hand, by denouncing mainstream popular works like the film *Le fabuleux destin d'Amélie Poulain*). This desire to support values in competition with commercial values is expressed, however, in a complex manner (which is far from being a radical opposition), since, like other specialist music reviews, *Les Inrockuptibles* is a business that must take into account the expectations of its readership, and which needs to retain professional relations with the cultural industry whose diary of events, in a way, imposes itself on theirs (record releases, film releases, tours, festivals etc.)

As we have shown elsewhere,[9] *Les Inrockuptibles* now extends and exacerbates the position that was occupied by its sister publication *Rock & Folk* during the 1970s and 1980s. Founded in 1967, this magazine appeared in 1966 as a supplement to another monthly magazine, *Jazz Hot*, which itself had been set up in 1935 and whose editorial director during the 1960s, Philippe Koechlin,

---

[9] See Teillet, Philippe (2002), 'Les cultes musicaux. La contribution de l'appareil de commentaires à la construction de cultes – l'exemple de la presse rock', in Le Guern, Philippe (ed.), *Les cultes médiatiques,* Rennes: Presses Universitaires de Rennes.

was also editor of *Rock & Folk* from its creation until 1990. For a long time *R & F* represented an informed approach to rock (both scholarly and aesthetic), despite which it found a relatively high readership. But after two decades of development,[10] at the end of the 1980s the magazine's economic situation progressively deteriorated and it was consequently sold to another publisher. Several years later one of its former journalists, Philippe Manoeuvre, became its editor and endeavoured to manage the magazine's inheritance and symbolic capital, while both defending a certain conception of rock (which in his opinion is still embodied by the Rolling Stones) and writing about current events within this type of music. However, as regards an intellectual approach to rock, *Les Inrockuptibles* has henceforth supplanted its predecessor.

Indeed, the writers of *Les Inrockuptibles* have different social characteristics and greater cultural resources. They have more links with intellectual milieux (whether with various celebrities or with *France-Culture*). The diverse content of their issues is a good reflection of the eclecticism and hybrid character found in the cultural world of the most cultivated (and minority) fringes of the population.[11] It would therefore be tempting to think that the intellectualization of rock is attributable to the almost mechanical effect of its gradual appropriation by social groups with an intellectual dimension (secondary-school pupils and students first of all, the intellectual professions – teachers – and professionals in culture and the media), an appropriation which *Les Inrockuptibles* reflects. There may be some truth in this remark (and it will be seen indeed that the need of these categories to achieve distinctiveness was partly satisfied by the positions adopted by *R & F*'s writers and subsequently continued by their heirs in *Les Inrockuptibles*), but it is not sufficient to explain how the component parts of the intellectual dimension that has been progressively conferred on rock (etc.) in France have been constructed. In effect, if firstly *Rock & Folk* and secondly *Les Inrockuptibles* have contributed to the intellectualization of the music that forms their subject matter, it is by bringing to them a particular perspective that gives the French reception of rock its singularity.

---

[10]   In 1974, *R & F* printed over 77,000 copies (for a circulation of over 53,500). In 1984, its print run exceeded 182,000 copies for a circulation of almost 134,400. Thus it outstripped its competitor *Best* who printed 164,000 copies for a circulation of 112,000 in the same year. However, these monthly magazines only reached the weekly results in Britain where, in 1982, approximately 150,000 copies of *Melody Maker* were in circulation, 189,000 of *New Musical Express*, 100,000 of *Record Mirror* and 114,000 of *Sounds*. On this point, see M. C. Bonzom, (1987), 'Rock & Folk: l' idéologie du rock sous presse', DEA thesis in political studies, Université de Rennes I, 104–108.

[11]   People termed as 'branchés' (switched-on) by Olivier Donnat, even if they are not all readers of *Les Inrockuptibles* and even if the readership of this magazine does not restrict itself to this category within the population. See Donnat, Olivier (1994), *Les Français face à la culture*, Paris: La Découverte, 342–43.

An unusual intellectualization

French rock press was first of all a 'fans' press (*Disco Revue* created in 1961 by Jean-Claude Berthon, *Salut les copains* taken from the 1962 radio programme of the same name broadcast on Europe 1 and presented by Daniel Filipacchi and Franck Ténot). Then, once the above two publications had either disappeared (*Disco Revue*, in 1966) or fallen back on mainstream French pop (*Salut les copains,* from the same year[12]), the French rock press slowly started to specialize in different types of music and to promote artists that were rare or at least less prominent in the media. In comparison to the United States, Great Britain and indeed other European countries, France has long stood apart in terms of the difficulties experienced within the world of rock music (few suitably adapted concert halls or venues, indifference – even hostility – from the mainstream media, the distinctive strength of cultural hierarchies). It has therefore seen the development of a specialized press whose function has in part been to provide its readers through its articles with a substitute musical life. The lack of concerts and tours in France (except for large cities), geographical distance (from concert halls or well-stocked record shops), the linguistic barrier and the inability of most French fans to get immediate access to rock lyrics, in effect rendered indispensable the mediating role that the specialized written press claimed it was playing – mainly *Rock & Folk* and *Best*, until the end of the 1980s. Like any other mediator, these magazines in part co-constructed the representation of music and musicians on whom they were commentating. A more specific study of the work of *R & F*[13] shows that the contents of this review were more or less consciously directed by a wish to escape rival forms of cultural recognition.

Indeed, it seems that it tried to avoid the reproduction of scholastic forms of recognition to which, nevertheless, other specialist papers turned, such as rankings or other forms of hierarchy of works presented as universal. A famous article by one of *R & F*'s no less famous critics, Philippe Garnier, is a perfect example of this point. Entitled 'Mes années lumières' [My light years], it presented a series of records considered to be important. However, the following rider was found in the introduction:

> this is not a universal Top Twenty like the Top One Hundred published by the NME: this type of undertaking pleases everyone, but stinks of pantheonization, and the high priests take as their starting point that these records have intrinsic value independent of the context that caused them to be made in the first place, and which led listeners to discover them. It is the theory of the little pink cloud of creation, and it is the coward's way out. What gives rock its value, if it has any, is you and me. ... All I want to do here is to mention some records that have touched

---

12   Assayas, M. (ed.) (2000), *Dictionnaire du rock*, Paris: Robert Laffont (Bouquins), 1439–40.
13   See Teillet, 'Les cultes musicaux'.

me personally AND which I knew belonged to the collective awareness of my entire age group.[14]

It seems therefore that the journalists from *R & F* have managed to escape traditional forms of celebration by disqualifying objects (work or artists) proposed for the admiration of their readers. Effectively, traditional celebrations are typified by the search for 'masterpieces', for perfection and summits in writing or performing. On the contrary, this journal's writers regularly emphasize the imperfections, limits or defects of what they paradoxically come to celebrate.

In this way, Philippe Garnier wrote about Jonathon Richman and Modern Lovers in a paper that was, in fact, full of praise:

> The group, need it be said, remains relentlessly below the threshold of competence; and Jonathon's voice, already desperately plain and as flat as the Dead Sea on disk, is very whimsical, and sometimes even decides to disappear completely.[15]

On the subject of home-produced discs, manufacturing flaws were exposed by a more ordinary musical critic who was therefore more concerned for the listening quality of his readers (but what seems more important than the music here are the song titles by Willie Loco Alexander):

> I put the disk on the turntable, and it was obviously warped, unplayable. But in the three seconds that I could hear before the stylus bit the dust, there was this superb voice, these Jagger-like mannerisms, and the titles, of course the titles: 'Kerouac' and 'Mass. Ave'...[16]

Thus, a very particular method of negative evaluation developed that underlined the faults and the limits of what is nevertheless noted as a valuable object. It was not about a musician but about a writer, Charles Bukowski, that the same Philippe Garnier wrote:

> Buk's feet and gob stink, and he has a ring of eggs round his anus. The sign of a great writer (that and cats; but Buk doesn't like Jews. He doesn't like anybody). In fact, Bukowski is a nasty piece of work, and the things he draws on for inspiration are about as romantic as an enema.[17]

Equally, this is an approach that we can see towards actors in cinema:

> I am part of the silent rank of Tuesday Weld unconditionals and here is another opportunity to take part in the ritual: to suffer, ecstatically, in front of another of her shitty films. There are cults and actors like that. Elliot Gould is another; I'm going

---

[14] No. 98, March 1975.
[15] No. 113, June 1976.
[16] No. 119, December 1976.
[17] No. 112, May 1976.

to see all his films ... but it seems like that the bastard is doing it on purpose to get mixed up in the most unwatchable of films.[18]

To make it absolutely clear, the rejection of the traditional characteristics associated with cultural value here has nothing to do with anti-intellectualism. The complete opposite in fact: as these efforts to present artistic productions as admirable when they appear to be nothing of the sort, recall the formal transgressions of contemporary art, rather than artistic populism.

But, beyond the rejection of any kind of creeping 'pantheonization', the writers of *R & F* were equally looking for a way to distance themselves from the most naive methods of expressing admiration for French *variété* singers, male and female (the *yéyé* singers and their successors). In more or less conscious contrast to the blissful love-affairs of nice, smiling stars, *Rock & Folk* developed a sense of the tragic, a form of almost morbid fascination with various rock stars whose moment of glory was as brilliant as it was brief.

Without doubt, this was a gradual development, even if the early years of the magazine featured many notable deaths (Otis Reading, Brian Jones, Janis Joplin, Jimi Hendrix, Jim Morrison). This tragic mode of presenting rock and its heroes became an increasingly distinctive mark of the magazine. If regular news of deaths of celebrities gave the opportunity for more or less voluminous articles suggesting that the people concerned had by dying illustrated some general law of rock, other angles also allowed this tragic dimension to be reinforced. Whether it be madness, failure, depression, sadness, ageing or a career that was now well over, every chance of dramatic treatment of the music world seems to have been exploited. Philippe Koechlin in fact brought to the magazine a characteristic page set-up appropriate to the dramatic atmosphere of their approach to rock, inspired by the German magazine *Twen* which during the 1960s used a page set-up described as 'austere, dominated by black and white, with big, grainy photos, and much use of space'.[19] This tragic setting of the rock scene can also be found in *Rock Dreams,* the book by Guy Peelaert (photography) and Nik Cohn (text) initially published in 1974, the French translation[20] supplied by Ph. Paringaux, editor of *Rock & Folk.*

This work, called 'a seventies Sistine Chapel' by the periodical *Interview,* was republished with a preface by Michael Herr where, as in the texts by Nik Cohn, we find the same tonality that the management of *R & F* wanted for their monthly magazine.

If this sensitivity to the tragic succeeded in fascinating the paper's readers, it is because it broke with the more positive, cheerful and carefree tone of other publications treating music for and by young people. In this way the intellectual

18 Garnier, Philippe (1978), 'Hollywood', *R & F*, 138.
19 Koechlin, Philippe (1992), *Mémoires de Rock et Folk*, Paris: Mentha, 132–33.
20 Paris: Albin Michel, 1982, for the French translation.

dimension that *Rock & Folk* and later *Les Inrockuptibles* bestowed on rock comes not only from their writers' erudition, or from their social and cultural properties or those of their readers. It comes also and perhaps especially from a more or less conscious strategy of the magazines' management to challenge the cultural values and attitudes of musical products supported by the main audio-visual media. As we have seen, this intellectual dimension has favoured a tragic dimension being conferred on rock, a dimension that has allowed rock to share the symbolic privilege that drama enjoys to the detriment of comedy (or the comic).[21] It also conferred on rock music the status of an adult form of artistic expression, that is, capable of recreating the often painful experiences of maturity, and not simply the caricatured forms of adolescent growing pains. Moreover, the dependence of these journalists and their attempts to become independent of the record and entertainment industries and from the media, led them to introduce into the rock world (which is nevertheless strikingly marked by the strong presence of these industries) an opposition between aesthetic values and cultural values upon which the autonomy of the cultural field is constructed.[22] In this way France has experienced, principally through these two publications, a new representation of rock, conferring upon it, at least in the eyes of some and for part of what rock covers, greater seriousness and greater artistic expectations than had been initially thought. This is what we have called rock's intellectual dimension.

Today, it appears that the development of more 'festive' musical genres (discotheque and *dance floor* culture) has in some sense erased this tragic dimension. The most frequently used criteria in value judgements on rap and electronic music come from traditional parameters: for rap work on language (word-play)[23] and social references, and for electronic music invention, the art of sound collage, and style (the famous *French touch*). Nevertheless there remains a distancing from tastes that have been pre-constructed by the record industry and the media that for these types of music as for the most noble art forms is an indicator of artistic value that is rarely challenged.

However, without being able to develop the various different points here, it is important to note that the intellectualization of rock cannot be attributed solely to these publications. Beyond the growth and renewal of 'intellectual' social groups, other factors can be considered. The ageing of rock and more specifically its mutations and successive hybridization has led it to cross over into other creative domains (notably the visual arts – Pop art – cinema and literature), as the multidisciplinarity of today's *Les Inrockuptibles* demonstrates.

---

[21]   The first rock songs sung by Henri Salvador (alias Henri Cording), from lyrics written by Boris Vian, were parodies of the first American hits. These jazz fans could, in this way, take account of the low regard they had for this new type of music that threatened the music they were considered specialists in and performers of.

[22]   See Bourdieu, Pierre (1992), *Les Règles de l'art*, Paris: Le Seuil.

[23]   See Shusterman, Richard (1991), *L'art à l'état vif*, Paris: Minuit, 1991.

Moreover, even though the more nostalgic of the specialists may regret it, these forms of musical expression, which were relatively simple and limited in their original expressive functions, have, like other popular art forms, adopted a more ambitious and complex content linked to certain parts of scholarly culture[24] (in the same way as comic strips, crime fiction – which besides its established position in school or university circles has become a literary genre sometimes endowed with social and political ambitions – or, more recently break-dancing and electronic music).

Finally, in contrast to other forms of criticism (such as literary or film criticism), rock criticism has not gained a foothold in university institutions or in training in the arts. These publications have remained its sole institutions. The result is that this intellectualization has not been disseminated widely, particularly among musicians. Indeed rock musicians rarely appear to consider themselves as artists and seem rarely tempted, or even capable of discussing their own work in a relatively elaborate fashion. In other words, when listening to them or observing them, at least until very recently, our hypothesis may leave the reader sceptical. It remains, however, that *Les Inrockuptibles*'s position, and even that of other publications such as *Technikart*, and the integration of a rock critic on the staff of *Le Monde* are all a reflection of the conditions in which France has seen important changes in the position of rock in the hierarchy of cultural values. It is surprising, however, to observe that its integration into cultural policy-making may be hardly or not at all linked to its intellectualization. This is a further example of the relative autonomy of this sector (the cultural pole) within the cultural field.

Rock and local political culture

Another unusual element of French rock history comes from its integration, now 20 years ago, into public policy-making in the cultural field. There has already been one attempt to write the history of the national construction of French cultural policy.[25] We would like to focus here more specifically on the local level and examine the integration of the actors associated with rock music into municipal cultural politics. At the same time, it is impossible to discuss this subject without looking back to the actions of the state in this domain.

---

[24] Such as late nineteenth-century French poetry (Baudelaire, Verlaine, Rimbaud) for artists such as Patti Smith, Richard Hell or Tom Verlaine.

[25] On this point see my PhD thesis (1992), 'Le discours culturel et le rock, l'expérience des limites de la politique culturelle de l'Etat', University of Rennes 1.

The birth of 'rock policy'

One unusual feature among others within French cultural policy is that 'rock policy', at a budgetary level, accounts for a limited number of participating institutions and agents, and is a mini-policy which cannot be compared with more legitimate musical sectors such as classical music or contemporary music, or other disciplines that are better supported (or supported instead of rock) by the state (the cultural heritage, museums, books and reading, theatre, the visual arts). There is no space here to present every detail of public intervention (by the state and the local authorities) in the domain of rock and 'current music', but it must not be forgotten that low investment in material terms in this sector by the state's cultural services has nonetheless had a considerable impact symbolically, and has led to the use of this policy to represent, for good or for ill, the huge changes in cultural policy made under the responsibility of the socialist Minister of Culture, Jack Lang. Since this meeting at the national level did not solve all the problems posed by the integration of rock into the field of intervention by public authorities in cultural affairs – problems we shall return to, a rapid review of the conditions that might make this possible is necessary.

No request for state intervention had been forthcoming from any actor within rock – quite the opposite in fact, as the determination to challenge traditional cultural hierarchies, noticeable in the enlightened fans that were the specialist journalists, made it impossible for them to make applications to the Ministry of Culture. The idea of an 'official' institutionalized rock was used at the beginning of the 1980s to definitively disqualify anyone who was tempted to compromise rock with the representatives of legitimate culture. It was in fact reflection by the state cultural services themselves on the failure of cultural democratization (that is, the democratization of access to legitimate cultural works) that led on the one hand to the invention of a policy based on a plural approach to culture (including 'major' and 'minor' arts; regional or ethnic cultures; scientific culture), and on the desire to encourage a wide range of activities which did not have the pre-established norms of 'real' cultural practices on the other. A policy of this type, embodied by Jack Lang, was inconceivable without a gradual cognitive change in cultural officials' ways of understanding the field in the years preceding Lang's appointment. This change in the order of representations was principally the consequence of sociological analyses undertaken by the Study and Research Department (le services des études et recherches – SER) (now called the Study and Prospect Department (le département des études et de la prospective, DEP) in the Ministry of Culture. It was these studies that showed up the extent of the failure of cultural democratization, and that identified, amongst the cultural activities of French people, practices hitherto ignored by the state, and notably rock music among young people. In this way, it became possible to conceive of state intervention in culture to support the type of music that had been defined as being the musical identity of young people.

It is therefore during Lang's first spell as Minister (1981–86) that some officials in the Ministry, supported by certain agents of the SER, decided to put into action this reorientation of cultural policy, by measures aimed at the young and cultural forms that were attributed to them. These various important people were put in touch with those running non-profit-making associations in the rock music world who took responsibility for defining how state intervention in this domain could be useful. Caught between the double constraint of needing to justify the intervention to the Ministry for Culture to both the government and its officials on the one hand and to other actors within the rock world in France on the other, these early 'representatives' of rock set about stressing that measures could not be limited to the idea that this was simply 'the music of the young' nor to adopting an exclusively socio-cultural approach to this music. However, the rejection of this status that was judged to be ignoring the artistic vitality of the sector could not be accompanied by an artistic-recognition type discourse using the habitual criteria (formal complexity, or works that had stood the test of time). Therefore there gradually developed a discourse (or set of arguments) about the place of rock within the music industries and about its professionalization, discourse that, while referring to the 'entrepreneurial'[26] myth and using management vocabulary, allowed weight and maturity to be given to this domain without bending it in the direction of criteria of legitimacy and artistic gravity. This discursive register, which favoured the setting up of public actions in partnership with professional organizations,[27] had the additional advantage of distinguishing rock from (or even opposing it to) traditional sectors of cultural policy that had been relatively protected from market forces. Thus, much to the satisfaction of many of its fans, there was no question that rock be assimilated to other artistic disciplines that had received the recognition of public cultural and educational institutions.

Despite the existence of specialist critics (as described above), it would appear in fact that rock (etc.) musicians and their entourage have always found it difficult to accept any criterion of success other than an increase in audience (measured by number of spectators and/or number of records sold). This attachment to a criterion of recognition that is, in the end, close to market logic, allowed those responsible for rock policy to defend its integration of rock into the field of state cultural intervention without coming into too much conflict with fans' common representations of it. Basically, it was a case of accepting government aid without adopting the criteria of value typical of the subsidized sector. This argument could be accepted in so far as state intervention could give priority to emerging artists, who had not yet attracted the vast audiences of the

---

[26] See Le Goff, Jean-Pierre (1995), *Le Mythe de l'entreprise*, Paris: La Découverte.

[27] To such an extent that we no longer notice that it could be different and that rock could be appreciated in ways that are more independent of commercial logic. See Roussel, Daniel (1995), 'L'Etat, le Rock et la chanson', *Regards sur l'actualité*, November, for a 'mixed-economy' approach to rock.

star system. It was just correcting the worst effects of commercial logic. Thus, those responsible for nascent rock policy offered the actors of the rock world an acceptable representation of their music, a representation simultaneously hostile to cultural hierarchies and embarrassed by commercial success. Because, as Simon Frith has remarked, 'Rock is a mass-produced music that carries a critique of its own means of production.'[28]

This brief reminder of the genealogy of public policy on rock and of the issues involved has, hopefully, brought out its cognitive dimension (that is, what this policy owes to a change in ways of seeing and treating cultural problems) and the impact of relations between the rock field and the cultural policy sector on the content of the policy.

Cultural policies and local identities

The local dimension in cultural policies frequently translates itself on the ground into a wish to give policies an identity dimension, either to promote a positive and attractive image of the town externally, or, internally, to encourage the integration of population groups who, for social, spatial and cultural reasons (often combined), tend to be subjected to varying degrees of exclusion.[29] In Great Britain as in the United States, public initiatives in the musical domains we are looking at can have a strong tourism dimension, based on the built heritage (concert halls, recording studios and various historical sites), as well as on the important contribution made by musicians from these countries to the history of this field of music.

If the French contribution to music is today still far more modest, the will of local councillors to intervene in cultural affairs is on the other hand more obvious and often driven by the overall goals (such as local development) to which the cultural sector is invited to contribute.[30] The different aspects of local government intervention, encouraged and helped by the state, are thus united by this notion of identity, conscious of the need to promote the cultural expression of social and ethnic identities, to further identify a town on a European, national or regional scale, or to confer greater legitimacy to cultural intervention by government, which is still seemingly marginal (or is this a myth?) in its impact on the local population. It must, however, be recognized, as Alan Faure asserts,[31]

---

[28] Frith, Simon (1983), *Sound Effects: Youth, Leisure, and the Politics of Rock'n' Roll*, London: Constable, 11.

[29] See Rizzardo, R. (1995), *Identités et politiques culturelles*, in J. P. Saez, *Identités, cultures et territoires*, Paris: Desclée de Brouwer.

[30] See Morel, A. (1993), 'Politiques culturelles, production d'images et développement local', in J.-P. Saez, *Identités, cultures et territoires*; and Gaudin, J.-P. (1993), *Les nouvelles politiques urbaines*, Paris: PUF, 68–74.

[31] Faure, A. (1995), 'Les Politiques locales, entre référentiels et rhétorique', in A. Faure, G. Pollet and P. Warin, *La construction du sens dans les politiques publiques*, Paris: L'Harmattan, 69–83.

that if local councillors 'take over the intellectual field' and seek to redeem their area's 'cultural virtues', as well as 'the unique public characteristics inscribed in the history of their geographical community', it is often by using rhetoric which is consensual and uncontroversial, often one representative of local identity, which presents a decision-making framework that lacks transparency and is on the whole hardly restrictive. Policies based on identity may be relatively easy to use in terms of argument or discourse, but whatever the size of the efforts put into constructing and differentiating the promotion of a particular identity, the success of these identity policies depends upon the aptitude of this identity to find its place in local customs and practices that will ensure that these policies become grounded socially and territorially, and thus give them the necessary credibility. Public decision makers looking for symbols to represent this identity can find this particular quality (an undeniably local grounding) in a local music scene.

Rock scenes and cultural identities

The notion of a 'rock scene' is in part the outcome of the cumulative history of the field of rock – and its agents – which has remembered the particular contribution of certain cities to music production (through artists, groups or record labels).[32] But, contained as it is within a history that is not taught in schools, this notion also depends on other non-academic methods of commentary (reports, reviews of concerts and records, and interviews with musicians and producers – essentially in the written press) inspired by these forms of musical expression. In this way, this history, maintained by more or less specialized press bodies, and partially constructed (through obscuring, selection and interpretation of facts) projects a memory which today is more sensitive and weightier, and is often employed, through subtle references to the past, in promotional business strategies.

For example, several years ago, the competition between the British groups Blur and Oasis was presented by the press (no doubt aided if not by the band members themselves then by their respective entourage) as a repeat of past battles (Beatles/Rolling Stones) or as traditional city rivalries (in this case London and Manchester) presented as social class rivalries at the cost of a rather forced (even if not completely false) construction of the social identity of these cities.[33]

---

[32] Amongst others: Liverpool, London, Manchester, Glasgow and most recently Bristol in Great Britain; Memphis, Detroit, San Francisco, Los Angeles, New York, and most recently Athens or Seattle in the USA; Rennes, Lyon, Bordeaux, Le Havre, Rouen, Nancy, Marseille, and even Angers, in France.

[33] See the examples, amongst others: 'La nouvelle bataille de la pop passionne la Grande Bretagne' in *Le Monde*, 28 October 1995; 'La bataille d'Angleterre', *Télérama*, 1 November 1995.

It is thus within musical commentary and music discourse that is to be found the mechanism of symbolic representation at work in writing about 'local scenes'. Out of the four functions of representations outlined by Maurice Godelier,[34] at least three appear clearly in this particular case. Firstly, the notion of a local scene enables an intellectual understanding of these musical practices; it gives these external realities a presence in the thoughts of an individual. It is actually easier to understand a set of musical productions in terms of the locality where they first appeared and of the common sensibilities and proximities supposedly favoured by this locality. Secondly, the reference to this notion is always an interpretation of reality, a reading of reality that is both founded and yet erroneous (actors of these 'local scenes' often make play of denying or nuancing their connections to the scene that this notion seems to describe). Finally, representations (and this one in particular) give or deny legitimacy to the relationships of individuals and groups to each other. It would indeed appear that in these musical domains integration or the lack of integration to a particular local scene can have an influence, positive or negative, on the legitimacy of artistic proposals.

Yet, like all symbolic representation, the representations that pervade the notion of local scene would not have such an impact without some connection to reality. It is therefore necessary to note that this notion can rely upon concrete and practical elements of music. Firstly, since rock and assimilated music is accessible to amateurs because of its relatively small demands for musical skill, rock is capable of attracting a far greater number of practitioners than other forms of musical expression which require far longer musical apprenticeship and prove to be noticeably more selective disciplines. The human population group here concerned is then for this reason far greater in number and thus more visible. Secondly, urban locations pose a multitude of practical problems for performers and audiences of this type of often highly amplified music. Whether for staging concerts or for rehearsals, these forms of music require specially adapted buildings to cope with noise pollution. Moreover the hierarchy of cultural productions favouring the forms approved of by schools encourages the exclusion of this music from the benefits of the more substantial public sector interventions in favour of culture. For this reason, often because of their age, their financial means or the cultural status of their music, musicians who all hail from the same locality and social group are led to conceive of their situations in terms of community of interests and shared conditions. Thirdly, the lack of opportunities for recognition independent of the market and its logic (schools and cultural institutions), means that musicians in this field have no real form of recognition other than their audience. Its size and dynamics are the most reliable indicators of their artistic success, beginning with a measurable small-scale success, which can be offered by their local scene and its public.

---

[34]   Godelier, Maurice (1984), *L'idéel et le matériel*, Paris: Fayard, 199–200.

At the crossroads of these logics, the incorporation of actors from musical scenes into local cultural policy-making may seem both coherent in terms of the modes of artistic production in these domains, and useful in the construction of 'strategic identities'[35] by local authorities.[36] Councillors can actually draw on this to prove the existence of a genuine cultural identity, pre-existing their intervention, and also to show an aspect of their cultural policy which will not have to prove its grounding in the local fabric, or which will avoid the expense of costly implantation procedures.[37] One can add to these virtues the impact of the evolution of cultural practices which, in most European states, is tending to favour the domain of image and sound to the detriment of words as an artform. This is why the vitality and wealth of a local music scene and of its talented performers, when amply exposed to the media, can more effectively contribute to a town's fame. This integration remains impossible, however, without resolving the difficulties resulting principally from the reversal of functions between the fields of rock and of local culture.

Issues in the instrumentalization of rock scenes to create local cultural identities

The use of a rock scene to identify a local authority area within which it exists assumes firstly that the local political officials are publicly as much in favour of this music and those dedicated to it as officials at Ministry level. However, at present, policies concerning rock music are far from being conceived in absolute consensus, and numerous local situations have demonstrated the reticence or hostility of councillors to take on this often vulgar, difficult-to-master social ground, which is liable to create more conflict than consensus. It is true to say nonetheless that over the years, the national example as well as that of several provincial towns has undoubtedly helped overcome the fears of town councillors, with backing for rock events and facilities becoming relatively common in the cultural policies of medium and large towns. Moreover, rock's increasing popularity among the most educated groups of the population has encouraged the emergence of mediators capable of staging projects while working alongside local authorities – as well as completing all the form-filling that is necessarily involved – and of satisfying local councillors with the external signs of

---

[35] The notion of strategic identity refers to the products of the construction of a personal identity, whose architects are the politicians themselves and their entourage, and which can then be put to use to support the different causes in which they are involved. See Collovald, A. (1988), 'Identité(s) stratégique(s)', *Actes de la Recherche en Sciences Sociales*, 73, June.
[36] See, on this point, the conflicting relations between Toulouse town hall and the musical group, the Fabulous Troubadors, who re-enact the tradition of Occitan troubadours from the Middle Ages, giving their act a modern twist by crossing it with an ethno-musicological reading of rap.
[37] One can here cite the examples of Rennes and, to a lesser extent, Marseille.

competence and responsibility.[38] The difficulties surrounding this point today are more acute with rap music where these mediators are, no doubt temporarily, harder to find, and where questions concerning control of public order during concerts are more frequently raised.

Another point is that building local cultural policy around the theme of identity logically encourages the highlighting of the natural and architectural heritage or of strong cultural traditions. It is based therefore on the legitimacy of the long tradition of local history. Musical scenes have only appeared comparatively recently and can hardly claim to possess the same legitimacy. Also, the outside recognition of these music scenes is the result of a long, complex and relatively haphazard process, which often involves the intervention of many people. Conversely, the nomination of an artist or a cultural manager with a national or international reputation to chair a local institution is a decision within the bounds of local officials' expertise, and its effects on the identity and identification of the community for which they are responsible could be swiftly felt. This no doubt explains why, without necessarily cutting themselves off from supporting their local scenes, elected councillors have preferred, as regards rock and other similar music, to concentrate their efforts on prestigious events which provide the sought-after visibility and widespread public support with greater certainty.[39]

Further, if the notion of local scene symbolizes a community of like-minded musicians united by their sensibilities and by sharing the common space required by their musical activities (concert or rehearsal rooms, bars, record shops), its integration into local cultural policy assumes a strong and visible representation emerging from this movement (in the shape of one or more emblematic personalities). This representation, which (as in many other cases) crystallizes the formation of the group represented,[40] will therefore depend on 'representatives' (legitimate, self-proclaimed or selected by the local authorities) or on the existence of 'representative' events (concerts and festivals which give visibility, both within and outside the town, to the artists who live there). As it is, the reality of musical activities means that fields of artistic production emerge which are less like fraternal communities and more like spaces of conflict waged over ideological conceptions and relatively divergent interests. Whatever the mode of recognition of their status, the emergence of representatives is necessarily accompanied by opposition from other people in the field, who question their dominant position. They may contest, for example, their close relations with the public authorities, in the name of a 'rebel' ethic or, after the

---

[38]   There is no systematic study of the social definitions and strategies of the mediators who have helped establish these local policies supporting 'current music'.

[39]   This is notably the case of the festival 'Les Eurockéenes' created in 1989 by the Local Council of Belfort (Conseil général du Territoire de Belfort).

[40]   See, among others: Boltanski, Luc (1982), *Les Cadres*, Paris: Minuit.

resources have been allocated to them – an appointment as director of a theatre, or grants – as a form of ingratitude and remoteness from local artists.

In addition, the public acknowledgement of these music scenes, in the shape of various types of support, and the integration of their actors into local cultural fields can rekindle internal struggles within these fields and call into question the overall coherence of public interventions in culture. As late-comers into these fields, and often the least financially secure, the representatives of music scenes tend to oppose the culture professionals (who, especially in large towns, at the head of more prestigious, traditional institutions, look like outsiders who have been parachuted in and like representatives of a cultural elite) about, on the one hand, their regional 'anchorage' and on the other hand, their 'popular' dimension or, at least, the existence in their domain of a more substantial public (quantitatively and qualitatively – younger and less advantaged socially than the traditional cultural public). It must be added that if, originally, cultural decentralization came about through a regional planning logic being applied to the whole of the country in an attempt to create cultural facilities in the provinces reminiscent of those which up to that point were unique features of the capital, it now favours the investment by local authorities in this domain, which obey a quite different logic, notably competition between towns. It is at this point that contradictions inherent in certain cultural instruments being employed to promote the locality (as they are at the same time attached to a territory but also escape from it by participating in regional, national and even international competition[41]) run the risk of being denounced by representatives of the local music scene. Whilst the latter may often be underprivileged when it comes to the distribution of subsidies and various symbolic payments that councillors can award cultural officials, they will find in their regional grounding and in their ability to participate more legitimately in the theme of identity, solid arguments to obtain from the public authorities the material means they lack to further their development.[42]

Within the framework of the Minister of Culture's legitimization of public-sector intervention to promote rock and 'current music', towns and cities were given the idea that support for their local music scene could help promote their identity. At the (provisional) end of the period of support that has been granted, it seems that this notion of a 'local scene' tends to disappear. The existence of these scenes seems therefore in part linked to the cohesion of musical milieux at

---

[41] On this point, see the works of Guy Saez on cultural policies in the major cities: 'Etat, villes et culture: un modèle métropolitain d'intervention publique', contribution to the conference *Décentralisation, régionalisation et action culturelle municipale*, Montréal, 12, 13 and 14 November 1992; 'Le dilemme culturel de la métropole: villes, identités et politiques publiques', in M. Bassand and J.-Ph. Leresche, *Les Faces cachées de l'urbain*, Bern: P. Lang, 1994.

[42] See, on this point, Castagnac, G. (1991), 'L'enjeu des scènes locales', *Yaourt*, hors série no.4, November.

an earlier stage when public authorities were more often indifferent, if not hostile, towards them. The development of local cultural policies and of competition between towns has encouraged a type of support that has no doubt not harmed the music scene in these towns (on the contrary). But it has seriously affected these local scenes as symbolic constructions.

This study has essentially attempted to show that the dissemination and integration of rock in France cannot be limited to the history of its performers and its fans. This musical genre, however ill defined it is, has, via the people who have claimed in their different ways to represent it, entered social fields where symbolic representations of reality are constructed and where public cultural policy is made and negotiated. Rock was initially looked down on, even mocked, but has gradually been partially endowed with some cultural value as a function of a more intellectual representation that has been made of it. Rejected or ignored by those in charge of public sector culture that became institutionalized at about the same time as the first French rockers appeared (1959), rock made its first entry into the cultural policy sector (particularly the local cultural policy sector) during the 1980s. This chapter has attempted to describe this double move.[43] The most surprising thing is doubtless that despite their links the first change has (as we have seen) not been the cause of the second.

---

[43]   Virginie Millot has undertaken work with a similar aim on rap and the integration of break dancing in the cultural sector. See 'Les fleurs sauvages de la ville et de l'art. Analyse anthropologique de l'émergence et de la sédimentation du hip-hop lyonnais', doctoral thesis, University of Lyon II, 1997; and Millot, Virginie (2002), 'La mise en scène des cultures urbaines ou la fabrique institutionnelle du métissage', *L'Observatoire*, 22, 14–22.

Chapter 11

Globalization, Americanization and hip hop in France

Steve Cannon

What David Toop describes as a movement from 'African rap to global hip hop',[1] has seen France emerge as the world's second-largest market for hip hop musical products. Whilst it might initially seem strange to be discussing hip hop in a book on *French* popular music, where the *chanson* tradition might be the expected focus, the latter's status as 'text-song', which clearly contributes significantly to its cultural legitimacy, is paralleled in French hip hop, with MC Solaar in particular not only making cultural reference to *chansonniers* such as Gainsbourg, Boby Lapointe and Jacques Dutronc, but creating texts which are complex and inventive in their own right, full of alliterative word-play that many a poet would envy.[2]

The big-sellers in France have included homegrown examples as varied as MC Solaar, Suprême NTM, Doc Gyneco and Saïan Supa Crew, which, since the early 1990s, have established a significant place in mainstream popular music in terms of sales, play-listing and numbers of new releases. Part of the explanation for hip hop's success in France lies in the presence in France of approximately 15 million people who are either officially 'foreign', or whose family is of minority ethnic origin. The role of young people of minority ethnic origin in the production and consumption of hip hop is not the focus of this chapter, nor is it my intention to focus on the history and evolution of hip hop in France here.[3]

---

[1]   Toop, David (2000), *Rap Attack 3: From African rap to global hip-hop*, London: Serpent's Tail. The attempt to trace hip hop's cultural antecedents leads Toop back to African bardic traditions, while Lapassade, G., and Rousselot, P. (1990), *Le Rap, ou la fureur de dire*, Paris: Editions Loris Talmart, make connections to *griot* singers and other aspects of African vernacular expression.

[2]   The notion of 'text-song' is briefly discussed in Looseley's chapter in this volume. See also, on *chanson*, Hawkins, Peter (2000), *Chanson: the French Singer-Songwriter from Aristide Bruant to the Present Day*, Aldershot: Ashgate. It is significant that 'the present day' is represented in Hawkins's survey by MC Solaar.

[3]   See Bazin, Hugues (1995), *La Culture hip-hop*, Paris: Desclée de Brouwer; Cannon, Steve (1997), '"Paname City Rapping": B-Boys in the *banlieues* and beyond', in Alec G. Hargreaves and Mark McKinney (eds), *Post-colonial Cultures in France*, London: Routledge, 150–66; and Warne, Chris (1997), 'Articulating Identity from the Margins: *Le Mouv'* and the Rise of Hip-hop and Ragga in France', in Sheila Perry and Maire Cross (eds), *Voices of France*, London: Cassell, 141–54, for a fuller discussion.

But a brief description of its adoption and adaptation should introduce some of the key questions which might be raised by the importation and subsequent flourishing development of an (African-) American cultural form in France. We will then 'go local', examining hip hop in Marseille as a case study, and specifically the work of IAM, one of the best-known and most successful groups in France.

From the Bronx to the *banlieues*[4]

Hip hop developed in the South Bronx area of New York in the mid-1970s, a culture of interconnected street arts including graffiti and dance as well as music, though it is principally in the form of the latter, known as 'rap', that it has been commercialized and distributed globally. Tricia Rose defines rap as 'rhymed storytelling accompanied by highly rhythmic, electronically-based music',[5] the latter supplied by a DJ using twin turntables (and later digital sampling technology) to mix fragments or sections of vinyl recordings together to create a new piece of music.[6]

Hip hop came to France in the autumn of 1982, when radio station Europe 1 financed a tour featuring all three of its elements: music (Afrika Bambaataa), graffiti (Futura 2000) and break-dancing (the Rock Steady Crew). This tour, combined with images in films like *Flashdance*, helped create a short-lived vogue for break-dancing (in France labelled 'le smurf'), including a weekly television show on TF1.

While that fad soon ended, hip hop sounds and styles found a new home amongst a fervent minority in France, particularly in the Paris *banlieues*, and although white individuals such as Dee Nasty played a pioneering role, it was particularly amongst the region's minority ethnic communities that hip hop found an echo.

The classic Parisian initiation into rap would begin with seeing Afrika Bambaataa on tour, perhaps joining the French branch of the Zulu Nation[7] that

---

[4]   I am retaining the French term throughout this chapter as it clearly has directly opposed connotations to 'suburbs'.

[5]   Rose, Tricia (1994), *Black Noise: Rap Music and Black Culture in Contemporary America*, Hanover, NH: Wesleyan University Press, 2.

[6]   See Toop, *Rap Attack*; Hager, Steven (1984), *Hip Hop: The Illustrated History of Breakdancing, Rap Music and Graffiti*, New York: St Martin's Press; and Hebdige, Dick (1987), *Cut 'n' Mix Culture: Identity and Caribbean Music*, London: Methuen, ch. 16: 'Rap and hip hop: the New York connection', 136–48.

[7]   The Zulu Nation was an important source of collective values, founded by Afrika Bambaataa in New York to overcome inter-project rivalries and gang wars. It established a branch in France, with its own 'King and Queen' in 1984 after a visit by Bambaataa. With its own fanzine *The Zulus' Letter* and *soirées* called 'Zulu's Party' (*sic*) it was one of the first organizations which attempted to rally the disparate forces of hip hop in France

he established, forming a 'posse' whose spray-painted 'tag' decorates their estate, or the metro system, becoming part of the hardcore fanbase visiting import record stores, nightclubs, clothes shops and eventually pirate radio stations, the key loci of hip hop apprenticeship.[8]

Graffiti and break-dance sessions usually preceded any musical activity, but independent radio stations such as Nova and Radio 7 began to open up their microphones to the unofficial 'freestyle' champions of each *banlieue*. As Geoff Hare explains, the 1980s was a period where the so-called state monopoly of the airwaves was broken up: new commercial stations mushroomed, highly dependent on heavily segmented audiences for specialist music, with Nova functioning as provider to its Parisian audience of hip hop, dance and 'world' musics.

Following Nova presenter Dee Nasty's self-produced mini-album *Paname City Rapping*, and a successful compilation of rap in French, *Rapattitude*, released in 1990, the major labels began to sign up francophone rappers and MC Solaar, IAM, Suprême NTM, Alliance Ethnik and subsequently countless others established successful careers and substantial sales, such that by the end of the 1990s, rap in France represented billions of francs to the music industry.

One view of this arrival of hip hop in France might be that it represents a further example of Americanization of 'French' popular culture, part of the eradication of cultural difference that more pessimistic analysts of cultural globalization have detected. The unequal flow of media influence and imagery imposes a 'numbingly standardized',[9] homogeneous world culture, which an early generation of French resistance to 'cultural imperialism' termed 'coca-colonization', but which Ritzer has updated in referring to 'McDonaldization'.[10]

More optimistic approaches, or at least those more sceptical about the supposed uniformity of effect of cultural globalization, might see it as an example of 'cultural reterritorialization',[11] viewing cultural products as resources that can be reinscribed with meanings, adapted and reworked to relate to local contexts.

The discussion that follows, focusing on Marseille's principal exponents of rap, IAM,[12] will explore the intersection of the local and the global, will

---

during the late 1980s. However despite this desire for unity, the relatively prescriptive 'charter' regulating behaviour of official members of the Nation, which, for example, forbade tagging as a form of delinquency was unlikely in the end to achieve it.

8   Bazin, *Culture hip-hop*; Cannon, *B-boys in the banlieues*.
9   '[C]ulture has been expropriated of its variety ... in its place has been put ... numbing standardization.' Aguiton, Christophe, Petrella, Riccardo and Udry, Christophe-André (2001), 'The Mechanics of exclusion', in F. Houtart and F. Polet (eds), *The Other Davos: the globalization of resistance*, London: Zed, 31.
10   Ritzer, George (1993), *The McDonaldization of Society*, Newbury Park, CA: Pine Forge Press.
11   Lull, J. (1995), *Media, Communication, Culture: a global approach*, Cambridge: Polity.
12   There is now a flourishing hip hop scene in Marseille, partly inspired by the success of IAM and the establishment of their label, *Coté Obscur*, including groups such as 3e Oeil, Uptown, Fonky Family and Soul Swing 'n' Radical.

hopefully illustrate the complexity of meanings in the best francophone rap and perhaps allow us to move beyond the potentially reductive trend of seeing rap in France simply as 'une réponse des banlieues' [a reply from the *banlieues*].[13]

What I will argue is that hip hop in Marseille has developed around a different kind of relationship between centre and periphery than the dominant scenes of Paris and its *banlieues*, and that the sense of the local for IAM in particular, and perhaps for Marseille hip hop in general, is a rather different one than that expressed in Parisian *banlieue* rap. So a few remarks on the specificities of Marseille first, before looking in detail at some aspects of IAM's practice.

'De la planète Mars(eille)': Global and local identities in Marseille hip hop

Albert Londres's somewhat poetic description of Marseille emphasizes its place as gateway to France, particularly from Africa: 'en résumé, une porte monumentale, où passeraient, flux et reflux, les cent visages du vaste monde' [a giant door through which might ebb and flow the 100 faces of this vast world].[14]

This aspect is echoed in more negative images and stereotypes associated with the city – as a kind of Achilles' heel of France's immigration controls, as a city of illegal immigration and racism, criminality, corruption and drugs. Its marginality, despite being one of France's largest cities, is linked to its geographical position, as well as these social ills. From the centre, from Paris, Marseille truly seems, in Edward Said's characterization of the marginal space, to be on the edge of civilization,[15] as if its place on the French side of the Mediterranean gives it one foot in the 'other' continent, in Africa.

Murray Forman's recent article on race, space and place in rap describes its obsessive preoccupation with 'spatialized themes of intense locality',[16] citing examples from Compton and Watts. Similar preoccupations can be found in francophone rap, for example in the names of Parisian crews such as Suprême NTM 93 (93 being the number of the *département* in which their *banlieue* town is located) or 113 (more local still – the number of the block on the housing estate/project in which group members live). In the case of IAM, it is a whole city that is celebrated and validated in their work, rather than one housing estate, *quartier*, or *banlieue*. And it is Marseille in its historical, social and mythical contexts, 'warts and all', which is being placed at the centre in their work.

13   Calio, Jean (1998), *Le Rap: une réponse des banlieues?* Paris: Aléas.
14   Londres, Albert (1994), *Marseille, porte du Sud*, Paris: Le Serpent à plumes, 18.
15   Said, Edward (1978), *Orientalism*, New York: Vintage.
16   Forman, Murray (2000), '"Represent": Race, space and place in rap music', *Popular Music*, **19** (1), 76.

What's in a name?

The group had been called Lively Crew by its two founders, Philippe Fragione and Eric Mazel in 1986, then B-Boy Stance from 1987 to 1989, while also referring to themselves as part of 'le Criminosical Posse' (a compound of criminal/music), a collective much wider than the actual musical or dance performers.

These terms *crew*, *posse*, *b-boy* (abbreviation of breaker-boy or bad-boy) all represent identification with, and belonging to, the global hip hop movement, and obviously reflect its origins in the USA. But by 1989, as the group expanded to comprise six members, they chose the name IAM.

The name has multiple significations, and the group have deliberately encouraged this multiplicity of meanings of their name and their identity: the discussion that follows, of their image, their music and the hybrid identities they express, will be organized around five versions of the meaning of the name IAM.

IAM's first-degree meaning is its English one, 'I am': 'IAM ça veut dire "je suis", j'existe. Pour dire à ceux qui nous dirigent qu'on est autre chose que des chiffres.' [It means I am, I exist. To say to those in power that we are more than just numbers.][17]

So 'I rap therefore I am', an idea which reflects the important role of rap as establishing a right for repressed voices, for the traditionally excluded, to have a say, to have a place. This is reinforced by the centrality of *naming* in rap and hip hop. As Tricia Rose points out, 'hip hop's prolific self-naming is a form of reinvention and self definition'.[18]

Below we have the names of the six individuals in IAM, as well as their complex mixture of family backgrounds and ethnicities, which will not be discussed here in detail.

Philippe Fragione/Chill (Phil)/Akhénaton/ Abd-El-Hâkim/Filippo/Sentenza, born Marseille, Italian (Neapolitan/Sicilian) parents (rapper/lyricist).
Geoffroy (Jo) Mussard/ Shurik'n Chang-Ti, born Marseille, parents from Madagascar/ la Réunion (rapper/lyricist).
Eric Mazel/Mr Crazy Mix/DJ Khéops, born Marseille, Spanish/Marseillais parents.
Pascal Pérez/Imhotep, l'architecte du son [architect of sound], born Algiers, Spanish/French *pied noir* family.
Malek Brahimi/Abdel Malek Sultan/Freeman, born Marseille, Algerian parents (dancer/rapper).
François Mendy/le Divin Képhren, born Paris, Senegalese parents (dancer).

Philippe Fragione initially adopts the abbreviation Phil, to play more 'americano', then when visiting Italian-American relatives in New York, falls in

---

[17]   Chill, quoted in Obadia, E. (1991), 'IAM: Planète Mars'. *BEST* Hors série no. 2, 82.
[18]   Rose, *Black Noise*, 36.

with a hip hop crowd, including the Jungle Brothers and MC Choice, the latter allowing him to record the b-side of his single, under the name Chill Phil, a nickname they had dubbed him with as he was so laidback. Back on the streets of Marseille, he retains the name Chill, but when forming IAM, under the twin influences of his own reading about Egypt and of Afrocentrism that he picked up in hip hop circles in New York, he renames himself Akhénaton, after one of the pharaohs. In the course of IAM's career and his own solo recordings, however, he has also written and performed raps in the names of Abd-El-Hâkim (the name he took when converting to Islam, when he married a Moroccan woman in 1993); Filippo, the Italianization of his given name; and a pseudo-character from a spaghetti western, Sentenza.

Eric Mazel similarly adopts a name in keeping with his function or particular technical prowess within hip hop, as a mixer, a DJ, then as IAM is formed takes the name, as does Pascal Pérez, of an Egyptian *architect*. Finally Malek Brahimi, who wished to retain some Islamic cultural influence when choosing a pseudonym in joining IAM as a dancer, hence adopts that of a Sultan of the Ottoman Empire, rather than an Egyptian name, and interestingly he has recently taken the name Freeman, now that he has recorded raps of his own, perhaps or perhaps not a comment on the internal politics of the group.

The fact that Chill went to New York might seem anecdotal, but his repeated visits every summer, taking other members of the fledgling group with him, offered them a different relationship with the source than the Parisian scene. Without access to that growing network of Parisian locations, Chill establishes a Marseille/New York axis that continues to exist, rap producers such as Nick Sansano having been brought across to work in Marseille.

I would argue that this direct contact gave IAM more confidence more quickly to abandon their influences and branch out, forging a style very much rooted in Marseille, rather than slavishly seeking to emulate West or East Coast styles from the USA. One key example is Chill/Akhénaton's exploration of his own Italian origins and the role of southern Italian migration to Marseille:

nous avons commencé par imiter nos maîtres. Quand on évoquait la drogue, on parlait de crack comme si on habitait à LA, alors que, en France, ça n'était pas le problème ... Il a fallu du temps pour qu'on se recentre sur ses propres racines. Pour que je me rende compte, par exemple, que mes origines italiennes me donnaient une richesse différente.

[We began by imitating those who had taught us. When we spoke of drugs we mentioned crack, as if we lived in LA, whereas in France that wasn't the problem ... it took a while to draw on our own roots. For me to realize, for example, that my Italian origins offered a different richness.][19]

---

[19]   Chill, quoted in Blanchet, Philippe (1995), 'Bourges: le printemps du rap', *Evénement du Jeudi*, 20–26 April, 79.

This 'richesse' is explored in a marvellously evocative track, *Où sont les roses?* [Where are the roses?] from *Ombre est lumière* [Shadow is light], the group's second album.[20] To the accompaniment of Tino Rossi-esque Italian ballad samples, it offers a moving account of a family's emigration from Naples, the racism faced in transplanting in Marseille and the bitter irony that the descendants of that generation of Italian immigrants are now some of Front National leader Jean-Marie Le Pen's fiercest supporters in the South,[21] seeking to 'se la jouer plus autochtones que les vrais' [pose as more French than the French]. It was further developed on his solo project, *Metèque et Mat*,[22] recorded in Naples, packaged with sepia-tinted family photos and, on tracks such as *La Cosca* and *L'Americano*, again sampling popular Italian and Sicilian ballads.

Imperial Asiatic Men

Already in the rudimentary packaging of the self-produced *Concept* cassette, Afrocentrism was an important influence on the group, with the red, black and green of the Black Nationalist flag accompanied by the crescent and star of Islam, also incorporated into the group's logo, circled by Arabic lettering. One of their earliest recordings was entitled *Red, Black and Green*, sampling influential Black Nationalist rappers Brand Nubians. Afrocentrism also influences the second version of their name, Imperial Asiatic Men.

This represents a validation of early non-European civilizations, from Africa to China,[23] forming a composite pre-capitalist 'empire' to which they claim allegiance. But in contrast to US rappers' Afrocentrism, which might be described as broadly separatist in outlook, there is an emphasis on universality.[24]

---

[20]   Since the *Concept* cassette was a self-produced, mail order run of only 500 copies, I am referring to the first widely released album, ... *de la planète Mars* as the first, and so on (see discography).

[21]   The Front National is a fascist party which has risen from virtual obscurity in 1981 to garner the votes of upwards of 15 per cent of the French electorate, and, spectacularly, in the Presidential elections of 2002, Le Pen took almost 18 per cent of the vote and pushed the Parti Socialiste into 3rd place. Provence has traditionally been one of its strongholds, partly due to the presence there of significant numbers of resettled *pieds noirs* (European Algerians returning to France following Algerian independence in 1962), and the FN currently runs the municipalities of several towns and cities in the Marseille area: Marignane, Orange, Toulon and Vitrolles.

[22]   An untranslatable pun on 'échec et mat' (checkmate) whilst its literal meaning employs the archaic insult 'métèque', giving us something like 'dago and dark'.

[23]   Shurik'n Chang-Ti, the name adopted by Jo Mussard, is a Chinese martial arts weapon.

[24]   1960s black nationalist politics and political figures were popularized by Public Enemy, and by KRS-1/Boogie Down Productions who adopted its slogans and styles (berets, clenched fist salutes) from the late 1980s onwards. From followers of Louis Farrakhan's Nation of Islam or the Five Per Cent Nation to a more culturally influenced

Whether African or not, anyone can find their own authentic values in the Motherland, returning to the source of all human life precisely for authenticity, the essential.

There is also, here, a rather different relationship with Afrocentric ideas than their US influences, perhaps reflecting the closer physical and therefore less mythical relationship of rappers in Marseille to the 'pays d'origine'. Chill read and studied Senegalese academic Cheikh Anta Diop, particularly *Nations nègres et cultures*,[25] whereas only selections from Diop's work exist in translation in English, and it has only fairly recently become influential amongst African-American academics. The key argument in Diop's work is that Egypt was essentially an African civilization, that it shared elements with other civilizations on the continent, and indeed, horror of horrors for the ideological supports of colonialism, that the Pharaohs were black.[26]

So Egypt, hieroglyphic and pyramid imagery play a significant role in the stage sets and CD or cassette packaging of IAM's early 1990s work. On the cover of the single *Donne-moi le micro* [Give me the mike], this took a somewhat humorous form of recognizable hieroglyphic representations of human figures clutching microphones, grouped around a DJ's turntables, while the album *Ombre est lumière* and its accompanying tours featured a more sombre representation of the columns of a ruined temple and hieroglyphics which were worn away and virtually effaced.

From the specific perspective of Marseilles, there is also an emphasis on the city being founded 2600 or so years ago by Phocean settlers, from Asia Minor, giving it a history far longer than 'France' and reversing the centralist notion of the capital's culture enlightening the provinces. There is a further, cheeky, mythologizing of the Mediterranean, civilizing place of Marseille in the history of European civilization: the suggestion that, at some unspecified point, due to continental drift the deltas of the Rhône and the Nile were separated.

Afrocentrism, the influence of a variety of black nationalist ideas is now widespread in hip hop. See the interviews in Eure, J. D. and Spady, J. G. (eds) (1991), *Nation Conscious Rap*, New York: PC International Press; and analysis in Decker, Jeffrey L. (1994), 'The State of Rap: Time and Place in Hip Hop Nationalism', in Ross, A. and Rose, T. (eds), *Microphone Fiends: Youth Music and Youth Culture*, London: Routledge, 99-121; and Zook, K. B. (1992) 'Reconstructions of Nationalist Thought in Black Music and Culture', in Garofalo, Reebee (ed.), *Rockin' the Boat: Mass Music and Mass Movements*, Boston: South End Press.

[25] Diop, Cheikh Anta (1955), *Nations nègres et cultures*, Paris: Présence africaine.

[26] While there is an element of racial romanticism in Diop's work, it nonetheless represented a powerful ideological challenge to the justifications of Colonialism and Imperialism that meant all Africans had to be seen as primitive, innocent savages and the civilizing mission of the colonial powers could thus be rationalized. Above all in that view of Africa and its History, any evidence of African civilization, be it in Zimbabwe or the Nile delta, had to be called into question, and any connection between Egypt and 'black' Africa denied.

Chill's choice of the pseudonym of Akhénaton is not a random one: Aton was the sun god, a monotheistic deity that Akhénaton, also known as Amenophis III, sought to encourage under his reign as Pharaoh. There is a strong element of religious mysticism in the group's earlier work, a syncretism that seeks to combine elements of Taoism, Buddhism and Islam.

These ideas have had a significant influence on the group in another sense: Oriental and Maghrebi samples have played a key role in establishing a distinctive IAM sound, with wailing clarinets alongside percussion instruments forming the basis for tracks such as *Le Feu* [The Fire] and *J'aurais pu croire* [I could've believed] on the second album, and the title track of the third, *L'école du micro d'argent* [The School of the silver mike]. Their contribution to the album of music inspired by the film *la Haine* (Mathieu Kassovitz, 1995), *la 25ᵉ image* [The 25th Image] is marked by a tragic violin chord sampled from a contemporary Egyptian musical film.

This is an important innovation in their sound which contrasts markedly with the heavily West Coast-influenced Parisian rappers or with MC Solaar, the chief commercial force in francophone rap, who relies more on jazz. The interest in such music was taken further by Imhotep on his solo album *Blueprint*, for which he travelled to Essaouira in Morocco to make recordings of street sounds and local musicians, which form the basis for the mixes on the album.

Invasion Arrivant de Mars

The poster advertising IAM's main Paris dates in the early 1990s featured Parisian landmarks in silhouette, with a cone of light projecting the band's logo from a hovering flying saucer. This 'Invasion Arriving from Mars' represents the group as 'aliens', emphasizing their difference from France/Paris (or indeed Aix-en-Provence, Marseille's chic and wealthy neighbour that has been the butt of frequent satirical comment by IAM), a willing and symbolic adoption of 'otherness' which also turns the jargon of 'invasion' in racist discourse (by 'illegal aliens' for example) against the oppressor. This is made explicit in the title track of the first album, ... *de la planète Mars*, which refers to Le Pen and the Front National as invaders and those who vote for him locally as collaborators: 'Marseille elle-même a subi des tentatives d'invasion / des hordes ténébreuses lors des élections ... Je m'en rappelle ce jour-là, la peur / quand 25% ont collaboré avec l'envahisseur.' [Marseille herself has suffered attempted invasion / From dark hordes at times of election ... I remember that day, the fear / When 25% collaborated with the invader.]

This metaphorical use of UFO imagery is one of a chain of popular cultural references in IAM's work. Continuing the science fiction theme, and the representation of Marseille as the planet Mars, Imhotep's compilation of other local groups was entitled *Chroniques de Mars* (echoing Ray Bradbury's *Martian*

Chronicles). All of their albums feature snatches of real or invented film dialogue: from epic peplum movies; from gangster films, providing Akhénaton with mafia imagery on his solo excursion to Naples and Sicily (although elsewhere in the group's work Al Pacino in Oliver Stone's *Scarface* (1980) is a particular favourite); and from spaghetti westerns, DJ Khéops' solo album *Sad Hill* packaging and organizing its numerous guest appearances around that concept.

IAM's new logo, adopted for their third album, is a kind of combination of a Chinese warrior and Darth Vader's helmet. Retaining the UFO symbolism, the stage set for the 1998 tour had this as a structure descending into the centre, from which the rappers emerged to perform.

That album features a track entitled *L'Empire du coté obscur* (*Star Wars'* 'darkside') both reworking the 'Imperial' of their name and developing an ongoing interest in the *Star Wars* films. Interestingly, however, they take an 'oppositional' reading of the films' Manichean world-view, associating themselves with Vader, and dismissing Marseille's current right-wing mayor as 'ce niais de Jean-Claude Gaudin Skywalker' [That simpleton …].[27] 'Mon rêve,' said Chill, in a Canal+ interview, 'c'est que tout le monde apprenne à connaître l'autre coté' [My dream is that everyone should get to know the other side].

Indépendantistes Autonomes Marseillais[28]

This version of the name again represents a metaphorical strategy, rather than reflecting a serious political commitment to regionalism, or autonomy for Marseille. Such ideas became popular, however, in 1994, when the city's football team, l'Olympique Marseille (or l'OM as it is popularly known) suffered enforced relegation to the second division and were stripped of their titles of French and European champions due to allegations of match-fixing by the then owner, Bernard Tapie. This led to outraged demonstrations, and to the circulation of posters and leaflets celebrating the French national team's (or 'l'équipe du F. F. F.'[29] as the posters put it) failure to qualify for the World Cup (USA 1994), often underlining the fact that 'Marseille, c'est pas la France' [Marseille is not France].

Le Feu, traditionally the group's signature tune, opening both the second album and the tour shows, uses the tune of *Roll Out the Barrel*[30] for its chorus, having its origins on the terraces of the Stade Vélodrome, OM's home ground. Ironically, in the light of the 1994 hostilities, it is now sung by supporters across

---

27   The group's own record label is also called 'Coté Obscur'.
28   Marseille Independent Autonomists.
29   Fédération Française du Football, the French football federation, thereby associating the national team with the very authorities penalizing OM.
30   Known thus in Britain, anyway – a Cockney drinking song. It is rumoured to be a Polish folk tune in origin.

France, including by the national team's fans and undoubtedly the canonization of Zinedine Zidane (like Malek Brahimi from the Castellane housing estate in Marseille) following his key role in France's victorious World Cup 1998 and Euro 2000 teams will have done something to mend fences between Marseille football fans and the national team.

The group insists, however, on their independence from the Paris-dominated French music industry. It was widely assumed that they would set up in Paris following their initial success, but the group steadfastly refused. The single *Independenza*, first performed at the annual music awards ceremony in 1998 (IAM were receiving an award for Best Album, for *L'école du micro d'argent*, following their 1995 award for Best Group) can be read as a statement of intent about their career. On a bare stage, the rappers appeared behind a table covered with a black banner bearing the word 'Independenza' (Italian for independence), their faces concealed behind ski masks. While the lyrics play with imagery of the *maquis*, very much of local resonance in southern France,[31] the performance mobilized rather more global symbols of resistance to centralized power and profit, resembling one of the infamous press conferences of Sub-Comandante Marcos and the Zapatistas.

Morley and Robins suggest that the global-local nexus can develop in contrasting ways: 'giving rise to an energetic cosmopolitanism in certain localities. In others, however, local fragmentation may inspire a nostalgic, introverted and parochial sense of local attachment and identity.'[32] The sense of the local in IAM's work is by no means a parochial, uncritical celebration, refusing to deny the problems, specifically that of racism, that beset their city.

In response to a Marseille city hall poster campaign 'L'avenir de Marseille s'appelle Florence, Philippe, Véronique' [The future of Marseille is called ...], Imhotep rejoindered: 'Non, l'avenir de la ville s'appelle Farida, Bruno, Mamadou, Rachid ... Marseille se fera avec tous ou ne se fera pas' [No, the future of the city is called Farida, Bruno, Mamadou, Rachid ... Marseille will be built by all of us or not at all].[33]

Their celebration of Marseille is based on an awareness of the history of the city, and the fact that immigration and cultural mixing are its lifeblood. While their most angry denunciation of Parisian centralization, *Mars contre-attaque* [Mars counter-attacks] (*Ombre est lumière*), contains what might sound like a regionalist proclamation that 'ici on est marseillais bien avant d'être français' [Here we are Marseillais long before we're French], this is, in the context of racist immigration laws and growing restrictions on access to national identity, more a statement of fact.

---

31 The *maquis* was the name adopted by Resistance fighters who took to the hills in the South during the Second World War, the term itself referring to the scrubland terrain.
32 Morley, D., and Robins, K. (1995), *Spaces of Identity: Global media, electronic landscapes and cultural boundaries*, London: Routledge, 118.
33 Obadia, *IAM: Planète Mars*, 84.

Le Mia

The final version of the name is an anagram of 'mia'. The group's first major success, the single *Je danse le Mia* [I'm dancing the mia], spent most of the summer of 1994 at the top of the charts, totalling 600,000 sales. It became a 'phénomène de société' [social phenomenon], with kids in playgrounds across France calling out its heavily accented catchphrases. It is the reason why the group became well known all across France, and the pretext for ritualized denunciations from self-styled 'underground' or 'hardcore' Parisian hip hop fanzines.[34] The group have to some extent been forced to try to live down the single ever since, for example changing the name of their fanclub (known pre-1994 as 'L'Association des mias'). IAM's third album is noticeably less nostalgic, featuring less humorous and satirical asides, perhaps in reaction to the perceived commercialism of the single. It should also be said, however, that the album also places less emphasis on mysticism, with a much greater focus on social realism (in keeping with developments in the French cinema and television of the late 1990s) and the denunciation of class differences (e.g. *Petit frère, Nés sous la même étoile*) [Little brother, Born under the same star].

I would begin to explain ... *le Mia*'s phenomenal success by suggesting it offers a very interesting combination of the local and the universal, digging back into the prehistory of rap (partly through sampling George Benson's *Gimme the Night*), including their own pre-rap days as funk/soul boys, ... *le Mia* is a nostalgic, cinematic account of nights in clubs and bars of Marseille in the 1980s, dominated by half-drunk medallion men, known locally as *mias*. But its evocation of dance competitions, brawls, egotistical smalltime DJs and cheap promotional giveaways at teenage discotheques is recognizable far beyond the streets where that term has currency. Despite the hostility of the 'underground' it would also be important to point out that its success also took place against the backdrop of Charles Pasqua's nomination as Minister of the Interior in the Balladur government, placing him at the head of both the police forces and immigration/nationality policy. Pasqua was seen as responsible both for encouraging the proliferation of police *bavures* ('cock-ups' i.e. injuries or deaths in custody) such as the one which starts the riot in *La Haine*, and for opening up the mainstream Right in France to the ideas of Le Pen and the fascist Front National, particularly in his repressive Nationality Law. The presence at the top of the charts and on television of a group of confident, multiracial rappers posed at least an implicit alternative to the racist atmosphere he was fostering.

---

[34] Fanzines such as *Yours, From Da Underground, Down With This* (which, despite their English names, only deal with the French hip hop scene). The latter denounced the 'programmation abusive' (excessive playlisting) of IAM's *Je danse le Mia* and the 'attitude commerciale' shown by their 'enchaînement de passages télé' (string of TV appearances), *Down With This: fanzine hip hop français*, no. 4, 1994, 11.

Conclusion

Without going into great detail, clearly there are limitations in IAM's work: although avoiding the misogyny of some US gangsta rap, for example, there is nonetheless little attempt to create a space for women. The hybrid identities they work with are principally young, male identities.

The examples provided illustrate, however, the complex web of sources and influences from which they draw: Afrocentrism, the work of Cheikh Anta Diop; ancient Egypt and its representation in peplum movies; football and the fan culture of OM; science fiction and other forms of popular cultural narrative; North African, African-American and Italian popular musical forms.

This multiplicity of identities, this representation of some of the '100 faces of the vast world' passing through Marseille, has been an important factor in the group's success and appeal way beyond Marseille, clearly offering attractive alternatives to the dominant ideas, and proving, perhaps, that you can be universal without being metropolitan, that you can 'think locally and act globally'.

This intersection of the local and the global, and the wholehearted adoption of *métissage* (mixing of cultures) contrasts starkly with France's traditions: centralization, a strong sense of the national, culturally, politically and economically, and a predominantly white ethnic self-image, reinforced by a top-down assimilationist model of integration of immigrant communities.

Hip hop is clearly, therefore, an important genre for France's future: as Dauncey illustrates, the French state has, somewhat ironically, funded cultural attachés in London to promote 'French' hip hop to the 'Anglo-Saxons' and Geoff Hare describes how broadcasting quotas directly benefited the nascent francophone rap.

We can view hip hop in France, then, as representing and revealing the social modernization of French society, redefining, as Middleton has suggested, who 'the people' are, uncovering hitherto-ignored elements of France's socio-cultural heritage, being in many senses 'prophetic' in the way that Attali suggests.

IAM-Selected Discography

Concept (Roker Promocion, 1990)
... de la planète Mars (Labelle Noir, 1991)
Ombre est lumière (Delabel, 1993)
L'école du micro d'argent (Delabel 1997)

Akhénaton *Métèque et mat* (Delabel 1995)
Khéops *Sad Hill* (Delabel 1997)
Imhotep *Blueprint* (Delabel 1998)
Shurik'n *Où je vis* (Delabel 1998)
Imhotep *Chroniques de Mars* (Coté Obscur 1999)

Chapter 12

Flaubert's sparrow, or the Bovary of Belleville: Édith Piaf as cultural icon

Keith Reader

Édith Piaf is almost certainly the best-known voice France has ever produced. A December 1999 poll conducted for the newspaper *Le Parisien* and the television channel La Cinq showed that for 54 per cent of French people she was the 'singer of the century'; her recording of 'Milord' became the first song entirely in a foreign language to enter the British charts; at least two of her other songs, 'La Vie en rose' and 'Non, je ne regrette rien', form an established part of the 'standard' repertoire; she has been the subject of numerous books and of a big-budget feature film, Claude Lelouch's *Édith et Marcel* of 1983. Piaf is undoubtedly a 'star,' in the sense in which the term is used by Edgar Morin:

> The star is the actor or actress who absorbs part of the heroic – in other words godlike and mythical – substance of film heroes, and who, in return, enriches this substance with her/his own contribution. What we mean when we talk of the myth of the star is in the first place the way in which the film actor comes to seem godlike, becoming in the process the idol of the masses.[1]

Morin is, to be sure, referring specifically to film stars; but among other post-war icons of French femininity, it is precisely only film stars – Brigitte Bardot and Catherine Deneuve in particular – who can lay claim to equal prominence. An important part of the 'star phenomenon' is the interplay between the on- and off-screen or stage persona, exemplified by Bardot's hectic sexual activity and Humphrey Bogart's world-weary tippling both in their film roles and in real life. Piaf's many love-affairs, frequently turbulent and sometimes seemingly blighted by destiny, were copiously referred to in the popular press of the time, and appeared at once to mirror and to feed into the universe of tormented but ultimately triumphant passion evoked in so many of her songs. Between the end of the war, when her career really took off, and her death in 1963, French cinema was for much of the time in a somewhat quiescent state, and television of course within the reach of only a minority, so it is no exaggeration to say that Piaf was

---

[1]   Morin, Edgar (1972), *Les Stars*, Paris: Seuil, 39.

probably France's biggest star, and certainly icon of femininity, for much of that period.

Yet there is very little serious analysis of her from this point of view in the books devoted to her. Some sample titles – *Piaf mon amour, The Piaf Legend, Édith Piaf: l'hymne à l'amour* (one in a series entitled *Amoureuses du monde entier*, including books on Colette, Coco Chanel and Lucrezia Borgia (!)) – suggest the hagiographic mummification to which she has been subjected. Her self-styled half-sister Simone Berteaut earned notoriety with a scurrilous, and factually dubious, first-person memoir entitled simply *Piaf*[2] in which sexual promiscuity, financial imprudence, drunkenness and drug abuse figure large, constructing Piaf as a rock star *avant la lettre*, albeit one with a strong sentimental and superstitious streak. A more sober and carefully researched biography by Pierre Duclos and Georges Martin, also called *Piaf*, takes Berteaut to task for her 'presumptuous exaggerations, not to say inventions'.[3] The facts about Piaf's early years in particular are, unsurprisingly, considering the impoverished and poorly documented milieu from which she came, often difficult to establish, and this biographical problem may in part account for the dearth of serious analysis of her. More generally, however, it is probably true to say that – with a few exceptions such as the analyses of Bardot by Simone de Beauvoir and Catherine Rihoit – there has been comparatively little work done on French stars in France from what in an Anglo-American context is known as a 'star studies' perspective.[4] Morin's study focuses almost exclusively on Hollywood, in keeping with the tenacious love–hate relationship with American culture so characteristic of post-war France – one likely reason for the anomaly under discussion. Another is that French feminism, certainly in its 1960s/1970s heyday, tended to concentrate on theoretical, particularly psychoanalytically based elaboration, rather than feeding into what became known in an Anglo-American context as the domain of 'cultural studies'. Yet another may simply be the French cultural establishment's comparative disdain, at any rate up till about 1968, for popular culture, with the significant exceptions of the cinema, *le septième art* and of course a French invention, and *chanson* treated as a branch of poetry – Brassens, Brel, Ferré are the canonical names here. The contrast between the two most high-profile culture ministers of the Fifth Republic is revelatory here. André Malraux, under de Gaulle, instituted the Maisons de la Culture in order to extend the audience for high culture, whereas Mitterrand's appointee Jack Lang built a career on broadening the remit of his ministry to encompass rap, strip cartoons and even the circus – what David Looseley has described as 'the politics of fun'.[5] Piaf had her *entrée* into the world of Parisian

2   Berteaut, Simone (1972), *Piaf*, Paris: Robert Laffont.
3   Duclos, Pierre and Martin, Georges (1993), *Piaf*, Paris: Seuil, 26.
4   Dyer, Richard (1998) *Stars*, London: BFI; and Vincendeau, Ginette (2000), *Stars and Stardom in French Cinema*, London: Continuum are excellent examples of this approach.
5   Looseley, David (1995), *The Politics of Fun*, Oxford/New York: Berg.

high culture, best illustrated by her relationship with the actor Paul Meurisse and her close friendship with Jean Cocteau, who died a matter of hours after pronouncing a radio valediction to her; but the audience to which she appealed was overwhelmingly a popular and largely female one, vividly and movingly illustrated by the huge number of working-class women who turned up at her funeral or to mourn outside her home in the up-market sixteenth *arrondissement.*

The only text known to me which suggests what a star studies approach to Piaf might look like, particularly in a gendered perspective, is Ginette Vincendeau's 'The *mise-en-scène* of suffering: French *chanteuses réalistes*'. Vincendeau treats Piaf as the final exponent – after such as Fréhel and Mistinguett – of a genre which 'proposes a city of working-class *faubourgs*, rainy streets, and tall buildings ... in which proletariat and underworld, pimps and prostitutes, enact a scenario of crime and doomed passion'. This phraseology irresistibly calls to mind, as Vincendeau points out, 'the 1930s "poetic realist" films of Carné, Clair, Renoir'[6] – to which one might also add Jacques Becker's *Casque d'or* of 1952, the last of its cinematic line much as Piaf is the last of its musical correlative, and starring Simone Signoret, whose autobiography is famously entitled *La Nostalgie n'est plus ce qu'elle était* [Nostalgia isn't what it used to be]. By the time Piaf died, the Paris her songs evoke was, and had been for some time, on the wane. Her work and persona – the two are indissociably linked – are thus, and have perhaps always been, shot through with backward-lookingness, in a manner which may make particularly appropriate comparison of her with an icon of vulnerable womanhood from an earlier era, Flaubert's Madame Bovary. In an age when rock, rap, hip hop have long since supplanted *la chanson française* in the affections of the young, Piaf now appears more *passé* than ever; as Vincendeau points out, her records and cassettes are generally to be found 'in the nostalgia section, of course'.[7] Matthieu Kassovitz's *La Haine* (1995), the first film to bring the problems of the contemporary *banlieue* before a wide audience, makes ironic reference to her obsolescence in mixing the rap group Suprême NTM (Nique ta mère) [Fuck your mother] with Piaf singing 'Non, je ne regrette rien'. Yet obsolescence – which can be seen as the negative counterpart of nostalgia – can also be a powerful part of a work's, or a performer's, appeal. Jean-Pierre Jeunet's *Le Fabuleux Destin d'Amélie Poulain/Amélie* (2001), a film that has enjoyed extraordinary popularity both within and outside France, is a striking recent example of a text whose success, for better or for worse, is largely grounded in its appeal to a bygone age – Montmartre reconstructed as a semi-bucolic village community, buildings as free from graffiti as the streets are from violence, even a running gag about malfunctioning photo-machines reminiscent of Truffaut's

---

6   Vincendeau, Ginette (1987), 'The *mise-en-scène* of suffering: French *chanteuses réalistes*', in *New Formations*, 3, Winter, 107.
7   Ibid., 125.

'Antoine Doinel' film cycle. *Amélie*, more self-consciously but no less surely than Piaf's songs, builds nostalgia into its present.

This is not to suggest that Piaf's *œuvre* is any kind of 'feelgood' phenomenon. For every 'La Vie en rose' or 'Heureuse' – songs whose titles bespeak their emotional optimism – there is a 'Les Flonflons du bal' with its memories of loss or a 'Les Mots d'amour' with its cynicism about the perpetual recurrence of words of love from one relationship to the next. Rather, it is to suggest that her continuing appeal – not least to British Francophiles – resides in her coming at the end of a line – what the literary theorist Harold Bloom might call her 'belatedness'.[8] Attempts were made in the 1960s to market Mireille Mathieu as her successor, but it did not take long for the difference between a fairly bad pop singer and the last of the great *chanteuses* to become apparent.

Piaf's life

Piaf was born Édith Giovanna Gassion, the daughter of a strolling acrobat and a singer, on 19 December 1915 – not, as the most tenacious of the many myths surrounding her was to claim, in the street outside her parents' home in the rue de Belleville, but in the Hôpital Tenon nearby. Twenty or so years later, she was to be discovered by the impresario Louis Leplée singing in the street near the Place de l'Etoile, a circumstance that was doubtless read romantically back on to the supposed place of her birth. A plaque outside 72 rue de Belleville, unveiled by Maurice Chevalier in 1966, claims that it was on the steps of the house that Piaf was born – a myth that it would thenceforth be virtually impossible to deny.

With her father generally away on war duties and her negligent mother concerned primarily with pursuing her own singing career, the young Édith was largely brought up by her grandmother, who ran a brothel in the small Norman town of Bernay. It was here that Édith was reputed to have temporarily lost her sight, which she supposedly recovered thanks to the miraculous intercession of the 'local' saint, Thérèse of Lisieux. This appears to be another mythical exaggeration, the somewhat more prosaic reality having been an inflamed cornea which impaired her sight badly and took some time to heal. The religious element is even more marked here than with her alleged birth in the street, thrown into relief by the fact that she was living in a brothel at the time. Édith was of course far too young to play any part in the brothel's activities, but the contrast between sexual *laissez aller* and a simple, even superstitious faith so characteristic of her in later life is strikingly prefigured here. We may think in this connection of Maupassant's short story *La Maison Tellier*, the inspiration for one of the episodes of which Max Ophuls's film *Le Plaisir* is made up. *La Maison*

---

[8]   See Bloom, Harold (1982), *Agon: Towards a Theory of Revisionism*, New York and Oxford: Oxford University Press, for a development of this concept.

Tellier recounts the emotions of a group of Norman prostitutes, from an earlier version of the kind of establishment in which Édith lived, at a first communion, at which they shed floods of tears – doubtless for their lost innocence, though Maupassant is careful not to spell this out too explicitly. Their 'evident faith' and 'living piety', extolled by the priest,[9] stand in ironic contrast to the way in which they earn their living. Such an antithesis is, *mutatis mutandis*, an important factor in the Piaf myth too.

Maupassant was of course from Normandy – like Édith's father (whence the Bernay connection), like Sainte Thérèse, like Flaubert and Emma Bovary. Piaf was to maintain a fervent devotion throughout her life to Sainte Thérèse, provocatively paralleled with Madame Bovary in Micheline Hermine's *Destins de femmes, désir d'absolu*. Between the cloistered virgin of modest origins and the adulterous doctor's wife there may at first seem to be little in common, but Hermine sees both as in some sense rebelling against the constraints of their gender ('Femininity is damned for both'[10]), and even compares Thérèse to Teresa of Avila and John of the Cross in her desire, less fully realized than with her Spanish predecessors, to 'suffer and experience ecstasy *at the same time* within a being consumed with love'.[11] That is not a bad description of the intensity of many of Piaf's songs, which 'appeal to a generalized notion of womanhood as suffering, dependent, and submissive, but at the same time driven by sexual passion'.[12] The dependence and submissiveness are less uniform than Vincendeau may seem to imply, but the interplay of suffering and passion is a constant in Piaf's work from the first, as might be said the ground on which those two forms of ecstasy that are love and religion meet.

Piaf was to return to Paris sometime in her teens, and it was with that city that her name was ever afterwards to be associated. Leplée was to give her the stage-name 'La Môme Piaf', after that quintessentially urban bird the sparrow, since 'he wanted something really Parisian, which went well with the style of his protégée'.[13] That style was in large measure determined by her height – less than five feet, in striking contrast to the dark resonance of her voice, extravagantly praised by Cocteau and the novelist Robert Sabatier. Piaf's 'Parisianness' had nothing in common with the self-conscious elegance often associated with that city – something that was to baffle audiences on her first tour of the US – nor indeed with conventional views of French femininity, for her stage presence was curiously non-sexual, whence Adrian Rifkin's description of her as 'an oddly inverted *travesti*, a figuring through the crushed body of the city-*pute* of a

---

9 Maupassant, Guy de (1983), *La Maison Tellier*, Paris: Albin Michel, 39.
10 Hermine, Micheline (1997), *Destins de femmes, désir d'absolu*, Paris: Beauchesne, 171.
11 Ibid., 110.
12 Vincendeau, 'The *mise-en-scène* of suffering', 118.
13 Duclos and Martin, *Piaf*, 12.

missing element in masculinity'.[14] She was an instant and immense success on stage, but almost from the outset her offstage life attracted as much attention, notably with the murder of Louis Leplée in 1936, for which undeserved suspicion briefly fell on her. Sacha Guitry's remark that 'her life has been so sad that it is almost too beautiful to be true'[15] has a sharp edge of truth to it. Her only child, a daughter whom she had with a manual worker in 1933, had died of meningitis only two years later. According to her half-sister, Piaf – for the first time in her life – resorted to prostitution to pay the burial expenses, though there is a suspiciously sentimental quality to her claim that when the client discovered this he gave her the money and asked for nothing in return. Had Berteaut taken something of a leaf out of Maupassant's book?

Accounts differ about whether she could not have more children or chose not to do so because of the demands of her profession. What seems certain is that her maternal impulses found an outlet in her protective relationships with a number of young male singers, most famously Yves Montand and Charles Aznavour. She married twice, first (1952) the singer Jacques Pills whom she divorced in 1956, then in 1962 a much younger hairdresser of Greek origin, Theophanis Lamboukas, whom she launched on a far from illustrious singing career under the name of Théo Sarapo and to whom she was still happily married at the time of her death. Sarapo was killed in a car crash a few years later, the third of her *grandes amours* to meet a violent death. The American painter Doug Davis, whose portrait of Piaf adorns both the cover of *L'Hymne à l'amour*[16] and the sleeve of her celebrated 1960 Paris Olympia recording, was killed flying back to the USA in 1962. Davis's death, however, received scant attention compared with the tragedy that had afflicted Piaf 13 years before, and more than any other single phenomenon contributed to the perception of her as the greatest star-crossed lover of her time.

Édith and Marcel

Piaf regularly performed in the United States (though curiously I have been able to find no record of her appearing in the UK), and it was in New York, in October 1947, that she first met Marcel Cerdan, who the following year was to become world middleweight boxing champion. Cerdan had a wife and two children in his native Morocco (then of course a French colony), which did not stop a passionate relationship from developing between Piaf and himself. Assertions that the two were 'just good friends' fooled nobody, as evidenced by a story in *France-*

---

[14]   Rifkin, Adrian (1993), *Street Noises*, Manchester/New York: Manchester University Press, 155.
[15]   Quoted in Berteaut, *Piaf,* 9.
[16]   Piaf, Édith (1994), *L'Hymne à L'amour*, Paris: Librairie Générale Française.

Dimanche announcing that: 'Cerdan sees Édith Piaf every day. She goes to all his fights. He goes to hear her sing every night. Piaf is an attractive woman for Cerdan because she talks to him about music, literature and poetry, which is new for him and gives him social status.' This unconvincingly sanitized account was largely belied by the story's title: 'Piaf brings Cerdan bad luck!' – this just after Cerdan had lost his European championship. Pygmalion she may have been, but for *France-Dimanche* she was something of a Delilah as well.

Cerdan and Piaf were as celebrated a couple in their day as David and Victoria Beckham are now – with, of course, added spice because the relationship was an illicit one. Piaf was to proclaim: 'No, Marcel Cerdan will never get divorced. If I were to take a man away from his home and children, I couldn't sleep, I couldn't live. If I were to separate Marcel from his family, I'd kill myself.'[17] The cynicism with which a contemporary Anglo-American audience is likely to view that statement requires tempering from two points of view, one biographical, the other cultural. After Cerdan's death, Piaf took his widow and family under her wing, inviting them to stay in her Paris home and sharing with them what appears to have been a strong and genuine affection – borne out by the fact that Cerdan's son, also called Marcel, played his father in Claude Lelouch's *Édith et Marcel*. More generally, France, like other Mediterranean Catholic cultures, traditionally frowns on divorce and sees adultery, or even parallel families, as a price well worth paying to prevent it. The most striking recent example of this is of course then-President François Mitterrand's second family, with Anne Pingeot and their daughter Mazarine, which coexisted with his lawful wedded union for upwards of 20 years. This largely accounts for the lack of press and media scandal provoked by Piaf and Cerdan's relationship. 'Édith and Marcel', from modest origins both, came close to being national sweethearts, as *L'Humanité* was to assert in its presentation of the Lelouch film ('Piaf. Cerdan. We loved them both, for the way in which their lives were like a revenge on society. The fact that they loved each other made this modern fairy tale complete, at a time when the wireless and newspapers printed on grey paper were not yet known as the media.')[18]

The fairy tale, however, was to have a tragic ending, thereby securing itself a kind of immortality. The plane in which Cerdan was flying back to New York for a bout in October 1949 crashed in the Azores; there were no survivors. That evening, Piaf insisted on going ahead with a concert in Paris, announcing to the audience: 'Tonight, I'm singing for Marcel Cerdan, only for him.' She was able to complete only part of her programme before collapsing.

Lelouch's film was a major media event in France, dedicated to Patrick Dewaere who was meant to play the role of Cerdan but, in a further stroke of tragic irony, committed suicide before shooting started. The film is a

---

[17]   Here and in the previous paragraph quoted in Duclos and Martin, *Piaf*, 197; 206.
[18]   *L'Humanité*, 13 April 1983.

monumentally unsubtle blockbuster, aptly compared by Serge Daney to 'swimming up a river of jam',[19] and in the event was poorly received by critics and public alike. Lelouch made claims for the film whose extravagance is their prime interest, declaring in an interview that 'it could just as well have been called "Edith, Marcel and God", so much is it a film about God, superstition and parapsychology – about lack of culture too'.[20] We may be forgiven for wondering whether the lack of culture is that of Piaf, depicted attempting to get in touch with the dead Cerdan through mediums and table-turning, or of the film's condescendingly middlebrow director. For Frantz Gévaudan – and it is difficult to disagree – the film was not only fatalistic but also misogynistic, preaching as it does that 'happiness is always matched by unhappiness, we should expect nothing from adulterous love and it is impossible to mistrust women enough'.[21] We are back here, it would seem, with the view put forward by Ginette Vincendeau, for whom the songs of Piaf and her predecessors embody 'a longing for archaic gender relations',[22] and their performances constitute 'a self-display of pain, a *mise-en-scène* of suffering'. Vincendeau does, however, assert that '[c]ourage, strength, and tenacity in the face of mounting obstacles are also part of Piaf's and Fréhel's repertoire',[23] which brings out an ambiguity the remainder of this chapter will seek to explore.

Piaf and Emma Bovary

That ambiguity is, I shall argue, never more marked than in the songs' attitude towards love – the *summum bonum* of the Piaf universe. For Simone Berteaut, 'it was not men who counted for Édith, but love; she had to believe in it, she could not do without it. Without love, she could not have lived or sung.'[24] That centrality, always important in her work, became massively more so after Cerdan's death. Yet it would be an oversimplification to conclude that that work is uncomplicatedly predicated upon the desirability of love and the inevitability of suffering. Many of the songs, and Piaf's matchless delivery of them, suggest something more – a *déjà vu* in the always-new that may well call to mind her provincial 'neighbour' and alter ego Madame Bovary, of whom Flaubert tells us: 'Emma was rediscovering in adultery all the platitudes of marriage.'[25] *Les Incarnations de Madame Bovary*, a 1933 collection of short stories edited by Roger Dacosta, updates the Bovary myth in an intriguing variety of ways. Odette

---

[19]   *Libération*, 16 April 1983.
[20]   *Première*, December 1982, 66.
[21]   *Cinéma*, June 1983, 56.
[22]   Vincendeau, 'The *mise-en-scène* of suffering', 118.
[23]   Ibid., 125.
[24]   Berteaut, *Piaf*, 513–14.
[25]   Flaubert, Gustave (1986), *Madame Bovary*, Paris: Flammarion, 364.

Parmentier's story transforms the clothes-seller Lheureux into a drug-dealer, while Georges de la Fourchadière has Emma and her most youthful admirer Justin killed in a plane crash – both transformations that may bring Piaf to mind,[26] suggesting that her songs and story may profitably be read as in some sense avatars of *bovarysme*. Stephen Heath draws attention to Emma's 'yearning for *something else* that the affairs cannot give, themselves in the end mere repetitions of the same banality',[27] and comments on how the songs in the novel, 'for all their stylistic inanity and musical imperfections, afford a glimpse of sentimental realities'.[28] The duc de Brissac notoriously observed apropos of a Piaf recital: 'The French language contains 250 000 words. What a pity that this show uses only 150!' and by and large her repertoire does tend to the lexically repetitive – what Flaubert would have termed the *idée reçue*. Those *idées reçues* are, however, not always to be taken at face value. The songs, and Piaf's delivery of them, often operate a process of ironic distanciation from – even demolition of – the myths of love they might appear enthusiastically to endorse. Diana Knight observes that '[t]hough Emma's language is clichéd and while her tragedy is partly tied up with the misunderstanding or abuse of words, she is not properly speaking inarticulate, and is quite at home in a verbal atmosphere'[29] – something clearly true of Piaf in real life (for example, her introduction of the sometimes bemused Cerdan to the world of literature), and something borne out in many of her songs, alive to the 'misunderstanding or abuse' of words that the lover's discourse systemically generates. (Roland Barthes's *Fragments d'un discours amoureux*[30] hinges on the inevitability of this generation.)

Knight retrieves the assertive, even subversive, potential of what Jules de Gaultier had labelled, a touch judgementally, *le bovarysme* in asserting that '[t]he old definition of *bovarysme* as a condition in which we delude ourselves as to what we are and as to life's potential ... would surely be better recast as the condition of "knowing life's potential and refusing to be satisfied with it".'[31] The immense popularity of Piaf's songs among working-class women – even more likely then than now to be trapped in a 'life's potential' of painful restrictiveness – can in this context be read positively. *Hymne à l'amour* is no more, and no less, escapist than the culturally more elevated mirages – though they are not only that – of true love in Marguerite Duras's *L'Amant* or *Moderato Cantabile*. In the brief analyses of Piaf songs that follow, I shall be attempting to show how her work

---

[26] See Buisine, Alain (ed.) (1997), *Figures mythiques: Emma Bovary*, Paris: Autrement, 25–28.

[27] Heath, Stephen (1992), *Madame Bovary*, Cambridge/New York: Cambridge University Press, 2.

[28] Heath, *Madame Bovary*, 75.

[29] Knight, Diana (1985), *Flaubert's Characters*, Cambridge/New York: Cambridge University Press, 32.

[30] Barthes, Roland (1977), *Fragments d'un discours amoureux*, Paris: Seuil.

[31] Knight, *Flaubert's Characters*, 82.

operates simultaneously as a naïve celebration of the joys and sorrows of love and as a suggestion that these, while they may be our last best chance of happiness, nevertheless depend on inescapable mechanisms of illusion and repetition – similar in this respect to the omnipresent but delusive Lacanian imaginary. What I cannot, alas, convey is what Roland Barthes[32] terms 'the grain of the voice' – the distinctive vocal timbre, at once beguiling and harsh, that makes a Piaf performance so unmistakable. Like Ginette Vincendeau, I shall have to make the 'beauty and power' of Piaf's voice 'the absent signifier of this article'.[33] The songs I analyse, however, are widely available in the UK, so that any hypotheses I put forward can readily be corroborated or refuted. I deal with them in chronological order, giving the date as quoted in *L'Hymne à l'amour* after each title.

'Mon légionnaire' (1936)

This song, written by Raymond Asso and Marguerite Monnod, was banned under the Occupation (when of course the Foreign Legion was on the 'enemy' side), and – presumably because of the Legion's unsavoury reputation in the decolonizing period of the 1950s and 1960s – rarely figured in Piaf's repertoire in her later years. It is of interest here because it stands at the intersection of two important myths, what Adrian Rifkin calls 'the literary *imaginaire* of North African sexual pleasure and the popular journalistic literature of the Légion'.[34] Asso was gay, and the homoerotic has always loomed large in representations of the Legion, right through to Claire Denis's 2000 film *Beau travail*. Serge Gainsbourg was to record the song not long before he died accompanied by an explicitly homoerotic – not to say paedophiliac – video clip. At the same time, Piaf was to claim that the song was inspired by a lover she had met outside a barracks in the working-class Parisian suburb of Romainville, and Simone Berteaut alleges that when Asso spoke to Piaf of his life as a legionnaire, 'she would listen to him with her heart thumping and her eyes full of mirages'.[35]

Gay, straight or queerly undecidable, 'Mon légionnaire' is clearly a romantic reinscription of rough trade, figured alike through the legionnaire's anonymity ('J'sais pas son nom, j'sais rien de lui') [I don't know his name, I don't know anything about him] and through his tattoos:

Il était plein de tatouages
Que j'ai jamais très bien compris,
Son cou portait: 'pas vu, pas pris,'

---

[32] Barthes, Roland (1982), 'Le Grain de la voix', in *L'Obvie et l'obtus*, Paris: Seuil.
[33] Vincendeau, 'The *mise-en-scène* of suffering', 125.
[34] Rifkin, *Street Noise*, 139.
[35] Berteaut, *Piaf*, 132.

Sur son cœur on lisait: 'personne,'
Sur son bras droit un mot: 'raisonne'.

[He was covered in tattoos
that I never really understood:
on his neck ' If nobody knows it doesn't matter',
over his heart 'nobody',
on his right arm: 'use your head'.]

The cynicism of this literal body language resembles that – when Emma is not there – of *Madame Bovary*'s Rodolphe, but it is redeemed in the song's denouement, in which the legionnaire is buried in the warm sand of which he smelt and he is forgiven for what he did not know ('Il ne savait pas ... Je lui pardonne'). [He didn't know ... I forgive him.] What did he not know? – presumably that the narrative voice, Asso's or Piaf's, had really loved him, in an archetypally romantic retrieval of the brevity and anonymity of their encounter through an assertion of its unavowed importance. That voice's fantasy that she and the legionnaire 's'en iraient seuls tous les deux / Dans quelque pays merveilleux Plein de lumière' [We would go away alone together to some wonderful country full of light] may recall Emma's dreams of enraptured yet lasting departure ('going away to those sonorously-named countries where the days after marriage are suavely idle'[36]). In 'Mon légionnaire', however, the fantasy of departure comes only after the legionnaire has been killed, foregrounding the romanticization of death that haunts so much of Piaf's work, and that, as we have seen, was an important strand in the myth of Piaf-as-star.

'L'Accordéoniste' (1942)

This song, by Michel Emer, like 'Mon légionnaire' disappeared comparatively early from Piaf's repertoire – largely because it placed too much vocal strain upon her, but also perhaps because its evocation of wartime loss of life was a particularly painful one. The song tells of a couple – a prostitute or (ironically named) *fille de joie* and her accordionist lover, 'un drôle de p'tit gars ... Qui sait jouer la java.' [A funny little fellow ... who's really good at playing the *java*].[37] Her passion as she watches the accordionist playing is explicitly erotic ('Ça lui rentre dans la peau / Par le bas, par le haut') [It really gets under her skin, above and below], but then he has to go off to war, and their dreams of stability and happiness on his return ('Quand y r'viendra d'la guerre / Ils prendront une maison / Elle sera la caissière / Et lui, sera le patron') [When he gets back from

---

[36] Flaubert, *Madame Bovary*, 100.
[37] The *java* was an erotic form of popular waltz, much performed in working-class cafés and dance-halls in the earlier years of the last century.

war they'll run a bar; she'll be the cashier and he'll run the show][38] are shattered by his death. So too is her – literal – street credibility: 'Les filles qui font la gueule / Les hommes n'en veulent pas' [Men don't want girls who look miserable].

This is of course a far more *louche* and plebeian milieu than any inhabited, or even fantasized, by Emma Bovary. Yet the street-girl's unhappiness ('Son homme ne reviendra plus') [Her man will never come back] is not dissimilar to Emma's 'reverie about what will never return'[39] after Léon has departed for Rouen, both suggesting in different ways the melancholy that the loss of the object of desire can bring about for the desiring female subject. Important in both texts also is fatality – the arbitrariness of war in 'L'Accordéoniste', for Emma what Stephen Heath calls 'the term of a whole romantic ethos of tragic destiny ... but ... also the acknowledgement of the inexorable'.[40] Fatality is closely associated with repetition, as the Roman goddess of fate, Fortuna, and her endlessly-revolving wheel suggest, and repetition is what above all else Emma seeks to break away from, often unsuccessfully as her rediscovery in adultery of 'all the platitudes of marriage' indicates. The 'clichéd language of love'[41] that is her affective habitat is also, of course, as the duc de Brissac scathingly observed, prominent in Piaf's songs – at once an assertion of the uniqueness of (a) passion and a recognition that it inexorably resembles other passions past and to come.

This is strikingly figured in the closing stanzas of 'L'Accordéoniste', where the *fille de joie*'s 'jambes tristes / L'emmènent au boui-boui / Où il y a un autre artiste / Qui joue toute la nuit.' [[Her] sad legs take her along to the local flophouse, where there's another artist who plays all night long]. The slowing of the tempo and the weariness of Piaf's voice give these lines a sense of deep lethargy and inevitability rather than of the exhilaration a new love might have been expected to yield. Eros, we might say, is fighting what it knows will be a losing battle with Thanatos – the drive towards repetition that can only culminate in death. In a France traumatized by Occupation, 'L'Accordéoniste''s final lines would doubtless have suggested even more powerfully than they do today that the *fille de joie*'s new love will be a repetition of the tragedy she has just experienced rather than, or at least as much as, an exorcism of it.

'Hymne à l'amour' (1951)

'Hymne à l'amour', with music by Marguerite Monnod and words by Piaf herself, was first performed by Piaf not long before Marcel Cerdan's death, and

---

[38]   The kind of 'maison' this might have been is doubtless deliberately not specified – just as well since the Liberation was to see the effective outlawing of brothels in France.

[39]   Flaubert, *Madame Bovary*, 188.

[40]   Heath, *Madame Bovary*, 89.

[41]   Knight, *Flaubert's Characters*, 32.

remains more than any of her other songs imperishably associated with his memory. The lyrics printed in the book *L'Hymne à l'amour*[42] give the song's date as 1951, presumably because that was when the sheet music was published, but it seems to be a matter of record that the song was among those Piaf sang in her Paris concert immediately after learning of the fatal crash. The words are a resounding, if also somewhat clichéd, declaration of faith in love lasting even beyond the grave, twice evoking the colour blue ('Le ciel bleu sur nous peut s'effondrer' / 'Nous aurons pour nous l'éternité Dans le bleu de toute l'immensité') [The blue sky can fall in upon us / We shall have eternity together in all its blue vastness]. Emma Bovary's amorous universe is likewise periodically coloured blue – just before she surrenders to Rodolphe her face is described, through her veil, as 'bathed in transparent blue, as if she were swimming beneath azure waves',[43] and afterwards, as she gazes at herself in the mirror, 'a bluish immensity surrounded her'.[44] The association of blue and infinity is a romantic cliché that derives particular force in 'Hymne à l'amour' from Cerdan's death in the 'ciel bleu' evoked by the song's first line. Piaf, we may remember, had said of Cerdan : 'Il est mort dans le ciel, donc il y est.' [He died in the sky/heaven, so that's where he is].

'Hymne à l'amour' is not, however, so uniformly optimistic and affirmative as we may at first think. Immediately after the evocation of 'l'éternité Dans le bleu de toute l'immensité', Piaf sings 'Dans le ciel, plus de problèmes' [No more problems in heaven], before quizzically asking: 'Mon amour, crois-tu qu'on s'aime?' [My love, do you think we love each other?] – a sudden calling into question of the loving bedrock on which the song has been built. To be sure, no sooner has the doubt been raised than surging strings and a final triumphant affirmation that 'Dieu réunit ceux qui s'aiment!' [God reunites those who love each other] work to dispel it; but even this most biographically hallowed of Piaf's quasi-religious affirmations of the power of love cannot uncritically believe its own assertions.

'Padam ... padam ...' (1951)

Literally, 'dee-dah, dee-dah' – an evocation of rhythm rather than sense – this song, with words by Henri Contet and music by Norbert Glanzberg, makes mocking allusion to the irony with which a love song can be imbued when love itself has gone. In this respect it can be seen as something of a companion piece to 'Les Mots d'amour', suggesting that the tropes and clichés of love pre-date as they outlive the all too ephemeral emotion itself. This is shown by the fact that

---

42   Piaf, Édith, *L'Hymne à l'amour*, Paris: Librairie Générale Française,195–96.
43   Flaubert, *Madame Bovary*, 226.
44   Ibid., 229.

the tune – 'Cet air qui m'obsède jour et nuit' [This tune that obsesses me day and night] – 'parle toujours avant moi / Et sa voix couvre ma voix' [Always speaks before I do, and its voice covers mine]. Repetition, here as in 'L'Accordéoniste', is of the essence, itself repeated in the song's references to 'Des "je t'aime" de quatorze-juillet ... Des "toujours" qu'on achète au rabais ... Des "veux-tu" en voilà par paquets.'[45] ['I love yous' from 14 July ... Cut-price 'forevers' ... 'Will yous' in bulk]. The final verse is among the most ironic in Piaf's repertoire:

Faut garder du chagrin pour après
J'en ai tout un solfège sur cet air qui bat ...
Qui bat comme un cœur de bois ...

[I must keep some sorrow for later ...
I've got a whole musical scale of it here in this tune,
whose rhythm is like a heart of wood.]

The mechanics of love – its 'solfège' as exemplified in a hundred songs (including of course many of Piaf's own), its beating like an artificial surrogate heart – are what underlie the apparently joyous melody and rhythm of 'Padam ... padam ...'. This may make us think of La Rochefoucauld's maxim 'There are people who would never have been in love if they had never heard of love'[46] – prominent among them of course Emma Bovary whose imagination is fuelled by the romantic novels she avidly reads. Piaf here seems more aware of the illusory rhetoric of love than her nineteenth-century counterpart.

'Milord' (1956)

This Georges Moustaki song has a strong claim – certainly for the present author – to being Piaf's masterpiece. The protagonist is 'une fille du port ... une ombre de la rue' [A girl from the port, a shadow of the street] – a prostitute, picked up by the wealthy dandy of the title, who has seen him earlier that day with a woman clearly of his own social class ('Mon Dieu! ... Qu'elle était belle ... J'en ai froid dans le cœur') [Oh Lord, how beautiful she was! It strikes chill into my heart]. The song alternates lively dance rhythms with mournful recitative, and it is in and through this alternation that the singer is to assume a benignly dominant role, telling Milord that she knows all about 'La douce aux yeux si tendres / Qui n'a pas su comprendre Qu'elle brisait votre vie' [That gentle woman with such tender eyes, who simply didn't understand that she was smashing your life to pieces] by sailing away on a ship. Cynical philosophizing on love, as we have seen common in Piaf's work, follows:

---

[45]   14 July – Bastille Day – is the traditional time for street parties in France.
[46]   La Rochefoucauld (1976), *Maximes et réflexions diverses*, Paris: Gallimard, 65.

L'amour, ça fait pleurer
Comme quoi l'existence
Ça vous donne toutes les chances
Pour les reprendre après.

[Love makes you weep;
life gives you every chance,
only to take them all back one by one.]

By this stage (about two-thirds of the way through the song) the singer is clearly in command, inviting Milord into her 'royaume' [kingdom] and, crucially, telling him: 'Vous avez l'air d'un môme' [You look just like a kid]. The move here is from one archetype of Catholic womanhood to another, the prostitute becoming a mother-figure who 'soigne les remords' and 'chante la romance'. [Heals remorse and sings of romance]. Her exclamation 'Mais vous pleurez, Milord? Ça ... j'l'aurais jamais cru!' [But you're crying, Milord? That I'd never have believed] has been likened by Gilles Costaz to '"a very faint echo" of Racine's *Bérénice*: "You are an emperor, my lord, and you are weeping!"'.[47] The song ends with her inviting Milord to laugh, sing and dance – her specifically sexual role occluded by that of the playful mother-figure, Milord coming to resemble those men who reputedly pick up prostitutes as confidantes rather than sexual partners, and perhaps even evoking a dim memory of the punter who allegedly paid the bereaved mother Piaf for her daughter's funeral expenses while taking nothing in return.

It is the strength of Piaf's character (as the song's prostitute may quite properly be called) that makes this song for me so remarkable, exemplifying the 'courage and strength' commented upon by Vincendeau. The 'little sparrow' here is at her most worldly-wise yet nurturing, in the process creating as un-Bovaryesque a persona as we shall find anywhere in her work.

'La Foule' (1958)

The similarities between the universe of Piaf's songs and that of Marcel Carné's films have, we have seen, been observed by Ginette Vincendeau. Nowhere are they more pronounced than in 'La Foule', despite the fact that the melody, by Angel Cabral, is Peruvian. Michel Rivgauche's words are, however, resolutely in the popular Parisian vein of Carné and Jacques Prévert, above all that of *Les Enfants du paradis* – a world of bustling street life in which we follow one of 'Padam ... padam ...'s '"je t'aime" de quatorze-juillet'. *Les Enfants du paradis* is, to be sure, set well over a century before 'La Foule', but it was at about that time that the crowd became a leitmotif of texts about Paris (as classically in the work of Baudelaire), so that 'La Foule' inscribes itself in a tradition at once venerable and popular.

---

47   Duclos and Martin, *Piaf*, 273.

'La Foule' is about loss, the singer being almost forced by the crowd into contact with a man whom she (could have) loved ('le flot sans effort / Nous pousse, enchaînés l'un et l'autre / Et nous laisse tous deux Épanouis, enivrés et heureux') [The flow effortlessly pushes and chains us together, leaving us fulfilled and intoxicated with happiness], but who is instantly taken from her thanks to that very same crowd ('la foule vient l'arracher d'entre mes bras') [the crowd tears him away from my arms]. What the end of the song in particular evokes, with its *bal-musette* rhythms and harmonies and its steady crescendo of despair, is Jean-Louis Barrault/Baptiste's despairing pursuit of Arletty/Garance at the end of *Les Enfants du paradis* – probably French cinema's most widely known moment of love lost, and one to which Rivgauche's lyrics pay implicit but unmistakable homage in their evocation of '[l]'homme qu'elle m'avait donné et que je n'ai jamais retrouvé' [The man the crowd gave me, whom I was never to see again].

'Les Mots d'amour' (1961)

'La Foule' does not particularly evoke the universe of Flaubert (Emma may lose Léon first to Rouen, then to Paris, but it is not a festive crowd that takes him from her) – certainly not compared to Dumont and Rivgauche's 'Les Mots d'amour'. The gentle waltz-like melody may on a first hearing occlude from us the profound cynicism of the lyrics, which strikingly echo Rodolphe's disenchantment with Emma as he becomes aware of 'the eternal monotony of passion, which always takes on the same forms and *uses the same language* [my italics]'.[48] Emma is of course a victim of that linguistic repetition, for, as Tony Tanner says, she 'becomes repetitious (or suffers repetition) in her quest for originality',[49] and Piaf in this song lays that repetitiousness pitilessly bare. The song begins with a verse that would have been grist to the duc de Brissac's mill, dispensing one amorous cliché after another:

> C'est fou c'que j'peux t'aimer
> C'que j'peux t'aimer des fois
> Des fois, j'voudrais crier
> Car j'n'ai jamais aimé
> Jamais aimé comme ça
> Ça je peux t'le jurer
> Si jamais tu partais
> Partais et me quittais
> Me quittais pour toujours
> C'est sûr que j'en mourrais

---

[48]   Flaubert, M*adame Bovary*, 259.
[49]   Tanner, Tony (1979), *Adultery and the Novel*, Baltimore/London: Johns Hopkins University Press, 268.

Que j'en mourrais d'amour
Mon amour, mon amour ...

[It's crazy how I can love you,
how much I can sometimes love you
so much that I could shout aloud.
I have never loved, never loved like this,
that I swear.
If ever you went away,
went away and left me,
left me for ever,
it's certain that I'd die,
that I'd die of love,
my love, my love ...]

By the end of the stanza the lyrics are close to getting bogged down in a
hypnotic monotony of repetition – which, of course, is precisely the point. He
who spoke those words of love, the next verse tells us, in the end left her 'sans
dire un mot' [Without saying a word] – which has not stopped her from repeating
the words in her turn to another lover ('C'est moi qui les redis / Avec autant
d'amour / A un autre que lui') [Here am I saying them again, just as lovingly, to
somebody else]. Vaucaire and Piaf, long before Roland Barthes, realize that these
words are uttered not by this or that lover, but by the very lover's discourse of
which they are part:

Au fond ce n'était pas toi
Comme ce n'est même pas moi
Qui dis ces mots d'amour
Car chaque jour ta voix
Ma voix, ou d'autres voix
C'est la voix de l'amour.

[In the end it wasn't you,
and it isn't even me,
who is speaking these words of love.
For every day your voice,
my voice, the voices of others
– they are only the voice of love.]

The cynicism here is not quite so destructive as that of the Flaubert for whom
'human language is like a cracked cauldron on which we beat out melodies for
bears to dance, when we should like to move the stars' – largely because of the
haunting melody and the lilting accordion, anything but a 'cracked cauldron'.
But in this song as much as in any of her others Piaf refutes the widespread view
of her as simply one of the more gullible *amoureuses du monde entier* (to reprise
the title of the series in which one book on her appeared). Love fills the horizon
of her work, to the all but total exclusion of other experiences or emotions; but
perhaps precisely because of that it is an emotion to whose discursive repetition

and sameness-in-difference she is frequently, and acutely, sensitive. Piaf may not have been exactly a second Flaubert, but in the last resort she was not exactly a second Emma Bovary either.

Conclusion

Singing icons of suffering femininity are not of course the sole prerogative of France. American blues, jazz and musicals provide a number of striking examples – Bessie Smith, Billie Holliday, Judy Garland, Janis Joplin the best known among them – and the Egyptian *chanteuse* Oum Kalsoum shows that the phenomenon is not confined to the 'developed' world. European high musical culture too has its repertoire, as Puccini's Madame Butterfly and the women misused by Mozart's Don Giovanni illustrate. Piaf thus forms part of a tradition of representations of femininity that may be seen ambiguously as endorsing or as countering the subordinate status of women, proclaiming that woman's destiny is to suffer for and through man while, in hallowed Romantic vein, redeeming that suffering through its transmutation into art. At the same time, as we have seen, her work is quintessentially 'Parisian' – the quotation marks there to suggest that it is representative of a Paris that scarcely now exists other than in memorialized and citational form, the world of the *bal-musette*, the *fille de joie* and the traditional life of the urban street.

This suggests a twofold datedness to Piaf – icon at once of a femininity regarded at best as suspect and of a Paris now redolent of the theme park – which I have suggested accounts for the lack of serious analysis of her work. Yet the 'grain' of her voice works with the irony of many of her lyrics – not a few we should remember written by her – to cut across that datedness and to call into question its sugary and subordinate mythical foundations. Marguerite Duras's work, as I have suggested, does something not dissimilar, ambivalently endorsing and waxing ironic about the myth of romantic love; but Duras is a high-cultural icon and thus endowed with *carte blanche* in this area, if only because high culture is generally credited with more ironic self-awareness than its popular counterparts. Recent work on women's magazines and the tropes of popular romantic fiction[50] has gone some way towards combating this attitude of condescension. Yet the dearth of similar work on Piaf, and indeed other *chanteuses réalistes*, suggests that such an attitude is still prevalent when the texts concerned are sung rather than 'simply' written down. As one of the key figures in post-war French popular culture, as apotheosis of and arguably farewell to a whole *chanson* tradition, as the 'voice of Paris' par excellence, Piaf

---

[50]   See Paizis, George (1998), 'Romantic novels', in Alex Hughes and Keith Reader (eds), *Encyclopedia of Contemporary French Culture*, London/New York: Routledge, 474, whose bibliography includes a number of French works analysing this area.

the singer and Piaf the myth stand at the crossroads of nowadays widespread types of cultural analysis. Gender studies, cultural topography, the sense(s) of the 'popular' all have rich insights to offer into the 'Piaf phenomenon'. Such tools, as I hope I have shown, need not be deployed solemnly or with undue gravitas. My aim here has been to analyse Piaf's work, but also, and as importantly, to celebrate it.

Chapter 13

French electronic music: the invention of a tradition

Philippe Birgy

Historically, American techno and house reached France – as they did Spain, Belgium or Germany – in 1989, shortly after their first exposures in London and Ibiza. Sensational media coverage of the epic nature of the raves and the cosmopolitan mores of their potential publics certainly played a role in this penetration. But while the new genres had been enthusiastically welcomed by British youth and had immediately started resonating in their new environment, France offered a more hesitant and diffuse response. Their early importation into Great Britain had been undoubtedly facilitated and legitimized by a common language and, above all, by previous interactions between American and British musical traditions, from rhythm'n'blues to rock and pop. Hence it had certainly sounded more familiar to their ears. Conversely, France was in a less comfortable position to receive techno for it lacked the tradition that would have made the new genre readily acceptable.[1]

Of course, the shared 'Anglo-Saxon' element is not the only significant criterion determining the reception of a genre. In Germany, the integration of techno and house was made possible because the country could boast a tradition of experimentation from Stockhausen to Krautrock, Can, Neu! and Kraftwerk, prolonged throughout the 1980s by an electronic 'industrial' scene. Hence techno could ideologically be related to a lineage that had often intersected youth cultures.

Questions of filiation and musical credentials are not what we intend to discuss in this chapter, for such arguments are unavoidably part of the discourse elaborated by the actors of a subculture in an attempt to legitimize its existence and officialize it. What we will observe is the manner in which an 'exotic'

---

[1] For some other perceptions of techno in France, see Lentin, Eric (1995), *Rave*, Montpellier: Climats; Demougin, Thierry, 'Historique du mouvement dance, du disco à la techno', www.fran-techno.fr/Reports/Reports/Techno History/; Fontaine, Astrid, and Fontana, Caroline (1996), *Raver*, Col. Anthropos. Paris: Economica; Grynszpan, Emmanuel (1999), *Bruyante techno: réflexion sur le son de la free-party*, Nantes: Mélanie Séteun; Guibert, Gérôme (1998), *Les nouveaux courants musicaux: simples produits des industries culturelles?* Nantes: Mélanie Séteun; Strazulla, Jérôme (1998), *La Techno*, Paris: Casterman.

(Anglo-Saxon) trend and a new aesthetic gradually manage to establish and root themselves on foreign ground (France), thereby giving themselves a local existence.

When they reached France, techno and house were first endowed with the attractiveness of imported articles and they were adopted by hedonistic young men and women who were not disinclined to clubbing. Yet their transformation into valuable fashion items proved problematic, for most French youth remained suspicious of the genres' unpleasant associations with the facile enjoyment offered by the *discothèque*. Easy detachment or careless jocularity clearly went against the ethics and aesthetics of rock and independent pop – favoured by middle-class youth – which prized political awareness and a more or less desperate form of gravity. This is a simplification, of course, and the range of popular music associated with youth cultures in France is far more varied than we are suggesting here. But as far as the line of our argument is concerned, what matters is that the musical forms mentioned above generally shy away from the obvious and the simply euphoric.

This prejudice is at the origin of the most common representation of the field of *techno* in France. Participants and external observers generally identify a dividing line which cuts across the field and isolates the domain of *confidential* free parties and *illegal* gatherings from that of official clubbing. The former is reportedly characterized by minimalism and sonic aggressiveness (hardcore and jungle are frequently quoted as examples of this attitude) while the latter is typified by kitsch and an acknowledgement of light music and disco (as in house).

In the accounts given by people interviewed about *techno*, the cardinal values of each scene are expressed as a series of dichotomies which are roughly superimposed (gravity/naivety, enthusiasm/passiveness, amateurism/ professionalism, integrity/corruption, subversion/innocuousness). But when asked for specific names of musicians, DJs, clubs or events that would fall within each category, each subject significantly draws the line in a different manner, suggesting that the characteristics are diffuse and volatile and cannot be supported by objective criteria. A brief observation of the size of record distribution channels and independent labels confirms that small productions and 'underground' activity are not the privilege of any subgenre. Each musical style is also segmented by other factors such as relative accessibility or difficulty of approach. The same accusations of commercialism will be heard everywhere. And here, again, discourse about success is relative: a successful producer may develop 'evangelical' arguments about spreading the movement, while another will find in his limited popularity an incentive for radicalism and a confirmation of his talent and subversiveness.

Estimations of illegal practice – drug use, for instance – prove even more inconclusive. As researches by the International Research Centre on

Environment and Development demonstrate, traffic and consumption are almost as developed in clubs as in free parties.[2]

As for the discourse of political assertiveness – we are using the term 'discourse' since commitment in itself can hardly be measured – it is as conspicuously absent from the songs themselves in one scene as it is in the other. This statement needs to be qualified, for the communication that surrounds free parties is far more politically aggressive than anything that is to be found in the sphere of clubbing. Yet this communication is concerned with the organization of the techno event or, in other words, with the professional activity of DJs and organizers which is constantly threatened by police forces and local administrations.

Colombier, Lalam and Schiray have argued that free parties in France are a form of alternative economy generating profits and not entirely different, in an economic perspective, from the 'overground' exploitation of techno.[3] Consequently, they also see the ravers' theoretical insistence on freedom of action as an ideological formulation of a sort of professional protectionism. The actual claim underlying it – they suggest – might be first and foremost a claim for freedom to carry out one's activities, the right of free enterprise. In one sense, it would be a liberal argument, both in the French and the British understanding of the word. But the questions of commitment, and of subversiveness, are too complex and elusive to be tackled in this introduction. They will be developed in the last part of this chapter.

All in all, the same categorizations can be applied at every level of this complex cultural system, that is: inside each of the supposedly antagonistic provinces as well as within subgenres.

What is remarkable and probably unique with techno – and this applies to France as well as the rest of Europe – is that though it covers a wide variety of styles, sounds and practices, all these distinctions do not fragment the community as a whole and estrange its members one from another: participants never question the basic assumption of their belonging to a single overall movement. This *esprit de corps* is reinforced by the tenor of their common ideology, which extols the virtues of universality, hybridity and acceptance of difference (the DJ's practice of the mix being in itself a dramatization of such qualities).

Whether formulated in the discourse of the intellectual exponents of techno – who frequently use Deleuze's concept of 'deterritorialisation' and Hakim Bey's notion of 'temporary autonomous zones' as theoretical backing to articulate their

---

[2] Colombier, Thierry, and Nacer, Lalam (1998), *Etudes des filères produits psychotropes à partir des soirées de musique techno*, intermediary report, Paris: International Research Center on Environment and Development, 20.

[3] Colombier, Thierry, Nacer, Lalam, and Schiray, Michel (2000), *Drogue et techno: les trafiquants de rave*, Paris: Stock, 78–112.

refusal of fixed territories (we will come back to this terminology)[4] – or phrased in a more sentimental and idealistic language foregrounding the ravers' spiritual communion and their cosmic consciousness, the same values (openness, centripetal expansion, and the sense of some universal spirit infusing itself in all the parts of the scene to totalize them) dominate techno and account for the irresistible progression of the movement. One of the consequences of this common spirit, for instance, is that the success of a particular artist, however marginal and even denigrated by the rest of the scene, ultimately benefits all of the participants. Attempts to understand this secret harmony will be put forward in the third part of our study.

Techno in France: the institution of a genre

Witnesses of the development of techno agree on a number of founding events in the chronology of the French adoption of the genre.

The first specialized record shops were set up at the end of the 1980s (BMP in Paris or USA Import in Nice, later joined by Rough Trade which, interestingly, had turned from independent pop and 'experimental' subgenres to a frank endorsement of techno). Early French labels Rave Age and F. Communication[5] appeared respectively in 1989 and 1994 on the initiative of Manu Casana, Eric Morand and Laurent Garnier, but vinyl pressing was not limited solely to a few well-known labels: white labels[6] equally flourished at the same period. Radio FG, the mouthpiece of the gay community, whose authorization to broadcast had been threatened by French authorities because of mismanagement, was reconstructed by Henry Maurel in 1991 and from then on became an important channel for the diffusion of electronic music. Radio Nova had included techno in its programmes ever since 1988 but it was only in 1993 that it started giving special time slots or 'residencies' to famous DJs. Maximum, the first all-dance music station to broadcast on a national scale, also featured late-night *techno* programmes, but it disappeared after two years of broadcasting (1990–92). From then on, major commercial FM radios (Skyrock, Energy and Fun to a lesser degree) sporadically attempted to introduce electronic music but these experiments remained tentative. Hence they never managed to capture a long-standing audience.[7]

---

[4]   Deleuze, Gilles, and Guattari, Félix (1980), *Mille Plateaux*, Paris: éditions de minuit; Bey, Hakim (1991), *Temporary Autonomous Zones. Ontological Anarchy, Poetic Terrorism.* Brooklyn: Autonomedia.

[5]   Morand had already managed the label when it was still a division of FNAC music stores.

[6]   Independent productions whose characteristic white sleeves offer no information on the artist, producer or record company, thereby revealing the unpremeditated and unofficial quality of the record.

[7]   See the discussion of new music and new radio stations given by Geoff Hare in this volume.

As raves and parties started to proliferate in the early 1990s, a whole economy developed around the Paris scene, including diverse activities: publication of fanzines, graphic designing, clubwear, decoration, as well as various forms of craftsmanship.

The foundation of *Coda*, a monthly magazine specializing in techno (1993), contributed to the music's visibility. It was soon complemented by *Trax*, another monthly with a more critical bias (*Vibration* also had a role to play in publicizing electronic genres with a series of compilations). Meanwhile, reports in the general-purpose or sensational press either expressed moral panic or proposed pedagogical reductions (with glossaries and who's whos of the scene).[8]

Participants identify a watershed in 1995, the year when a ministerial circular addressed to all prefects warned the mayors and the police against dangers of techno gatherings, recommending vigilance. This text, quite similar in spirit to the Criminal Justice Bill passed by the British government at about the same time, strongly encouraged mayors to refuse cooperation with the parties' organizers and thus initiated a repressive policy.

In February 1996, as a result of pressure from a group of disco owners and managers in Lyon, a major gathering (Polaris) was prevented from taking place at the last minute. This prompted a number of actors on the scene to create Technopol, an association aimed at promoting 'electronic cultures'.

Such initiatives, together with the increasing popularity of a number of DJs and producers, certainly helped to change the public and governmental attitudes towards the scene, to such an extent that, eventually, the 'Planète' night organized by the management team of French festival 'Les Transmusicales' held in December in Rennes (for a long time it had fulfilled the function of a showcase where new musical genres and individual talents were discovered and exposed) was honoured by the visit of Minister of Culture Catherine Trautman and Minister Jack Lang who had already started championing the project of a techno parade in Paris.

At about the same time, 15 million francs were allotted by the Ministry of Culture to the promotion of 'musiques actuelles' (December 1997). The first techno parade took place in Paris in September 1998 and 200,000 people attended the event. In 1999, there were 350,000. Tangible progression of sales are evidenced by a 3.5 per cent rise in FNAC record stores in one year (from 2.5 per cent to 6 per cent of global sales, that is from marginal to considerable). Over the same period, sales of vinyl soared from 120,000 units to 295,000.[9]

---

8   Examples of moral panic can be found in *L'Humanité* (15 June 1993) and *Le Nouvel Observateur* (17 April 1997). Guides of the scene were devised by *Le Nouvel Observateur* (25 July 1996); *Paris Match* (March 1997), *Elle* (6 March 1998), among others.
9   These figures as well as those contained in the following paragraphs have been found on the site of a national agency (www.diplomatie.gouv.fr) and tally with the information given in the specialized press.

What really set French electronica apart in the history of the country's musical traditions was its being recognized worldwide as a *school* or *movement*. Prior to it, French popular music had rarely been approved of by English-speaking audiences. Isolated songs or artistic personalities might occasionally have aroused some interest (Serge Gainsbourg is an obvious example of a lasting influence), but the case of techno is unprecedented because it was the whole of a scene that was favoured by a British audience (the phrase 'French touch' itself was coined by the British press). And contrary to variety songs with a more consensual content and conventional orchestration, it was aimed at a public attaching tremendous importance to originality, innovation and change, whose tastes were thus highly unstable.

The period of gradual international expansion for French electronica began in 1995. By 1997, it had reached considerable proportions. Daft Punk's 'Homework' album was the first instance of massive success with 1.5 million copies sold. In 1998, after having been marketed for eight months, Stardust's single 'Music sounds better with you' sold a total of 1.2 million units. Cassius's single '1999' rose to the seventh position in British charts in early 1999. In the wake of this first commercial success – which paved the way for Cassius's subsequent releases – the album (bearing the same name) was simultaneously released in 33 countries and enthusiastically welcomed, getting decent scores in European charts and selling 250,000 in Europe in three months (50,000 in France). Alex Gopher only sold 25,000 copies of 'Me, My Baby and I', but considering the untypical, often atmospheric content of the songs and their unusual tempi (which meant that they did not qualify for exploitation in the clubbing circuits), this volume of sales cannot be ignored.

More recently, and four days after the release of his 'Flat beat' single (F Communications/PIAS), Mr Oizo had reached the heights of the British Top 40 and boasted sales of 440,000 copies. By October 1999, 3 million units of 'Flat beat' had been distributed (700,000 in Great Britain).

In all these cases, the conquest of an English-speaking (preferably British audience) had authenticated and confirmed the worth of the French musical products, facilitating their reception in France. Somehow, they had to be pointed out for the public's admiration by (British) outsiders and the same rule still obtains for more confidential productions. This mediation has always been necessary because of the unsafe position occupied by the French community in the field of techno.

Early connoisseurs were highly conscious that the genre had not naturally developed on French soil but had been implanted there at a time when it had already reached an advanced state of development elsewhere.[10]

---

[10]   This complex is partly based on a misrepresentation. If techno and house undoubtedly developed in America, they did not achieve public success here between 1985 and 1995. It is only when they were imported to England and Ibiza that they generated such a craze.

Somehow this sense of foreignness and exoticism added to the fascination. But together with it came the feeling that the French public's claim on techno was not *grounded*. They lacked some elementary cultural heritage to absorb it. This reaction is interesting to observe in the light of Bourdieu's remarks on strategies of distinction, myths of naturalness, and instinctive tastes. Obviously, we are presented here with a case where social or cultural markers (the capacity to respond to music, the natural ease with which one moves in its milieu) are so closely associated with individual subjects that, from an external point of view, they seem to be intrinsic qualities of the said subjects (Sarah Thornton's application of Bourdieu's theses to club culture is a stimulating example of a sociological approach).[11]

This deception is intimately linked to the belief that *popular* forms, being 'grassroots' cultures, emanate from a context and a situation; that they are born in response to them. Hence the insistence on the *underground* milieu as birthplace: it is the soil from which popular cultures spring, the ur-place in the myth of origins devised by the community. As France was obviously devoid of such a nurturing milieu, no one could initially boast possession or mastery of the genre (ownership of symbolical and subcultural capital). Of course there is no such thing as an instinctive taste, or an innate capacity of distinction: this is only how the British musical community is envisaged and subsumed; this is the place which is assigned to it. But we suspect that there is more in the term 'subculture' than a suggestion of deviance and secrecy. The *underground*, in the mind of those who use the phrase, lies at the root of official national culture. Hence the participants' frequent insinuations that mainstream entertainers and subsidized artists alike 'recuperate' or draw inspiration from it. Interpreting literally their own territorial metaphor, specialists strongly resent the 'exploitation' of techno by show business as though the stock of phrases, motifs and structures that constitute its aesthetic code were a limited quantity of natural resources that could be exhausted. This metaphorical displacement reflects intense anxieties in a field where no intellectual and artistic property can be legally protected. Besides, symbolical capital can actually be depreciated by appropriations or mimetic behaviour. But what it loses then is the power to confer prestige and identity upon those who endorse techno cultures, not the share of creativeness which is present in artistic products (the songs themselves).

Foreignness as style

Coming back to the recent recognition of French electronica outside France itself, we will argue in the following section that this has paradoxically

---

[11] See Thornton, Sarah (1996), *Club Cultures: Music, Media and subcultural Capital*, London: Wesleyan University Press – University Press of New England, and Gelder, Ken, and Thornton, Sarah (eds) (1997), *The Subcultures Reader*, London: Routledge.

confirmed the national specificity of the genre and caused it to develop into a coherent cultural field on its own native soil.

Etienne de Crecy's *Superdiscount* project achieved an award in France after having achieved respectability in Great Britain. 'If it works in London', De Crecy commented, 'Europe starts caring about it.'[12] Initially signed to Glasgow's Soma records label, Daft Punk's first single hit France on the rebound after its international diffusion, establishing the duo as authoritative members of the global techno community. The Micronauts deplored the fact that though their first productions were released on pioneer French labels Rave Age and Fnac Music (later to become F-Com), they only encountered success in foreign countries. But this acknowledgement has unquestionably added to the prestige they enjoy now, a prestige manifested by the tribute which is paid to them in the specialized press. Devoting themselves consistently and obdurately to their musical activities in the absence of any local public response, they have ultimately strengthened their position: an investment of time has resulted in heightened respectability.

Because of the authority of the Anglo-Saxon model, French techno, in its infancy, strove to capture the exact tone and style of the foreign product from which it derived. Flyers advertising raves and special events in traditional venues were done in imitation of British prototypes. Characteristically, they were often drafted in English. The jargon was largely borrowed from the idiom of British *techno* culture and it still prevails as the language of the scene. Borrowings include warm up, rave, clubbing, line up, live act, set, bleep, smart drink, chill out, dancefloor, guest, free party, overground and underground, before and after (used as substantives when referring to introductory and closing parties bracketing the main techno event). Even aesthetic appreciations such as cheesy or dark are preferred to lexically equivalent *ringard* or *sombre* because of their different connotations (above all, they are not derogatory). All generic appellations of subgenres have equally passed into this idiom untouched (hardcore, speed garage, drum n' bass, deep house ...).

Literal translations are sometimes substituted to English words: vinyl records are known as *plaques*, in imitation of the term plate (short for dubplate, a special imprint of a recording used by DJs). But linguistic invention remains limited.

In time, French techno gradually got beyond the purely mimetic, and started to affirm openly its French-ness abroad, using it as a promotional rationale. And somehow, the unprecedented acknowledgement it then received in foreign countries not only reinforced its credibility among French connoisseurs but also validated its French character in their eyes. To put it differently, it confirmed that the main reason why the music was prized outside France was that it was distinctively French.

'French connection' – one of the catchphrases used to describe the new wave

---

[12]   *The Face*, 16, 121.

of popular electronic music – explicitly confirms the global significance of the scene as a network of artists and aficionados. It can be understood as a declaration of principle in which criminal connotations are less important than the suggestions of a secret society whose members are interdependent and closely knit (Laurent Garnier had contemplated using it as a pseudonym for one of his early recordings). The tendency to aggregate and set up networks of influences and loyalties is not specific to electronica. Yet a number of factors may explain why the temptation might be stronger in this field.

The role played in France by associative structures, offering special flexible status that allowed commercial ventures without heavy taxation, was an incentive for isolated individuals to put resources together. Besides, the desire to receive recognition from one's peers is of particular importance in a field where the absence of tradition leaves artists isolated. Since the principle which dominates their creation is novelty, they are placed in an uncomfortable position to defend aesthetic choices which may just appear eccentric or unprofessional. Mutual recognition and support often allow them to pass from marginality or deviance to integration in a 'school'.

As an illustration of these French connections, one might consider the case of Alex Gopher, Xavier Jamoux, Jean Benoît Dunckel and Nicolas Godin, all of whom had played in the same band (Orange) and resided in Versailles at the beginning of their career before becoming notorious as active exponents of the French touch (respectively under the name of Gopher, Bang Bang and Air). Versailles, an affluent residential suburban location, seems to have participated in the elaboration of Dunckel and Godin's public image as well as in the symbolical construction of their musical universe. They have frequently suggested in interviews that the situation of this peaceful traditional town, removed from the exuberant effervescence of Paris, reflected their artistic temperament. This preference is at one with their avowed taste for French 'variety' of the 1960s (Françoise Hardy, Gainsbourg) and lounge music such as Francis Lai's or Burt Bacharach's (with the sense of measure and peaceful harmony it conveys). Their first record conjures up, with a measure of nostalgia, sentimental memories of the France of bygone days (more accurately, it resuscitates its taste).[13]

Of course if we posit that the work of art – even minor – is a closed system, these extra-musical circumstances can only be brought up at the risk of a confusion between levels of representation. Yet there is rarely such a neat closure delimiting the products of popular cultures.

Each in their own way, famous producers Dimitri from Paris and Ludovic Navarre (known as St Germain) capitalised on the ironic evocation of a France

---

[13] In an interview given to magazine *The Face*, the journalist reports that the two musicians brought him into the forest in search of an old tree in which Dunckel and Godin used to play as children. But they could not find it, even though they were convinced they stood on the place where it once had stood. See Hooper, Mark (1998), 'Paris is Burning', *The Face*, 97–110.

of yore (after the Second World War).[14] But beyond the retro touch of local colour that outmoded references conferred upon their productions – a distinctive feature in a scene where futurism and technological images dominate – such forms of recuperation link back the whole genre to a Parisian tradition of clubs where jazz enthusiasts could go and listen to American records played by a Disc Jockey. This tradition was discontinued in the 1970s (or was only maintained as folklore for the tourists) yet it remained available as a source of imaginative origins. Le Costes, (another famous jazz café and a symbol of Parisian elegance that fires the imagination of the non-Parisian public) was recently used as a marketing argument for a series of compilations.

One might also think of Lab Insect's album *Il est cinq heures, Paris s'éveille* including such titles as 'Faubourg St Germain' (the title of the record is taken from Jacque Dutronc's song evoking the picturesque atmosphere of Paris in the 1960s, but seen from the point of view of a distanced and slightly amused observer who goes to sleep when the town wakes up to its humdrum life). Ark's *De derrière les fagots* (an expression referring to some choice product – for instance an excellent vintage – that has been kept in store for a special occasion) is deliberately outdated. Bosco's intention might have been similar when they carefully picked up an Anglicized French term in the British lexicon to serve as a title for their second LP (*Paramour*). Likewise 'Sacrebleu' (Dimitri from Paris's first album) is an archaic interjection that clearly announces a parodic intention.

Taken together, all similar musical endeavours serve as the vehicle of a discourse on the legitimacy of French electronica and more particularly on its legitimacy abroad.

In order to affirm a French identity in a pan-cultural movement, one has to recant one's words at the very moment the national claim is expressed. But whatever the exact tenor of the message, the national message remains inscribed in the music, in the press and in public opinion. Thus, the jacket cover of Air's *Moon Safari* bears the mention 'French Band', an appellation which previously would have been derogatory.

What is striking in all these evocations of France is that they are neither realistic nor documentary reflections but rather images of the country as perceived and reinvented by foreigners, with its reductions and clichés. They are mythologies of France in foreign consciousness (of course all cultural and racial representations involve an amount of subjectiveness, but the point is too general to be discussed here). Consequently, parody signals French people's awareness of an identity that is imposed from the outside and over which they have no control. Conforming with the cliché is a circular way of reappropriating this identity and achieving mastery over it by giving it an aesthetic value (again the

---

[14] Dimitri from Paris, *Sacrebleu*, Yellow, 1996. St Germain, *Boulevard*, F Communications, 1996.

term kitsch applies to define this manipulation). As Bourdieu contends in *La distinction*, when 'high art', as defined by an elite or aristocracy, is not accessible, another class or social group may affirm their right to institute as art what had not been intended as such and was disregarded by other privileged classes.[15]

The role which *kitsch* and parody play in the legitimization of *techno* as a genre in France can also be extended to different aspects which are not specifically national. But these will eventually bring us back to the question of French techno being still in its infancy or simply copied from a foreign original and uncritically consumed as a ready-made product.

For instance, Etienne de Crecy's 'Superdiscount' project consists of a series of singles whose front sleeves copy the gaudy and vulgar commercial adverts that signal articles for sale. Thus, it deliberately brings the public's attention to bear on the commercial value of the record: it anticipates and forestalls accusations of commercialism and superficiality by turning them into an aesthetic code. It is easy to understand that these strategies are imposed by a context. Because of the hedonistic bias and melodic simplicity of the most publicized brand of techno, the genre as a whole has brought upon itself charges of immaturity and lack of seriousness (here, the same process of generalization that sustains the utopia of the 'techno nation' operates in public opinion). Le Tone's 'Joli dragon' [Pretty Dragon] extracted from his album 'Le petit Nabab' [Little Nabob] (1998) gets ahead of such criticism thanks to his pastiche of the imaginary world of children's tales (diminutives 'little', 'pretty' or 'cute' indicate the vein of ironic self-depreciation that runs through the French touch). Roudoudou (the name of a children's sweet) adopts a similar strategy on his first record entitled *Tout l'Univers* [The whole universe, the name of a children's encyclopaedia]. The record contains among other things a cover of a tune taken from Walt Disney's version of *The Jungle Book* with English lyrics.

This last detail has its importance. Indeed it refers us to another arresting characteristic of the French touch that we have still not accounted for: the notable persistence of Anglo-Saxon imagery and language (predominantly American) across the range of its productions. To begin with, lyrics are frequently sung in English. Yet this does not contradict in any way the demonstration we have made in the first part of the chapter. Concerning those borrowings, the most common explanation proposed by musicians is that since electronic music is frequently exported to Europe and America, the use of English is a practical choice to ensure a good understanding of the music.

In most cases, the textual content of these electronic productions is limited to catchphrases, mottoes or slogans (very often sampled voices of English speakers or singers). Or, as in Air's case, it is reminiscent of sentimental and old-fashioned

---

[15] Bourdieu, Pierre (1984), *Distinction. A Social Critique of the Judgement of Taste*, Cambridge, MA: Harvard University Press.

ballads (predominantly French, but often sung in poor English) which are only acceptable because they are part of a coherent kitsch reconstruction. A more radical example of 'Americanism' would be the back sleeve of Bob Sinclar's 'Paradise' EP which features a cheap advertisement written in English that reads 'Get Bob Sinclar's aftershave and achieve sexual climax'. The ad displays a bottle of aftershave lotion and quaint images of success and seduction.[16] Again, the techno tune is ironically presented as a product – this is not an isolated case and certain labels, such as Apricot, have capitalized on this form of pastiche of a consumer society -and the American culture of the 1960s is recuperated and debunked as outmoded, yet also rehabilitated as an element of style.

Sarah Thornton, drawing on Bakhtin, has argued that parody is not strictly an exclusion but an ambivalent response to embarrassing influences.[17] Parodying is a way of acknowledging one's debt to the holders of tradition, while at the same time showing one's right freely to use their inheritance. In parody, irreverence is coupled with a very clear admission that the art of the new generation would not even be possible without these precedents which are used as raw material.

Local tensions and global significance

Of course, actors on the French electronic scene have never made any explicit statement concerning their personal aesthetic intentions. But, collectively, their visual and musical manipulations constitute a form of resistance against all criticism addressed to them. As models of an essentially ambivalent communication, these parodies rely on the proceeds of double entendre and they imply irony which, by definition, cannot openly announce its duplicity: it is only efficient when it excludes some of those who receive the message from communication. It is on this condition that it can create between the author and the listeners an intimacy facilitating this communal feeling praised by technophiles.

The most patent example of this combination of respect and diffidence is probably that of Thomas Bangalter and Guy-Manuel de Homem-Christo – especially since they initiated the whole phenomenon of expansion of French techno. Their first attempt at penetrating the world of pop music with a single was harshly criticized by British specialists and a journalist described the band as 'daft punks'. Surprisingly, rather than ignoring the insult, Bangalter and de Homem-Christo endorsed the identity that had been thrust upon them and, moving from pop music to electronica, they symbolically turned the insult upon those who had first uttered it by conquering the British charts as 'Daft Punk'.

---

[16]   Bob Sinclar is the hero of an openly anti-British cinematic parody of James Bond. The part was played by French actor Jean-Paul Belmondo.

[17]   Thornton, *Club Cultures*.

The title of Daft Punk's debut album (*Homework*) and the inclusion of a song which consisted of an enumeration of the great masters of house and techno ('Teachers') helped to turn it into it a statement of moderate ambitions issued by two humble pupils. The collection of Americana that decorated the inside jacket, with its many references to artists of the 1970s, could not possibly be a reminiscence of their youth (they would not even have been born at that time): it was a memorial tribute to the infancy of techno.

Significantly, Daft Punk (who sold over a million and a half copies of *Homework*) were the first French band with a reputation of underground and anti-commercial integrity to have the satisfaction of seeing their name and picture on the front pages of the British musical press since French punk outfit Stinky Toys (who had once posed for the cover of an issue of the *New Musical Express*). Thus, they were admitted by the Anglo-Saxon press as representatives of an alternative French musical culture. By comparison, mainstream Francophone best-sellers such as Vanessa Paradis or Celine Dion were never granted the same status (neither did they or their public demand it, for that matter: their songs were just not addressed to the same audience).

But it is also significant that the only precedent of full-page coverage should have been a self-styled punk band whose leader, Jacno, rapidly confirmed his French identity in his solo career, and subsequently seduced the French audience with naive electronic tunes sung by Elli Medeiros and partly derived from the same sources of inspiration as those to which the neo-retro band Air later laid claim (namely, the *nouvelle vague* and its spearheads: Gainsbourg, Françoise Hardy ...).

Perhaps at this point some more detail on punk would be useful, for it undoubtedly played a role in the formation of the part of techno culture represented by free parties and *teknivals* as well as by the establishment of the independent circuit of labels and record shops which are not specific to free parties.

Of all the imported movements that have reached France during the past 30 years, punk is the one with which French youth identified themselves most strongly. Thus when a new generation went in search of a pop history on which to ground their own French electronic culture, punk was one of the few milestones they could willingly and even passionately claim as a national reference point – especially because it had been so closely related to *situationism*. Therefore it fitted within a chain of events including the 1968 Paris uprising and Guy Debord (in other words, a long tradition of protests that has been almost entirely recuperated in the French raver's counterculture).[18]

As we can see, the course of this analysis has taken us from the notion of facile kitsch amusement to that of countercultural movement. In other words we have

---

[18] Political statements made on sites such as www.techno.org or www.kanyar.fr evidence this political inclination.

been brought back to the dichotomy mentioned in our introduction. But having considered now various cultural aspects of the 'French touch', as defined by an English-speaking public, we are better equipped to confront critically the problem of this supposedly essential division in the field of techno. And in order to understand the nature of the controversy we will be led to discuss various sociological analyses developed by French commentators.

But the first obvious remark that can be made is that a large share of the supporters of free parties (those who live this experience to the full) would not accept the French touch (understood in the strictest sense) as a significant extension of their own cultural field. To do so would go against their belief in global cultures and multiculturalism and would be at cross purposes with their rejection of the notions of state and national frontiers.

Yet a French and sometimes regional identity (as in the case of Brittany) expresses itself on the techno scene in spite of its abhorrence of particularisms. The existence of geographical centres of intense activity (the Mediterranean hinterland from Nice to Montpellier as well as the Parisian region) is also indicative of its dependence on a local public.[19]

Even if we accept that multiculturalism is a cardinal value of techno, the raver's claim that this ideological programme is better realized in the sphere of free-partying than in the more conventional world of clubbing nonetheless invites discussion.

This claim can be questioned firstly, because the multitude of French 'tribes' which now possess their own sound system principally stem from a single British root (the Spiral Tribe). These travellers and squatters fled England towards the continent when the repression of raves and illegal parties started hampering their activities. But their nomadic existence is not the rationale of the movement. There is a confusion between permanent members who disregard geographical boundaries and intermittent workers who join them, yet frequently go back to their sedentary life. Besides, the scene is composed of a majority of simple users whose attendance can vary from assiduousness to occasional presence. In this way, on the whole, raves are not cut off from the social environment.

Secondly, this 'free' scene is not indifferent to the developments of the overground official circuit. As soon as well-reputed musical festivals such as Les Francofolies (La Rochelle) or Le Printemps de Bourges opened up to electronic music, fringe festivals were set up in their surroundings. A 'F*** Borealis' party is known to have taken place every year on the day of the famous official Borealis rave in Montpellier. On these yearly occasions a section of the audience has always joined the alternative party after having attended the main event. And

---

[19]   To be absolutely accurate, we must admit that regionalism is less at variance with the ravers' belief in small tribal communities than nationalism. Ravers and regionalists are both in conflict with the state and similarly vindicate independence (Britanny is a pregnant example of the trend).

when Heliocolor succeeded to the defunct Borealis in August 2000, French techno-tribes changed the name of their own party into 'F*** Heliocolors'.

In addition, the fact that ravers pitch camp in the vicinity of such sites at crucial dates, improvising alternative gatherings, suggests that they partly define their identity in opposition to 'overground' manifestations. Entering a competition, they implicitly recognize their opponents as members of the techno nation, albeit degraded by commercial compromises. Travellers[20] in the free parties circuit will admit, for example, that the award Laurent Garnier won at the Victoires de la Musique is an asset of the techno movement but they will deny that Garnier belongs to their sphere since he has never played in free parties.[21]

It is important at this stage to distinguish between ideological arguments, national identities and musical preferences because it is the complex interactions between these three factors that obscure the debate.

Free parties are defined by oppositional tendencies. The rave being idealistically a moment of abstraction from the social world, the audience attaches vital importance to ritual expressions of personal and collective difference. Due to the consequent isolation of the 'free' scene, penetration by other musical styles proves more difficult. Independent record-shop owners note that if travellers are using the network of specialized retailers to distribute their own independent productions and advertise their nights, they do not lend an attentive ear to musical genres which do not symbolically and aesthetically reflect their political extremism. Consequently, illegal raves are often accused of musical immobilism and of reduced musical creativity. Yet jungle and breakbeats entered free parties some years ago and house is liable to be played on certain occasions.

A large number of free party-goers also patronize clubs and authorized raves. Moreover, free parties are supported by a young public who are taking advantage of it to assert themselves by fleeing the family milieu and flouting conventions. It is a transitional experience or rite of passage that will often lead them towards other less oppositional forms of participation in the musical techno culture.

Gradually, we come to understand that the fate of the supposedly antinomic groups (ravers v. clubbers) is inextricably linked because they are two components of the same movement. Yet they are bound to oppose each other since the affirmation of national identity is perceived by some as an obstacle to the realization of 'autonomous zones'. Conversely others will be frightened by what they interpret as sectarianism: that is, an excessive literalness in the application of these common principles that they also endorse and value.

---

[20]   The term has been adopted in French to describe all people whose radical involvement in the rave culture causes them to live a nomadic life.

[21]   A flagrant example of such a contradiction (or what sounds like a contradiction) is to be found in the transcription of an interview with a traveller reproduced in full in Colombier et al., *Drogue et techno*, 227–48.

Ultimately, it appears that it is the tension between the ethical and the aesthetic which is at stake in this confrontation of points of view. And we may suspect that such conflicts just highlight inherent tensions in the global culture itself, problems that techno necessarily encounters when actualizing its potentials in a given social environment. Above all, divergences proceed from the more or less literal interpretation of the programme defined by techno.

In order to account for the vitality of the rave culture in France, Gaillot – following Fontaine and Fontana – ventures the hypothesis that the rave re-actualizes a Dionysian principle or a tribal feeling which has not been entirely eradicated from contemporary European societies because it is necessary to their equilibrium. Gaillot traces the rave back to 'happenings' as an art form in which immediacy, presence and participation are rated more highly than the work of art itself, the final outcome and materialization of the artist's creative process encapsulating all meanings generated by his talent and inspiration. In 'happenings' as in techno culture, Gaillot contends, objective palpable artworks (musical recordings) only serve as a pretext for the social moment.[22]

Prolonging this argument, one might infer that the music played at raves and techno events performs only an instrumental or functional role. Such meetings can be held and a whole range of activities develop without having to be supported by and articulated around a recognizable musical form possessing a strong identity. In turn, this argument invites reflection: it is stimulating because it implies that a milieu (a space where techno exists as a cultural practice) can constitute itself without a 'scene' (a national character), and this might explain why raves, as a social phenomenon, caught on and lasted in France in the absence of a local thematic. Meanwhile, the French scene was given time to constitute itself and find its formulas, motifs, and themes. Resorting to foreign music to establish a local 'sociality' could not be considered as bringing discredit on the movement: it was sufficient that the songs reflected the universal and abstract values of the scene. They did not have to resemble the French audience to assemble them together.

This might be a plausible explanation of the divergence we have repeatedly mentioned: a section of the community might continue along the original path without having radically to alter its directions while, simultaneously, others will feel that deviations are absolutely vital to the achievement of techno as a cultural project.

Of course, for a philosopher such as Gaillot, the emphasis on the 'here and now' has implications different from those we have suggested above. In his assessment of techno, the author opposes art as representation (that is an art whose purpose is to represent certain abstract values such as truth or beauty) and art as presentation (a place where 'individual existences' are put forward and

---

[22]   Gaillot, Michel (1999), *Sens multiple. La techno, un laboratoire artistique et politique du présent*. Paris: Dis voir, 58–65.

exposed but not exhibited, where each participant is given a chance to inhabit the present). When Gaillot posits the dichotomy between free parties and those where there is a charge for admission, he is reformulating the ravers' argument that the authentic rave, as a gratuitous waste of time and energy, is a political manifestation of dissatisfaction with rational time and production-oriented mainstream society.[23] This has always been the ground on which the ethical superiority of free parties and teknivals over official raves and club events has rested. In this perspective, clubbing is an attempt at reintegrating the movement within an economic system. But, advocates of free partying will argue, this attempt at assimilation is bound to fail because it perverts the true nature of the fête or feast. When turned into a leisure activity, it becomes a spectacle, a *simulacrum*.[24]

Such is the theoretical argumentation that backs the division between free parties and the commercial recuperation of techno in clubbing. But this explanation is partly based on false assumptions, considering that the origins of that genre are easily traceable to Chicago, Detroit and New York gay clubs whose customers were of Afro-American and Latin origins.

If we side with ethnologists and anthropologists and admit that the fête or feast performs the function of a safety valve, preserving the balance of the community and allowing the dissipation of violence and unwanted social tensions at specified moments (village feasts and yearly celebrations traditionally functioned as cathartic moments of expurgation in France), this hypothesis still only confirms that raves are adaptations of these ceremonies to the contemporary environment. But these considerations are not of great help when it comes to understanding their content, the special aesthetic codes they have developed and the choices which presided over their maturation. Nor does it tell us why the music created its own tradition and how it filled up the new space of freedom it created.

Now these questions, if they are to be properly discussed, force us to leave the domain of sociology and enter another province, that of artistic representation.

Electronic culture, because it is intimately linked to the new technologies of sampling and the expertise of the DJ, is a culture of synthesis and hybridization. One of the *raisons d'être* of the rave, for instance, is to stage and dramatize a utopian reverie: the conciliation of differences. From a musical point of view, the techno event is the moment when everything falls into place, when every song miraculously fits within its slot and plays its role. It is this immediate observation that has prompted commentators to extrapolate political inferences, sometimes at the risk of repeating the same confusion that had already made communication so difficult between the different subgroups of the techno culture.

---

[23]   Ibid., 78–80.
[24]   Today many DJs and organisers pragmatically deny the relevance of this dichotomy and they urge technophiles to go beyond this schematic representation and consider the quality of the music and sound system, the attention paid to the choice of the venue and the way it has been fitted up.

But as far as the musical aspect of the problem is concerned, the first direct implication is that any song which comes forward as a self-sufficient composition and exposes a neat aesthetic closure that makes it stand out is banished from the mix. Tunes are destined to be the elements of a composite work elaborated by the DJ. He is animated by a federating ambition, and, because he is the kingpin of this global culture, because he is visibly and audibly bringing its fragments together, the DJ is given the role of ambassador. The fantasy of the invisible network is projected upon him: he embodies techno as a culture branching and linking up references, defining constellations, drawing large ensembles in which the whole matters more than the parts. Laurent Garnier owes his reputation largely to his capacity to embrace a wide variety of styles in a set. British journalists have frequently suggested that the attraction exercised by French electronica is partly due to its eclecticism, its ability to combine heterogeneous references (for instance, Bosco have distinguished themselves by the eccentricity of their musical collages). Being in a position from which the internal complexities of foreign cultures (say British culture) are not perceptible, electronic musicians addressing a foreign public are perhaps less anxious about cultural incoherence, bad taste and indecorous references and feel freer to favour incongruous associations. Conversely, in the eyes of a foreign audience which receives this rearranged version of a (perhaps too) familiar construction, the offence is excused by its extraneous origin, and it is the conscious dissociation between the aesthetic product and any national discourse which allows the expected and necessary defamiliarization that fertilizes the exchange between technophiles. Otherwise it would just be a circulation of records, fashion items and ready-made attitudes.

This restriction of cross-cultural interactions to electronic music is not a rhetorical figure or a partisan statement. The ease with which electronica imports musical blocks or fragments – lifting them straight from an original piece of music thanks to sampling and other modern recording techniques and freely rearranging the chosen passages with no regard for the integrity of the base product – is something which definitely sets the genre apart.

A very general and tentative conclusion to this chapter would be that cultural renewal must apparently be expected to come from the outside, and in the form of national codes that have escaped the limits of the national discourse which once originated them. More specifically, it suggests that the international programme of techno can be ultimately achieved in an acknowledgement of national and local cultural specificities, even if these are deliberate misrepresentations – but only as long as they are cut off from any political or racist intention. In this sense, DJ-ing and techno are musical *projections*: the aesthetic rendering of a social ideal. But actualizing them remains another problem. Perhaps it is not a musical question at all.

Conclusion

French popular music, cultural exception and globalization

Hugh Dauncey and Steve Cannon

In a series devoted to 'Folk and Popular music', a book on specifically French popular music represents a somewhat bold attempt to break away from the lazy English speaker's assumption that popular music is – and almost has to be – sung in English, or at least derived from English-speaking countries. Popular music in this world-view is thus Britney and Kylie and their predecessors and successors and also, in a generous acknowledgement of those who choose to sing in English, all those bands and artists from Abba to the Hives whose musical success has been achieved by espousing the dominant format of popular musical popularity. The French describe the US and the UK as the 'Anglo-Saxons', and have always preferred to believe that their own cultural and musical traditions – as well as their ways of running politics and economics – are different, and have something to offer a world dominated by the 'Anglo-Saxon' neo-liberal economic consensus and by US-driven cultural globalization. This book tries to demonstrate how the French understand and approach popular music, how popular music in France has reflected and helped shape French society and culture since the Second World War, and how French popular music and culture have engaged culturally, cinematographically and commercially with the dominance of 'Anglo-Saxon' music in an increasingly globalized world.

A survey of who and what British or American music enthusiasts would consider to be French popular music would provide a wide range of responses, from embarrassed silence to passionate enumeration, but it is fair to suggest that depending on age and other factors, a fairly standard list of artists would be mentioned. Such a list might well include Chevalier, Trenet, Piaf, Brel, Brassens, Ferré, Aznavour, Hallyday, MC Solaar, Air, Daft Punk, and, depending on the degree of Francophilia of the respondent, other rarer musicians, such as perhaps Serge Gainsbourg, Jean-Michel Jarre or Les Rita Mitsouko. The point is that French popular music has managed to escape from France, often by virtue of its artists consenting to sing in English (but also sometimes because they sing – so charmingly – in French) and also by virtue of being instrumental. Another point is that although the majority of the artists mentioned above are exponents of *chanson*, others (increasingly as we move towards the present day) are not. If Aznavour is borderline *chanson/variétés* [easy-listening], Johnny Hallyday is the father of French rock, MC Solaar is perhaps the best known of a new generation of French rappers, and Air and Daft Punk are currently bringing French techno to the world.

The genre of French popular music which has attracted the most academic attention – certainly in the field of UK and US research in modern languages – has always been *chanson*. Peter Hawkins, the author of the most recent and arguably most authoritative study of the *chanson* (although he focuses on merely one aspect of the *chanson* tradition, namely the contemporary singer-songwriter) provides a list of the 'ingredients that go to make up the hybrid form of French popular culture which is *chanson*' which includes being a form of popular music with links to classical music and to poetry, theatre and live performance. For Hawkins, *chanson* has an 'ambiguous, hybrid status' and is a 'deceptive and elusive phenomenon'.[1] Hawkins's invaluable study also investigates how the work of the famous singer-songwriters he discusses – from Piaf, through Ferré and many others, to MC Solaar – has negotiated the huge changes in mediation through recording, and the media, but the perspective he adopts is closely linked to textual analyses of song lyrics, doubtless in recognition of the curious nature of *chanson* as a genre which, for all its undoubted status as popular music, can nevertheless still occupy an intermediate position in the hierarchy of musical practices.

As we have intimated above, this present volume of studies of French popular music – generously defined – includes consideration of *chanson*, but also investigates other genres and other aspects of the 'field' (to use Bourdieu's terminology) of French music. Those chapters which consider artists do so with reference to their socio-political and socio-cultural significance, and are flanked by other chapters which contextualize the work of the musicians and the music itself within more general developments and trends in French society overall. Thus studies of the *chansonniers* Chevalier, Piaf, Ferré and Brassens discuss them in relation to France's experience of Occupation and then the difficulties of society and politics in the post-war decades. Thus chapters on the mediation of popular music by business, radio, television and the specialist press and French government attitudes towards rock music provide an informative background to discussions of the symbiotic cultural relations obtaining between France and the US in the areas of film music, musical films, French rap and hip hop and French techno.

The study of popular music is of course a relatively new academic pursuit, as is touched on by Middleton in his introductory comments, and in France itself – a country as we know imbued with pride in the claimed superiority of its high

---

[1]   Hawkins, Peter (2000), *Chanson: the French Singer-Songwriter from Aristide Bruant to the Present Day*, Aldershot: Ashgate, 5.

culture – examining popular music has until very recently been an activity undertaken only by the foolhardy or those brave enough to aspire to academic 'distinction' through the intellectual analysis of the Low-Other. The status of popular music as an object of study in France is addressed by a survey-chapter of sociological research into various forms of (non-classical) music and musical practices. It becomes clear from this survey that the French themselves are somewhat unclear as to what precisely constitutes 'popular music' within the context of their musical traditions, and such uncertainty strengthens our resolve to look at French popular music defined in the widest sense.

It is doubtless easier to define popular music as what it is not, rather than what it is, so this volume does not consider any forms of classical music or jazz (except to the extent that they figure as music in popular films) or any forms of what in French are actually termed *musiques populaires* which is more folk music than popular music of mass consumption. The French state (as chapters by Le Guern and Teillet demonstrate) has evolved a variety of terminologies to help it manage the social, cultural, political and commercial impacts of non-classical, non-folk music (live music, amplified music, contemporary music), but the fundamental form of popular music that French researchers seem to have focused upon is rock. French rock is a rather singular musical genre once famously compared by the newspaper *Libération* to English cuisine. Deriving from imported US rock and roll in the 1950s, the classic age of French rock was the 1960s when stars such as Johnny Hallyday and Eddie Mitchell created a Frankensteinian hybrid which appealed to the young generation of the baby boom. Although Johnny is still around, many face-lifts later, 'rock' has been adopted by French musicians and constitutes merely one genre among others in the panoply of popular music styles. The most popular genres in the 1990s have been hip hop and techno, and it is the US influences behind these, along with the American roots of rock, and before that, French jazz, which brings this chapter to its next point, which is the delicate relationship between France and the US concerning culture and language in general, and, in most cases combining the two, in music.

A recurrent theme in this volume has been that of France's cultural exceptionalism and the challenges to the French language (the two are closely, if not inextricably, linked). Since the age of Empire and before, France has always prided herself on the originality and quality of her cultural practices and productions, but in the period covered by this volume – the second half of the American Century – such a pride has been systematically undermined by France's declining status as a world power. But undermined or not, French belief in the value of her culture – whether it be art, fashion, literature, film, philosophy, or music – has remained, perhaps even enhanced by the realization that this is now simply all that France can lay claim to in the world system as a marker of her distinction amongst nations. The Atlantic – or the French Atlantic, as some are coming to term it – has been the mediator of cultural cross-fertilization between France and the US, and music has not escaped this fecund symbiosis. The issues of cultural exception and French concerns to defend her cultural specificity and identity against Americanization, Coca-Cola-ization, McDonaldization and globalization are discussed in a variety of the chapters of this volume; they are indeed the backdrop to much of the cultural and social importance of popular music in France today. Jazz figures only briefly in our analyses – mainly because it is difficult to see it clearly as a popular genre – but, as Stilwell reminds us, the reception and adaptation of jazz in France in the early part of the twentieth century provides a model of the processes of cultural interdependency to be reiterated by rock, hip hop, techno and other genres. Although the simple model of 'cultural imperialism' is – as Middleton points out – no longer to be taken seriously, its discourses are often still apparently influential. The studies by Powrie and Stilwell of French film music and of French film musicals engage with these issues, discussing how far American culture and commerce threaten French musical and cultural forms with disintegration and how far there has always existed a creatively conflictual, reflexively recursive relationship between form and content across the Atlantic. Cannon and Birgy's analyses of hip hop and techno likewise show how France 'gives as it good as she gets' in the field of popular music, although the predominantly instrumental techno is clearly more readily exported, and even in the realm of commerce, Dauncey suggests that France is not completely defenceless against global capitalism. Sometimes it seems that the unreconstructed thesis of 'cultural imperialism' is only still fully adhered to in the corridors of power of French cultural policy.

In his preface to this study, Richard Middleton sets out what could be termed the general musicological context to an analysis of French popular music. His outline of the status of popular music as an object of study locates it at the focal point of a number of debates which recur at different points throughout the volume. Middleton's starting point is that music is inescapably social, whatever traditional approaches to music and musicology may have tried to assert in the past in theories of music which stress its supposed autonomy. As Middleton points out, the notion of autonomous music was of course itself the result of various trends in music and how it was perceived in views imposed by a bourgeois elite, namely the pre-eminence of instrumental rather than vocal music, a stress on musical works rather than practices, and the elaboration of a canon of musical masterworks. Within this late-modern *Weltanschauung* of music, popular music was a problematic phenomenon, based as it was and is fundamentally in practices, vocal and instrumental and without any officially sanctioned canon of masterpieces.

Several of the other analyses presented in this book investigate the contemporary reverberations of these elite views on music which have traditionally banished popular music to the realms of Low-Other, from Le Guern, whose survey of current French research into popular music reveals a focus on amateur and popular practice inspired by de Certeau and other theoreticians of the everyday, to Looseley and Teillet, who describe the French state's recent conversion to a role in cultural policy which includes the encouragement of 'culture for all' rather than simply the preservation of masterpieces for posterity. Birgy, in his study of the reception and spread of techno in France in the 1990s addresses simultaneously issues of instrumental music production and practice. Middleton points out (perhaps partly in explanation of the French state's 'enlightened' attitude towards popular music since the 1980s) that it is precisely French theoreticians on music such as Attali and Hennion who have helped think through the links between music and society: while for Attali music is anticipatory and 'prophetic' of change in society, for Hennion, what is called 'music' is made up of its mediations. Both Attali and Hennion meet in agreement, Middleton reminds us, over the lesson that the ways in which music features in people's lives tell us about their social world: the mechanisms of practice and orders of discourse through which sites of music enable the building and upkeep of identities both social and psychological (as Middleton adds to Hennion's call for a 'musicology of society') are also addressed by a number of contributions to this book. Lloyd and Tinker, for example, investigate some of the socio-political dimensions of French popular music during the Occupation and in the post-war decades; Powrie and Stilwell describe the ways in which music is mediated by film and how musical films have mediated Franco-American cultural relations; Cannon looks at how music negotiates and constructs youth and ethnic minority identities; Hare and Pires consider the mediation of music by radio, television and the music press.

Middleton situates these issues and debates over music and society, over the value and meaning of art, over the use of music in world-building and identity-formation as typical of the modern period and of its founding interrogations about the relations between the People and the Elite and notions of the popular, the vernacular, the everyday, the Low and the elite, the erudite, the rare, the High in terms of culture in general and music in particular. Just as France was central to the birth of modernity in the late eighteenth century, Middleton indicates how France is nowadays paradoxically both at the centre and the periphery of the global music-media system: 'France stands, fascinatingly, in more than one role and at more than one level in this multivalent system.' Again, chapters by Dauncey, Hare, Powrie, Stilwell, Birgy and others respond to this in discussing France's role in protecting music rights in the e-economy, the ambitions of Vivendi-Universal, France's attempt to protect French-language music through radio quotas, the cultural dialogue between France and the US and many other instances of the ways in which France occupies different spaces in the system of conflict, tension and interdependence between cultures, genres, identities and economies.

In the brief synopses which follow, we try to give accurate summaries of what each chapter says about popular music in France and how each analysis links to others and to general themes in the study of popular music and France itself. The way in which the book itself is structured means that successive chapters are intended to build up an overall picture of the French system of popular music.

Like Richard Middleton's piece, the chapter by Philippe Le Guern provides more detail on the theoretical context to the study of French popular music. Le Guern gives a survey of recent work by French sociologists and musicologists on various aspects of what is seen in France as popular music. The starting point of the survey is that in French research there has been a relative neglect of the sociology of music in general and of the sociology of contemporary and popular musics in particular. As perhaps in Britain and the US before interest in popular music arose in the 1970s, Le Guern explains that this neglect arose from a combination of factors such as the lack of cultural legitimacy of popular musics, the negative image of rock and pop music as musics of revolt and protest, the practical difficulties of fieldwork and the terminological confusion surrounding popular music. Reminding us that those who interest themselves in popular music in France play a proselytizing role, Le Guern summarizes the issues addressed by French research as threefold: what are the typologies and classifications of popular music?; how can the origin and development of popular music be analysed?; how can the impact of popular musics be gauged?

Concerning typologies and terminologies, Le Guern's summary suggests that compared with British and US research into popular music, the French approach is somewhat handicapped by its over-reliance on the term 'rock' (alongside 'chanson') almost to the point of using it to describe everything which is clearly not serious classical music or jazz (which occupies an intermediate position in cultural hierarchies). Three approaches highlighted by Le Guern which seem useful are that of Menger, who simply defines *musique populaire* as a music of 'mass consumption' (as opposed to musics of restricted consumption), that of constructivist sociology, which takes popular music to be all those practices which go to make it up and which are recognizable as *not* serious music, and that of those who seek to define music teleologically in terms of its role in creating trance-like states, enhancing emotions or creating personal, local or other identities. Looking at the origin and development of popular music, Le Guern surveys studies investigating who, how, where and why people do music in France, whether this be 'rock', music played in the Paris métro or 'everyday' amateur music, and reveals how French research has linked these practices to the social, emotional and identity realities of their participants (Birgy's chapter provides an example of this for techno music). Le Guern provides a brief overview of the musical 'field' in France, and then concludes his survey with a consideration of the mediation of music and its audiences, focusing in particular on attempts to gauge the impact of popular musics and the audiences they attract.

David Looseley's analysis of the ways in which both *chanson* and French pop music have (during different periods) acquired cultural legitimacy provides an informative and thought-provoking context for many of the studies which follow.

Looseley argues that *chanson* and pop music in France – *chanson* the indigenous popular music form and pop music the imported genre – started from positions of cultural domination, and that both genres, by similar processes and developments, have now attained a legitimacy as cultural objects which allows them to figure in official discourse and to play a role in government thinking on cultural and economic policy. Looseley briefly demonstrates how *chanson* developed its own legitimacy through the nineteenth century, as government policies towards (often satirical) popular music evolved and institutions such as the SACEM (musicians' rights association) created a context in which popular music could provide the way to make a living.

Allied to these changes in the second half of the nineteenth century, were developments in the nature of the venues in which popular music was performed, France's *cafés-concert* and music-hall tradition adapted from the UK, allowing the creation of the modern notion of the 'star' and his/her audience. Looseley cites Chevalier and Piaf (discussed in subsequent chapters in this volume) as typical of this early generation of *chanson* stars whose commercialization of the genre contributed to dissolving its dissidence and moving it towards legitimacy. He also discusses Brassens, Brel and Ferré, who in the 1950s and 1960s arguably represented the culmination of the *chanson* genre, and who were presented as more 'authentic' artists of the *chanson* genre, as *chanson* increasingly came into competition with pop music, and, through a process of laying claim to cultural value through reference to its lyrical qualities (*chanson* as 'text-song') came to distinguish itself from the newer forms of popular music typified by rock, pop, French rock, alternative rock, world music and rap in the 1970s, 1980s and 1990s.

In demonstrating his thesis that French rock and pop in the latter half of the twentieth century followed the same process of legitimation as *chanson*, Looseley shows how these popular musical forms have similarly developed 'mainstream' and 'commercial' varieties, allowing the more prestigious forms to acquire the status of culturally legitimate objects (through the growing confidence of the genre, the influence of the specialist press and the role of the Ministry of Culture). Such a new legitimacy has allowed pop music to become instrumentalized in the context of French music export and employment policies (see Dauncey's discussion of the French Music Export Bureau), but Looseley suggests that techno (see Birgy's analysis) may yet set a new challenge to the French state's approaches to popular music.

Hugh Dauncey provides an overview of the French music business, linking the current state of the industry to two examples of issues which characterize firstly France's reaction to the challenge posed by the internet, and secondly France's attempts to affirm her cultural and commercial identity in the global market for music. Whereas the French music industry is generally considered to be fragile and complex, but nevertheless possessing some strengths (notably linked to the French state's support for France's cultural industries in general) Dauncey's presentation of these case studies shows how both the government-sponsored French Music Export Office and the private-sector strategies of the French-owned multinational Vivendi-Universal are giving French leadership to questions of the protection of national cultural and commercial identities in the world popular music industry.

Geoff Hare's discussion of popular music on French radio and television provides a comprehensive coverage of the political, social and economic underpinnings of the mediation of music through the traditional audiovisual media. He sets these mediations within the context of France's socio-political *difference* from her neighbours – particularly the UK – firstly in terms of her state tradition, and secondly in terms of the state's willingness to protect French language and culture against globalization. Hare's analysis sets out how popular music and song's mediation by radio and television has been informed by these twin features of French exceptionalism.

Music on radio can be divided into three periods, as Hare points out: the early period (pre-Second World War) of state-controlled radio and a few commercial stations; the post-war state radio monopoly; and the post-1981 rise of independent radios. Although during the first two periods popular music was catered for by radio (principally by commercial radio, but also by generalist public sector stations), it was in the 1980s and 1990s that there was an explosion of new FM radio outlets and a massive increase in music specialization. Politically, music was crucial to the development of the radio sector, as it was behind the end of the state monopoly and also the foremost issue of the 1990s as France instituted linguistic quotas on music played by French radio stations in order to protect French musical culture.

In terms of television, Hare shows how programming of popular music has in some senses duplicated the trends set by radio, but identifies two major television phenomena which have structured music television, namely the French TV tradition of the variety show, and the long-awaited dedicated French music TV channel. Hare's conclusion is that music programming on radio and television has moved from supplying a standardized repertoire to a mass audience to offering a varied range of music formats and genres to highly segmented audiences. He suggests that popular music on radio and television exemplifies paradoxes within French exceptionalism.

Mat Pires considers the popular music press since its beginnings in the 1950s, and his analysis reveals how the mediation of popular musics by the specialized press developed through a number of phases, the *Presse des jeunes* (youth-interest press) in the 1950s, the *Presse des idoles* (the singing scene, focusing predominantly on stars) and since the late 1960s, the *Presse musicale* (a more standard music press covering specialist magazines and, increasingly, coverage of popular music in quality newspapers).

Quite markedly, this survey of the music press illustrates the social and emotional realities of popular music for its (predominantly youthful) readership.

Pires's consideration of the two major titles of the *presse des jeunes* in the 1950s – the Catholic Church's *Rallye–Jeunesse* and the French Communist Party's *Nous les garçons et les filles* – shows how music merged with socio-political factors as well as the emotional traumas of emerging identities in adolescence.

Similarly, Pires's narrative links the popular music press to the development of French society, as in the 1950s and 1960s France modernized economically, socially and demographically – one of the implicit features that his analysis suggests is that the music press in these decades contained within it a generation gap between the young fans of *yéyé* music and the journalists who reported on it to them. Perhaps the most famous titles of France's popular music press are *Salut les copains* (launched 1962) and *Rock & Folk* (1966): Pires discusses how *Salut les copains* transformed the youth music press and how *Rock & Folk* anticipated future music coverage and took the genre forwards until other titles, such as the current market leader *Les Inrockuptibles* (also discussed by Teillet, in another perspective) and the music columns of such quality papers as *Libération* and *Le Monde* started to cover popular music in the 1980s and 1990s.

Phil Powrie provides a broad historical survey of popular music in French film soundtracks, from the sound era onwards. Seeing popular music as an index of social change, and as a key mediator of the relationship between France and the US, he discusses a 'slow disintegration of specifically French cultural norms' in the shift to jazz and pop-inflected soundtracks. Seeing the use of *chanson* in pre-1945 films as constitutive of a specifically French 'community', he explains its demise partly due to increased distribution of American films in the post-war period and partly due to 1960s cinema's greater concern with individuality and self-expression, for which jazz seemed to fit the bill.

The nostalgia of 'heritage' film-making in the 1980s is accompanied by classical music signifying loss, the loss of community, while the playfulness of the *cinéma du look* film makers' mixing of high- and low-cultural forms represents a refusal to hierarchize, but also speaks of multi-culturalism and marginality. Powrie sees the developing trend towards an Anglo-American-dominated compilation score as a logical outcome of the 'slow infiltration' of American music which accompanies the on-screen deterioration of French community.

Robynn Stilwell analyses France's best-known exponent of the musical, Jacques Demy, situating his films amongst a cross-fertilization of musical and dance styles back and forth across the Atlantic from the 1920s onwards. She demonstrates, therefore, that despite the musical being seen as distinctly American, signifying 'Hollywoodness', the MGM musicals of Minelli and Kelly/Donen were themselves products of an interweaving of French and American influences. Demy's films of the 1960s, the New Wave era of stylistic and generic complexity, pay homage to the musical genre as a whole, but blend their references and homage with treatment of issues of great significance in France: the Algerian war in *les Parapluies de Cherbourg* and regionalism, throwing the spotlight on non-Parisian France, in both that film and *les Demoiselles de Rochefort*. Stilwell also discusses the films' ambivalent subtext about economic change and modernization (or Americanization?).

Chris Tinker, like Lloyd, looks at *chanson*, as incarnated by two of France's most famous exponents of the genre, namely Léo Ferré and Georges Brassens, who during the 1950s and 1960s created significant repertoires of politically and socially committed songs. As Tinker points out, during a period of great social and political change typified by the aftermath of Occupation, the Algerian war in the late 1950s and early 1960s, the secularization and liberalization of society, Ferré and Brassens used *chanson* and their status as stars of this traditional form of popular music to challenge received social and personal identities and to explore new possibilities.

The 'oppositional discourses' elaborated by Ferré and Brassens were aimed at the institutional structures of bourgeois power and domination that at the time were represented by the Catholic Church and the state. Ferré in particular attacked the repressive influences of the Church and state but also targeted the bourgeois family, (state) radio and television, while Brassens, reading behind the state and its most evident manifestations, attacked the repressive forces of law and order and, even further, nationalist identities.

As Tinker demonstrates, these oppositional stances were not without their difficulties, paradoxes and omissions: for instance, Ferré's anti-nationalism did not prevent him from wishing to protect French culture from encroaching Americanization, and neither Ferré nor Brassens made any protest against patriarchy, despite their strong libertarian and anarchist sympathies. Tinker's analysis investigates the social and political *engagement* (commitment) of these artists and shows how their songs provide a singular viewpoint from which to understand the turbulence of French society in the post-war decades and to consider the role of the musician as social, political and ultimately moral guide.

Chris Lloyd's study of popular music during the troubled years of the Occupation of France by German forces from 1940 to 1944 provides another case study of the ways in which musical practices and the mediation of music through radio performance and critical appraisal is, as Middleton suggests, 'irreducibly social'. Lloyd shows how the ways in which music – more specifically singing – functioned during the Occupation contributed to the construction and upkeep of social, political, ideological and emotional identities. Taking two informally defined corpuses of songs (the political anthems of opposing groups and the entertainment songs of singers such as Maurice Chevalier), Lloyd's analysis reveals the complexities of singing in the Occupation, either in terms of the ideological commitment of mass-singing or in terms of the more problematic 'singing for entertainment' perpetrated by star singers.

Lloyd shows how the well-known anthems 'Maréchal, nous voilà' (in favour of the Vichy collaborationist government) and 'Le Chant des partisans' (the song of the Resistance) both mirrored and created social realities during the years of the Occupation, underlining the importance of their status as songs to be sung collectively. But the songs of popular entertainers such as Chevalier – who was seriously criticized during and after hostilities for having 'collaborated' with the Germans through his readiness to continue performing – are shown by Lloyd to play a more ambiguous role in 'world-building'.

In contrast to the anthems (perhaps predictably, but contrary to what has often been imagined) these songs of entertainment serve a purpose simply of 'oblique commentary on everyday life' in which the star's performance of a song provides, through an aestheticized mediation of common experience, the possibility of solace and solidarity. By studying Chevalier's lyrics and career, Lloyd is able to demonstrate that he was not at all an active promoter of the Vichy régime, and concludes with a comment on the role of stars of popular music that doubtless holds true in times of both strife and peace: 'The distractions of song are more than egocentric frivolity; by creating a parallel universe (which comments indirectly on the real one and contains its horrors) the singer undertakes a form of cultural resistance in which his or her listener participates and achieves a brief moment of liberty.'

Philippe Teillet looks at the ways in which rock music in France has been accepted into the French cultural field, after having started, as an imported genre, in a position of subordination and domination. His analysis considers how rock, and, more generally, contemporary popular musics, have been integrated through two main mechanisms: firstly gaining acceptance in the hierarchy of cultural values; and secondly, gaining a place within state cultural policies. Teillet illustrates how rock interests both the Ministry of Education and the Ministry of Culture in France, in reflection of its rise from a dominated position in the cultural field to a place where it is a valid object both of cultural policy and academic enquiry.

It was the state which became interested in rock as a component of cultural policy, rather than rock seeking state attention, as government thinking on cultural policy realized that the interventionism of the state since the 1960s to democratize access to culture through traditional definitions of 'works of art' of had failed, and that an emphasis on minor arts, regional and ethnic cultures and cultural practices would be more appropriate. On a national level rock and associated musics gained entry to the established hierarchy of cultural values, an acceptance which was taken up by layers of government at local and regional level, who were ready to use rock as a vehicle for developing local economies and identities.

This integration of rock into 'culture' was complemented by a status as an object of serious discussion and scientific research by the instrumental work of 'intellectual' music magazines such as *Les Inrockuptibles* and *Rock & Folk* (see also Pires's treatment of these and other press mediation) which, as Teillet demonstrates, effected a transformation in the representation of rock in the 1970s and 1980s through discourses of double opposition to both traditional definitions of culture and tastes imposed by media and commerce. Thus rock is, through its development as a practice and a genre, an example of popular music's 'irreducibly social' status (Middleton) and of the value of Hennion's 'musicology of society'.

Steve Cannon looks at the success of hip hop in France since the 1980s, investigating some of the ways in which hip hop's global expansion has seen France emerge as the world's second-largest market for hip hop product, including homegrown, francophone examples which have established a significant place in mainstream popular culture in France, in terms of sales, play-listing, numbers of new releases and 'official' critical reception. Cannon examines French hip hop's significance within debates about the effects of globalization on culture in France and French politics, culture and society in general. To what extent has French state cultural policy encouraged and shaped the francophone hip hop scene? Does the adoption by youth in France of hip hop forms and styles represent homogenization of youth culture on a global scale, a further stage of Americanization of French cultural life? Do the localized forms of expression emerging from cities such as Marseille, on the other hand, offer a means of expressing and celebrating diversity?

Focusing principally on the group IAM, one of the biggest commercial and artistic successes of hip hop in France, this chapter outlines the ways in which their texts, the musical forms that they sample, produce and reproduce and the images that they mobilize in packaging, merchandising and performing their work, articulate a hybrid identity or identities situated between the local and the global.

Examples are discussed illustrating the complex web of sources and influences from which they draw: Afrocentrism and the work of Diop; ancient Egypt and its representation in epic movies; football and the fan culture of Olympique Marseille; science fiction and other forms of popular narrative and North African and Italian popular musical forms.

Keith Reader's study of 'France's best-known voice', Édith Piaf, offers a chance to consider female exponents of *chanson*. He argues that her place in French culture derives in part from her 'belatedness', the last in a line of 'realist *chanteuses*' who garnered significant high-cultural credibility, but whose audience was overwhelmingly popular and predominantly female. Reader adopts a 'star studies' approach developed amongst analysts of cinema, appropriately enough, since among her contemporaries, only Bardot and Deneuve achieved equal prominence. Piaf's often tragic 'offstage' life and in particular her turbulent love-affairs (especially with boxing champion Marcel Cerdan) and media coverage of them, contributed to the construction of a worldly-wise, suffering survivor persona on stage.

Reader's detailed analysis of some key songs reveals their ambiguous attitude towards 'love' and he compares her with an earlier icon of 'vulnerable femininity', Flaubert's Emma Bovary. Even in their day, Piaf's songs were nostalgic for a Paris that was ceasing to exist, similar to the Paris of Carné's films. Reader concludes that there is a 'twofold datedness' to Piaf – icon both of an archaic femininity and of a Paris 'now redolent of the theme park', though her voice and the irony of her lyrics call into question the mythical foundations of the former at least.

Philippe Birgy's chapter analyses the process by which the 'exotic' trend of techno has not only rooted itself successfully in France, but gained worldwide recognition and commercial success for the 'French touch' of artists such as Air, St Germain etc. While tracing its evolution and mediation through specialist shops, fanzines and radio shows, Birgy demonstrates that the eclecticism of French electronica, their use of irony and lack of anxiety about 'bad taste' in recycling cliché and double entendre made it distinctive in a scene characterized by futurism and technologies.

Beyond these issues of cultural exchange (and successful export), Birgy not only points out how techno renegotiates France's musical identity on the world stage, but also assesses the ways in which the techno scene(s) and their raves offer a space for the conciliation of differences and the forging of a, possibly utopian, hybrid identity, in the face of periodic moral panic and state repression.

Conclusion

This survey of popular musics in France has shown how they have both reflected and helped create social, political, cultural and emotional identities throughout a period of great change. Whether popular musics since 1940 have in any way anticipated or prefigured socio-political developments (or to use Attali's expression, have been 'prophetic') in France is an intriguing question. Undoubtedly, the debates over the role and responsibilities of musical performers and their music pertaining to Chevalier in the Occupation and Ferré and Brassens in the 1950s and 1960s were still relevant in the 1990s, as rap and hip hop brought new form to political *engagement* (commitment) through music. Equally certain is the way in which the mediation of music in the 1990s and 2000s is playing a role in both developing new techniques such as MP3 and reflects their own progress as technology. According to Hennion, there is no such thing as music, but only the things which go together to make up what we – the general public, popular opinion – understand to *be* music, so whatever is seen to be music is automatically at one and the same time, prophetic, constructive and reflective of social, political, cultural and psychological realities.

Since the 1940s French society has changed in radical ways; France has been transformed more profoundly and more extensively than perhaps any other comparable Western European nation, and this transformation has been undertaken within a context of antagonistic internal forces informing her modernization. France has arguably been modernized by her elites, despite constant interference in their modernizing projects from the French people themselves, who seem to retain an attachment to the past which tempers moves for change. Culturally (and the cultural sphere is inseparable from the ways in which France organizes herself socially, politically and economically) France is similarly torn between the (elite and popular) desire to maintain her (traditional) identity and the (mainly popular) desire to succumb to a fascination with all things American. It is the theme of the US-Other – and of France's national cultural identity 'threatened' by an Americanized world culture – that has been the most visible thread in the fabric of analyses woven by this volume. Debate and analysis in this volume has shown that the period from the 1980s onwards has been a crucial one for popular music in France, politically, culturally, socially and in terms of technology. The governments of the Mitterrand years began to revise traditional attitudes to the cultural role of the state, as well as 'liberalizing' the broadcast media in ways which fundamentally altered access to and consumption of popular musics; these trends have continued during the 1990s, and as hip hop, web radios, European integration and globalization increasingly influence the development of French music, cultural modernization will continue apace.

Bibliography

Aaron, Didier (2001), 'L'évolution de la programmation musicale en radio', *Dossiers de l'audiovisuel* (97), 9–12.

——, Leboeuf, D., and Samyn, C. (2001), 'MCM: nouvelles gammes', *Dossiers de l'audiovisuel* (97), 36–37.

Achard, Maurice (1996), 'Avant Rock&Folk', *Rock & Folk*, hors-série 12, '30 ans de rock et de folk', November, 8–12.

Achard, Pierre (1995), '50 ans de paillettes', *Notes: le journal de la SACEM* (144), January, rep. in *Dossiers de l'audiovisuel* (97), 2001, 14–17.

Adair, Gilbert (1983), 'Racine of Dreams (review)', *Sight and Sound*, **52** (2), 144.

Aguiton, Christophe, Petrella, Riccardo, and Udry, Christophe-André (2001), 'The Mechanics of exclusion', in F. Houtart and F. Polet (eds), *The Other Davos: the globalisation of resistance*, London: Zed.

Allinson, E. (1994), 'Music and the Politics of Race: It's a Black Thing – Hearing How Whites Can't', *Cultural Studies*, **8** (3), October, 438–56.

Altman, Rick (1987), *The American Film Musical*, London: BFI Publishing.

Andrews, Chris (2000), 'The social ageing of *Les Inrockuptibles*', *French Cultural Studies*, 11, 235–48.

Andrex (1989), *On ne danse plus la java chez Bébert*, Paris: Presses de la Renaissance.

Anon. (1945), *La France nouvelle. Chansons de la Résistance*, Paris: Éditions Salabert.

Anon. (1947), *Les Procès de la radio*, Paris: Albin Michel.

Anon. (1994), 'La première une de "Rock & Folk"', *Libération* (*Le Magazine de Libération* supplement), 26 November, 63.

Anon. (2001), 'Le Midem témoigne du succès à l'export de la musique française', *Le Monde*, 22 January, 24.

Aron, R. (1968), *La révolution introuvable: réflexions sur les événements de mai*, Paris: Fayard.

Assayas, M. (ed.) (2000), *Dictionnaire du rock*, Paris: Robert Laffont (Bouquins).

Attali, Jacques (1985), *Noise: The Political Economy of Music*, trans. Brian Massumi, Manchester: Manchester University Press.

Badinter, E. (1986), *L'Un est l'autre*, Paris: Odile Jacob.

Balen, N. (1992), *Charles Trenet: le fou chantant*, Monaco: Editions du Rocher.

Bara, Guillaume (1998), 'Cocoriquotas ou quotallergie', *Télérama* (2516), 1 April.

Barthes, Roland (1977), *Fragments d'un discours amoureux*, Paris: Seuil.

—— (1982), 'Le Grain de la voix', in *L'Obvie et l'obtus*, Paris: Seuil.

Bazin, Hugues (1995), *La Culture hip-hop*, Paris: Desclée de Brouwer.

Beckman, J., and Adler, B. (1991), *Rap: Portraits and Lyrics of a Generation of Black Rockers*, New York: St Martin's Press.

Behr, E. (1993), *Thank Heaven for Little Girls: the True Story of Maurice Chevalier's Life and Times*, London: Hutchinson.

Bellaïche, R. (1994), 'Jean Ferrat', *Je chante*, Paris: Chelles.

Belleret, R. (1996), *Léo Ferré: une vie d'artiste*, Arles: Actes sud.

Bergfelder, Tim (2000), 'Between Nostalgia and Amnesia: Musical Genres in 1950s German Cinema', in Bill Marshall and R. Stilwell (eds), *Musicals: Hollywood and Beyond*, Exeter: Intellect Books, 80–88.

Berteaut, Simone (1972), *Piaf*, Paris: Robert Laffont.

Berthomé, Jean-Pierre (1982), *Les Racines du Rêve*, Nantes: L'Atalante.

Bey, Hakim (1991), *Temporary Autonomous Zones; Ontological Anarchy, Poetic Terrorism*, Brooklyn: Autonomedia.

Blair, M. E. (1993), 'Commercialisation of the Rap Music Youth Subculture', *Journal of Popular Culture*, **27** (3), Winter, 21–33.

Blanchet, Philippe (1995), 'Bourges: le printemps du rap', *Evénement du Jeudi*, 20–26 April, 78–81.

Bloom, Harold (1982), *Agon: Towards a Theory of Revisionism*, New York and Oxford: Oxford University Press.

Bloomfield, T. (1991), 'It's sooner than you think, or Where are we in the History of Rock music?', *New Left Review*, 190, Nov.–Dec., 59–81.

Bohlman, Philip (2002), *World Music: A Very Short Introduction*, Oxford: Oxford University Press.

Boltanski, Luc (1982), *Les cadres, la formation d'un groupe social*, Paris: Minuit.

Bonnafé, A. (1963/1988), *Georges Brassens – l'anar ... bon enfant*, Paris: Seghers.

Bonzom, M.-C. (1987), 'Rock & Folk: l' idéologie du rock sous presse', unpublished DEA thesis in political studies, Université de Rennes I.

—— (1991), 'Le Noir, la Femme, et le Sudiste. Une mythologie du rock sous presse', in Patrick Mignon and A. Hennion (eds), *Rock, de l'histoire au mythe*, Anthropos, coll. Vibration, 6, 65–74.

Bood, M. (1974), *Les Années doubles: journal d'une lycéenne*, Paris: Laffont.

Born, Georgina, and Hesmondhalgh, Dave (eds) (2000), *Western Music and Its Others: Difference, Representation and Appropriation in Music*, Berkeley, CA: University of California Press.

Boucher, Manuel (1998), *Rap: expression des lascars*, Paris: Harmattan.

Bourdieu, Pierre (1984), *Distinction. A Social Critique of the Judgement of Taste*, Cambridge, MA: Harvard University Press.

—— (1984), *Questions de sociologie*, Paris: Editions de Minuit.

—— (1992), *Les Règles de l'art*, Paris: Le Seuil.

Boyer, J.-A. (1991), *J'ai rendez-vous avec vous*, Cinétévé/INA Entreprises/La Sept.

Brandl, Emmanuel (2000), 'La sociologie compréhensive comme apport à l'étude des musiques amplifiées/actuelles régionales', in Anne-Marie Green (ed.), *Musique et sociologie. Enjeux méthodologiques et approches empiriques*, Paris: L'Harmattan, coll. Logiques sociales, 256–300.

—— (2002), 'Légitimation et normalisation des "musiques amplifiées" en région', *Volume*, 1, 91–102.

Briet, Sylvie (1997), 'Chanson française: les quotas radio font moins de couacs', *Libération*, 21 January, 26.

Briggs, A. (1970), *The History of Broadcasting in the United Kingdom*, vol. 3, *The War of Words*, Oxford: Oxford University Press.

Bromberger, Christian (ed.) (1998), *Passions ordinaires*, Paris: Hachette Littératures.

Brulard, Inès (1997), 'Linguistic policies', in Sheila Perry (ed.), *Aspects of Contemporary France*, London: Routledge, 191–207.

Brunschwig, C., Calvet, L.-J. and Klein, J.-C. (1981), *Cent ans de chanson française*, Paris: Seuil.

Buisine, Alain (ed.) (1997), *Figures mythiques: Emma Bovary*, Paris: Autrement.

Burleigh, M. (2000), *The Third Reich*, New York: Hill & Wang.

Buxton, David (1985), *Le rock: star-système et société de consommation*, Grenoble: La Pensée Sauvage.

Calio, Jean (1998) *Le Rap: une réponse des banlieues?* Paris: Aléas.

Calvet, L.-J. (1976), *La Production révolutionnaire: slogans, affiches, chansons*, Paris: Payot.

—— (1981), *Chanson et société*, Paris: Payot.

—— (1981/1993), *Georges Brassens*, Paris: Lieu Commun.

Cannavo, R. (1993), *Monsieur Trenet*, Paris: Lieu Commun.

Cannon, Steve (1997), '"Paname City Rapping": B-Boys in the *banlieues* and beyond', in Alec G. Hargreaves and Mark McKinney (eds), *Post-colonial Cultures in France*, London: Routledge, 150–66.

—— (2000), 'Let's film to the sound of the underground?' The uses of hip hop and reggae in recent French films', in Bill Marshall and and R. Stilwell (eds), *Musicals: Hollywood and Beyond*, Exeter: Intellect, 163–70.

Caradec, F., and Weill, A. (1980), *Le Café-concert*, Paris: Hachette.

Cardona, J., and Lacroix, C. (1996), *Statistiques de la culture: chiffres clés 1996*, Paris: La Documentation française.

Castagnac, G. (1991), 'L'enjeu des scènes locales', *Yaourt*, hors série no. 4, November 1991.

Chambers, Ian (1985), *Urban Rhythms: Popular Music and Popular Culture*, London: Macmillan.

—— (1994), *Migrancy, Culture, Identity*, London: Routledge.

Charman, T. (1991), '*Chantons sons l'occupation*: Maurice Chevalier and Collaboration in Occupied France', *Imperial War Museum Review*, 6, 96–108.

Chevalier, M. (1946), *Ma route et mes chansons*, Paris: Julliard.

—— (1948), *Tempes grises*, Paris: Julliard.

—— (1960), *With Love: the Autobiography of Maurice Chevalier*, London: Cassell.

—— (1970), *Les Pensées de Momo*, Paris: Presses de la cité.

Chion, M. (1985), *Le Son au cinéma*, Paris: Cahiers du cinéma.

—— (1995), *La Musique au cinéma*, Paris: Fayard.

—— (1994), *Audio+Vision: Sound on Screen*, ed. and trans. Claudia Gorbman, New York: Columbia University Press.

Chocron, Catherine (1994), 'La perception du rock dans la presse quotidienne: L'exemple de "Libération"', in A.-M. Gourdon (ed.), *Le Rock: aspects esthétiques, culturels et sociaux*, Paris: CNRS Editions.

Chollet, J.-J. (1997), *Georgius, l'amuseur public no 1*, Paris: Christian Pirot.

Claus, Horst, and Jäckel, Anne (2000), '*Der Kongress Tanzt*: UFA's Blockbuster *Filmoperette* for the World Market', in Marshall, Bill and R. Stilwell (eds), *Musicals: Hollywood and Beyond*, Exeter: Intellect Books, 89–97.

Clech, Thierry, Strauss, Frédéric, and Toubiana, Serge (1988), 'Entretien avec Jacques Demy (Suite)', *Cahiers du Cinema*, 414, 57–62.

Cleveland, L. (1994), *Dark Laughter: War in Song and Popular Culture*, Westport, CT: Praeger.

Clifford, James (1988), *The Predicament of Culture: Twentieth-Century Ethnography, Literature and Art*, Cambridge, MA: Harvard University Press.

Collovald, A. (1988), 'Identité(s) stratégique(s)', *Actes de la Recherche en Sciences Sociales*, 73, June.

Colombier, Thierry, and Nacer, Lalam (1998), *Etudes des filères produits psychotropes à partir des soirées de musique techno*, intermediary report, Paris: International Research Center on Environment and Development, 20.

——, Nacer, Lalam, and Schiray, Michel (2000), *Drogue et techno: les trafiquants de rave*, Paris: Stock.

Commission nationale des musiques actuelles (1998), *Rapport de la Commission nationale des musiques actuelles à Catherine Trautmann, Ministre de la culture et de la communication*, September; unpublished.

Conte, C. (2001), interview, *Time Out Paris Free Guide,* 'The Music Issue', Autumn, 15–17.

Cornu, Francis (1997), 'La colère sourde d'un indépendant', *Le Monde*, 2 June, 3.

Costello, M., and Wallace, D. F. (1990), *Signifying Rappers: Rap and Race in the Urban Present*, New York: Ecco Press.

Cottet, J.-P. (1990), *Georges Brassens: Histoire de copains et de copines*, Collection les Grands, FR3.

Coulonges, G. (1969), *La Chanson en son temps de Béranger au juke-box*, Paris: Les Éditeurs Français Réunis.

Crémieux-Brilhac, J.-L. (ed.) (1975), *Les Voix de la liberté. Ici Londres 1940–1944*, 5 vols, Paris: La Documentation française/Le Club français des bibliophiles.

Cross, Brian (1993) *It's Not About a Salary ...: Rap, Race and Resistance in Los Angeles*, London: Verso.

Crozier, M. (1968), *La Société bloquée*, Paris: Points Seuil.

Dac, P. (1972), *Un Français libre à Londres en guerre*, Paris: Editions France-Empire.

D'Angelo, Mario (1997), *Socio-économie de la musique en France: diagnostic d'un système vulnérable*, Paris: La Documentation française.

—— and P. Vesperini (1993), *Avenir et devenir des indépendants français du disque*, 2 vols, Paris: IDEE Europe.

Darré, Alain (ed.) (1996), *Musique et politique. Les répertoires de l'identité*, Rennes: Presses Universitaires de Rennes, coll. Res Publica.

Dauncey, Hugh (1994), 'Reality shows on French television: Télé-vérité, Télé-service, Télé-civisme or Télé-flicaille?', *French Cultural Studies*, 5, 85–98.

—— and Hare, Geoff (1999), 'French youth talk radio: the free market and free speech', *Media, Culture and Society*, **21** (1), 93–108.

Davet, Stéphane (1997), 'Jean-François Michel, secrétaire général du Bureau européen de la musique', *Le Monde*, 2 April, 22.

—— (1997), 'L'Europe supplante les Etats-Unis sur le marché de la musique populaire', *Le Monde*, 2 April, 2.

de Bechade, Chantal (1982), 'Eveiller le sentiment amoureux ... Entretien avec Jacques Demy', *La Revue du cinéma*, 377, 26–27.

Decker, Jeffrey L. (1994), 'The State of Rap: Time and Place in Hip Hop Nationalism', in Ross, A. and Rose, T. (eds), *Microphone Fiends: Youth Music and Youth Culture*, London: Routledge, 99–121.

Deleuze, Gilles, and Guattari, Félix (1980), *Mille Plateaux*, Paris: éditions de minuit, 1980.

Demougin, Thierry «Historique du mouvement dance, du disco à la techno». www.france-techno.fr/Reports/Reports/Techno History/

DeNora, Tia (2000), *Music in Everyday Life*, Cambridge: Cambridge University Press.

Deramat, J. M. (1964), *Pourquoi tous ces copains?* Paris: Librairie Charpentier.

Dillaz, S. (1973), *La Chanson française de contestation: des barricades de la Commune à celles de mai 1968*, Paris: Seghers.

—— (1991), *La Chanson sous la Troisième République, 1870–1940*, Paris: Tallandier.

Diop, Cheikh Anta (1955), *Nations nègres et cultures*, Paris: Présence africaine.

Dister, Alain (1990), 'Les enfants de la passion', *Nouvel observateur*, 18 October, 76.

Dompnier, N. (1996), *Vichy à travers chants*, Paris: Nathan.

Donnat, Olivier (1994), *Les Français face à la culture*, Paris, La Découverte.

—— (1998), *Les pratiques culturelles des Français, Enquête 1997*, Paris: La Documentation française.

Douchet, Jean (1990), 'Entrechats et loup', *Cahiers du cinéma*, 438, 52–53.

Dransart, S. (1994), 'La Chanson de variété en France sous l'Occupation (1941–1943)', unpublished mémoire de maîtrise, Université de Paris I.

Dubois, Vincent (1999), *La politique culturelle. Genèse d'une catégorie d'intervention publique*, Paris: Belin, coll. Socio-Histoires.

Duclos, Pierre, and Martin, Georges (1993), *Piaf*, Paris: Seuil.

Duneton, Claude (1996), 'Dix menaces qui pèsent sur la langue française', *Le Figaro,* 8 February.

Dutheil, Catherine (1991), 'Les musiciens de rock nantais', in Patrick Mignon and A. Hennion (eds), *Rock: de l'histoire au mythe*, Paris: Anthropos, coll. Vibration, 150–51.

Duverney, A.-M., and d'Horrer, O. (1979), *Mémoire de la chanson française depuis 1900*, Paris: Musique et Promotion.

Dyer, Richard (1998), *Stars*, London: BFI.

Eck, H. (ed.) (1985), *La Guerre des ondes. Histoire des radios de langue française pendant la Deuxième Guerre mondiale*, Paris: Armand Colin.

Ellen, Mark (1994), 'Getting my mojo working', *Guardian*, 20 June, II, 17.

Eure, J. D., and Spady, J. G. (eds) (1991), *Nation Conscious Rap*, New York: PC International Press.

Evein, Bernard (1990), 'L'école de Nantes', *Cahiers du cinéma*, 438, 46–47.

Faure, Alain (1995), 'Les Politiques locales, entre référentiels et rhétorique', in A. Faure, G. Pollet and P. Warin (eds), *La construction du sens dans les politiques publiques*, Paris: L'Harmattan, 1995, 69–83.

Feld, Steve (2000), 'The Politics and Poetics of Pygmy Pop', in Georgina Born and Dave Hesmondhalgh (eds), *Western Music and Its Others: Difference, Representation and Appropriation in Music*, Berkeley, CA: University of California Press, 254–79.

Finkielkraut, Alain (1987), *La défaite de la pensée*, Paris: Gallimard.

Flaubert, Gustave (1986), *Madame Bovary*, Paris: Flammarion.

Fléouter, C. (1996), *Léo*, Paris: Laffont.

Fontaine, Astrid, and Fontana, Caroline (1996), *Raver*. Col. Anthropos, Paris: Economica.

Forbes, J., and Kelly, M. (eds) (1995), *French Cultural Studies: an introduction*, Oxford: Oxford University Press.

Forman, Murray (2000), '"Represent": Race, space and place in rap music', *Popular Music*, **19** (1), 65–90.

Fourment, Alain (1987), *Histoire de la presse des jeunes et des journaux d'enfants (1768–1988)*, Paris: Eole.

Frith, Simon (1983), *Sound Effects: Youth, Leisure, and the Politics of Rock'n'Roll*, London: Constable.

—— (1998), *Performing Rights: Evaluating Popular Music*, Oxford: Oxford University Press.

Fumaroli, M. (1991), *L'État culturel: une religion moderne*, Paris: Éditions de Fallois.

Gaillot, Michel (1999), *Sens multiple. La techno, un laboratoire artistique et politique du présent*, Paris: Dis voir.

Galinier, Pascal (1998), 'Du mouvement chez les indépendants du disque', *Le Monde*, 8 July, 24.

Galtier-Boissière, J. (1992), *Journal 1940–1950*, Paris: Quai Voltaire.

Garnier, Philippe (1978), 'Hollywood', *R & F*, 138.

Garofalo, Reebee (ed.) (1992), *Rockin' the Boat: Mass Music and Mass Movements*, Boston: South End Press.

—— (1993), 'Black Popular Music: Crossing Over or Going Under?', in Tony Bennett et al. (eds), *Rock and Popular Music*, London: Routledge, 231–48.

Gatfield, C. M. (1975), 'La formation du vocabulaire de la musique pop: Étude morpho-sémantique d'une langue de spécialité', unpublished thesis, Universities of Toulouse II – Le Mirail and London Ontario Canada.

Gaudin, J.-P. (1993), *Les nouvelles politiques urbaines*, Paris: PUF.

Gauthier, A. (1967), *Les Chansons de notre histoire*, Paris: Pierre Waleffe.

Gelder, Ken, and Thornton, Sarah (eds) (1997), *The Subcultures Reader*, London: Routledge.

Genton, Louis (2000), *Le Rap, ou la révolte?* Paris: Place d'Armes.

George, Nelson (1988), *The Death of Rhythm and Blues*, London: Omnibus.

—— (1994), *Buppies, B-boys, Baps and Bohos: Notes on Post-soul Black Culture*, New York: Harper Perennial.

Gervereau, L., and Peeschanski, D. (1990), *La Propagande sous Vichy*, Paris: BDIC.

Gibson, O. (2002), 'Kerrang! rocks its way to the top', *Guardian*, 15 February.

Gilroy, Paul (1987), *There Ain't No Black in the Union Jack: The Cultural Politics of Race and Nation*, London: Hutchinson.

—— (1993), *The Black Atlantic: Modernity and Double Consciousness*, London: Verso.

Giolitto, P. (1999), *Volontaire français sous l'uniforme allemand*, Paris: Perrin.

Girod, Francis (1966), *Manuel de la pensée yéyé*, Paris: Julliard.

Godelier, Maurice (1984), *L'idéel et le matériel,* Paris: Fayard.

Godfrin, Jacqueline and Philippe (1965), *Une Centrale de presse catholique: la Maison de la Bonne Presse et ses publications*, Paris: PUF.

Green, Anne-Marie (1986), *Les adolescents et la musique*, Issy-les-Moulineaux: Editions EAP.

—— (ed.) (1998), *Musiciens de métro. Approche des musiques vivantes urbaines*, Paris: L'Harmattan, coll. Logiques Sociales.

—— (ed.) (2000), *Musique et sociologie. Enjeux méthodologiques et approches empiriques*, Paris: L'Harmattan, coll. Logiques sociales.

Grynszpan, Emmanuel (1999), *Bruyante techno: réflexion sur le son de la free-party*, Nantes: Mélanie Séteun.

Guérin, André (1963), 'Le yéyé tel qu'on le parle', *L'Aurore*, 9 December, 2a.

Guibert, Gérôme (1998), *Les nouveaux courants musicaux: simples produits des industries culturelles?* Nantes: Mélanie Séteun.

—— (2001), 'Industrie musicale et musiques amplifiées', in *Chimères*, **40**, 103–16.

—— and Migeot, Xavier (1999), 'Les dépenses des musiciens de musiques actuelles: éléments d'enquêtes réalisées en Pays-de-Loire et Poitou-Charentes', in Teillet, P., *Politiques publiques et musiques amplifiées actuelles*, hors série *La Scène*.

Guitry, S. (1947), *Quatre ans d'occupations*, Paris: Editions de l'Elan.

Gumplowicz, P., and Klein, J.-C. (eds) (1995), *Paris 1944–1954. Artistes, intellectuels, publics: la culture comme enjeu*, Série Mémoires no. 38, Paris: Editions Autrement.

Hager, Steven (1984), *Hip Hop: The Illustrated History of Breakdancing, Rap Music and Graffiti*, New York: St Martin's Press.

Halimi, A. (1976), *Chantons sous l'Occupation*, Paris: Olivier Orban.

Hare, Geoff (1992), 'The law of the jingle: a decade of change in French radio', in R. Chapman and N. Hewitt (eds), *Popular Culture and Mass Communication in Twentieth Century France*, Lampeter: Edwin Mellen Press, 27–46.

Hawkins, P. (2000), *Chanson: the French Singer-Songwriter from Aristide Bruant to the Present Day*, Aldershot: Ashgate.

Heath, Stephen (1992), *Madame Bovary*, Cambridge/New York/Port Chester/Melbourne/Sydney: Cambridge University Press.

Hebdige, Dick (1987), *Cut 'n' Mix: Culture, Identity and Caribbean Music*. London: Methuen.

Heinich, Nathalie (2002), *La sociologie de l'art*, Paris: La Découverte.

Hennion, Antoine (1981), *Les professionnels du disque. Une sociologie des variétés*, Paris: Metaile.

—— (2003), 'Music and Mediation: Towards a New Sociology of Music', in *The Cultural Study of Music: A Critical Introduction*, ed. Richard Middleton, Trevor Herbert and Martin Clayton, London and New York: Routledge, 80–91.

——, Maisonneuve, Sophie and Gomart, E. (2000), *Figures de l'amateur. Formes, objets, pratiques de l'amour de la musique aujourd'hui*, Paris: La Documentation française.

Hermelin, Christian (1965), 'L'interprète-modèle et "Salut les Copains"', *Communications*, 6, 43–53.

Hermine, Micheline (1997), *Destins de femmes, désir d'absolu*, Paris: Beauchesne.

Hirsch, Jean-François (ed.) (1971), 'La pop music' (dossier), *Musique en jeu*, 2, 66–110.

Hirschhorn, Clive (1974), *Gene Kelly: A Biography*, London: W. H. Allen.

Hooper, Mark (1998), 'Paris is Burning', *The Face*, 97–110.

IPSOS (1997), *Bilan Radio Aircheck* 1997, Paris: IPSOS Music.

Irvin, Marjory (1973), 'It's George, Not Jazz: Gershwin's Influence in Piano Music', *American Music Teacher*, 23, November–December, 31–34.

Irving, K. (1993), '"I Want Your Hands On Me": Building Equivalences Through Rap Music', in *Popular Music*, **12** (2), 105–21.

Jameson, F. (1990), '*Diva* and French Socialism', in *Signatures of the Visible*, New York and London: Routledge, 55–62.

Jamet, Michel (1983), *La presse périodique en France*, Paris: A. Colin.

Jeanneney, Jean-Noël (2001), *L'Echo du siècle. Dictionnaire historique de la radio et de la télévision en France*, Paris: Hachette Littératures/ARTE Editions (1st edn 1999).

Johnson, William (1996), 'More Demy: In Praise of The Young Girls of Rochefort', *Film Comment*, **32** (5), September–October, 72–76.

Jouffa, François (1978), *Idoles Story*, Neuilly: Alain Mathieu.

Jouvenet, Morgan (2001), 'Emportés par le mix. Les DJ et le travail de l'émotion', *Musique et émotion*, Terrain 37, septembre, 48.

Kassabian, A. (2001), *Hearing Film: Tracking Identifications in Contemporary Hollywood Film Music*, New York and London: Routledge.

Kirgener, C. (1988), *Maurice Chevalier*, Paris: Vernal/Lebaud.

Kitwana, Bakiri (1994), *The Rap on Gangsta Rap – 'Who run it?': Gangsta Rap and Visions of Black Violence*. Chicago: Third World Press.

Knight, Diana (1985), *Flaubert's Characters*, Cambridge/New York/Melbourne: Cambridge University Press.

Knox, Donald (1973), *The Magic Factory: How MGM Made* An American in Paris, New York: Praeger Publishers.

Koechlin, Philippe (1992), *Mémoires de Rock et Folk*, Paris, Mentha.

Konstantarakos, M. (1999), 'Which Mapping of the City?: *La Haine* (Kassovitz, 1995) and the "Cinéma de banlieue"', in Powrie, Phil (ed.), *Contemporary French Cinema: Continuity and Difference*, Oxford: Oxford University Press, 152–61.

Labarde, Philippe (1998), 'Interview: Les quotas encore en question', *Vive la Radio*, March.

Lack, R. (1997), *Twenty Four Frames Under: A Buried History of Film Music*, London: Quartet.

Lacombe, Alain (1984), *La Chanson dans le cinéma français*, Paris: Import Diffusion Music.

Lacombe, A., and Porcile, F. (1995), *Les Musiques du cinéma français*, Paris: Bordas.

Laing, Dave (1986), 'The Music Industry and the "Cultural Imperialism" Thesis', in *Media, Culture and Society*, **8** (3), 331–41.

—— (1992), '"Sadeness", Scorpions and Single Markets: National and Transnational Trends in European Popular Music', *Popular Music*, **11** (2), 127–40.

Lapassade, Georges, and Rousselot, Philippe (1990), *Le Rap, ou la fureur de dire*, Paris: Editions Loris Talmart.

La Rochefoucauld (1976), *Maximes et réflexions diverses*, Paris: Gallimard.

Layani, Jacques (1987), *Léo Ferré – la Mémoire et le temps*, Collection Paroles et musiques, Paris: Seghers.

Le Boterf, H. (1997), *La Vie parisienne sous l'Occupation*, Paris: Editions France-Empire.

Le Gall, Yves (1966), 'La presse à grand tirage et les magazines', in *Mass media 1. La Presse d'aujourd'hui*, Paris: Bloud & Gay, 19–63.

Le Goff, Jean-Pierre (1995), *Le Mythe de l'entreprise*, Paris: La Découverte.

Le Guern, Philippe (ed.) (2002), *La célébration. Œuvres cultes et culture fan*, Rennes: Presses Universitaires de Rennes, coll. Le sens social.

Lebœuf, D. and Samyn, C. (2001), 'Dix ans de musique en télévision: 1990–2000', *Dossiers de l'audiovisuel* (97), 21–26.

Legrand, Michel (1990), 'Pianissimo', *Cahiers du cinéma*, 438, 44–45.

Legras, M. (1994), 'Léo, Come on, Boy …' *Chorus: Les Cahiers de la chanson*, Bréziolles: Les Editions du Verbe.

Lentin, Eric (1995), *Rave*, Montpellier: Climats.

Letailleur, Laurent (2001), 'Les variétés à la télévision', *Dossiers de l'audiovisuel* (97), 17–21.

Letellier, C. (1993), *Léo Ferré: L'Unique et sa solitude*, Paris: Nizet.

Light, Alan (1992), 'About a Salary or Reality? – Rap's Recurrent Conflict', in A. DeCurtis (ed.), *Present Tense: Rock 'n' Roll and Culture*. London: Duke University Press, 219–34.

Lindeperg, Sylvie, and Marshall, Bill (2000), 'Time, History and Memory in *Les Parapluies de Cherbourg*', in Bill Marshall and R. Stilwell (eds), *Musicals: Hollywood and Beyond*, Exeter: Intellect Books, 98–106.

Lloyd, C. (1997), 'Maurice Chevalier et l'Occupation', in *La Culture populaire en France*, ed. P. Whyte and C. Lloyd, Durham Modern Languages Series, 79–92.

—— (2001), 'Comic Songs in the Occupation', *Journal of European Studies*, 31, 379–93.

Londres, Albert (1994), *Marseille, porte du Sud*, Paris: Le Serpent à plumes; 1st published 1927, Editions de France.

Looseley, David (1995), *The Politics of fun*, Oxford/New York: Berg.

—— (2003), *Popular Music in Contemporary France: Authenticity, Politics, Debate*, Oxford and New York: Berg.

Lull, J. (1995) *Media, Communication, Culture: a global approach*, Cambridge: Polity.

Madiot, Béatrice (1991), 'Les musiciens de jazz et de rock', in Patrick Mignon and Antoine Hennion (eds), *Rock: de l'histoire au mythe*, Paris: Anthropos, coll. Vibration, 6, 183–93.

Magny, Joël (1990), 'En ville, la tragédie', *Cahiers du cinéma*, 438, 34–36.

Marc, Edmond (1972), *La Chanson française*, Paris: Hatier.

Marny, Jacques (1965), *Les adolescents d'aujourd'hui*, Paris: Le Centurion.

Marshall, Bill, and Stilwell, Robynn (eds) (2000), *Musicals: Hollywood and Beyond*, Exeter: Intellect Books.

Marshall, P. (1993), *Demanding the Impossible: A History of Anarchism*, London: Fontana.

Martin, Jean-Clément, and Suaud, Charles (1992), 'Le Puy du Fou, l'interminable réinvention du paysan vendéen', *Actes de la recherche en Sciences Sociales*, 93, June, 21–37.

Mauboussin, Elisabeth (1999), 'Quel avenir pour les quotas de diffusion de chansons d'expression française?', *Légipresse* (162), June, II, 76–77.

Maupassant, Guy de (1983), *La Maison Tellier*, Paris: Albin Michel.

Menger, Pierre-Michel (1983), *Le paradoxe du musicien*, Paris: Flammarion.

Mesnil, Michel (1991), 'Demy ou le génie du lieu', *Esprit*, 1, 31–36.

Messier, Jean-Marie (2001), 'Vivre la diversité culturelle', *Le Monde*, 10 April, 1.

Middleton, Richard (2000), 'Musical Belongings: Western Music and its Low-Other', in Georgina Born and Dave Hesmondhalgh (eds), *Western Music and Its Others: Difference, Representation and Appropriation in Music*, Berkeley, CA: University of California Press, 59–85.

—— (2003), 'Locating the People? Music and the Popular', in Richard Middleton, Trevor Herbert and Martin Clayton (eds), *The Cultural Study of Music: A Critical Introduction*, London and New York: Routledge, 251–62.

——, Herbert, Trevor, and Clayton, Martin (eds) (2003), *The Cultural Study of Music: A Critical Introduction*, London and New York: Routledge.

Mignon, Patrick (1988), 'La production sociale du rock', *Cahiers 'Jeunesses et sociétés'*, 10, February, 3–32.

—— (1991), 'Paris/Givors: le rock local', in Mignon and Hennion (eds), *Rock: de l'histoire au mythe*, Paris: Anthropos, coll. Vibration, 197–216.

—— (1997), 'Evolution de la prise en compte des musiques amplifiées parles politiques publiques', *Politiques publiques et musiques amplifiées*, Adem, FL: Gema, 23–31.

——, and Hennion, Antoine (eds) (1991), *Rock: de l'histoire au mythe*, Paris: Anthropos, coll. Vibration, 6.

Miller, G. (1988), *Les Pousse-au-jouir du Maréchal Pétain*, Paris: Livre de poche.

Millot, Virginie (1997), 'Les fleurs sauvages de la ville et de l'art. Analyse anthropologique de l'émergence et de la sédimentation du hip-hop lyonnais', unpublished doctoral thesis, University of Lyon II.

—— (2002), 'La mise en scène des cultures urbaines ou la fabrique institutionnelle du métissage', *L'Observatoire*, 22, Spring, 14–22.

Milton, G. (1951), *T'en fais pas Bouboule*, Paris: Editions de la Vigie.

Morel, A. (1993), 'Politiques culturelles, production d'images et développement local', in J.-P. Gaudin (ed.), *Les nouvelles politiques urbaines*, Paris: PUF, 68–74.

Morin, Edgar (1972), *Les Stars*, Paris: Seuil.

Morley, D., and Robins, K. (1995), *Spaces of Identity: Global media, electronic landscapes and cultural boundaries*, London: Routledge.

Mortaigne, Véronique (1996), 'Le complexe de la chanson française', *Le Monde*, 18 April, 13.

—— (1996), 'La musique est le principal loisir des Français', *Le Monde*, 19 July, 21.

—— (1998), 'La Commission nationale des musiques actuelles vient de rendre son rapport', *Le Monde*, 18 September, 29.

—— (1998), 'La musique occupe la première place dans les loisirs des jeunes', *Le Monde*, 22 July, 22.

—— (1999), 'La chanson, éternelle oubliée', *Le Monde*, 9 November, 16.

—— (2001), 'Le droit d'auteur est-il dépassé?', *Le Monde*, 2 August, 1.

—— (2001), 'L'idée est de réunir notre offre musicale autour d'un label "France"', *Le Monde*, 22 January, 24.

—— and Sylvain Siclier (2001), 'Le financement de la culture mis à mal par l'Internet', *Le Monde*, 18 January, 17.

Musso, Pierre (2000), 'Vivendi-Universal: l'Amérique gagnante', *Le Monde*, 8 December, 17.

Mussou, Claude (2001), 'M6 gardera-t-elle le tempo', *Dossiers de l'audiovisuel* (97), 38–40.

Negus, Keith (1992), *Producing Pop: culture and conflict in the popular music industry*, London: Edward Arnold.

Obadia, E. (1991), 'IAM: Planète Mars', *BEST* Hors série no. 2, 82–85.

O'Shaughnessy, M. (2001), 'The Parisian popular as reactionary modernisation', *Studies in French Cinema*, **1** (2), 80–88.

Paizis, George (1998): 'Romantic novels', in Alex Hughes and Keith Reader (eds), *Encyclopedia of Contemporary French Culture*, London and New York: Routledge, 474.

Papadimitriou, Lydia (2000), 'More than a Pale Imitation: Narrative, Music and Dance in Two Greek Film Musicals of the 1960s', in Bill Marshall and Robynn Stilwell (eds), *Musicals: Hollywood and Beyond*, Exeter: Intellect Books, 117–24.

Pascal, René (1964), 'Les journaux des fans', *Esprit*, 2 (NS), 247–52.

Peelaert, Guy and Cohn, Nik (1974), *Rock Dream*, New York: Popular Library, 1973. French trans. Paris: Albin Michel, 1982.

Perkins, E. (ed.) (1994), *Droppin' Science: Critical Essays on Rap Music and Hip Hop Culture*, Philadelphia: Temple University Press.

Perrault, G. (1987), *Paris sous l'Occupation*, Paris: Belfond.

Pessis, J. (1992), *Pierre Dac*, Paris: Editions François Bourin.

Peterson, Richard A. (1991), 'Mais pourquoi donc en 1955? Comment expliquer la naissance du rock', in Patrick Mignon and Antoine Hennion (eds), *Rock: de l'histoire au mythe*, Paris: Anthropos, coll. Vibration, 6, 9–39.

Piaf, Édith (1994), *L'Hymne à l'amour*, Paris: Librairie Générale Française.

Pires, Mat (1997), 'Les stars noires et *Salut les copains, 1962–1968*', *Communication et langages*, 111, 59–71.

—— (1998), 'Popular music reviewing in the French press, 1956–1996', unpublished PhD thesis, University of Surrey.

Pistone, Danièle (2000), 'De l'histoire sociale de la musique à la sociologie musicale: bilans et perspectives', in Anne-Marie Green (ed.), *Musique et sociologie. Enjeux méthodologiques et approches empiriques*, Paris: L'Harmattan, coll. Logiques sociales, 83.

Pluvinage-Paternostre, Anne (1971), *L'adolescent et sa presse. Analyse de contenu des publications destinées aux jeunes*, Brussels: Editions de l'Institut de sociologie de l'Université libre.

Poirrier, Philippe (ed.) (2002), *Les collectivités locales et la culture*, Paris, Comité d'Histoire du Ministère de la culture, La Documentation Française.

Powrie, P. (1997), *French Cinema in the 1980s: Nostalgia and the Crisis of Masculinity*, Oxford: Clarendon Press.

—— (2001), *Jean-Jacques Beineix*, Manchester: Manchester University Press.

Ragache, G. and J.-R. (1988), *La Vie quotidienne des écrivains et des artistes sous l'Occupation*, Paris: Hachette.

Raskin, R. (1991), 'Le Chant des partisans', *Folklore*, 102, 62–76.

Rifkin, Adrian (1993), *Street Noises*, Manchester/New York: Manchester University Press.

Rioux, J.-P. (ed.) (1990), *La Vie culturelle sous Vichy*, Paris: Editions Complexe.

Rioux, L. (1994), *50 ans de chanson française*, Paris: L'Archipel.

Ritzer, George (1993), *The McDonaldization of Society*, Newbury Park, CA: Pine Forge Press.

Rizzardo, R. (1995), *Identités et politiques culturelles,* in J.-P. Saez, *Identités, cultures et territoires*, Paris: Desclées de Brouwer.

Robine, M. (1994), *Anthologie de la chanson française: Des trouvères aux grands auteurs du dix-neuvième siècle*, Paris: Alban Michel.

—— (1994), 'Ni Dieu ni maître' *Chorus: Les Cahiers de la chanson,* Bréziolles: Les Editions du Verbe.

Rochard, L. (1996), *Brassens: orfèvre des mots*, Pont-Scorff: 'Imprim'art'.

Rose, Tricia (1990), 'Never Trust a Big Butt and a Smile', in *Camera Obscura*, 23, May, 108–31.

—— (1994), *Black Noise: Rap Music and Black Culture in Contemporary America*, Hanover, NH: Wesleyan University Press.

Rositi, Franco (1969), 'Studio sull'ambivalenza culturale – Il caso della cultura giovanile', *Ikon*, 19 (71), 9–38.

Ross, A. and Rose, T. (eds) (1994), *Microphone Fiends: Youth Music and Youth Culture*, London: Routledge.

Ross, Kristin (1995), *Fast Cars, Clean Bodies: Decolonization and the Reordering of French Culture*, London: October Books.

Roussel, Daniel (1995), 'L'Etat, le Rock et la chanson', *Regards sur l'actualité.*

Saez, Guy (1992), 'Etat, villes et culture: un modèle métropolitain d'intervention publique', contribution to the conference *Décentralisation, régionalisation et action culturelle municipale*, Montréal, 12, 13 and 14 December.

—— (1994), 'Le dilemme culturel de la métropole : villes, identités et politiques publiques', in M. Bassand and J.-Ph. Leresche, *Les Faces cachées de l'urbain*, Bern: P. Lang.

—— (1995), 'Villes et culture : un gouvernement par la coopération', *Pouvoirs*, 73, 115.

Said, Edward (1978), *Orientalism*, New York: Vintage.

Sallée, A. (1991), *Brassens*, Paris: Solar.

Sartre, J.-P. (1948), *Situations II, Qu'est-ce que la littérature*, Paris: Gallimard.

Saumade, Frédéric (1998), 'Le rock, ou comment se formalise une passion moderne', in Christian Bromberger (ed.), *Passions ordinaires*, Paris: Hachette Littératures, 309–29.

Seca, Jean-Marie (1988), *Vocations rock*, Paris, Meridiens Klincksieck.

—— (2001), *Les musiciens underground*, Paris: PUF, coll. 'Psychologie sociale', 3.

Sermonte, J.-P. (1988), *Brassens: le prince et le croque-note*, Paris: Editions du rocher.

Sève, A. (1975), *Toute une vie pour la chanson*, Paris: Editions du centurion.

Shusterman, Richard (1991), *L'art à l'état vif*, Paris: Minuit.

Siclier, Sylvain (2000), 'La Sacem s'allie à quatre sociétés d'auteurs pour protéger le droit des créateurs sur Internet', *Le Monde*, 28 December, 24.

Simsi, S. (2000), *Ciné-Passions: 7e art et industrie de 1945–2000*, Paris: Editions Dixit

SNEP (1997), *L'Economie du disque*, Paris: SNEP (Syndicat national de l'édition phonographique).

Sotinel, Thomas (1990), 'Le blues de la presse rock', *Le Monde*, 1 August, 6.

Stephens, Greg (1992), 'Interracial Dialogue in Rap Music: Call and Response in a Multicultural Style' in *New Formations*, 16, Spring, 62–79.

Stokes, Martin (2003), 'Globalisation and the Politics of World Music', in Richard Middleton, Trevor Herbert and Martin Clayton (eds), *The Cultural Study of Music: A Critical Introduction*, London and New York: Routledge, 297–308.

Strazulla, Jérôme (1998), *La Techno*, Paris: Casterman.

Strode, Louise (1999), 'Language, Cultural Policy and National Identity in France, 1989–1997', unpublished PhD thesis, University of Loughborough.

Suquet, Patrick (1998), 'Moins de titres francophones à la radio en 1997', *Ecran Total*, 11 February.

Swedenburg, Ted (1992), 'Homies in the 'hood: Rap's Commodification of Insubordination', *New Formations*, 18, Winter, 53–66.

Taboulay, Camille (1990), 'Lettre d'une inconnue', *Cahiers du cinéma*, 438, 48–51.

—— (1996), *Le cinéma enchanté de Jacques Demy*, Paris: Cahiers du cinéma.

Tanner, Tony (1979), *Adultery and the Novel*, Baltimore/London: Johns Hopkins University Press.

Tarr, C. (1999), 'Ethnicity and identity in the "Cinéma de banlieue"', in Phil Powrie (ed.), *Contemporary French Cinema: Continuity and Difference*, Oxford: Oxford University Press, 162–73.

Teillet, Philippe (1991), 'Une politique culturelle du rock', in Patrick Mignon and Antoine Hennion (eds), *Rock: de l'histoire au mythe*, Paris: Anthropos, coll. Vibration.

—— (1992), 'Le discours culturel et le rock, l'expérience des limites de la politique culturelle de l'Etat', PhD thesis, University of Rennes.

—— (1996), 'L'Etat culturel et les musiques d'aujourd'hui', in Alain Darré (ed.), *Musique et politique. Les répertoires de l'identité*, Presses Universitaires de Rennes, coll. Res Publica, 120.

—— (1999), '"Musiques amplifiées", "musiques actuelles", "musiques populaires", "musiques d'aujourd'hui", etc. ou la querelle des principes de vision et de division', in *Actes des 2ème rencontres nationales Politiques publiques et musiques amplifiées/actuelles, La Scène. Le Magazine professionnel des spectacles*, Hors série, Ed. Millénaire, Avril, 115.

—— (1999), *Politiques publiques et musiques amplifiées actuelles*, hors série *La Scène*.

—— (2002), 'Eléments pour une histoire des politiques publiques en faveur des musiques amplifiées', in Philippe Poirrier (ed.), *Les collectivités locales et la culture; les formes de l'institutionnalisation, 19ème–20ème*, La Documentation Française/Comité d'histoire du ministère de la Culture, 361–93.

—— (2002), 'Les cultes musicaux. La contribution de l'appareil de commentaires à la construction de cultes: l'exemple de la presse rock', in Philippe Le Guern (ed.), *La célébration. Œuvres cultes et culture fan*, Rennes, Presses Universitaires de Rennes.

Thornton, Sarah (1996), *Club Cultures: Music, Media and subcultural Capital*, London: Wesleyan University Press / University Press of New England.

Todorov, T. (1995), *Les Abus de la mémoire*, Paris: Arléa.

Toop, David (2000), *Rap Attack 3: From African rap to global hip-hop*, London: Serpent's Tail.

Toubiana, Serge (1982), 'Jacques Demy ou le retour au pays des rêves', *Cahiers du Cinema*, 341, 5–13.

—— (1990), 'Jacques Demy ou le bel entêtement', *Cahiers du cinéma*, 438, 4–5.

—— (1990), 'Le premier qui m'ait vue … Entretien avec Catherine Deneuve', *Cahiers du cinéma*, 438, 38–41.

Touché, Marc (1998), *Mémoire Vive*, Annecy: Association Musiques Amplifiées/Le Brise Glace.

Valérian, P. (1996), *Chansons et chanteurs des années noires*, Mallemort: Editions Proanima.

Van Moppès, M. (1944), *Chansons de la BBC*, Paris: Editions Pierre Trémois.

Vecchiali, Paul (1990), 'Le touche Demy', *Cahiers du cinéma*, 438, 42–43.

Vernillat, F., and Charpentreau, J. (1977), *La Chanson française*, 2e édition revue et corrigée, Que Sais-Je?, no.1453, Paris: Presses Universitaires de France.

Vicherat, Mathias (2001), *Pour une analyse textuelle du rap*, Paris: Harmattan.

Victor, C., and Regoli, J. (1978), *20 Ans de rock français*, Paris: Albin Michel.

Vincendeau, Ginette (1987), 'The *mise-en-scène* of suffering: French *chanteuses réalistes*,' in *New Formations*, 3, Winter, 107–28.

—— (2000), *Stars and Stardom in French Cinema*, London: Continuum.

Vincent, François (1986), 'Rock & Folk, du pareil au même ...', *La Revue des revues*, 2, November, 55.

Vovelle, M. (1998), 'La Marseillaise: War or Peace', in P. Nora (ed.), *Realms of Memory*, vol. 3, *Symbols*, English edn, ed. L. R. Kritzmann and trans. A. Goldhammer, New York: Columbia University Press.

Warne, Chris (1997), 'Articulating Identity from the Margins: *Le Mouv'* and the Rise of Hip-hop and Ragga in France,' in Sheila Perry and Maire Cross (eds), *Voices of France*, London: Cassell, 141–54.

Yonnet, P. (1985), *Jeux, modes et masses: la société française et le moderne 1945–1985*, Paris: Gallimard.

Zago, Léonie (1995), 'Musiques actuelles et politiques culturelles à Rennes, 1983–1995', unpublished Political Science dissertation at the Institut d'Etudes Politiques de Rennes.

Zilbertin, Olivier (1999), 'Trois questions à Catherine Keer-Vignale, membre du directoire de la Sacem', *Le Monde*, 24 February, 2.

Zook, K. B. (1992), 'Reconstructions of Nationalist Thought in Black Music and Culture', in Reebee Garofalo (ed.), *Rockin' the Boat: Mass Music and Mass Movements*, Boston: South End Press.

Index